# THE FORMER SOVIET UNION'S DIVERSE PEOPLES

Other Titles in
ABC-CLIO's
ETHNIC DIVERSITY WITHIN NATIONS
Series

*Canada's Diverse Peoples,* J. M. Bumsted

*The Former Yugoslavia's Diverse Peoples,* Matjaž Klemenčič and Mitja Žagar

*Nigeria's Diverse Peoples,* April A. Gordon

# THE FORMER SOVIET UNION'S DIVERSE PEOPLES

## A REFERENCE SOURCEBOOK

*James Minahan*

A B C 🞄 C L I O

Santa Barbara, California   Denver, Colorado   Oxford, England

Library of Congress Cataloging-in-Publication Data
Minahan, James.
  The former Soviet Union's diverse peoples : a reference sourcebook / James Minahan.
    p. cm. — (Ethnic diversity within nations)
Includes bibliographical references and index.
  ISBN 1-57607-823-X (hardcover : alk. paper) ISBN 1-57607-824-8 (e-book)
  1. Former Soviet republics—Ethnic relations—Political
aspects—History. 2. Ethnology—Former Soviet republics. 3. Nationalism—Former
Soviet republics—History. 4. Ethnic conflict—Former Soviet republics—History.
5. Former Soviet republics—Race relations—History. I. Title. II. Series.

DK33.M54 2004
305.8'00947—dc22
                              2003025599
07  06  05  04    10  9  8  7  6  5  4  3  2  1

This book is also available on the World Wide Web as an e-book.
Visit abc-clio.com for details.

# Contents

## Rebirth of Ethnic Consciousness

7    Cold War Stagnation and the
Rebirth of Nationalism, 1971–1991    217

# Series Editor's Foreword

WE THINK OF THE UNITED STATES AS A NATION OF PEOPLES, with some describing it as a mosaic, a stew, an orchestra, and even yet as a melting pot. In the American vision of diversity the whole is perceived as greater than the sum of its parts—groups of peoples unify into a national identity. Not all Americans have shared that vision, or, to the extent that they initially did, they considered diversity as groups of people with shades of difference—such as shades of whiteness or variants of Protestantism. Many of the early newcomers would come to represent the core of an American society wherein distinctions were expected to fade by and large because a unity was anticipated that would be greater than any one homogeneous racial or ethnic national community. That unity would be forged through a common commitment to the American system of republicanism and a shared set of political principles and values—collectively, America's civic culture. For decades the diversity that was recognized (essentially in terms of religion and nationality) did not appear to be so formidable as to constitute a barrier to nationhood—as long as one did not look beyond the whiteness to the African and Native American (and later Latino and Asian) peoples. By rendering such groups invisible, if not beyond the pale, majority groups did not perceive them as representing a challenge to, or a denial of, the national unity. They were simply left out of the picture until, eventually, they would compel the majority to confront the nation's true composition and its internal contradictions. And, even before that more complex confrontation took place, streams of (mostly) European newcomers steadily stretched the boundaries of the nation's diversity, requiring a reexamination of the bonds of nationhood, the elements of nationality, and the core society and values. By World War II and in the ensuing two decades it became more and more difficult to ignore the impact of a dual development—the expanding Latino and Asian immigration and arrival of far more diverse groups of European newcomers. To secure their national vision, Americans had (albeit reluctantly and not without conflict) to make rather profound and fundamental adjustments to many of those components that had served as the nation's bonds, particularly the perception of America as a multicultural society and the belief that pluralism was a legitimate and inherent part of American society and culture.

To what extent has this scenario of a nation of peoples been present elsewhere in the world? Where have others struggled to overcome racial, religious, tribal, and nationality differences in order to construct—or to preserve—a nation? Perhaps one might even ask where, by the late twentieth century, had others not experienced such struggles? In how many of the principal nations has there long been present a homogeneity of people around which a nation could be molded and shaped with little danger of internal discord threatening the overall fabric of national unity? On the other hand, in how many countries has there been present a multiplicity of peoples, as in the United States, who have had to forge a nation out of a disparate array of peoples? Was that multiplicity the product of in-migrations joining a core society as it has been in the United States, or was there a historic mosaic of tribes, bands, and other more-or-less organized entities that eventually adhered together as their discovered commonalities outweighed their differences? Or, do we see invasions from without and unity imposed from above, or the emergence of one group gradually extending its dominance over the others—installing unity from below? Did any of these variations result in nation-states comparable to the United States—the so-called first new nation— and, if so, what have been the points of similarity and difference, the degrees of stability or unrest? Have their diversities endured, or have they been transmuted, absorbed, or suppressed? How much strain have those states experienced in trying to balance the competing demands among majority and minority populations? In other words, where nation-states have emerged by enveloping or embracing (or subjugating) diverse peoples, what have been the resulting histories in terms of intergroup relations and intergroup strains as well as the extent of effective foundations of national unity?

The challenges of coexistence (voluntarily or otherwise) remain the same whether two or twenty people are involved. The issue is what traditions, institutions, concepts, principles, and experiences enable particular combinations of peoples to successfully bond and what factors cause others to fall prey to periodic unrest and civil wars? Finally, many upheavals have taken place over the past 150 years, during which in-migrations have penetrated nations that were previously homogenous or were sending nations (experiencing more out-migration than in-migration) and were less prepared to address the rather novel diversities. Have these nations had institutions, values, and traditions that enabled them to take on successfully such new challenges?

Examples abound beyond the borders of the United States that require us to examine the claims of American exceptionalism (that America's multiculturalism has been a unique phenomenon) or, at the very least, to understand it far better. Canada and Australia have had indigenous peoples but have also long been receiving nations for immigrants—however, usually far more selectively than has the United States. Brazil and Argentina were, for decades in the late nineteenth and early twentieth centuries, important immigrant-receiving nations, too, with long-term consequences for their societies. Long before there were Indian and Yugoslavian nation-states there were myriad peoples in those regions who struggled and competed and then, with considerable external pressures, strained to carve out a stable multiethnic unity based on tribal, religious, linguistic, or racial (often including groups labeled "racial" that are not actually racially different from their neighbors) differences. Nigeria, like other African countries, has had a history of multiple tribal populations that have competed and have endured colonialism and then suffered a lengthy, sometimes bloody, contest to cement those peoples into a stable nation-state. In the cases of South Africa and Russia there were a variety of native populations, too, but outsiders entered and eventually established their dominance and imposed a unity of sorts. Iran is representative of the Middle Eastern/Western Asian nations that have been for centuries the crossroads for many peoples who have migrated to the region, fought there, settled there, and been converted there, subsequently having to endure tumultuous histories that have included exceedingly complex struggles to devise workable national unities. In contrast, England and France have been tangling with about two generations of newly arrived diverse populations from the Asian subcontinent, the West Indies, and Africa that are particularly marked by racial and religious differences (apart from the historic populations that were previously wedded into those nation-states), while Germans and Poles have had minorities in their communities for centuries until wars and genocidal traumas took their toll, rendering those ethnic stories more history than ongoing contemporary accounts—but significant nonetheless.

The point is that most nation-states in the modern world are not like Japan, with its 1 percent or so of non-Japanese citizens. Multiethnicity and multiculturalism have become more the rule than the exception, whether of ancient or more recent origins, with unity from below or from above. Moreover, as suggested, the successes and failures of these experiments in multiethnic nation-states compel us to consider what traditions, values, institutions, customs, political precedents, and historical encounters have contributed to those successes (including that of the United States) and failures. What can Americans learn from the realization that their own history—by no means without its own conflicts and dark times—has parallels elsewhere and, as well, numerous points of difference from the experiences of most other nations? Do we come away understanding the United States better? Hopefully.

An important objective of the Ethnic Diversity Within Nations series is to help readers in the United States and elsewhere better appreciate how societies in many parts of the world have struggled with the challenges of diversity and, by providing such an understanding, enable all of us to interact more effectively with each other. Thus, by helping students and other readers learn about these varied nations, our goal with this series is to see them become better-informed citizens that are better able to comprehend world events and act responsibly as voters, officeholders, teachers, public officials, and businesspersons, or simply when interacting and coexisting with diverse individuals, whatever the sources of that diversity.

*Elliott Robert Barkan*

# Preface

A S A CHILD GROWING UP DURING THE COLD WAR—the twentieth century's most protracted political confrontation—I learned that the Soviet Union was a multiethnic empire but an empire that was united in its desire to spread the evils of communism. Like many of the people who witnessed the rapid decline and the collapse of the Soviet state in 1991, I was astounded by the number and variety of ethnic groups that suddenly found their long-silenced voices. The Soviet leadership's lie that ethnic diversity had been transformed into a glorious new Soviet nationality was one of the first casualties of the collapse of the Soviet Empire during the formation of fifteen newly independent states.

When Elliott Barkan, the editor of ABC-CLIO's Ethnic Diversity Within Nations series, suggested that I contribute a volume to the series, I was eager to research and write about the evolving ethnic situation but also daunted by the size of the region and its hundreds of ethnic groups.

Many books, particularly those written since the Soviet collapse, have focused on the larger and better known of the ethnicities of the former Soviet Union, even though many of the region's ethnic problems involve smaller groups almost unknown in the West. I was enthusiastic about the Ethnic Diversity Within Nations series and fascinated by the many ethnic groups inhabiting the vast territory that formerly comprised the Union of Soviet Socialist Republics but still wary of focusing too closely on just the largest of the region's ethnic groups. The result of long deliberation was to include ethnic groups as they evolved during the long sweep of Russian and Soviet history. There are abundant works spotlighting the more numerous of the region's peoples but few that attempt to include the smaller groups, those that are currently making headlines and those that may do so in the future, in a comprehensive and historically accurate account. Thus, this volume chronicles the evolution of the many ethnicities that have so long been forgotten or lumped into a larger Russian or Soviet identity. Certainly one of the most important points of this study is to highlight the historical evolution, and the historic grievances, that continue to color ethnic relations within the states that succeeded the Soviet Union in the early 1990s. This is not to suggest that all of the groups are intent on establishing independent homelands, but the future relations between the various ethnic groups in each of the former Soviet states will be dictated as much by historical relationships as by those that are currently evolving.

The nationalist revival that accompanied the Soviet collapse first reduced the Soviet Empire to the borders of the USSR when client states in Eastern Europe and elsewhere reasserted their historical identities. The actual downfall of communist domination in the Soviet Union sparked yet another reduction of historical Russian influence when the major nationalities of the non-Russian republics declared their homelands independent states, thus reducing historical Russia to its European heartland and the vast territories to the east that were colonized mainly by ethnic Russians. At first it seemed that the new Russian Federation, still with more than 100 distinct nationalities, would follow the pattern of the Soviet Union and splinter along ethnic lines. This further splintering was prevented partly by redirecting the historical relationships between the Russians and the many non-Russian groups, including considerable cultural, linguistic, and political autonomy. Many of the ethnic groups included in this book played little or no role in the historical development of the huge region before the Soviet collapse, but since that time ethnic assertiveness has replaced their common Soviet past making the ethnic diversity of the former Soviet Union one of the most fascinating and most quickly evolving in the world.

I would like to thank all those who gave of their time and knowledge, particularly the staff of the excellent North American and British libraries in Barcelona for their assistance and good humor. I would also like to thank Elliott Barkan for his editorial assistance and his encouragement.

# Maps

# From Tribes
# to Nations

# CHAPTER ONE

# Prehistory to A.D. 1500

THE FORMER UNION OF SOVIET SOCIALIST REPUBLICS (USSR), until its dissolution in 1991, was the world's largest country in area and one of the largest in population. The Soviet Union was the home of more than one hundred recognized national and ethnic groups (see Significant People, Places, and Events in this chapter) and many other distinct groups that were never recognized as official nationalities by the Soviet authorities. The origins of this immense empire included not only the Russians, the historically dominant nationality, but also many other national, ethnic, and religious groups that developed distinct cultures or that came as migrants or invaders from other areas of Europe and Asia. In order to understand the development of the diverse ethnic groups of the nations now collectively called the former Soviet Union, the Russian Federation, and the other states that emerged from the collapse of the Soviet Union, it is necessary to look back on the historical development of the region.

The Russian Federation, which succeeded the USSR as the world's largest country in area, also inherited the majority of the ethnic groups—still numbering more than one hundred—that inhabited the Russian and Soviet Empires. The Russian Empire, the enormous state established by the conquest and colonization of vast territories in Europe and Asia, collapsed in revolution in the early twentieth century and was replaced by the world's first Communist state, which quickly became an empire in all but name. The Soviet successor to the Russian Empire, like its predecessor, splintered along ethnic lines even though the majority of the territory and population was included in the newly independent Russian Federation. The other states that emerged from the breakup of the Soviet Union are dominated by their titular ethnic group but, like the Russian Federation, have ethnically mixed populations that are often the result of Soviet-era population movements. The one ethnic group that forms substantial minorities in all of the other Soviet successor states is the Russians. The ethnic Russians, the historically dominant people in both the Russian and Soviet Empires, colonized a huge tract of land stretching from central Europe on the west to the Pacific Ocean on the east between the sixteenth and early twentieth centuries. The Russian settlement of northern Asia, the huge territory east of the Russian heartland between the Ural Mountains and the Pacific Ocean, has many parallels with the westward colonization of North America.

## Physical Setting

The great Eastern European Plain, known as the Russian Steppe or the Russian Plain, extends east from the borders of the member states of the European Union to the Ural Mountains, which, by convention, divide the European continent from Asia. To the south this great plain ends at the Caucasus Mountains. The Caucasus, lying between the Black and Caspian Seas, are also considered to divide Europe from Asia. The boundless steppe lands are mostly flat prairies in the south and rolling wooded areas or grasslands in the north. Beyond the mountain passes of the Urals and the Caucasus that serve as gateways to the flat steppe lands in the east and south, the huge territory presents few natural obstacles to migrations or invasions. The steppe retains numerous archeological remains indicating human habitation by the early Paleolithic period, although the southern Caucasus region is considered the most probable original home of the Caucasian peoples. Beyond the Russian Steppe, east of the Ural Mountains, is another vast plain, the Siberian Steppe, which, like the Russian Steppe, connects the various geographic regions, from the frozen tundra bordering the Arctic Ocean south to the deserts and oasis of Central Asia.

## Ethnic Diversity

Each of the many national and ethnic groups of Russia and the other states of the former Soviet Union has a separate and complex foundation. The origins of the Russian state, later the Russian Empire and the Soviet Union, however, are principally those of the Eastern Slavs, the ancient peoples that evolved into the Russian, Ukrainian, and Belarussian nations. The major pre-Soviet Eastern Slav states were Kievan Rus', Muscovy, and the later Russian Empire. Kievan Rus' represented the first territorial state established by the Eastern Slavs. It disappeared during the Mongol invasion of Europe in the thirteenth century, and Muscovy eventually emerged as the Eastern Slavs' new center. Muscovy, the territory around the city of Moscow, began the territorial conquests and expansion that eventually became the Russian Empire and the later Soviet Union. During the long history of the Eastern Slavs, three other nations—the Poles, the Lithuanians, and the Mongols—also played significant roles in the historical development of the Russian Empire.

A very important component of Russian history has been continual territorial expansion. The experience of Mongol/Tatar domination between the twelfth and fifteenth centuries culminated in Muscovy's attempts to consolidate Eastern Slav territory as Tatar control waned. Territorial expansion soon went beyond the ethnically Eastern Slav regions; by the eighteenth century the Tatar-dominated principality of Muscovy had developed and expanded to become the enormous Russian Empire, stretching from the western borders with Poland, Austria, and other central European states eastward to the Pacific Ocean. Its immense territorial expanse and its military might made the Russian Empire a major world power, but its acquisition of immense territories inhabited by non-Russian national groups began a historic pattern of ethnic confrontations and nationality problems that continue to the present day.

## Tribes and Migrations

Tribal peoples related to the ancient Persians were the first recorded inhabitants of the steppe region west of the Ural Mountains. Ancient peoples migrated across the vast territory to settle, or were displaced by migrations of other peoples farther to the east or south. Finnic tribes from their homeland on the Volga River dispersed across a large area from the Volga River valley to the Baltic Sea in several migrations that ended in the eighth century A.D. The Baltic peoples, the ancestors of the Lithuanians and Latvians, probably from origins farther east, migrated to northeastern Europe around 2000 B.C. Turkic peoples from Central Asia came in waves of migration from the fourth through the fourteenth centuries, including the large numbers that settled the Volga River basin as part of the Mongol invasion of Europe in the thirteenth century. The Slavs expanded from their original homelands in Poland and Ukraine between the sixth and eighth centuries to eventually dominate most of central and eastern Europe. The eastern branch of the Slavs continued their territorial expansion to eventually reach the Pacific Ocean in northeastern Asia. But the most ancient organized societies in the huge territory that comprised the former Soviet Union are believed to have been in the Caucasus region, in Armenia and Georgia.

## The Caucasus Region

### Armenians

Scientists and archeologists generally agree that the first organized, settled societies in the territory that later comprised the Soviet Union appeared in the Caucasus region in ancient times. According to the local folk tales and traditions, the Armenians are the descendants of Japheth, one of the sons of Noah, whose ark landed on Mount Ararat, where he and his descendants settled. Although it is sometimes difficult to separate the Armenians' history from their strong cultural traditions and legends, they now form a separate branch of the Caucasian peoples and speak the only surviving example of the Thraco-Phrygian group of the Indo-European languages. Their language is derived from a very early form of Indo-European and uses an alphabet that developed around A.D. 400. The uniqueness of the language and alphabet, along with the Armenians' cherished Christian religion, has allowed the Armenians to survive as a distinct nation for more than 3,000 years. However, sovereign Armenian states, with varying borders, have existed for only relatively short periods during their long and turbulent history.

Influenced by the advanced civilizations of the Fertile Crescent and the eastern Mediterranean, the Armenians developed a sophisticated civilization in what are now the Transcaucasus and eastern Anatolia regions. Because of its strategic location as a bridge between Europe and Asia, the southern region of the Caucasus, the mountainous Transcaucasus, was frequently invaded or overrun by migrating tribes. During the Bronze Age large tribal confederations were formed, laying the basis for the evolution of the early Armenian and Georgian states. By the sixth century B.C. the Armenians had formed a homogenous nation, called Utartu in the inscriptions left by the ancient Assyrians. Traditionally, the foundation of the Armenian nation was set in the year 624 B.C., making it one of the earliest of organized societies. The Armenian territories formed part of the ancient Persian Empire until the invasion of the Greeks led by Alexander the Great. Independent under a native dynasty starting from 189 B.C., the first Armenian kingdom faced the growing power of Rome in the west and the empire of the Parthians, later called Persians, in the east. While both Rome and Parthia were occupied in other areas, the Armenians extended their rule over a large territory in modern Turkey, Iran, and Azerbaijan, making Armenia an imperial power. However, this period of Armenian greatness was short lived. Rome sent its legions to restore its prestige in Asia Minor and Mesopotamia while the Parthians advanced from the east. The Armenians were restricted to their former boundaries, and they resumed their policy of trying to maintain a balance between their powerful neighbors.

The struggle for influence in Armenia was settled by treaty in A.D. 64. The brother of the Parthian ruler was accepted as king of Armenia but was to be crowned in Rome by the Roman emperor, Nero. Although the new dynasty, the Arsacid, began as a branch of the Parthian dynasty, it quickly became a distinctly Armenian monarchy. During the four-century rule of the Arsacid dynasty the Armenians became the first nation to embrace Christianity as their national religion, in A.D. 303. The Armenian national church was established in 491, when it separated from the Greek rite that dominated Christianity in eastern Europe and the Middle East. Religious fervor inspired a level of learning and cultural achievements unknown in other parts of Europe in the fourth and fifth centuries. The Armenian language, written in a script invented by St. Mesrob, a monk and scholar, in the year 410, formed an important part of the flourishing Armenian culture.

The strength of the Persian successor of the Parthian Empire continued to threaten the Armenians. The Romans also intervened to maintain their influence. The two powers effectively partitioned Armenia in the late fourth century. The western part became a vassal state of the Roman Empire, as represented by Byzantium, and the east was incorporated into the Persian Empire. Byzantine policies aimed at the extension of direct rule to Armenia and the destruction of its strong feudal system. The Persians allowed the eastern Armenians to retain their feudal traditions but continued to oppose and suppress Armenian Christianity. In 451 the Armenians in the east rose against Persian rule. Their defeat created several legendary martyrs and fostered a spirit of rebellion. By the late fifth century the Armenians had assumed religious and political control of their homeland, including their religious separation from the Greek-rite Byzantine church, but in the late sixth century their country was again partitioned between the Byzantines and the Persians.

The invasion of the Muslim Arabs ended the historic rivalry for influence in the Caucasus region. The Arabs occupied the region but allowed local nobles to rule so long as they paid the required taxes. The Arabs accepted a new Armenian dynasty, the Bagratid, which succeeded in uniting Armenia in 885. The Bagratids continued to rule in Armenia until 1045 when the last of their strongholds fell to the invading Byzantines. Another branch of the dynasty, established in neighboring Georgia, ruled there until the nineteenth century. Renewed Byzantine attacks finally ended the Bagratid kingdom, and Armenia was incorporated into the Byzantine Empire. Byzantine rule lasted only until 1071 when the Seljuk Turks, having overrun Persia (Iran), to the east, moved west to defeat the Byzantines and take control of the Armenian homeland.

The Seljuk Turks, unlike earlier invaders, settled in Armenia and the other territories they conquered. The Armenians slowly lost their dominance in the Transcaucasus region as the population of Turks grew. Emigration, wars, and forced conversions to Islam further depleted the Armenian population, particularly in the lowlands of eastern Anatolia. Many Christian Armenians migrated west to Byzantine territory, including many nobles and political leaders. Those Armenians that remained in the historic homeland were left leaderless and virtually defenseless. The mountainous regions around Karabakh and Zangezour were the only parts of the traditional Armenian territories that retained an Armenian military leadership, a local nobility, and a church hierarchy. In these small highland regions the Armenians' oral histories and religious education continued to exist. By 1300 the arrival of the Mongols, the European withdrawal from the Middle East, and the resurgence of the Turks under the Ottomans ended all Armenian independence. The last of the independent Armenian states fell to Muslim rule in 1375. The Armenian populations of only a few regions in the Caucasus Mountains were able to retain any autonomy.

### Georgians

The Georgian homeland is just north of Armenia on the eastern coast of the Black Sea. Like the Armenians, the Georgians were frequently subject to invaders moving between Europe and Asia. The ancient inhabitants of the region formed tribal confederations as early as the Bronze Age. During the third century B.C. the tribal groups evolved as the first Georgian states, Colchis on the Black Sea and Kartli in the mountainous interior. Influenced by the Greeks to the west, particularly the Greek colonies around the Black Sea, and by the Persians to the east, the ancient Georgians developed an advanced culture that in turn influenced the other Caucasian peoples. Roman military power was extended to Georgia in 66 B.C., and the Georgian states became Roman vassal states as a unified kingdom. The Georgians remained nominal Roman allies for nearly 400 years. The Roman name for the region, Iberia, taken from the Greek name for the coastal peoples of the Caucasus, was also applied to early Spain, where the people of the Ebro delta were named for the Ebro River, which translates to Iberus in the Greek language.

Christianity, introduced by the Romans, was adopted as the Georgian kingdom's official religion in A.D. 337. The new religion greatly influenced the flowering of Georgian culture in the fourth and fifth centuries. A complex written language was invented, mostly for the religious writings of the autonomous Georgian church. The Byzantines, the inheritors of Roman power in the east, exerted great influence on early Georgian religion and culture, particularly in architecture and religion. Deeply involved in the rivalry between Byzantium and Persia, the Georgians came under Armenian rule in the sixth century. The Georgian homeland split into several rival states but was briefly reunited in 571. The Georgians, like the Armenians and other Caucasian peoples, became deeply engaged in the struggle between the Greeks of the Byzantine Empire, the successor state to the Roman Empire in the eastern territories, and the still powerful Persians. The rivalry between the Byzantines and Persians was particularly violent between the fifth and seventh centuries. The history of the Georgians is closely tied to that of the neighboring Armenians, both of the ancient nations playing pivotal roles in the wider Caucasian civilization.

The collapse of Roman power in the fifth century left the Christian Georgian nation vulnerable to invaders. Persians, Byzantines, White Huns, Khazars, and other groups overran the Caucasus, using the passes in the high mountains to move between Asia and the Eastern European Plain to the north. Many of the invaders remained, causing the Caucasus to gradually become a patchwork of different ethnic, religious, and linguistic groups (see Significant People, Places, and Events in this chapter for national and ethnic groups). The invaders also drove many of the Caucasian groups from the lowlands, forcing them into the less-accessible mountains. Each of the high mountain valleys became the center of a distinct cultural group.

In 645 Arab invaders, driven by religious fervor, conquered the Caucasus and introduced their new religion, Islam. Although the Christian Georgians of the Transcaucasus resisted the new religion, many of the other Caucasian peoples adopted Islam. Christian Georgian kings and princes, under Arab sway, were left to govern as traditional rulers but were subject to heavy yearly taxes and special restrictions as non-Muslims. The numerous revolts against Muslim rule, the Byzantine-Arab wars, and the frequent invasions of their homeland between the seventh and ninth centuries devastated the Georgian nation. By the eighth century the Georgian nation had declined, losing control of many territories to neighboring peoples, to the invading Arabs, or to the powerful Persians to the south. In the ninth century a resurgent Georgia, led by the Bagratid dynasty, reunified most of historical Georgia.

The arrival of Turkic migrants from Central Asia in the eleventh century ended Arab political power and added a strong Turkic element to the population of the Caucasus region. The Turks took control of the Arab Empire,

the caliphate, centered in Baghdad. Over time they expanded by conquer-
ing the Caucasus region and taking Asia Minor from the weakened Byzantine Empire. Although pressed by the rising power of the Muslim peoples to
the south, the Georgians threw off foreign rule and revived, under a string
of strong rulers, in the twelfth and thirteenth centuries, with a great flowering of literature, culture, and political power. However, when the Mongols
invaded the Caucasus in 1236, they ended the burgeoning cultures of the
Christian nations. By 1243 all the Georgian territories had been overrun. The
Mongol invasion began centuries of fragmentation and decline in the Caucasus, for the Mongols devastated the region, destroying what they could not
carry off. Massacres of the Christian populations forced many Christians to
flee. Tamerlane, or Timur, one of the successors of the Mongol's far-flung
empire, led a new invasion of the Caucasus in the fourteenth century, his
forces again massacring a majority of the Christians. For centuries the Caucasus was a frontier district at the confluence of the competing Persian and
Turkic Empires. The Persian Safavid dynasty, established in 1499, introduced
Shia Islam as the state religion in the territory under its control, including
the important Turkic-speaking Caucasian territory known as Azerbaijan, the
homeland of the Azeris.

### Azeris

The third of the major Caucasian national groups, the Azeris, are a people
of mixed Turkic and Caucasian heritage. Their homeland, lying in the eastern Transcaucasus and the region west of the Caspian Sea, extends from
modern Azerbaijan into northwestern Iran, a region known as Iranian Azerbaijan. Historically the Persians dominated the Caspian territories. A Persian
ruler, appointed by Alexander the Great, established an independent state in
the region in the fourth century B.C. Although long claimed by the Persians,
firm Persian control was finally established only in the third century B.C. Except for a brief period of Byzantine rule in the early seventh century A.D., the
territory remained under Persian domination until the Arab invasion of the
Caucasus in the eighth century.

   The Arab invasion and their conversion of many of the region's inhabitants to Islam began the separation of the Azeris from the Christian peoples
of the Caucasus. The Caspian territories remained part of the Muslim Empire, the caliphate, until the eleventh century, although the Persian language
and culture continued to prevail. The Seljuks, a Turkic people migrating from
Central Asia, overran Persia and moved into the Caspian region in the

eleventh century. The Seljuk Turks colonized the region and adopted the Muslim religion of the earlier inhabitants. Extensive mixing of the Seljuk Turks with the Caucasian and Persian inhabitants eventually resulted in the replacement of the Persian language and culture with a hybrid dominated by the Seljuks' Turkic language and culture. This combined culture evolved as the Azeris, a Turkic-speaking Caucasian national group.

The Azeris inhabited a mountainous territory that formed a frontier district at the junction of the Turkish and Persian Empires. The frequent change of rulers between the Turkish and Persian Empires reinforced the distinct Azeri culture, which continued to absorb influences from both. The Persian Safavid dynasty, established in 1499, from its beginnings in present Iranian Azerbaijan, took control of the region and introduced its official state religion, the Shia branch of Islam. In the subsequent centuries the Azeris lived on the cultural and religious fault lines that separated Christian from Muslim and the majority Sunni Muslims from the minority Shia Muslims.

## Other Caucasian Nations

The numerous Caucasian nations, of indigenous or Turkic origins, often inhabiting small mountainous territories, have historically maintained an inward-looking, xenophobic view of the outside world. Little is known of the origins of the various small Caucasian nations before the coming of the steppe and nomadic tribes who intermingled with the local peoples. Their mountainous homelands, forming part of the bridge between Europe and Asia, were regularly overrun by invaders. The invaders at times took control of some mountain valleys to become yet another Caucasian national group. The more remote tribal groups would retreat to mountain strongholds where they could hold out until the invaders departed. Historically trade ties were maintained with the Slavic peoples to the north and with the Byzantines. Famed as horsemen, they traded horses, but also honey, jewelry, and valuable furs.

Many of the ancient Caucasian peoples were known to Greek and Roman writers and historians. The Greeks, who colonized the coastal regions as early as the sixth century B.C., maintained trading and cultural contacts with the various Caucasian tribes. Latin culture began to penetrate the Caucasus following the Roman conquest of the Greek cities in 65 B.C. Many of the tribes, particularly those near the coastal trading centers, adopted Latin culture and learned the Latin language. The Christian religion was introduced to the Roman Caucasian territories in the third and fourth centuries. Christianity was often practiced as a combination of the Romans' beliefs and traditional pagan customs. The separation of the Roman Empire into western and eastern parts in the fourth century brought the Caucasians under Eastern Roman or Byzantine influence. Greek Byzantine cultural and religious authority gradually replaced the earlier Christian beliefs with the Byzantine version, Orthodox Christianity. Greek-speaking Orthodox monks were the first to bring Christian beliefs to many of the isolated tribes in the mountainous interior. The Caucasian tribes carried on an extensive trade with the Byzantines, receiving goods and luxuries unavailable in their homeland in exchange for horses, furs, and other goods.

The Mongol invasion of the thirteenth century drove many lowland tribes to seek refuge in the mountain strongholds, further fragmenting the Caucasian territories among the various tribal groups. The tribes, often so small that they inhabited just one or two mountain valleys, unlike the larger Caucasian nations, did not develop a strong sense of nationhood. Tribal loyalties and patriarchal clans remained more important than the ties of culture or language during the period of tribal consolidation. However, between the seventh and twelfth centuries the tribal groups gradually began to strengthen alliances into tribal federations, forming the basis of the later national sentiments and cultures. Many of the small Caucasian nations were originally settled agriculturists or cattle and horse breeders, but near constant invasions and war forced them to adopt a warrior culture in order to survive. Contact with Christian Byzantium ended with the thirteenth-century Mongol invasion.

By the fifteenth century a number of distinctive national groups had emerged in the region north of the high Caucasian peaks, although tribal and clan loyalties continued to supersede national sentiment until the twentieth century. The Caucasian Kabards and the Turkic Kumyks developed sophisticated state systems that dominated surrounding peoples between the eleventh and the thirteenth centuries. The Abkhaz united much of the western Caucasus in the ninth century, although the neighboring Georgians disputed their power, one of the historical grievances that continue to mark the region.

### The Steppe Lands: Tribal Migrations and the Eastern Slavs

Long before the emergence of the Slavs, groups related to the ancient Persians inhabited the steppe lands of present-day Russia and Ukraine. The best-known of the nomadic groups, the ancient Scythians, an Iranian people whose territory spanned a vast region from the Danube on the west to the borders of China on the east, dominated the flat steppe lands and flourished from the eighth century B.C. to about 200 B.C. Nomadic conquerors and skilled horsemen, they are believed by archeologists to have originated in the region of the Altai Mountains in western Siberia before expanding to the west to occupy the steppe of southern European Russia in the early first millennium B.C. Although the Scythians had no system of writing, the early Greeks recorded extensive contacts with the Scythian tribes. Items found in Scythian graves point to a widespread network of trade routes, including trading ties to the sophisticated Greek colonies around the Black Sea.

Over many centuries vast tribal migrations overran the flat, open plains, often driving earlier inhabitants before them. In the third century B.C., the Scythian tribes were displaced by related Sarmatians, who in turn were overrun by waves of Germanic Goths from the west in the second and third centuries A.D. Huns from north-central Asia overran the region in the fourth century, scattering the Goths and precipitating the great waves of migrations that eventually destroyed the Roman Empire and changed the human geography of Europe. The Avars, another nomadic group driven out of Central Asia in the fourth century by stronger tribes, moved west to plunder present European Russia and the Balkans. The Magyars passed through the region to eventually settle in central Europe. Although some of the migrating groups subjugated large territories, they left little of lasting historical importance. Around the same time, small Turkic-speaking tribes moved into the central and southern parts of the Russian steppe, the forerunner of the later migrations that brought Turkic peoples to the Caucasus, Asia Minor, and southeastern Europe. Some Caucasian tribes moved north into the Volga basin to escape the Arab invasion of the Caucasus in the mid-eighth century.

The Khazars, another Turkic people, appeared in the Transcaucasus in the second century A.D. They subsequently settled the lower Volga region and by the seventh century controlled the extensive steppe lands of the southern Russian Plain. Between the eighth and tenth centuries the Khazar Empire extended from the northern shores of the Black Sea and the Caspian Sea in the south to the Urals in the east and as far west as Kiev. The Khazars developed an advanced culture centered on the trade routes that crossed the steppe lands. Eventually, they controlled numerous tribal groups and levied tribute from the Eastern Slavs in present Poland and Ukraine. In the tenth century, they established friendly relations with the Byzantine Empire, partly as a military alliance against the Arabs. The Khazar nobility embraced Judaism in the eighth century, although Cyril and Methodius, Greek missionaries honored

for introducing Orthodoxy to the Slavs, converted some of the Khazars to
Christianity. Religious tolerance was complete throughout the Khazar territories. The highly evolved Khazar civilization ended with their defeat by the
forces of Sviatoslav, duke of Kiev, in 965. A joint force of Slavs and Byzantines destroyed the remains of the Khazar Empire in 1016, removing one of
the buffers between the Christian and Islamic peoples. Although the Khazars disappeared from history, they are believed by many to be the ancestors
of the majority of eastern European Jews.

*Kievan Rus', c. 1000*

## The Finnic, Volga, and Baltic Nations

### The Finnic Groups

The various Finnic tribes, believed to have settled the territories between the Volga, Oka, and Sura Rivers more than 2,000 years ago, were nomadic tribes roaming as far east as the Ural Mountains. The Finnic peoples were known in the valleys of the Volga and its tributaries as early as Neolithic times. They survived by slash and burn agriculture, hunting, fishing, and trading with neighboring peoples. The traditional religion of the Finnic peoples consisted of various shamanistic beliefs often revolving around veneration of ancestors. Byzantine records mention the tribes as seminomadic herders.

Although scholars dispute the exact dates, before the Christian era various migrations of Finnic tribes moved northwest to populate present Finland, Estonia, and northwestern Russia. Other groups moved north to the valleys of the Kama and Vychegda Rivers in northern European Russia. The Finnic peoples that remained in the Volga region began to divide into identifiable regional groups or tribes by the sixth century. Between the seventh and twelfth centuries their patriarchal and clan-based social systems gave way to more village-oriented social systems, as settled agriculture took hold among the scattered tribes. In the eighth century A.D., the Turkic Khazars established a nominal authority in the Volga region, but by the mid-ninth century most of the Finnic tribes had come under the rule of the ancient Bulgars, called the Black Bulgars or Volga Bulgars.

At the end of the sixteenth century, the various Finnic peoples of present European Russia had coalesced into distinct national groups. The tribal groups that settled in the northwest, along the Baltic Sea and north to the White Sea and the Arctic Ocean, included the Finns, Karels, Ingrians, Veps, Ludians, and Votes. Other Finnic tribal groups split from the northwestern migration to turn north into the fertile river valleys north of the Volga basin. Those Finnic peoples that remained in their ancestral home in the Volga River basin developed as the Mordvin and Mari nations, and mixed with the Turkic and Bulgar peoples as ancestors of the Tatars, Chavash, and Bashkorts.

### The Volga Bulgars

The ancestors of the Volga Bulgars are believed to have originated in the North Caucasus region between the Caspian and Black Seas. During the seventh and eighth centuries the Caucasian Bulgars began various migrations from their ancient homeland. Some of the tribes followed the coast of the Black Sea to finally settle in the southern Balkan Peninsula, others, some as early as the fifth century, moved in small groups to settle the middle Volga River basin, where they were joined by other clans over several centuries. The expansion of the Khazars in the seventh century and the Arab invasion of the Caucasus in the eighth century pushed other Bulgar groups to migrate north to the Volga region.

The Bulgars mixed with the earlier Finnic peoples of the Volga region, adopting many Finnic cultural traditions and establishing close ties to the neighboring peoples. The mixture of the Bulgar and Finnic groups developed a strong and distinct culture. Identifiable as a distinct national group by the tenth century, the Black Bulgars, later claimed to be the ancestors of the Chavash and the Tatars, adopted the Islamic religion brought to their territory by traders and adventurers. Adopting Muslim models of civic organization, the Black Bulgars created an extensive early medieval empire that eventually controlled many neighboring Finnic and Turkic peoples. At the height of its power from the tenth to the twelfth centuries, the Volga Bulgar state controlled a large territory on the upper and middle Volga, making it one of the largest European states of the time.

The Mongols overran the flourishing Bulgar state in 1236. Many Bulgars were absorbed into the ranks of the invaders to form the later Tatar national group. Others, calling themselves Chavash and known to the Slavs as Chuvash, migrated northward to escape Tatar raiders to eventually settle territory north of the Volga River. The Muslim Chavash, although under the nominal rule of the Tatar state known as the khanate of Kazan', were mostly converted to Christianity by Russian Orthodox monks venturing into the unknown east in the fourteenth century. By 1500 most of the Chavash had embraced Christianity and almost all traces of their earlier Muslim faith disappeared. About the same time the Chavash abandoned their seminomadic life as cattle breeders and settled in agricultural communities.

The Tatars, also claiming descent from the Black Bulgars, were first known as nomadic tribal groups living in northeastern Mongolia and in the area around Lake Baikal in the fifth century A.D. Migrating west, they mixed with other Turkic peoples and small groups first appeared in the Volga River basin in the eighth century. In the Volga region they mixed with the Finnic, Turkic, and Slavic groups to develop as part of the Black Bulgar culture. According to Tatar traditions, an embassy from the Muslim caliphate in Baghdad came to the region in A.D. 922 to introduce the Islamic religion. Like the other Black Bulgar groups they adopted the Islamic religion and gave up their

Turkic script in favor of the Arabic alphabet. The adoption of Islam stimulated greater ties to the brilliant civilization of the Muslims to the south, leading to a period of great advances in learning and art. Kazan' and other Tatar cities became centers of Muslim learning and dissemination.

The Mongol invasion of 1236 devastated the Volga lands. The fast-moving Mongols, by 1240, had moved west to capture Kiev, and later pushed into central Europe. Several tribes moving west with the Mongols settled in the fertile river valley where they mixed with the earlier Finnic and Bulgar peoples. After centuries of rebellions against the Mongols, the Bulgars, by then more ethnically mixed, finally accepted indirect rule as part of the Mongols' far-flung empire. By the mid-fifteenth century the khanate centered on Kazan', founded as the Tatar capital in 1401 and dominated by the Volga Tatars of Bulgar, Finnic, and Mongol ancestry, had emerged as the successor to the earlier Black Bulgar state. The Tatars, reflecting their mixed ancestry, became much more European physically than most Turkic-speaking peoples. The neighboring Finnic nations remained as subject peoples of the Tatar khanate but mostly retained their traditional religious beliefs and their clan structures.

## The Baltic Groups

Tribal groups that were the ancestors of the Baltic peoples, later known as Latvians and Lithuanians, arrived in northeastern Europe as early as 2000 B.C. They were mentioned in early chronicles as tribal peoples in the fertile valleys, but in the eighth and ninth centuries, they were pushed north by the expanding Slav population. They eventually settled along the eastern shore of the Baltic Sea south of the Finnic peoples. Their fierce resistance halted the expansion of the Slavs to the northwest. The Baltic tribes gradually split into two distinct groups, the ancestors of the Latvians and Lithuanians, who were pushed north into territory inhabited by Finnic tribes, and the Southern Balts, or Borussians, who moved south and were later eliminated or assimilated by the Germans, leaving behind only a version of their name as Prussia.

The territory of the Baltic tribes straddled the major trade routes between Scandinavia and the Mediterranean, leading to the development of a trading culture and contacts with many distinct nations. The Baltic peoples developed from a fusion of a number of distinct tribal groups. Culturally they adopted many traditions and traits from the neighboring Finnic groups, the Slavs, and the peoples living around the Baltic Sea, particularly the Scandinavians and Germans.

Christianity arrived in the Baltic region with German missionaries and armed religious crusaders in the twelfth and thirteenth centuries. During the thirteenth century, the German Teutonic Knights established an effective German presence in the Latvian territories. The Germans, intent on spreading Christianity to the pagan tribes, established a strong feudal state that controlled the homelands of the defeated Latvians and the neighboring Finnic peoples, the Livonians and Estonians. The Teutonic Knights eventually took the name German Knights of the Livonian Order. Great feudal land holdings were parceled out to German knights but were worked by Baltic peasants held as serfs—virtual slavery. German culture was so strong that in 1282, Riga, the major port of the region, joined the Hanseatic League, the vast network of mostly German trading cities that dominated trade in northern Europe.

The Lithuanians, farther to the south, successfully resisted the crusader onslaught. Although the Lithuanians were among the last in Europe to adopt Roman Catholicism, which was introduced to Lithuania by the neighboring Poles, the Catholic Church became a crucial part of Lithuanian national culture. The Lithuanian state began to expand in the fourteenth century, and by the mid-1300s, the Lithuanian Empire stretched from the Baltic Sea on the north to the Black Sea on the south. Lithuanian expansion rivaled that of the neighboring Poles by the end of the fourteenth century, making a political alliance welcome to both peoples. In 1385 the two states signed a treaty creating a dynastic alliance while retaining sovereignty in their respective territories. In 1399 the Lithuanians and Poles led a great Christian army against the Tatar invaders of Tamerlane. The battle ended without a clear victor, but Tamerlane was so weakened that he eventually returned to Asia. Beginning in 1501, the Lithuanian and Polish kingdoms were under the same ruler; after 1569, they shared a joint legislature. Over time, the Poles, with their larger population and more strategic territory, gradually became the dominant people of the empire. The Polish language and culture began to permeate the historically Lithuanian territories, particularly among the upper classes in Lithuania, Ukraine, and Belarus.

## Central Asia (Turkestan)

The original homelands of the Turkic peoples comprised an enormous territory stretching from Mongolia and northwestern China to the Caspian Sea on the west. Migrations from this region, between the fourth and fourteenth

*Nineteenth-century engraving of Genghis Khan (Free Library of Philadelphia)*

centuries, extended the Turkic languages and cultures to the Middle East, Asia Minor, Siberia, the Caucasus, and southeastern Europe. Inhabited as early as 3000 B.C., the region developed sophisticated civilizations along the trade route later known as the Silk Road, the great trade route between the Mediterranean and China. Divided into numerous tribal groups, many of the Turkic peoples of Central Asia came under Persian rule and cultural influences as early as 500 B.C. Geographical and historical factors made the region a bridge linking the Eastern and Western worlds, and the Turkic homelands formed part of the route taken by many of the great conquerors and migrating peoples.

The Silk Road, the most important trade route between Europe and Asia, traversed the homelands of the Turkic peoples. The Turkic groups developed wealthy, advanced cultures based on great trading cities, such as Samarkand, Bukhara, and Merv. An extensive system of irrigated agriculture added to the wealth and stability of the region. In the eighth century A.D., some nomadic tribes began to settle the vast plains to the northwest, later called the Kazakh Plain or Kazakh Steppe. Persians, Chinese, Greeks, and others were drawn to the region's legendary riches. Numerous conquerors controlled all or part of the territory over many centuries, although Persian rule and influence remained paramount until the expansion of the Mongols in the region to the east. In the thirteenth century the Mongols overran the Turkic tribes and states and absorbed many Turkic tribal groups into the vast Mongol armies that continued west into Europe.

Nomadic tribes of Mongols and Turkic groups, members of a loose confederation, were subsequently subdued and united under a tribal chief, Temüjin, later called Genghis Khan. After subjugating the various local tribes, he led the Mongol armies to conquer northern China, Turkestan, Afghanistan, and the North Caucasus between 1213 and 1224. The Turkic peoples, conquered and absorbed into the Golden Horde (see Significant People, Places, and Events, this chapter), formed a large part of the Mongol armies that invaded Europe in the early thirteenth century. The Mongol invasion, led by Batu Khan, overran the Russian Plain between 1231 and 1236 and moved into central Europe in 1241. The Mongol conquest ended the separate development of the small states that had been created by the diverse peoples of the vast region, including the previously discussed kingdoms of the Armenians and Georgians. Along with the Armenians, Georgians, and other Caucasian peoples, the Bulgar, Tatar, and Finnic peoples of the Volga basin were absorbed into the vast Mongol Empire. Many of the migrating Turkic and Mongol tribal groups settled the newly conquered territory between the Ural Mountains and the Volga River. Farther west, the

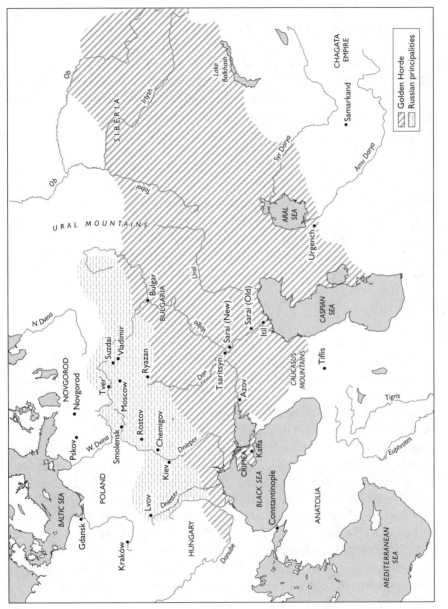

Khanate of the Golden Horde, c. 1300

Legend:
Golden Horde
Russian principalities

Mongol/Tatar invaders overran the Eastern Slav territories except for small regions in the west and northwest.

Questions of succession, a weakening of the warrior culture, and the growth of various power centers finally ended the authority of the Golden Horde, the part of the Mongol Empire that survived in eastern Europe and northwestern Asia. Following the disintegration of the Golden Horde in the fourteenth century, the Turkic groups, collectively called Tatars by the Slavs, established several successor states that dominated an enormous territory that included most of present European Russia, the Caucasus, and Central Asia. The fortress city of Kazan', founded as the capital of the Volga Tatars in 1401 in the Volga-Kama region, became the capital of the khanate of Kazan' in 1445. The powerful Kazan' khanate extracted tribute from the Eastern Slav states west of the Urals, including the emerging Muscovite state, as the price of continued Slav autonomy. Rich on tribute and trade, Kazan' fostered a second great flowering of Tatar culture, arts, and literature in the fifteenth and sixteenth centuries.

## The Eastern Slavs

Little is known of the origin of the Slavs. They are believed to have settled very early in the Carpathian Mountains or in territory now forming part of Belarus. Other theories place their origins in the marshy Polesie lowlands in the region of the present border between Belarus and Ukraine or farther west in Poland. They were probably dominated in succession by the Scythians and Sarmatians, the Goths, the Huns, and the Avars, whose westward expansion they shared. Agriculturists and beekeepers, although some were hunters, fishermen, herders, or trappers, they gradually formed a tribal federation that began to dominate neighboring peoples. By A.D. 600, the Slavs were the dominant ethnic group on the Russian Steppe. Between the sixth and eighth centuries the great Slav migrations extended Slavic culture into the Balkans and central Europe; the Western Slavs developed from those Slavic groups that moved into central Europe, and the Southern Slavs migrated into the Balkan Peninsula. By the ninth century, the Eastern Slavs had settled northern Ukraine, Belarus, Moldova, and northwestern Russia, driving the earlier inhabitants from the central parts of the great plains. The Eastern Slav expansion forced the non-Slavic peoples into the less-accessible territories, leaving the flat, fertile steppe lands to Slavic colonization. The Eastern Slavs, taking advantage of the river trade routes and the lack of geographical barriers, spread across the steppe lands from the

*Rurik, leader of the Viking Varangians 862–879 (Bettmann/Corbis)*

Baltic Sea to the Black Sea. Eventually they divided into three distinct ethnic groups.

The Slav migrations displaced many earlier peoples from the steppes, as noted, pushing the majority of the Finnic and Baltic peoples into present Finland, the Baltic countries, and northwestern Russia, and forcing the Turkic peoples to retreat into the Caucasus and Central Asia. Smaller tribal migrations established Slav communities east of the Oka River and in the basin of the upper Volga. A number of small Slavic principalities emerged, often warring among themselves. In the northeast, the Eastern Slavs colonized the territory around present Moscow by intermingling with the Finnic tribes already occupying the territory.

The origin of the Eastern Slav state coincides with the ninth-century arrival of the Scandinavian warriors and traders, the Vikings, called Varangians by the Eastern Slavs, whose migration paralleled those of the Norsemen and Vikings in the west. The Varangians followed the rivers, the major trade routes, establishing trading posts and fortified settlements. According to the *Primary Chronicle,* the first history of the Eastern Slav state, the Varangian leader, Rurik, established his authority and his dynasty at Novgorod, just south of modern St. Petersburg, in 862. From Novgorod the Varangians made their way down the great rivers and established important trade routes from Kiev to Byzantium. They repeatedly threatened the Byzantine capital at Constantinople in the ninth and tenth centuries before they gradually merged with the Eastern Slavs, often serving as soldiers of the various Slavic princes. Oleg, Rurik's heir, seized Kiev, to the south, in 879 and moved his capital there in 886. Oleg's Eastern Slav Empire, known as Kievan Rus' or Kievan Russia, included nearly all of present-day Ukraine, Belarus, and part of the Finnic homeland in northwestern European Russia. Oleg subdued the various Eastern Slav tribes, and in A.D. 907 he led a campaign against Constantinople. He signed a commercial treaty with the Byzantine Empire in 911, with the Eastern Slav state recognized as an equal.

Kievan Rus' prospered because it dominated the trade routes from the Black Sea to the Baltic Sea and had an unlimited supply of furs, honey, wax, and slaves for trade. Historians have long debated the role of the Varangians in the establishment and expansion of Kievan Rus'. It is possible that the name used for some Varangians, Rus' or Rhos, was extended to all the inhabitants of the Kievan state. Other theories trace the name *Rus'* to a Slavic origin. Russian historians—particularly during the Soviet era—have stressed the Slavic influence in the development of the Eastern Slav state. Although the origins of the state remain open to debate, it is known that the Slavic tribes had formed their own regional authorities by A.D. 860, but most historians now agree that the arrival of the Varangians greatly accelerated the development and expansion of Kievan Rus'.

Kievan Rus' reached the height of its power and influence in the tenth century. The powerful Slav state absorbed considerable Byzantine cultural and religious influence. Vladimir, later St. Vladimir, accepted baptism into the Byzantine church in 988. Orthodox Christianity was declared the state religion, and all subjects were ordered to accept baptism. Although many of Vladimir's subjects continued to adhere to their pre-Christian beliefs, Orthodox Christianity formed one of the pillars of the Eastern Slav state. Vladimir's choice of Eastern Orthodoxy as the official religion reflected his close personal ties to the Byzantine Empire, which dominated the Black Sea and therefore Kievan Rus's trade on its most vital commercial route, the Dnepr River, which flows into the Black Sea.

Adherence to Orthodox Christianity had important long-range political, cultural, and religious consequences for the Eastern Slavs. The church used a liturgy written in Cyrillic (see Significant People, Places, and Events, this chapter) and a body of translations from the Greek that had been produced for the South Slavs. The existence of this South Slav literature facilitated the Eastern Slavs' conversion to Christianity and introduced basic Greek philosophy, science, and historiography to them without the necessity of their learning Greek. Although educated people in medieval western and central Europe learned Latin, the Eastern Slavs learned neither Greek nor Latin, isolating them from both Byzantine and Western cultures. Orthodox Christian missionaries, responding to religious zeal, carried Orthodoxy and the Slavic language to the numerous non-Slav peoples outside the boundaries of Kievan Rus', winning many converts, particularly among the Finnic peoples of the Volga River basin and the north. Conservative Christian morality greatly influenced Kievan Rus's cultural development.

Between 1054 and 1073 civil law was codified in the Russkaia Pravda, the Eastern Slavs' first written laws. The laws clarified the relationships between the different social classes and set guidelines for relations between the dominant Slavs and the growing number of non-Slav groups in the state. The *Primary Chronicle*, composed in 1116, described the origins of Kievan Rus' and its expansion by the conquest and Christianization of the neighboring non-Slav peoples.

In 1147 a military outpost was founded on the Moskva River on the eastern edge of Kievan Rus' territory. The founder of the outpost, Yury Dolgoruky, constructed the first kremlin in 1156 as protection against the wild tribal peoples that raided Kievan Rus' territory from the south and east. The outpost, called Moskva or Moscow, became an important trading center. Following Kiev's decline in the mid-twelfth century, Moscow was made the capital of a separate principality, Muscovy. Moscow's expansion as a political entity paralleled the rapid decline of Kievan Rus'.

The zenith of Kievan Rus' territorial expansion in the eleventh century was followed by rapid disintegration during the twelfth century. The empire swiftly split into warring principalities and states. Powerful Novgorod, in the north, had obtained self-government in 997 and declared its independence from Kiev in 1136. The strength of the Novgorodian republic, called Great Novgorod, rested on its economic prosperity and its republican form of government. Situated on the great trade route to the Volga valley and the lands to the south, Novgorod became a westernized state through trade and cultural contacts with the cultures to the west. Along with London, Bruges, and Bergen, the Novgorodian capital formed one of the four chief trading centers of the Hanseatic League. The Novgorodians extended the power of their republic over the entire north of Russia and founded many colonies, some beyond the Urals, where they levied tribute from the indigenous tribal peoples. Novgorodian traders and Christian missionaries venturing north and east were often the first European travelers to encounter many of the small tribal groups of northern Russia and on both sides of the Ural Mountains. The rival Muscovite and Novgorodian states increasingly competed for influence among the various smaller Slavic states that emerged from the disintegration of the Eastern Slav Empire.

The Swedes conquered and Christianized the majority of the Finnic peoples of northeastern Europe in the twelfth and thirteenth centuries. In 1216 the pope confirmed Swedish title to much of Finland and granted missionary rights to territories to the east and north. The expansion of Sweden and the crusading Teutonic Knights in the northwest brought Western influence to a large area of the Baltic coast and northwestern Russia. In 1240 Alexander Nevsky of Novgorod defeated the Swedes and in 1242 stopped the eastward expansion of the Germanic Teutonic Knights, who retained control only of the Baltic territories. In 1323 a treaty divided the region east of Finland between Novgorod and Sweden. The Finnic peoples under Novgorodian rule mostly adopted Orthodox Christianity, while the Finns, the largest of the Finnic groups, were converted to Roman Catholicism and later adopted the Protestant Lutheran faith of their Swedish rulers. Traditionally, the division between the Finns and the Karels and other eastern Finnic peoples was based on the line that divided the Orthodox Christians from the Roman Catholic/Lutheran west.

## The Tatar Conquest

As noted previously, Batu Khan led the Mongol-Turkic invasion of European Russia and the Caucasus in the mid-thirteenth century. Although Batu Khan's troops defeated those of the Eastern Slav princes in 1228, they withdrew without attempting to follow up the victory. They returned in 1236 and, in less than four years, brought all the Eastern Slav principalities and states, except Novgorod, under their domination. The invaders virtually destroyed all the important Eastern Slav cities except Novgorod and Pskov, which escaped conquest in the northwest. The Tatar invaders established the Kipchak khanate in the Volga River basin, popularly called the Golden Horde for the gorgeous tents erected for the leaders along the Volga River. The Tatar invasion and the destruction of Kievan Rus' in 1237–1240 terminated the remaining political power of Eastern Slavs and destroyed the loose confederation of principalities that had gradually replaced centralized rule during the decline of the Eastern Slav Empire.

The impact of the Mongol-Tatar invasion on the Eastern Slav territories was uneven. Many important centers, such as Kiev, never recovered their former power. The Slav territories, already divided before the invasion of the Tatar-Mongol invasion, further split into a large number of semiautonomous states or principalities, often with numerous non-Slav populations. Under Tatar rule the various Eastern Slav states retained their own rulers and internal administration. However, they remained tributaries of the khan, who confirmed princely succession and extracted heavy taxes. Given that in the early fourteenth century the Empire of the Golden Horde adopted Islam as its official religion, most of the Eastern Slavs, the peoples of the Volga region, and the northern Caucasus were exposed to both Muslim and Asian influences. The separation of those Slavs under Tatar rule from the unconquered Slavs of the northwest began the development of three distinct Eastern Slav divisions. Internecine warfare among the Tatar leaders and attempts by various Slav princes to end Muslim hegemony contributed to the decline of the Golden Horde in the fourteenth century. The invasion from the east by other Turkic and Mongol groups led by Tamerlane splintered the Tatar Empire following the sack of the capital, Kazan', in 1395. After Tamerlane's death the Empire of the Golden Horde broke up into the independent khanates of Astrakhan, Kazan', Crimea, and Sibir', loosening the Tatar hold on the territories of the Eastern Slavs. The Slavs of the northwest continued to prosper; however, a new political entity, centered on the city of Moscow, began to flourish under loose Mongol-Tatar rule. Although the Muscovites felt strong enough to challenge Tatar power and even defeated the Golden Horde in

1380, Tatar domination of the Russian territories, along with the system of the Slavic princes paying tribute, continued until about 1480.

## The Russian Lands in 1300

Gradually, a number of distinct ethnic and linguistic groups developed in the vast steppe lands, although until the growth of national ideals five centuries later most identified with local cultures rather than as members of distinct national or ethnic groups. The three Eastern Slav nations culturally evolved as the Great Russians in the center and south, still under Tatar authority, and in the northwest under the independent Republic of Great Novgorod; the White Russians (or Belarussians) in the northwest, separated from the Great Russians by the Mongol-Tatar invasion; and the Little Russians, or Ukrainians, in the west and southwest. To the northwest of the Slavs were the Balts and the Finnic peoples. Other Finnic groups lived in the Volga basin under direct Tatar rule, and various Turko-Tatar groups had settled in the Volga region and in the North Caucasus. The Christian Armenians and Georgians, and Azeris and the smaller Islamic Caucasian peoples, under the rule of the Ottoman Turks or the Persians, inhabited the Caucasus Mountains region in the south. At the end of the thirteenth century, the Tatar-Mongol Golden Horde ruled all of European Russia except for small territories in the northwest, in western Ukraine, and in the Caucasus.

The great tribal migrations had ended, leaving a complicated pattern of religious, cultural, and linguistic groups in European Russia. These groups, with little national or cultural sentiment reaching beyond the local or tribal territory, mostly identified themselves by language, religion, kinship, or ancestry. The Turkic Khazars had disappeared, although Judaism remained. The Tatars had adopted the Islamic religion that spread from the south, but their subject peoples mostly retained Christian beliefs. The Eastern Slavs and some smaller Finnic groups, although mostly under the rule of the Golden Horde, identified themselves primarily as Orthodox Christians as opposed to the Islam of their Tatar rulers. Roman Catholicism remained the dominant religion in many areas of the northwest and in the Baltic region, where Scandinavian influence remained important. The Caucasus, particularly Christian Georgia and Armenia, was fought over by two Muslim powers, the Turks and the Persians. Islam had become the major religion in the eastern Volga region, the Tatar heartland, and was the predominant faith in the huge and varied territory in Central Asia known collectively as Turkestan.

## Timeline

| | |
|---|---|
| before 3000 B.C. | Caucasian race emerges in the Caucasus region. |
| 3000–2000 B.C. | Finnic and Baltic peoples migrate across the Steppe to settle the temperate zones of northeastern Europe. |
| 8th century B.C. | Armenians move into Asia Minor and settle the Transcaucasus. |
| 7th century B.C. | Scythians control the northern shore of the Black Sea and the Crimea. |
| 3rd century B.C. | The Scythians are displaced by the Sarmatians. |
| 3rd century A.D. | Germanic Goths invade from the west. |
| 4th century A.D. | Turkic Avars invade from the east. Turkic tribes called Tata, or Tatar, begin to settle the Volga River basin. |
| 7th century A.D. | The Turkic Khazars create a powerful state in southern Russia. |
| 8th century A.D. | The Eastern Bulgars (Chavash) establish an empire in the Volga region. |
| 9th century A.D. | Varangians, Vikings from Scandinavia, follow the rivers from the Baltic coast into central Russia. |
| 862 | A Varangian chief, Hrorerk, called Rurik by the Slavs, is accepted as ruler of Novgorod. |
| 922 | The Tatars adopt Islam as their official religion. |
| 965–967 | The Eastern Slavs conquer the major cities of the Khazars. |
| 971 | The Eastern Slavs conquer the Black Bulgar state on the Volga. |
| 988 | Vladimir, the grand duke of Kiev, accepts Byzantine Christianity. |
| 1016 | A joint Eastern Slav-Byzantine force destroys the remnant of the Khazar Empire. |
| 1054–1073 | Russkaia Pravda, the first Russian law, is written to clarify relations between the classes and the various ethnic groups. |
| 1116 | The first written history of the Eastern Slavs, the Povest' vremennykh let, the *Primary Chronicle*, is composed. |
| 1147 | Moscow is founded by Yury Dolgoruky. |
| 1216–1219 | The Mongols conquer Central Asia and begin to raid Kievan Rus' territory. |

| 1221–1231 | The Mongols invade the Transcaucasus from the south, conquering Armenia, Georgia, and other Caucasian territories. |
| 1228 | The Mongols defeat the combined forces of the Eastern Slav princes. |
| 1236–1242 | The Mongol-Turkic armies of the Golden Horde overrun the Volga Basin, the Russian Steppe, and the Caucasus region. Only the Slavs and Finnic and Baltic peoples in the northwest escape Mongol rule. |

### Significant People, Places, and Events

ARABS Driven by religious fervor, the Arabs from their homeland in the Middle East, invaded the Caucasus and Turkestan regions in A.D. 645, planting the seeds of the later conversion of most of the Caucasian and Turkic populations to Islam.

ARMENIA Region and ancient kingdom of Asia Minor and the Caucasus region. In Armenian tradition the kingdom was founded by Haig, or Haik, a descendant of Japeth, the son of Noah of Noah's Ark fame. Many scholars believe that the Armenians crossed the Euphrates River to settle the region in the eighth century B.C. and formed a homogenous nation by the sixth century B.C.

BALTS Distinct groups of Indo-European origin inhabiting the eastern shores of the Baltic Sea, traditionally divided into the now extinct Prussians and the closely related Lithuanians and Latvians.

BULGARS Also called Black Bulgars or Volga Bulgars. The ancestors of the Turkic-speaking Chavash and Tatars of the Volga River basin in eastern European Russia. Another branch of the same Bulgar group moved west into present Bulgaria, where they merged with local Slav tribes to form the Bulgarian nation.

BYZANTINE EMPIRE Also the Eastern Roman Empire. Successor to the Roman Empire in the east, which split into its eastern and western halves in A.D. 395, the Byzantine Empire was centered around ancient Byzantium, renamed Constantinople for the Roman emperor Constantine.

CAUCASIANS The indigenous peoples of the Caucasus region, possibly the original homeland of the Caucasian race. Caucasian peoples include the Armenians and Georgians and a number of smaller groups, the Abaza, Abkhaz, Adyge, Cherkess, Chechens, Ingush, Kabards, and the Dagestani peoples (Avars, Aguls, Dargins, Laks, Lezgins, Rutuls, Tabasarans, Tsakhurs, and smaller groups).

**CAUCASUS** Region and mountain range in southeastern European Russia. The mountain system extends from the mouth of the Kuban River on the Black Sea to the Apsheron Peninsula on the Caspian Sea. The Caucasus Mountains are considered a natural and political divide between the continents of Europe and Asia.

**CYRILLIC** The alphabet used in Russia, Ukraine, Belarus, and the Balkans. Traditionally ascribed to St. Cyril, it was probably devised by one of his followers. It was based on the glagolithic alphabet, which is still used by certain Balkan Catholics.

**EASTERN SLAVS** The eastern branch of the Slav peoples represented by the Russians, Ukrainians, and Belarussians. The Eastern Slavs form the largest of the major divisions of the Slav peoples.

**ETHNIC GROUP** A body of people that is classified by its association with a particular territory or by culture or linguistics. Most ethnic groups are identified by all three criteria—territory, culture, and linguistic affiliation—but there are many exceptions with ethnic groups being identified by only one of the usual classifications. The shared sense of nationhood, with unique histories, and shared values and traditions, has increasingly supplanted the traditional definition of an ethnic or national group. (See National Group.)

**FINNIC PEOPLES (FINNO-UGRIANS)** Peoples related to the Finns, mostly living in the Volga River basin and northwestern Russia near the Finnish border. The Volga Finnic groups include the Maris and Mordvins (Mordvinians). To the north of them live the Permian peoples, the Udmurts, Komis, and Permyaks, or Komi-Permyaks. In the northwest are the Karels, Ingrians, and the smaller groups, the Veps, Votes, Izhors, and others. The small, related groups in western Siberia are the Khant (Khanty) and Mansi, collectively called the Ob-Ugrians.

**GEORGIA** Historically the most powerful kingdom in the Caucasus region from about the fourth century B.C. There has been a standard Georgian literary language since the fifth century A.D. In Greek legend the Georgian kingdom of Colchis was the land where the Golden Fleece was sought by Jason and the Argonauts.

**GOLDEN HORDE** The Tatar-Mongol army that invaded Europe in the thirteenth century. The name is thought to refer to the gorgeous tents used by the leaders of the horde. The name was also applied to the empire established by Batu Khan, the grandson of Genghis Khan, which comprised most of European Russia, the North Caucasus, Ukraine, and the Ural Mountains region of Siberia.

**ISLAM** Islam is one of the three great monotheistic religions of the world. The adherents of Islam, called Muslims, include about a fifth of the world's total population. Muslims in the former Soviet Union are concentrated in the Central Asian republics, the Caucasus, and the Volga River basin. The Tatars, the largest component of the Golden Horde, according to their oral history, adopted Islam in the year 922. From their homeland in the eastern Volga region, the religion spread to many parts of their once extensive empire.

**KHAZARS** An ancient Turkic people who appeared in the Transcaucasus in the second century A.D. and subsequently settled in the lower Volga region. They emerged as a regional power in the seventh century, eventually controlling an empire that reached its height of power between the eighth and tenth centuries. In the eighth century the Khazar nobility embraced Judaism, which became the major religion of the empire. Many eastern European Jews are thought to be descended from the Khazars.

**KIEVAN RUS'** The united Eastern Slav state ruled by the Rukikov dynasty established by the Scandinavian Varangians in 862. The capital was transferred to Kiev in 886, the city then giving its name to the empire as Kievan Rus'. The state survived, although weakened and often divided politically, until its conquest by the Golden Horde in 1237–1240.

**MONGOLS** *Mongol* is the term used in Russian history to describe the various Mongol and Turkic groups that participated in the thirteenth-century invasion by the Golden Horde. Groups related to the Mongols living in modern Russia are the Buryats around Lake Baikal in southern Siberia and the Kalmyks in the North Caucasus.

**NATIONAL GROUP** A body of people, usually associated with a particular territory, that is sufficiently aware of its unity to develop a national consciousness. Unlike the definition of an ethnic group, national groups are not always based on a distinct culture or language. Also, during the Soviet period, from 1920 to 1991, many groups, although part of a larger ethnic group, were designated distinct national groups. Some examples are the Kabards, Adyge, and Cherkess, groups that were designated as national groups but who speak dialects of the same language and share the ancient Circassian culture; or the Volga Germans, who were designated a national group by the new Soviet government and were the first non-Russian group organized under the Soviet nationalities program in 1919.

**NOVGOROD** One of the earliest of Russian cities and the capital of the Viking Varangians from 862 to 886. Novgorod, known as Great Novgorod, became an independent republic in 1136, controlling the whole of north

Russia. It remained an independent state when most of Russia was conquered by the Golden Horde.

OLEG The son of Rurik, the first Varangian ruler of Novgorod. He united the Eastern Slavs and established his capital at Kiev, which became the center of a powerful Eastern Slav state known as Kievan Rus' or Kievan Russia.

PALEOLITHIC PERIOD Also known as the Old Stone Age, the Paleolithic period was the earliest period of human development and the longest phase of human history. Beginning about 2 million years ago, the Paleolithic period ended in various regions between 40,000 and 100,000 years ago and marked the evolution of humans from an apelike creature to true *Homo sapiens.*

PRIMARY CHRONICLE Annals of the Kievan Rus' state written in A.D. 1116. One of the earliest surviving historical documents that archives the events and rulers of the early period of Kievan Rus'.

ROMAN EMPIRE The Roman Empire, centered around Rome, Italy, at its greatest extent in the third and fourth centuries controlled territories in the Caucasus in the form of dependencies or client states. Roman cultural influence extended far beyond the limits of the boundaries of the empire. The Eastern Roman Empire, also called the Byzantine Empire, greatly influenced the development of Kievan Rus'.

RURIK Leader of the Viking Varangians, who was invited by the inhabitants of Novgorod to rule over them in 862. The dynasty he established later moved its capital to Kiev, which became the center of the first great Eastern Slav state, Kievan Rus'.

RUSSKAIA PRAVDA The first written civil laws in Kievan Rus'. Written between 1054 and 1073, the laws clarified the relationships between the various classes and between the Eastern Slavs and the subject peoples. A second version was written between 1125 and 1200.

SARMATIANS An Indo-Iranian tribal group that supplanted the related Scythians as the dominate peoples of the steppe lands of ancient Russia and Ukraine. A nomadic people, they left few archeological remains so their history and origins are still a matter of conjecture.

SCYTHIANS The earliest known inhabitants of the vast steppe that extends from European Russia to northern China. The Scythians were a nomadic Indo-Iranian tribal people related to the ancient Persians.

STEPPE The temperate grasslands of Eurasia, consisting generally of flat, mostly treeless plains. It extends over a vast region from the lower Danube River to northeastern China. The Russian Steppe covers most of European Russia, including the northern Caucasus, and extends into

Central Asia. The Siberian Steppe stretches from the Ural Mountains to the Pacific Ocean.

TATARS The descendants of the Tata tribes that migrated to the Volga region between the fourth and eighth centuries. Extensive mixing with the Bulgars and Finns gradually changed their physical appearance, which now ranges from blond and blue-eyed to the Mongol physical features of their distant ancestors. The name Tatar was later applied to all Turkic peoples by the Russians.

TIMUR, OR TAMERLANE Mongol tribal chief born in Samarkand in Turkestan. Claiming descent from Genghis Khan, he conquered part of the former Mongol Empire, a territory extending from Turkestan to southern Russia. His conquests helped clear the way for the expansion of the grand duchy of Moscow.

TRANSCAUCASUS A transitional region between Europe and Asia, lying between the Black and Caspian Seas, extending from the Caucasus Mountains to the Turkish and Iranian borders. The Transcaucasus, forming part of the Caucasus cultural and historical region, is now made up of the independent republics of Armenia, Georgia, and Azerbaijan.

TURKESTAN A historic region of Central Asia, the home of various Turkic peoples. The region was later divided into Russian Turkestan, Chinese Turkestan, and Afghan Turkestan. Russian Turkestan now forms the independent republics of Kazakhstan, Kyrgyzstan, Tajikistan, Turkmenistan, and Uzbekistan.

TURKIC PEOPLES Turkic peoples of the former Soviet Union, related to the Turks of Turkey, are divided into a number of national groups that include the Karakalpaks, Kazakhs, Kyrgyz, Turkmens, Uzbeks, and Uighurs of the Central Asian republics, historically called Turkestan. The Tatars, Bashkorts, and Chavash live in the Volga River basin in eastern European Russia. Other Tatars live in Belarus and the small Karaim nation is in Lithuania and Ukraine. In southeastern Europe are the Gagauz in Moldova, the Crimean Tatars of Ukraine, the Azeris of Azerbaijan, and the smaller Turkic groups settled in the Caucasus, the Balkars, Karachais, Kumyks, and Nogais. The Sakha, Altai, Tuvans, Khakass, Shors, Dolgans, and Tofalars are Turkic-speaking groups in Siberia.

URAL MOUNTAINS (URALS) An extensive mountain range in eastern European Russia and northwestern Kazakhstan, forming, together with the Ural River, the official boundary between the continents of Europe and Asia.

VIKINGS Called Varangians in Russia, the Vikings began to raid the eastern shores of the Baltic Sea in the ninth century. Their leader, Rurik, established himself at Novgorod in 862, laying the foundation for the development of Kievan Rus'.

## Documents

### The Varangians (Normans) and the
### Origins of the Russian and Ukrainian States

860–862 (6368–6370) The tributaries of the Varangians drove them back beyond the sea and, refusing them further tribute, set out to govern themselves. There was no law among them, but tribe rose against tribe. Discord thus ensued among them, and they began to war one against another. They said to themselves, "Let us seek a prince who may rule over us, and judge us according to the law." They accordingly went overseas to the Varangian Rus: these particular Varangians were known as Rus, just as some are called Swedes, and others Normans, Angles, and Goths, for they were thus named. The Chuds, the Slavs, and the Krivichians then said to the people of Rus, "Our whole land is great and rich, but there is no order in it. Come to rule and reign over us." They thus selected three brothers, with their kinfolk, who took with them all the Rus, and migrated. The oldest, Rurik, located himself in Novgorod; the second, Sineus, in Beloozero; and the third, Truvor, in Izborsk. On account of these Varangians, the district of Novgored became known as Russian (Rus) land. The present inhabitants of Novgorod are descended from the Varangian race, but aforetime they were Slavs; at Beloozero, Ves; in Rostov, Merians; and in Murom, Muromians. Rurik had dominion over all these districts, that since their deaths, their descendants were living there as tributaries of the Khazars. Oskold and Dir remained in this city, and after gathering together many Varangians, they established their domination over the country of the Polianians at the same time that Rurik was ruling at Novgorod.

863–866 (6371–6374) Oskold and Dir attacked the Greeks during the fourteenth year of the reign of the Emperor Michael. When the emperor had set forth against the Saracens and had arrived at the Black River, the eparch sent him word that the Russians were approaching Constantinople, and the emperor turned back. Upon arriving inside the strait, the Russians made a great massacre of the Christians, and attacked Constantinople in two hundred boats. The emperor succeeded with difficulty in entering the city. The people prayed all night with the Patriarch Photius at the Church of the Holy Virgin in Blachemae. They also sang hymns and carried the sacred vestment of the Virgin to dip it in the sea. The weather was still, and the sea was calm, but a storm of wind came up, and when great waves straightway rose, confusing the boats of the godless Russians, it threw them upon the shore and broke them up, so that few escaped such destruction. The survivors then returned to their native land.

*Source: The Russian Primary Chronicle.* Durham, UK: Department of Slavonic Studies, University of Durham.

## The Christianization of Russia, 988

987 (6495) Vladimir summoned together his vassals and the city elders, and said to them: "Behold, the Bulgars came before me urging me to accept their religion. Then came the Germans and praised their own faith; and after them came the Jews. Finally the Greeks appeared, criticising all other faiths but commanding their own, and they spoke at length, telling the history of the whole world from its beginning. Their words were artful, and it was wondrous to listen and pleasant to hear them. They preach the existence of another world. 'Whoever adopts our religion and then dies shall arise and live forever. But whosoever embraces another faith, shall be consumed with fire in the next world.' What is your opinion on this subject, and what do you answer?" The vassals and the elders replied: "You know, O Prince, that no man condemns his own possessions, but praises them instead. If you desire to make certain, you have servants at your disposal. Send them to inquire about the ritual of each and how he worships God. "Their counsel pleased the prince and all the people, so that they chose good and wise men to the number of ten, and directed them to go first among the Bulgars and inspect their faith. The emissaries went their way, and when they arrived at their destination they beheld the disgraceful actions of the Bulgars and their worship in the mosque; then they returned to their own country. Vladimir then instructed them to go likewise among the Germans, and examine their faith, and finally to visit the Greeks. They thus went into Germany, and after viewing the German ceremonial, they proceeded to Constantinople where they appeared before the emperor. He inquired on what mission they had come, and they reported to him all that had occurred. When the emperor heard their words, he rejoiced, and did them great honour on that very day.

On the morrow, the emperor sent a message to the patriarch to inform him that a Russian delegation had arrived to examine the Greek faith, and directed him to prepare the church and the clergy, and to array himself in his sacerdotal robes, so that the Russians might behold the glory of the God of the Greeks. When the patriarch received these commands, he bade the clergy assemble, and they performed the customary rites. They burned incense, and the choirs sang hymns. The emperor accompanied the Russians to the church, and placed them in a wide space, calling their attention to the beauty of the edifice, the chanting, and the offices of the archpriest and the ministry of the deacons, while he explained to them the worship of his God. The Russians were astonished, and in their wonder praised the Greek ceremonial. Then the Emperors Basil and Constantine invited the envoys to their presence, and said, "Go hence to your native country," and thus dismissed them with valuable presents and great honour. Thus they returned to their own country, and the prince called together his vassals and the elders. Vladimir then announced the return of the envoys who had been sent out, and suggested that their report be heard. He thus commanded them to speak out before his vassals. The envoys reported: "When we journeyed among the Bulgars, we beheld how they worship in their temple, called a mosque, while they stand ungirt. The Bulgarian bows, sits down, looks hither and thither like one possessed, and there is no happiness among them, but instead only sorrow and a dreadful stench. Their religion is not good. Then we went among the Germans, and saw them performing many ceremonies in their temples; but we beheld no glory there. Then we went on to Greece, and the Greeks led us to the edifices where they worship their God, and we knew not whether we were in heaven or on earth. For on earth there is no such splendour or such beauty, and we are at a loss how to describe it. We know only that God dwells there among men, and their service is fairer than the ceremonies of other nations. For we cannot forget that beauty. Every man, after tasting something sweet, is afterward unwilling to accept that which is bitter, and therefore we cannot dwell longer here." Then the vassals spoke and said, "If the Greek faith were evil, it would not have been adopted by your grandmother Olga, who was wiser than all other men." Vladimir then inquired where they should all accept baptism, and they replied that the decision rested with him.

After a year had passed, in 988 (6496), Vladimir marched with an armed force against Kherson, a Greek city, and the people of Kherson barricaded themselves therein. Vladimir halted at the farther side of the city beside the bay, a bowshot from the town, and the inhabitants resisted energetically while Vladimir besieged the town. Eventually, however, they became exhausted, and Vladimir warned them that if they did not surrender, he would remain on the spot for three years. When they failed to heed this threat, Vladimir marshalled his troops and ordered the construction of an earthwork in the direction of the city. While this work was under construction, the inhabitants dug a tunnel under the city wall, stole the heaped-up earth, and carried it into the city, where they piled it up in the centre of the town. But the soldiers kept on building, and Vladimir persisted. Then a man of Kherson, Anastasius by name, shot into the Russian camp an arrow on which he had written: "There are springs behind you to the east, from which water flows in pipes. Dig down and cut them off." When Vladimir received this information, he raised his eyes to heaven and vowed that if this hope was realised, he would be baptised. He gave orders straightway to dig down above the pipes, and the water supply was thus cut off. The inhabitants were accordingly overcome by thirst, and surrendered.

Vladimir and his retinue entered the city, and he sent messages to the Emperors Basil and Constantine, saying: "Behold, I have captured your glorious city. I have also heard that you have an unwed sister. Unless you give her to me to wife, I shall deal with your own city as I have with Kherson." When the emperors heard this message, they were troubled, and replied: "It is not meet for Christians to give in marriage to pagans. If you are baptised, you shall have her to wife, inherit the kingdom of God, and be our companion in the faith. Unless you do so, however, we cannot give you our sister in marriage." When Vladimir learned their response, he directed the envoys of the emperors to report to the latter that he was willing to accept baptism, having already given some study to their religion, and that the Greek faith and ritual, as described by the emissaries sent to examine it, had pleased him well. When the emperors heard this report, they rejoiced, and persuaded their sister Anna to consent to the match. They then requested Vladimir to submit to baptism before they should send their sister to him, but Vladimir desired that the princess should herself bring priests to baptise him. The emperors complied with his request, and sent forth their sister, accompanied by some dignitaries and priests. Anna, however, departed with reluctance. "It is as if I were setting out into captivity," she lamented; "better were it for me to die here." But her brothers protested: "Through your agency God turns the Russian land to repentance, and you will relieve Greece from the danger of grievous war. Do you not see how much evil the Russians have already brought upon the Greeks? If you do not set out, they may bring on us the same misfortunes." It was thus that they overcame her hesitation only with great difficulty. The princess embarked upon a ship, and after tearfully embracing her kinfolk, she set forth across the sea and arrived at Kherson. The natives came forth to greet her, and conducted her into the city, where they settled her in the palace.

By divine agency, Vladimir was suffering at that moment from a disease of the eyes, and could see nothing, being in great distress. The princess declared to him that if he desired to be relieved of this disease, he should be baptised with all speed, otherwise it could not be cured. When Vladimir heard her message, he said, "If this proves true, then of a surety is the God of the Christians great," and gave order that he should be baptised. The Bishop of Kherson, together with the princess's priests, after announcing the tidings, baptised Vladimir, and as the bishop laid his hand upon him, he straightway received his sight. Upon experiencing this miraculous cure, Vladimir glorified God, saying, "I have now perceived the one true God." When his followers beheld this miracle, many of them were also baptised.

Vladimir was baptised in the Church of St. Basil, which stands at Kherson upon a square in the centre of the city, where the Khersonians trade. The palace of Vladimir stands beside this church to this day, and the palace of the princess is behind the altar. After his baptism, Vladimir took the princess in marriage. Those who do not know the truth say he was baptised in Kiev, while others assert this event took place in Vasiliev, while still others mention other places.

Hereupon Vladimir took the princess and Anastasius and the priests of Kherson, together with the relics of St. Clement and of Phoebus his disciple, and selected also sacred vessels and images for the service. In Kherson he thus founded a church on the mound which had been heaped up in the midst of the city with the earth removed from his embankment; this church is standing at the present day. Vladimir also found and appropriated two bronze statues and four bronze horses, which now stand behind the Church of the Holy Virgin, and which the ignorant think are made of marble. As a wedding present for the princess, he gave Kherson over to the Greeks again, and then departed for Kiev.

When the prince arrived at his capital, he directed that the idols should be overthrown and that some should be cut to pieces and others burned with fire. He thus ordered that Perun should be bound to a horse's tail and dragged along Borichev to the river. He appointed twelve men to beat the idol with sticks, not because he thought the wood was sensitive, but to affront the demon who had deceived man in this guise, that he might receive chastisement at the hands of men. Great art thou, O Lord, and marvellous are thy works! Yesterday he was honoured of men, but today held in derision. While the idol was being dragged along the stream to the Dnepr, the unbelievers wept over it, for they had not yet received holy baptism. After they had thus dragged the idol along, they cast it into the Dnepr. But Vladimir had given this injunction: "If it halts anywhere, then push it out from the bank, until it goes over the falls. Then let it loose." His command was duly obeyed. When the men let the idol go, and it passed through the falls, the wind cast it out on the bank, which since that time has been called Perun's Shore, a name that it bears to this very day.

Thereafter Vladimir sent heralds throughout the whole city to proclaim that if any inhabitant, rich or poor, did not betake himself to the river, he would risk the prince's displeasure. Men the people heard these words, they wept for joy, and exclaimed in their enthusiasm, "If this were not good, the prince and his boyars would not have accepted it." On the morrow the prince went forth to the Dnepr with the priests of the princess and those from Kherson, and a countless multitude assembled. They all went into the water: some stood up to their necks, others to their breasts, the younger near the bank, some of them holding children in their arms, while the adults waded farther out. The priests stood by and offered prayers. There was joy in heaven and upon earth to behold so many souls saved. But the devil groaned, lamenting: "Woe is me! how am I driven out hence! For I thought to have my dwelling place here, since the apostolic teachings do not abide in this land. Nor did this people know God, but I rejoiced in the service they rendered unto me. But now I am vanquished by the ignorant, not by apostles and martyrs, and my reign in these regions is at an end."

When the people were baptised, they returned each to his own abode. Vladimir, rejoicing that he and his subjects now knew God himself, looked up to heaven and said: "O God, who hast created heaven and earth, look down, I beseech thee, on this thy new people, and grant them, O Lord, to know thee as the true God, even as the other Christian nations have known thee. Confirm in them the true and unalterable faith, and aid me, O Lord, against the hostile adversary, so that, hoping in thee and in thy might, I may overcome his malice." Having spoken thus, he ordained that churches should be built and established where pagan idols had previously stood. He thus founded the Church of St. Basil on the hill where the idol of Perun and the other images had been set, and where the prince and the people had offered their sacrifices. He began to found churches and to assign priests throughout the cities, and to invite the people to accept baptism in all the cities and towns. He took the children of the best families, and sent them to schools for instruction in book learning. The mothers of these children wept bitterly over them, for they were not yet strong in faith, but mourned as for the dead. When these children were assigned for study, there was thus fulfilled in the Russian land the prophecy which says, "In those days, the deaf shall hear words of Scripture, and the voice of the stammerers shall be made plain" (Isaiah, xxix, 18). For these persons had not ere this heard words of Scripture, and now heard them only by the act of God, for in his mercy the Lord took pity upon them, even as the Prophet said, "I will be gracious to whom I will be gracious" (Exodus, xxxiii, 19).

*Source: The Russian Primary Chronicle.* Durham, UK: Department of Slavonic Studies, University of Durham.

## Bibliography

Avrich, Paul. *Russian Rebels, 1600–1800.* New York: Schocken, 1972.

Crew, Allen F. *An Atlas of Russian History: Eleven Centuries of Changing Borders.* New Haven, CT: Yale University Press, 1970.

Hrushevsky, Mykhailo. *A History of the Ukraine.* New Haven, CT: Yale University Press, 1941.

Koestler, Arthur. *The Thirteenth Tribe: The Khazar Empire and Its Heritage.* New York: Random House, 1976.

MacKenzie, David, and Michael W. Curran. *A History of Russia and the Soviet Union.* Chicago: Wadsworth Publishing, 1987.

Subtelny, Orest. *Ukraine: A History.* Toronto: University of Toronto Press, 1988.

Suny, Ronald Grigor. *The Making of the Georgian Nation.* Bloomington: University of Indiana Press, 1994.

Vakar, Nicholas P. *Belorussia: The Making of a Nation.* Cambridge, MA: Harvard University Press, 1956.

Vernadsky, George. *The Mongols and Russia.* New Haven, CT: Yale University Press, 1954.

Walker, Christopher J. *Armenia: The Survival of a Nation.* New York: Palgrave Macmillan, 1990.

# From the Rise of Muscovy to the Establishment of the Russian Empire

THE DECLINE OF THE TATARS allowed the small principality of Muscovy to gradually throw off foreign rule and expand by taking control of neighboring territories. The territories controlled by the Muscovites progressively became known as Russia, after the dominant ethnic group that referred to itself as Rus', or Russian. Although Muscovy officially changed its name to the Russian Empire in the eighteenth century, the many Slavic regional and tribal groups that came under Muscovite rule continued to adhere to local identities rather than calling themselves after the small principality at the heart of the growing empire.

Muscovy was home to many distinct cultural and religious groups by the fourteenth century, but the separation of the population into the ethnic or national groups of the later Russian Empire had barely begun. The majority of the population continued to stick to a village-based political and social system and to identify with their religion, local area, or parish. The spread of serfdom, both in the Slav territories and in the German-controlled Baltic territories, was based mostly on class and local power structures rather than on an ethnicity or culture. Although Russian colonization of neighboring non-Slavic territories accelerated in the sixteenth and seventeenth centuries, the separation of the population into distinct national groups, including the Slavic groups, was mostly an outcome of the spread of nationalist ideals in the eighteenth and nineteenth centuries. Religion, geographical area, language, and blood ties continued to be the traditional measures of allegiance. Loyalty to the Russian state, like allegiances to a larger national or ethnic group, was a product of the growth of nationalist ideals that accompanied the spread of education and the growing influence of European culture.

## The Russian Heartland

The destruction of Kievan Rus' and the imposition of Mongol rule over most of the territory of the Eastern Slav state came at a crucial time for the Slavs and the other peoples of the region. Flourishing cultures and states that had been overrun and destroyed by the Tatar invaders never recovered. The Mongol invasion also allowed former rivals to take control of lands on the periphery of the territory controlled by the Golden Horde. In the west, the Roman Catholic Poles and Lithuanians began to expand into the territories formerly ruled by Kiev. The Scandinavian kingdoms, Denmark and Sweden, also began to expand their authority into northwestern Russia, particularly into the Finnic territories. The Germans continued to dominate the Baltic region, often under the nominal rule of neighboring powers.

The new center of Russian political power, the Muscovite principality, gradually became the center of the most powerful of the Eastern Slav territories under the hegemony of the Golden Horde. As the center of the Orthodox Church and therefore the focus of Eastern Slav loyalty, Muscovy gained enough strength to finally throw off Tatar rule and begin the political and territorial expansion that would later become the multiethnic Russian Empire. The defeat of the Tatar successor states to the Golden Horde in the sixteenth century accelerated that expansion and allowed the Russians to take control of the vast territories east of the Ural Mountains called Siberia. Russian expansion also brought increasing contacts with the Muslim peoples of Central Asia—through which Russia's increasing trade with the East flowed along the Silk Road—and brought the expanding Russian state into military conflict with the Muslim powers to the south, the Ottoman Empire of the Turks and Persia, which controlled part of the Caucasus and the southern coast of the Caspian Sea. The Russian Empire was forced to adopt many of the new ideas coming from western Europe; however, it remained a feudal state, its many peoples and nations oppressed and subjected to colonization and serfdom by an imperial elite.

The division between the Slavs under Tatar rule and those remaining under traditional rulers in the northwest, particularly the powerful Novgorod republic, accelerated the division of the Eastern Slavs into the three modern national groups: the Russians, Ukrainians, and Belarussians. The Slavs of the northwest continued to prosper; however, the new Eastern Slav political center, the city of Moscow, in the central part of European Russia, began to flourish under Mongol-Tatar rule. Although the Muscovites felt strong enough to challenge Tatar power and even defeated the soldiers of the Golden Horde in 1380, Tatar domination of the central Russian territories, with the system of the Slavic princes paying tribute, continued for another century.

The defeat of the Golden Horde by Tamerlane, another invader from Central Asia, was the beginning of the decline of the khanate of the Golden Horde in 1395. Between 1430 and 1466 the disintegration of the Golden Horde split the empire into a number of successor states. The Tatar khanates of Kazan', Astrakhan, and Sibir' each took control of part of the Slavic territories in central and southern Russia. They continued the practice of loose control of the vassal Slavic states, which paid tribute to retain their fragile freedoms under local princes or traditional leaders. In the Caucasus the Mongols began to lose ground to the fierce mountain tribes. The small Caucasian, Turkic, and Iranian peoples of the Caucasus, driven into the less-accessible highlands by the Mongol invasion, increasingly asserted their independence against the weakening Tatar authority, often aided by the growing power of the Ottoman Turks and Persians to the south.

## The Rise of Muscovy

In 1300 the metropolitan of Kiev, driven from his seat by the Tatars, established a new religious center at Vladimir, in a principality ruled as a vassal state of the Golden Horde. Vladimir-Suzdal, one of the small principalities under Tatar hegemony, began to gain influence in the late fourteenth century owing to its importance as a trade center, its central location, and its prestige as the Orthodox religious center. According to tradition, a military outpost founded on the Moskva River became a separate duchy under Daniel, the son of Duke Alexander Nevsky of Vladimir-Suzdal. Daniel's son, Yuri, launched a struggle to make Muscovy the predominate principality in central Russia. The Orthodox metropolitan moved his seat from Vladimir to Moscow in 1326, making Moscow the center of Slavic Orthodoxy and the focus of loyalty for the millions of Orthodox Christians, both Slavs and non-Slavs. While remaining loyal to their overlords of the Golden Horde, the Muscovites won the right to collect Tatar tributes from neighboring Slavic principalities. The Muscovites increasingly took on many of the trappings of autonomy, even though violent reminders of Mongol/Tatar power, such as the destruction of Moscow in 1408, were not infrequent. The defeat of Byzantium and the capture of Christian Constantinople by the Ottoman Turks in 1453 confirmed Moscow as the paramount center of the Orthodox religion. Orthodox missionaries, often accompanied by soldiers, were dispatched to work among the non-Christian tribes, particularly the Finnic peo-

*The first Russian monarch to use the title of czar, Ivan IV was known as Ivan the Terrible. During his long reign, he centralized the Muscovite state and set the stage for future expansion. (Library of Congress)*

ples of the Volga River region and the tribes of the Ural Mountains. Political influence often followed religious inroads, as the newly converted peoples looked to Moscow as the center of both religious and political power.

The Muscovite state, granted the title grand duchy, continued to expand by acquiring or subduing adjacent states, forming the basis of the later Russian Empire. A long rivalry with the Novgorodian state was ended by Muscovite invasions in 1456 and 1470, led by Ivan III (Ivan the Great). Ivan was the first Muscovite ruler to take the titles of czar and "Ruler of all Rus." Ivan's Muscovite state competed with the powerful Lithuanian duchy for control of the semi-independent principalities in the north and west and with Ottoman Turkey and Persia for control of the fertile steppe lands north of the Caucasus Mountains. A long, inconclusive war with Roman Catholic Lithuania, which didn't end until 1503, strengthened the hold of the Orthodox Church in the Eastern Slav land. In 1472, Ivan married Zoe (Sofia), the niece of the last Byzantine emperor, affirming Moscow's claims of being Constantinople's successor as the center of the Orthodox world. In 1478 Novgorod was brought under Muscovite rule, and in 1485 the Tver' principality was conquered, uniting most of the Great Russians in one state and bringing many more non-Slavic peoples under Russian rule. In 1510 the Muscovites conquered Pskov, the last important independent Slavic principality. By the early sixteenth century the Russians, aided by the Orthodox Finnic and Chavash peoples of the Volga, had thrown off the Tatar yoke and had consolidated their authority as the center of an expanding, powerful empire.

The expansion of the Great Russian state centered on Moscow incorporated many diverse peoples, although only the Great Russians and the Tatars of the Volga River basin had begun to develop a sense of nationhood. At the end of the fourteenth century Muscovite rule had been extended to the tribal Finnic peoples of the northwest and into the Volga River basin. Under Ivan IV (Ivan the Terrible), the Russians conquered the Tatar khanates of Kazan' (1552) and Astrakhan (1556), establishing Russian rule over a huge area of the middle and lower Volga and the North Caucasus and incorporating even more non-Slavic national groups. In 1598 a Russian expedition reached the Terek River in the Northern Caucasus, beginning centuries of conflict between the Russians and the various warlike tribes of the Caucasus Mountains. The conquest of the Tatar khanate of Sibir' in 1581 laid the basis for the colonization and annexation of Siberia. Russians colonized the conquered territories, and Orthodoxy was imposed as the only recognized religion. The many ethnic groups living in the newly acquired territories were most often treated as conquered and inferior nations, beginning a long tradition of Russian oppression.

A Tatar khanate established on the Crimean Peninsula in the late thirteenth century continually defeated Slavic attempts to expand to the south. Following the Turkish conquest of Constantinople in 1453, the Ottoman Turks proclaimed their sovereignty over the Crimean khanate, but the Crimean Tatars retained considerable independence under their own dynasty. Militarily the Crimean Tatars controlled most of the southern steppe lands of Ukraine and the North Caucasus and often provided well-trained soldiers for the campaigns of the Ottoman Turks. Crimean Tatar warriors continued to raid Slav settlements and attacked Moscow as late as 1572. Since Crimean Tatar military had kept Slavic settlers from moving to the areas of rich soil in the southern steppe lands, the colonists turned east to settle the Urals and moved into western Siberia.

The Orthodox religion played a large part in the expansion of the Russian state. The subject peoples, particularly the non-Christian groups in the northwest and the Volga River basin, were often forced to adopt Orthodox Christianity or were persuaded to join the Orthodox Church to enjoy certain rights of citizenship given to converts. Orthodox missionaries were often the first contact between the Russian authorities and the non-Slavic peoples inhabiting territories claimed as part of the widening Russian state. Colonization of tribal territories by the European Slavs seeking profit and power was often brutal, with entire tribes subjected to oppression, forced conversion to Orthodoxy, and the loss of traditional hunting and agricultural lands. Many of the subject non-Slav peoples, even the converts to Orthodoxy, were forced to work on the estates established by government officials or absentee landlords on confiscated lands. Serfdom accompanied Russian colonization of the territories east and south of the Eastern Slav heartland.

The later Russian state adopted many Muscovite political and cultural characteristics, including the subordination of the individual to the state. This idea of the dominant state derived from the Slavic, Mongol-Tatar, and Byzantine heritage, and it later emerged in the unlimited power of the czar and the state suppression of the growing empire's non-Slavic peoples. Individuals, national groups, and institutions—even the powerful Orthodox Church—were subordinate to the state as it was represented in the person of the czar.

The second characteristic of the Muscovite legacy to Russia was continual territorial expansion. Beginning with Muscovy's efforts to consolidate Russian territory as Tatar authority waned in the fifteenth century, expansion soon went beyond ethnically Slav territory. The acquisition of large territories inhabited by non-Russian peoples was the beginning of enduring nationality problems.

## Ukraine

The term *Ukraine,* meaning "at the border" or "borderland," came into general usage in the sixteenth century. At that time, Roman Catholic Poland-

Lithuania and the rising power of the Muscovites were vying for control of the vast area south of their borders that remained under the loose control of the Turkish Ottoman Empire through their vassals, the Crimean Tatars. Many Slavs, fleeing serfdom and religious persecution, escaped to the south, where they established a military order called the Zaporozhye Sich. These fugitives became known as Kozaks, or Cossacks, from a Turkic word for free or adventurer. The advance of serfdom and religious strife, the result of Catholic persecution of Orthodox Christians, sparked widespread opposition to Polish rule. In 1648, the Zaporozhye Cossacks, led by Bohdan Khmelnytsky (Bogdan Chmielnicki), successfully rebelled against Polish rule. However, realizing that the Ukrainians were too weak to retain their freedom, Khmelnytsky recognized the authority of Moscow over the territory of the Zaporozhye Cossacks, preferring an alliance with the Orthodox Muscovites to rule by the Roman Catholic Poles. By the terms of the 1654 Treaty of Pereyaslavl', seen by the Zaporozhye Cossacks as protection for the independent Ukrainian Cossack state, the Cossack Ukrainian state was recognized as an ally of the Muscovites, but Russian encroachments gradually eroded Ukrainian independence.

Russian attempts to impose their rule on the Ukrainian Cossack territories alienated many Ukrainians, who signed a separate treaty with the Poles in 1658 in an effort to reduce Russian influence. This set off a war between the Russians and the Polish-Lithuanian state, which finally ended with the partition of Ukraine between the two in 1667. Beginning in 1687, the leader of the Zaporozhye Cossacks hetman Ivan Mazepa tried to break free of both Russian and Polish rule. He formed an alliance with the Swedes and joined in the Northern War between Sweden and Russia. In 1709 he shared the Swedes' defeat by Peter the Great at the Battle of Poltava, which was fought in Ukraine. The defeat sealed the fate of Ukraine, as Ukrainian autonomy was further curtailed in all the territories, even those under Polish or Crimean Tatar control.

### Rivalries with Poland-Lithuania, Sweden, and Denmark

Poland and Lithuania were merged in 1386, bringing the two nations into a union under the Jagiello dynasty. The combined forces of the two countries defeated the Germanic Teutonic Knights at Tannenberg in 1410, opening the way for their political and territorial expansion and the establishment of the Polish-Lithuanian Empire. The northwestern Russian territories, along with western Ukraine and Belarus, were incorporated into the growing empire in the fourteenth century, coming under Lithuanian rule as they expanded at the expense of the neighboring Eastern Slav principalities weakened by the Tatar invasion. The centers of Eastern Slav political and economic life were transferred to the region out of Tatar control. The dynastic and military alliance between the two neighboring states was cemented by the adoption of a common Christian religion, Roman Catholicism. Western culture and Roman Catholicism spread through the Eastern Slavs of the medieval Polish-Lithuanian state, further dividing them from their Orthodox kin under Tatar rule. Many Slavs under Catholic rule converted to Catholicism to escape persecution and to acquire the benefits of belonging to the state-sponsored church. The Ukrainians and Belarussians under the rule of the united Polish-Lithuania state suffered the imposition of serfdom and the persecution of their Orthodox faith by the Roman Catholics. In 1596 the Ukrainian Orthodox bishops of the western Ukrainian provinces under Polish rule, confronted with the overwhelming power of the Roman Catholic Church, established a separate Uniate, or Greek Catholic, faith, which recognized papal authority but retained the traditional Orthodox rite.

### The Baltic Region

The Protestant Reformation came to the Baltic region from Germany in 1523. The Reformation had a significant impact on the Baltic peoples, except in Lithuania and the eastern part of Latvia, which remained under Catholic control. The rapid conversion of the German-populated towns to Protestantism increased the ethnic tensions between the German landlords and their Estonian and Latvian serfs, most of whom remained Roman Catholic until much later. Peasant uprisings against the Baltic German landlords spread rapidly, often provoked by religious zeal. Religious education, part of the growing religious conflict in the region, resulted in the publication of the first books in local languages. In 1525, the first book published in the Estonian language was a religious tract, which was seized by the German authorities and destroyed as heretical. A second book, a Roman Catholic catechism, was published in 1535.

Muscovite expansion to the northwest toward the Baltic Sea proved more difficult than the conquest of the declining Tatar khanates. The region, called Livonia, inhabited by Baltic and Finnic peoples—Lithuanians, Latvians, Livonians, and Estonians—was mostly controlled by Germans, the descendants of earlier religious crusaders known as the Teutonic or Livonian Knights. The region, with strong cultural and trading ties to western Europe, was contested by the Baltic powers of the time, Lithuania, Poland, and Sweden. In 1558 the Russians invaded Livonia, eventually embroiling Muscovy in a twenty-five-year war against Poland, Lithuania, Sweden, and Denmark. The Livonian War, fought for possession of the Baltic region with its valuable warm-water ports, continued from 1558 to 1583. To prevent a Russian conquest of the region, the ruling Germans of the Teutonic Order, except in some smaller territories in Latvia, placed their vast estates under the protection of the more powerful Polish-Lithuanian state in 1561. Under Polish authority the remains of Protestantism in the Baltic provinces was stamped out, and Catholicism was again proclaimed the official religion. The privileges of the German landowners (the Baltic Barons) were preserved, and the Baltic peoples, the Latvians, Livonians, and Estonians, although sharing the Catholic religion of the Polish-Lithuanian rulers, were reduced to serfdom on the feudal manors.

The Swedes, having controlled Estonia from 1521, took control of northern Livonia in 1558 during the Livonian War. Between 1561 and 1645 Swedish rule was extended to most of Livonia. Under the rule of the more lenient Swedes, the power of the German aristocracy was somewhat curtailed, and limited protection was extended to the Estonian and Latvian serfs. The Lutheran religion of the Swedes was introduced just as the stringent rules governing serfs were gradually being relaxed. Estonian and Latvian farmers were given representation in the Swedish parliament and could lodge complaints directly with the Swedish king. Schools were established across the region, including rural areas, and books were published in Estonian and Latvian as an aid to the spread of education. The Swedes founded the first Baltic university at Dorpat (Tartu) in 1632, allowing for some education in the Estonian language. The first Estonian grammar was published under Swedish rule in 1686. The first Bible was printed in Latvian in 1689. Only the Latvians in the eastern provinces, which remained under Polish rule, continued to adhere to the Church of Rome.

The Lithuanians, to the south, retained control of an extensive regional state that controlled territory in Ukraine and Belarus. The Lithuanian state, joined in a dynastic union with neighboring Poland since the fourteenth century, united with Poland to form a unified state in 1569. The Lithuanian upper classes gradually adopted the Polish culture and language, relegating Lithuanian to the status of a rural, peasant language. The Polish-Lithuanian state was a multiethnic empire embracing dozens of distinct cultures and peoples. Over decades the state increasingly came under the domination of the Poles and the Lithuanian aristocracy—Polish in culture and language. The ideas of humanism and the Protestant Reformation spread with the growth of printing and the opening of Vilnius University in 1579. A liberal code of law, the Statutes of Lithuania, stimulated the development of the Lithuanian culture. In the sixteenth and seventeenth centuries, wars with Sweden and Muscovy weakened the Polish-Lithuanian state, which rapidly declined in the late seventeenth century.

## Siberia

The immense territory east of the Ural Mountains, called Siberia after the conquered khanate of Sibir', was originally inhabited by small Turkic and Mongol tribes. Most of the southern part of the vast region was included in the Mongol Empire and then came under the authority of the khanate of Sibir', the local successor to Mongol power. Following the Russian conquest of Sibir' in 1581, Cossacks crossed the Urals, leading the Russian colonization of the vast, unknown land. The eastward expansion of the European Russians into Siberia paralleled the European conquest of North America. A line of Cossack forts gradually expanded the colonization against the resistance of the native peoples. The first colonists, mostly Cossacks and peasant serfs seeking land and independence in Siberia's vast open spaces, moved east along the rivers, the only means of transport and communication. By 1700 the Russians had extended their control to the Mongol peoples living around Lake Baikal and north to the Arctic Sea. In 1710 Siberia was organized as a separate province. It became a dumping ground for deportees, rebellious minorities, political prisoners, recalcitrant serfs turned over for deportation by landowners, convicted prostitutes, and Jews unable to pay their taxes. Antigovernment sentiment and a sense of separation from European Russia began a tradition of fierce independence among the scattered Siberians.

Farther east, the coastal regions on the Pacific had been under Chinese rule for centuries but remained remote, tribal territories sparsely populated by small ethnic groups. In the 1640s, Cossack explorers and Russian traders penetrated the Amur River area in the southeast, and the Russians soon challenged the long-standing Chinese territorial claim to the region. The Russians finally abandoned a line of Cossack forts and left the region to China under the terms of the Treaty of Nerchinsk in 1689. The treaty, confirming Chinese sovereignty in the Far East and defining the boundary between the two empires, was the first treaty signed between a European power and the Chinese Empire. Almost two centuries later (1858–1860), taking advantage of a weakened China, the Russians again took control of the Amur region.

## The Siberian Peoples

### Sakha

The Sakha, called Yakuts by the Russians, inhabit a region larger than western Europe in northeastern Siberia, bordering the Arctic Ocean. Considered the largest of the Altaic branch of the Turkic peoples, they are also the largest of the indigenous groups remaining in Siberia. Although they are considered a Turkic nation, their ancestry includes Turkic, Mongol, and Paleo-Siberian background, as evidenced by the presence of two physical types, Mongol and Turkic. Traditionally they were herders of cattle and horses driven from the southern Siberian territory around Lake Baikal in the Middle Ages by invading Buryats during the turbulent times following the collapse of the Mongol Empire. A Sakha legend traces their origins to a Tatar hero and a Buryat maiden who fled together from Lake Baikal. In the less-hospitable north, the Sakha settled the river lowlands where they found grass for grazing their herds and protection from the harsh northern winter. They showed remarkable flexibility in their adaptation to the severe conditions of their new homeland. Unlike their Turkic relatives in Central Asia, they were never affected by the spread of Islam but retained their ancient shamanistic beliefs.

Russian and Cossack traders and explorers crossed into Sakha territory in the sixteenth century. Trading tobacco and liquor for valuable furs to sell in European Russia, the newcomers quickly claimed the most valuable lands and properties. In 1632 a fort was founded at Yakutsk, which became a center of Slavic colonization and an important military center during the long war fought to subdue the Sakha between 1634 and 1642. By 1710 tens of thousands of Slavic colonists had occupied the more productive Sakha lands. Several rebellions fought the colonization of the Sakha homeland and the imposition of the *yasak,* the fur tax imposed on all Sakha trappers. Orthodox missionaries began to convert the Sakha to Christianity in the late seventeenth century. Many Sakha accepted baptism mainly because Christians were exempted from paying the hated fur tax.

### Buryats

The Buryats, the largest Mongol group in Russia, belong to the Central Asian branch of the Mongol peoples. Although physically they are Mongol, they also display some Turkic and Tungus cultural characteristics. Their origins, although disputed, are thought to include Mongol, Tungus, Turkic, Samoyed, and other strains. Historically they are a nomadic people, herding cattle, sheep, goats, and camels. The Buryat culture preserves much of the traditional Mongol culture, including their favorite sports—wrestling, horse races, and archery—and the traditional long poems, the *ugligers,* that preserve the Buryat oral history. The Buryats west of Lake Baikal are mostly Russian Orthodox, while those east of the lake continue to follow the Tibetan form of Buddhism. Traditionally the Buryats adhered to an intricate combination of shamanism and Buddhist practices.

The Turkic tribes east of Lake Baikal were loosely controlled by the Chinese until the mid-ninth century. Absorbed or driven north by waves of Mongol migrations from the south, the last of the Turkic tribes disappeared following the conquest of the region by the expanding Mongol Empire in 1205. Recognized as a separate Mongol people, the Buryats were first mentioned in a Mongol manuscript written in 1240. The various Buryat tribal groups formed part of the great Mongol Empire until its collapse in the fourteenth century. In the sixteenth century the last remains of Mongol rule ended in the Baikal region, allowing the Buryats to organize an independent tribal confederation. Slavic Cossacks, forerunners of Russian expansion into the region, reached Lake Baikal in 1643. The Russians gradually took control of the tribal lands, bringing the last Buryat tribes under Russian rule around 1700. Treaties signed by the Russian Empire and Manchu China in 1689 and 1727 established imperial boundaries and effectively cut off Buryat contacts with the other Mongol peoples to the south.

## Tuvans

The Tuvans, living in southern Siberia on the border between Russia and Mongolia, are a nation of mixed background. Physically the Tuvans resemble the Mongols, but culturally and linguistically they are more closely related to the Turkic peoples. Most anthropologists believe that the Tuvans are a historical mixture of Turkic, Mongol, Samoyedic, and other strains. Traditionally the Tuvans are divided into tribal groups, most engaged in herding and hunting. Their seminomadic way of life revolved around their herds, with small groups traveling across the steppe lands and living in large felt tents. Modern Tuvans are more likely to live in urban settlements in permanent homes or high-rise apartments. Their traditional culture is noted for its rich oral epic poetry and their distinctive music. Tuvan is a Turkic language belonging to the Northern Turkic group of the Altaic languages and is closely related to the Uighur language spoken in Chinese Xinjiang. In spite of the inroads made by the Russian language, Tuvan remains the mother tongue of about 99 percent of the Tuvan population.

The Tuvans' traditional oral history tells of an independent Turkish khanate in the region in the sixth century A.D. and periods of Uighur and Chinese domination until the ninth century. They were first mentioned in travelers' chronicles in the tenth century as a herder people living in the grasslands in tribal or clan groups. The Mongols overran the region in the thirteenth century, beginning three centuries of Mongol domination of the Tuvan homeland. The Tuvan tribes, often warring among themselves, emerged as a distinct cultural group in the early eighteenth century. Most Tuvans adopted the Tibetan form of Buddhism introduced to the region from Mongolia in the 1700s. Buddhism was adopted as the Tuvan national religion, but earlier shamanistic practices were also retained, producing a unique and enduring set of beliefs.

## Altai and Khakass

The related Altai and Khakass peoples are also of mixed Turkic and Mongol ancestry, mostly resembling the Mongols physically but retaining their Turkic languages and cultural characteristics. These people were traditionally divided into small tribal groups, and national sentiment is a very modern development, having come about during the Soviet era. Both the Altai and Khakass languages are Turkic languages, the Altai dialects, Telut and Oirot, belonging to the Northern Turkic languages and the Khakass belonging to the Hun branch. The Altai languages and Khakass didn't become standardized languages until the Soviet period. Officially both peoples are mostly Orthodox Christians, but shamanism remains an important part of local belief systems.

Historically the Altai and Khakass tribal groups lived as nomadic hunters, fishermen, and gatherers, although little is known of their early history. Remains of an advanced civilization have been found in the region, dating from about 600 to 300 B.C. Some of the tribal groups were mentioned in Chinese and Mongol records as nomadic tribes in the fifth century A.D. A Turkic khanate dominated the region from the sixth through the eighth centuries, introducing the Turkic language and culture adopted by the tribal peoples. The expanding Mongol Empire absorbed the tribal lands in the early thirteenth century. For more than two centuries the tribes lived as tributaries of the Mongols. In the fourteenth century Tamerlane overran the tribal lands, forcing some tribes to move west. One group of Oirots moved west to the

North Caucasus region of European Russia, the last Asian invaders to penetrate Europe. The collapse of Mongol power allowed the Altai to organize a powerful tribal federation that took control of territories as far west as Central Asia and north into the Khakass territories. Slavic Cossacks explored the mountainous region in the sixteenth century. By the late sixteenth century the Slavs were regularly collecting a tax, paid in valuable furs, from the tribal groups.

## Paleoasiatic Peoples

The Paleoasiatic peoples are small tribes of peoples who are historically and culturally related to the native peoples of the Americas. The largest of the native Siberian bands are the Chukots in the region opposite Alaska and the Koryaks in the northern Kamchatka Peninsula. In prehistoric times small nomadic groups migrated east from the Ural Mountains and the region of Lake Baikal across the vast stretches of wilderness into eastern Siberia. In pursuit of game, some groups crossed the land bridge that once connected the continents of Asia and North America at least 30,000 years ago. The small bands left on the Asian side, gradually pushed north by stronger enemies, spread out across the harsh landscape. Some bands took up reindeer herding in the interior, others settled along the coasts to become fishermen. The seasons; the reindeer herds; and the availability of sea mammals, fish, and other food directed communal life. The native peoples of northeastern Siberia, their homeland lying partly within the Arctic Circle, did not engage in large-scale warfare, although they could be formidable warriors. Land disputes, raiding, and fighting were common and somewhat ritualized, but few people were actually killed during such events. Captured enemies were often enslaved, but most disputes were not widespread and involved groups only at the clan or village level.

Russian expansion into eastern Siberia, led by Cossacks, reached the Pacific Ocean in 1640. Nominal Russian rule mostly consisted of collecting an annual fur tax, while leaving the native bands to their traditional way of life. The introduction of firearms and the demand for valuable furs greatly affected the local peoples. Furs were often bought with vodka, making alcoholism a major social problem. New diseases introduced from Europe also took a toll on the native peoples, particularly the smaller more isolated groups. When conflicts arose the natives most often lost, and many were killed in violent confrontations with the encroaching Europeans. The peoples of the Kamchatka Peninsula were finally subdued in two armed campaigns in 1690 and 1697–1698. By the beginning of the eighteenth century the number of tribal peoples in eastern Siberia had been greatly reduced and their traditional cultures badly damaged.

## The Caucasus

The Caucasus, devastated by the Golden Horde in the thirteenth century and by the invasion of another successor to the Mongol Empire, Tamerlane, in the fourteenth century, fell easily to the advancing Turks in the fifteenth century. The smaller tribal groups, after initial resistance, mostly welcomed the advance of the Turkish Ottoman Empire, but the Christians (Armenians, Georgians, and several smaller groups) were subjected to cruel restrictions and special taxes under Muslim rule. The Turks and the still-powerful Persians divided the Caucasus into spheres of influence in 1553. Turkish influence became paramount in most of the region. Several of the traditional tribal areas were established as protectorates or annexed as Turkish territory. The Persian conquest of eastern Armenia in 1639 effectively partitioned the Christians. Although often persecuted, the industrious Christians frequently acquired vital economic roles in the Persian and Ottoman states, some even rising to high office. Turkish influence in the region extended the Muslim religion to even the more remote mountains and introduced Turkish cultural traits to many local Caucasian cultures.

## Central Asia (Turkestan)

The Turkic peoples of Central Asia, long ruled by successive Parthian and Persian Empires, developed an advanced civilization as part of the Silk Road, the trade route stretching from China to the Mediterranean. Overrun by Arabs in 710–711, most of the inhabitants of Central Asia adopted the Arabs' new Islamic religion. The merging of the Turkic and Islamic Arabic cultures produced a great flowering of Turkestani culture in the ninth and tenth centuries. The region became a center of Muslim learning and of a Persian-influenced Muslim culture, with flourishing, sophisticated cities and advanced agriculture based on vast irrigation systems. Migrating Seljuk Turks conquered Central Asia in the eleventh and twelfth centuries before they moved west into Asia Minor. The Seljuks maintained the tradition of open trade and irrigated agriculture. They mixed extensively with the Persianized population, and their language and culture came to dominate the territory.

The invading Mongols devastated the brilliant civilization of Central Asia in the thirteenth century. The destruction of the extensive irrigation system had a profound influence on the development of the Central Asian peoples. The area again flourished under the rule of Tamerlane, who established his capital at Samarkand in the late fourteenth century. The various Turkestani peoples, the Uzbeks, Kazakhs, Kyrgyz, Turkmen, Tajiks, Karakalpaks, and some smaller groups, having formed part of the Mongol-dominated Golden Horde, set up local successor states following the breakup of the Mongol Empire in the fifteenth century. The Uzbeks conquered much of Central Asia between 1490 and 1505. In 1555 they moved the capital of the region from Samarkand to Bukhara. The Uzbek states developed strong trade ties with the expanding Muscovite state and served as conduits for trade and contacts between Russia and China.

Although dominated by the Uzbeks, ethnicity in Central Asia mostly remained a question of the Muslim religion, tribal affiliations, or local loyalties. The Uzbeks, as the most numerous and powerful of the Central Asian tribes, ruled the other peoples of the immense region but themselves remained divided along regional and clan loyalties. Although dominated by ethnic Uzbeks, the Central Asian states were multiethnic and multilingual yet united by their Muslim culture and religion. In the seventeenth and eighteenth centuries the mixed population, including the various Turkestani peoples, Arabs, Persians, and Bukharan Jews, formed one of the most advanced societies on earth. The cities along the Silk Road flourished as centers of the arts, sciences, and literature. The Uzbek states maintained trade and political contacts from China to the Mediterranean and allowed extensive freedom of religion and culture. Nonetheless, internal conflicts and interethnic wars split the Uzbek-dominated empire in the seventeenth century. The Uzbek states of Bukhara and Khiva emerged as the new regional powers. In 1619–1621 Russian expeditions visited the various regional states, establishing the first diplomatic contacts between Moscow and the Central Asians. The first Russian attempt to gain influence by military means led to a massacre of Russian troops at Khiva in 1717, ending Russian contacts with the Central Asian states for several decades.

## Russia's Time of Troubles

Internal consolidation of Muscovite power accompanied the outward expansion of the state. By the fifteenth century, the rulers of Muscovy considered the entire Russian territory as their collective property. The rulers of the ancient Rurik dynasty assumed the title of autocrat, literally meaning an independent ruler, but which came to represent unlimited power. Once Constantinople had fallen to the Ottoman Empire in 1453, the Muscovite czars considered themselves the only legitimate Orthodox rulers and claimed Moscow as the Third Rome, the successor to both Rome and Constantinople, the earlier centers of world power and Christianity. New laws, promulgated under Ivan the Terrible in the 1550s, reorganized local government, further subordinated the numerous non-Russian ethnic groups, and strengthened the Muscovite state in the face of continuous warfare. Efforts to curtail the mobility of the peasants, both Russian and non-Russian, by tying them to their land brought Muscovy closer to legal serfdom.

Under the rule of Ivan the Terrible the rapid expansion of Muscovite territory was undertaken as a holy crusade. In 1552, Moscow's military forces conquered the wealthy khanate of Kazan', the Tatar state that dominated the Volga River basin. The conquest of Kazan' was followed by the annexation of the Tatar lands to the east and the khanate of Astrakhan, on the shores of the Caspian Sea. Ivan's conquests greatly expanded the territory controlled by Muscovy and brought numerous non-Slavic national groups under Muscovite rule. Late in Ivan the Terrible's reign, Cossack expeditions began the conquest of Siberia, greatly extending the land area of his empire. Despite its rapid territorial expansion, the Muscovite-Russian state remained isolated from the rest of Europe, a semi-Oriental state distrustful of foreign ideas and innovations, especially those from the Roman Catholic West.

When Ivan the Terrible died in 1584, he was succeeded by his son, Fyodor (Fedor), who was unable to continue his father's authoritarian policies. Fyodor left most of the power to his brother-in-law, Boris Godunov, who became czar on Fyodor's death in 1598. Godunov's rule was never accepted as entirely legitimate and was challenged from several quarters. When Godunov died suddenly in 1605, the "Time of Troubles" began. For the next eight years rival claimants, supported by the Poles, led to the Polish occupation of Moscow from 1610 to 1613. Forces from the northern Russian cities and Cossacks organized the counterattack against the Poles. The upheaval was welcomed by many of Russia's non-Slavic peoples, because pressure to assimilate and to accept Orthodoxy eased for a time. In 1613, in an effort to reestablish czarist authority, Michael (Mikhail) Romanov was elected as czar, the first of the Romanov dynasty. The Romanovs promoted czarist absolutism as a necessary means to restoring order and unity in their enormous territories.

Under Romanov rule serfdom was extended to the non-Slavic peoples, particularly those living in the vast Volga basin. The Finno-Ugrian peoples of the Volga and the territories to the north were subjected to a harsh colonial regime. Most of the subject peoples were relegated to virtual slavery on the vast estates of Russian landlords. The Russian landlords had complete power over their peasants and bought, sold, traded, and mortgaged them. The peoples of the region were often offered tax incentives or exemptions from military conscription, but more often, Russian soldiers moved from village to village forcing the inhabitants to listen while an Orthodox priest read the liturgy and the *zakon bozhii,* God's Law. They were then considered Orthodox Christians and were given Christian, that is, Russian, family names. The best and most fertile lands were confiscated, often to be controlled by absentee landlords. Poverty became widespread. By the early seventeenth century, most of the non-Russians and many of the ethnic Slavs of the empire were tied to large Russian estates as serfs, unpaid agricultural workers with few rights. Kept in ignorance and poverty, their only escape was often the lower ranks of the Orthodox priesthood. Local languages and cultures were prohibited or relegated to rural, peasant cultures, whereas assimilation into the Russian language and culture became the official policy, often enforced with great cruelty.

Severe disruptions during the Time of Troubles led to widespread famine. Extreme poverty and hunger sparked numerous rebellions, particularly severe in the southern provinces and the Volga basin. The Chavash, Maris, and Mordvins of the Volga region attempted to throw off hated Russian rule in 1601–1603 but were defeated and subjected to savage reprisals. They again rebelled in 1670, joined by many other non-Slavic groups, Cossacks, and escaped serfs. The rebellion, led by a Cossack, Stenka Razin, affected a wide region from the Volga basin to the North Caucasus. Czarist troops finally defeated the rebels after they had occupied major cities along the Volga. Razin was publicly tortured and executed. The rebel minorities were subjected to renewed pressures to assimilate and restrictions on their languages and cultures.

## The Romanovs

The early Romanov rulers were mostly weak, often controlled by powerful ministers or political factions. Expansion westward and more contact with Western Europe sharpened Muscovy's awareness of its backwardness. The consolidation of centralized power had been obtained by forcibly depriving the nobility of their powers. In compensation, they had been granted vast estates and unlimited powers over the masses, both the Russians and the mi-

*Peter I (Peter the Great), czar of Russia 1682–1725 (Hulton Archives)*

nority peoples. The Romanovs officially changed the focus of Russian national sentiment from Muscovy to a wider Russian Empire, which encompassed numerous non-Russian national groups but focused on the Russian heartland. Forced to adopt Western technology to compete militarily in Europe, Peter I (Peter the Great), on becoming sole ruler in 1696, attempted to introduce Western materials and thought to the feudal empire. At the same time, the Russians continued to expand at the expense of non-Russian states on their frontiers. In 1696 they took control of Azov on the Black Sea, beginning a push into the North Caucasus. Peter the Great formally proclaimed Muscovy as the Russian Empire in 1721.

Swedish expansion in the Baltic region led to war in 1700. The conflict, called the Northern War, ended in 1721, with Russian control of the Baltic territories. Like the Swedes, the Russians allowed the German minority to retain their feudal privileges. Serfdom was instituted in the newly conquered territory, tying the native Estonians, Latvians, and Lithuanians to the estates of the Baltic Germans, the descendants of the Teutonic Knights. As a symbol of Russia's new position as a European power, in 1703 Peter founded a new capital, St. Petersburg, in territory inhabited by Finnic peoples at the head of the Gulf of Finland. The government of the Russian Empire was transferred there from Moscow in 1714.

The growth of the Slavic state centered around the small duchy of Muscovy was dramatic following the overthrow of the Golden Horde. Territorial expansion brought not only neighboring Slavic principalities under the rule of Muscovy but also numerous territories inhabited by non-Slavic ethnic groups. The hegemony of Muscovy, or Moscow, continued for hundreds of years, even after the official declaration of the Russian Empire and the founding of a new capital at St. Petersburg in the eighteenth century. The expansion of Moscow's political and territorial authority was sustained by the colonization of the non-Russian territories by reliable ethnic Slavs. The numerous non-Russian ethnic groups, including the other Slavic peoples of the empire, were subjugated and colonized in much the same manner as the colonization of the Americas, Asia, and Africa.

## Timeline

| | |
|---|---|
| 1242 | The Mongols overrun southern Russia. |
| 1243 | The Golden Horde is formed in the Volga River basin. |
| 1244 | The Mongols withdraw from southern Russia, but retain control through Slavic vassal states. |

| | |
|---|---|
| 1252 | Muscovy becomes a separate hereditary principality. |
| 1256–1259 | The Mongols conquer the North Caucasus. |
| 1302 | Muscovy expands by annexing neighboring Slavic states. |
| 1326 | Moscow becomes the seat of the metropolitan of the Russian Orthodox Church. |
| 1386 | Poland and Lithuania are united in a dynastic union that includes much of present Ukraine and Belarus. |
| 1436 | The khanate of Kazan' is established by the Tatars. |
| 1443 | The Crimean Tatar khanate is established on the Black Sea. |
| 1450 | The Golden Horde begins to disintegrate. |
| 1453 | The Ottoman Turks capture Constantinople. |
| 1478 | Muscovy annexes Novgorod. |
| 1547 | Ivan the Terrible takes title of czar. |
| 1552 | The Muscovites, increasingly calling themselves Russians, conquer the khanate of Kazan', bringing the Tatars and other non-Slavic peoples under their rule. |
| 1556 | The Russians conquer the khanate of Astrakhan, bringing the Chavash and several other non-Slavic groups into their growing empire. |
| 1578–1590 | The Ottoman Turks conquer the Transcaucasus region. |
| 1581 | Cossacks begin the conquest of Siberia. |
| 1598 | The Rurik dynasty established in 862 ends. |
| 1605–1613 | The "Time of Troubles" ends with the establishment of the Romanov dynasty. |
| 1649 | Serfdom is formally established. Serfdom, under other names, had existed in many areas prior to 1649 but without the rigid laws established at this time. |
| 1654 | The Ukrainian Cossacks establish an alliance with Moscow against Polish domination. A Russo-Polish war brings most of the Ukraine under Russian rule. |
| 1671 | Widespread rebellion of subject peoples and Cossacks is led by Stenka Razin. |
| 1700–1721 | The Northern War between Russia and Sweden ends with Russian control of the Baltic territories. |
| 1703 | St. Petersburg founded by Peter the Great in territory inhabited by Finnic peoples as Russia's "Window on the West." The Russian state, long centered on Muscovy, is officially reorganized as the Russian Empire. |

## Significant People, Places, and Events

**BALTIC BARONS** The German-speaking descendants of medieval crusaders originally formed in the Holy Land, but later organized to fight
pagans in eastern Europe. They eventually conquered the Baltic region,
eliminating or reducing to serfdom the indigenous peoples. Their
power as landowning nobility lasted until World War I. The German
minority remained influential in the independent states of Estonia,
Latvia, and Lithuania until they were evacuated to Germany during
World War II.

**BURYATS** The largest group of the Mongol peoples in Siberia. Living in the
region around Lake Baikal, the world's largest freshwater lake, the Buryats have retained much of their traditional culture and their religion, the
Tibetan form of Buddhism introduced in the eighteenth century.

**COSSACKS** Military groups composed of peasant-soldiers in various parts of
the Russian Empire. Personally loyal to the czars, they were originally
charged with expanding and protecting the frontiers of the empire. Incorporating cultural and military influences from neighboring non-Slav
peoples, many of the Cossack groups took on the trappings of distinct national groups.

**IVAN III (IVAN THE GREAT)** Grand Duke of Muscovy from 1462 to 1505, the
creator of the consolidated Muscovite (Russian) state. He was the first to
assume the title of czar. He conquered the rival Russian states such as Novgorod, Tver', Vyatka, and Yaroslavl and checked the eastward expansion
of Lithuania. In 1480 he freed Muscovy from allegiance to the Tatars of
the Golden Horde.

**IVAN IV (IVAN THE TERRIBLE)** Grand Duke of Muscovy from 1533 to 1584.
He conquered the successor states of the Golden Horde, the khanates of
Kazan', Astrakhan, and Sibir', thereby inaugurating the Russians' southern
and eastern expansion into the North Caucasus and Siberia.

**KAZAN', KHANATE OF** The major successor state to the Golden Horde in the
Volga River basin, established in 1445. The khanate was conquered and
the capital city, Kazan', was sacked by the Russians in 1552, allowing the
Russians to colonize a vast region formerly under Mongol and Tatar rule.

**KULIKOVO FIELD, BATTLE OF (1380)** The first military challenge by the Muscovites to the rule of the Golden Horde. Although the victory was the first
Russian defeat of the Tatars, it did not eliminate Mongol-Tatar rule,
which endured for another century.

**MANCHU CHINA** The name given the Chinese Empire during the rule of the
Manchu, who invaded and conquered China in the mid-seventeenth

century. Their rule continued from the conquest until the overthrow of
the Manchu dynasty in 1911.

**MUSCOVY, DUCHY OF** One of a number of states that emerged following the
Mongol invasion and the breakup of Kievan Rus'. Muscovy achieved
dominance over the Russian lands because of its strategic location at the
crossroads of medieval trade routes, its leadership in the struggle against
and the final defeat of the Tatars, and its position as the center of Orthodox Christianity.

**NORTH CAUCASUS** The region north of the Caucasus Mountains populated
by a large number of Caucasian, Turkic, and Iranian peoples along with
later Cossack and Slavic settlers. The area, with a relatively temperate climate, is an important agricultural and manufacturing region.

**PETER I (PETER THE GREAT)** Czar of Russia from 1682 to 1725; the major
figure in the development of imperial Russia. Partly to promote a grand
alliance of Christian nations against the Muslim Ottoman Empire and
partly to westernize his still feudal realm, he promoted Westernization, including moving the capital from Moscow to St. Petersburg, a new city built
on the Gulf of Finland.

**REFORMATION (PROTESTANT REFORMATION)** The religious movement that
swept northern Europe in the sixteenth century. Beginning as a movement
against the excesses of the Roman Catholic Church, the Reformation
eventually embraced a number of Protestant sects that gained widespread acceptance in parts of Europe, particularly in Germany, Scandinavia, and other parts of north and Central Europe.

**RUSSIAN ORTHODOX CHURCH** The largest of the churches to subscribe to the
ritual that developed at the patriarchate of Constantinople, the Byzantine
Rite. The church, centered at Moscow from 1326, greatly influenced the
creation and expansion of the Russian Empire. The church remained one
of the cornerstones of the empire until the Russian Revolution of 1917.

**SAKHAS** Called Yakuts by the Russians. The largest Turkic nation in Siberia,
inhabiting a huge territory bordering the Arctic Ocean. Many of the Sakha
are Orthodox Christians, never having been influenced by the Islam of the
southern Turkic peoples.

**SERFDOM** Serfdom in the Russian territories began in the sixteenth century,
when Ivan IV created a new landholding aristocracy. Beginning in 1581
laws were adopted inhibiting the free movement of the peasant tenants.
The peasants were later bound to the landowner rather than the land and
could be sold, traded, or mortgaged.

**SHAMANISM** The traditional belief systems and practices of many former
tribal peoples of Siberia and other regions. Although the beliefs vary

from region to region, most have belief in magic and spirits as a common ground.

SIBERIA A vast geographical region generally understood to comprise the northern third of the Asian continent, stretching from the Ural Mountains, which divide Asia and Europe, to the Pacific Ocean.

TEUTONIC KNIGHTS Crusaders against the pagan peoples of eastern Europe who conquered the Baltic coast in the thirteenth and fourteenth centuries. Their control of the region led to German domination that lasted in Estonia and Latvia until World War I.

TRANSCAUCASUS (TRANSCAUCASIA) The historical region just south of the Caucasus Mountains, including the southern slopes of the Caucasus Mountains lying between the Caspian and Black Seas. In the modern era the Transcaucasus is divided into the independent states of Armenia, Georgia, and Azerbaijan.

TUVANS A people of mixed ethnic background, physically resembling the Mongols but culturally and linguistically closer to the Turkic peoples. Ethnically the Tuvans incorporate Turkic, Mongol, Samoyedic, and Kettic influences, with the Turkic strain dominant. The Turkic and Mongol strains are dominant in western Tuva, the Samoyed strain is evident in both western and eastern Tuva, and the Kettic strain shows up mostly among the eastern Tuvans.

UIGHURS The Turkic nation inhabiting the large territory of northwestern China known as Xinjiang or Chinese Central Asia. Culturally and historically the Uighur form part of the Turkic peoples inhabiting Central Asia.

## Bibliography

Billington, James. *The Icon and the Axe: An Interpretive History of Russian Culture.* New York: Knopf, 1970.

Blum, Jerome. *Lord and Peasant in Russia from the Ninth to the Nineteenth Century.* Princeton, NJ: Princeton University Press, 1961.

Bushkovich, Paul. *Religion and Society in Russia: The Sixteenth and Seventeenth Centuries.* New York and Oxford: Oxford University Press, 1992.

Cracraft, James. *Peter the Great Transforms Russia.* Lexington, MA: D.C. Heath and Co., 1991.

Crummey, Robert O. *The Formation of Muscovy, 1304–1613.* London: Longman, 1987.

De Madariagha, Isabel. *Russia in the Age of Catherine the Great.* New Haven, CT: Yale University Press, 1981.

Evans, John L. *Russia and the Khanates of Central Asia to 1865.* New York: Associated Faculty Press, 1982.

Olson, James S., ed. *An Ethnohistorical Dictionary of the Russian and Soviet Empires.* Westport, CT: Greenwood Press, 1994.

Pelenski, Jaroslav. *Russia and Kazan: Conquest and Imperial Ideology, 1438–1560s.* The Hague: Mouton, 1974.

Rogger, Hans. *National Consciousness in Eighteenth-Century Russia.* Cambridge, MA: Harvard University Press, 1960.

# CHAPTER THREE

# National Consolidation and the
# Growth of National Sentiment

IN THE SEVENTEENTH CENTURY Russia remained isolated from the rest of Europe, a semi-Oriental empire distrustful of foreigners and innovations. Religion and location remained the focus of loyalty for the majority of the population. The consolidation of central power, spearheaded by two able rulers, Peter I and Catherine II, both called the Great, was accompanied by reforms and Westernization following the extension of Russia's borders to the Baltic Sea and into Central Europe. The enlightened ideals seeping into Russia from Western Europe also resonated beyond the European territories, particularly among the ancient peoples of the Caucasus and the newly conquered Muslims of Central Asia. The attempts to modernize the empire by importing ideas and technology from Western Europe opened the way for the appearance of liberal ideals unwanted by the Russian rulers. These ideals, particularly those of nation and nationalism, began to influence the empire's many ethnic groups. Revolutionary ideals also seeped into the empire, taking root among the growing number of poor factory workers in the cities. The nineteenth-century national revival that swept Western Europe and saved many smaller national groups from extinction resonated in the multiethnic Russian Empire. Ethnic groups across the immense Russian state began to coalesce as nationalist ideals took root. The many ethnic groups that had suffered the injustices of Russian domination quickly embraced national sentiment.

Throughout Europe nationalism became a widespread and powerful force. A political or philosophical movement that evolved from the ideals of the American and French Revolutions, nationalism was first embraced by governments to encourage the individual to believe that his primary duty and loyalty is to the nation-state. Russian nationalism implied national and Slavic superiority and glorified various national virtues but left no room for participation by the non-Slav nations of the Russian Empire. Nationalism

69

was extremely important in forming the bonds that held the Russian Empire together. Slavic colonization and domination of the non-Slavic populations was often undertaken in the name of nationalism. Assimilation became official government policy, and many non-Slavic languages were prohibited and non-Slavic cultures were suppressed. By the mid-nineteenth century nationalism was expressed by many of the non-Slav ethnic groups as a drive for national unification or independence from hated Russian rule. In the last decades of the nineteenth century Russian nationalism and assimilation policies were strengthened as a measure to tie the peripheral and non-Slavic provinces to the center.

The two outstanding Romanov rulers during the late seventeenth and eighteenth centuries, Peter the Great and Catherine the Great, very much changed the politics of the Russian Empire. Peter's series of reforms began the "Westernization" of the empire. The transfer of the capital to his new city at St. Petersburg became a symbol of Russia's new position as a major European power. A Romanov by marriage, Catherine II ruled Russia from 1762 to 1796, pursuing a policy of enlightened despotism, while continuing the aggressive foreign policy initiated by Peter I. She turned her armies against the Ottoman Turks to the south in order to win warm-water ports on the Black Sea, seen as necessary for the expansion of trade. Immense new territories were brought into the empire following a series of wars with the weakened Turks, including extensive territories in the region north of the Caucasus Mountains. Brutal attacks were carried out against the peoples of the newly acquired territories, particularly the Muslim peoples of the Caucasus, who resisted the imposition of Russian rule. In 1783 Catherine annexed the khanate of the Crimean Tatars, formerly a vassal state of the Ottoman Empire. The annexation opened the way to additional conquests in the North Caucasus following the Russo-Turkish War of 1787–1791. The best of the newly conquered lands were taken by Russian nobles, settlers, and Orthodox monasteries established to further the spread of Christianity among the non-Christian and Muslim subjects. The annexation of former Turkish and Crimean Tatar territory brought numerous new ethnic groups into the empire, particularly Muslim groups in the Caucasus. The Muslim religion, banned for two centuries, was again allowed during Catherine's rule in an effort to reconcile her new subjects to Russian authority. A law forbidding the building or repairing of mosques was rescinded in 1766.

In the late eighteenth century the first steps were taken to dismantle the system of serfdom, particularly the selling of serfs without land. The process was particularly embraced by the non-Slav ethnic groups, as it paralleled a new interest in education, national languages, and submerged cultures. The reform of serfdom was disrupted by Napoleon's invasion of Russia in 1812. Napoleon's military officers, in an effort to undermine support for the Russians, appealed to the national minorities to support the French invasion. Having burned Moscow, Napoleon was forced to retreat through the Russian winter, quickly losing the help of the non-Slav populations. In the early 1800s many Russian ministers, worried about the influence of so many distinct nationalities living in the Russian Empire, initiated a renewed and more intense policy aimed at assimilating the majority of the non-Slavic national groups into the Russian culture and language. National sentiments or support for non-Slavic cultures were seen as revolutionary and threatening. By the mid-nineteenth century, the Russian Empire had become the most reactionary state in Europe, acting as the policeman of the continent by combating all liberal tendencies, particularly in regard to national minorities. A clash between the reactionary Russian government and the major Western powers over the Ottoman Empire led to the Crimean War, which revealed the weakness of the near-feudal empire.

### The Crimean War

Russian territorial expansion finally led to war with the major Western powers allied to the Ottoman Empire. French and British troops landed on the Crimean Peninsula in the Black Sea and fought a long, bloody war against the Russians. The war, which ended with Russia's defeat in 1856, seriously divided Russia's military, which was also involved against the Muslims led by Imam Shamil in the Caucasus region. During the Crimean War a large exodus of Muslim peoples from Russian territory to the Ottoman Empire became so severe that some districts were virtually depopulated.

A liberal czar, Alexander II, who became ruler of the vast multiethnic empire in 1855, one year before the end of the Crimean War, was determined to modernize his defeated state. Among his reforms was the emancipation of the serfs and the end of official serfdom in 1861, which coincided with a gradual spread of education beyond the local religious and political elites. His rule also oversaw further Russian territorial expansion into the Caucasus region, Central Asia, and the southern regions of the Far East on the Chinese border. The Russian Empire reached its greatest territorial extent, with its borders extending to the frontiers of China, Afghanistan, and the Pacific Ocean in the mid-nineteenth century. In 1870 the empire was inhabited by an estimated 150 distinct ethnic and linguistic groups. Alexander II was assassinated in 1881. He was succeeded by the reactionary and conservative

*Famine-stricken former serfs travel to St. Petersburg during the late 1800s. The eman-
cipation act by Alexander II in 1861 freed serfs from the inhumane conditions of serfdom, but many emancipated serfs faced poverty and starvation. (Library of Congress)*

Alexander III, who rapidly reversed most of the reforms of his predecessor
and instituted a domestic policy that suppressed all manifestations of free
thought and progress. The motto "one law, one church, one tongue" became
the unwritten law of the empire. While great social and political changes
swept the rest of Europe, the Russian Empire remained mired in the traditional problems—feudal agrarian traditions, government policies that
pressed the assimilation of the national minorities, and the wasteful privi-
lege of the aristocratic classes. Although accomplishments such as the opening of the Trans-Siberian Railroad in 1892 made vast frontiers available for
development, they failed to resolve the fundamental problems facing the
mass of the empire's population. In 1894, Nicholas II, the last czar of the
Russian Empire, succeeded Alexander III.

Throughout the Russian Empire the ideas of nationalism and the rights
of individuals and ethnic groups resonated among the many oppressed nations. The Slavs had colonized every corner of the huge territory, and assimilation had been official government policy for centuries, but the various

ethnic groups, still clinging to national cultures and languages, quickly embraced the nationalism seeping in from Europe. Even those groups that had begun to assimilate into Russian culture responded to the new ideals. Nationalism became a central theme across the empire, particularly among the larger ethnic groups; however, even the smaller, weaker groups quickly embraced the ideas of nationalism and self-determination. The imperial government, viewing all nationalisms other than Russian nationalism as subversive and revolutionary, brutally retaliated against nationalist leaderships among the non-Russian peoples, creating even more resentment and hatred.

## Ukrainians

Between 1764 and 1775 the Zaporozhye Cossacks were brutally suppressed by the czarist government and all their former political autonomy was ended. The western Ukrainian territories, mostly under the rule of Poland-Lithuania, were divided by the eighteenth-century Polish partitions. The western part became part of Austria, while eastern Ukraine was added to the Cossack lands brought under Russian rule a century earlier. Although the Ukrainians were Eastern Slavs and closely related both culturally and linguistically to the Russians, cultural influences from the West and rule by the Roman Catholic Poles had raised significant cultural, linguistic, and religious differences. During the reign of Catherine the Great the Ukrainians were subjected to the traditional Russian policies of assimilation, national and cultural oppression, and economic exploitation. Although known as an enlightened despot, Catherine institutionalized serfdom in Ukraine and parceled out huge estates to her court favorites. The policies of Catherine's successors, even those who attempted reforms, proved equally repressive. In 1873 Alexander II totally banned the use of the Ukrainian language in publishing or education. Consolidated under czarist rule, eastern Ukraine was subjected to a policy of intense Russification in the eighteenth and nineteenth centuries.

The western Ukrainians, under somewhat more lenient Austrian rule, lived in an area called Galicia, a region of mixed Ukrainian and Polish populations. The revolutionary outbreaks in the Austrian Empire in 1848 led to a number of important reforms in Galicia. Serfdom was abolished and a regional parliament was created. Influenced by other ethnic groups in the multiethnic Austrian Empire, the Ukrainians began to embrace nationalist ideas of culture and self-determination. The Ukrainian national revival in Austrian territory stimulated a paralleled movement among the less-advanced pop-

*Catherine II became empress of Russia in 1762 after overthrowing Peter III with the help of the military and the royal guard. (Dmitry Levitzky. The Russian Museum, St. Petersburg, Russia)*

ulation in Russian Ukraine. Influenced by the romantic and liberal ideals of the European nationalist revival of the mid-nineteenth century, young Ukrainians began to take a renewed interest in their particular history and culture. Taras Shevchenko, a poet and artist, exercised tremendous influence on the development of the Ukrainian national consciousness in the late nineteenth century.

## Belarussians

The Belarussians also came under direct Russian rule as a result of the Polish partitions of 1772, 1793, and 1795. The official Russian policy of assimilation, particularly effective among the culturally and linguistically related Belarussians, achieved the conversion of the majority from Roman Catholicism to Russian Orthodoxy and reduced the Belarussian language to a rural, peasant dialect. The formerly prosperous Belarussian provinces declined under Russian rule. Widespread poverty fueled mass immigration in the early nineteenth century, mostly to North America. As a further attempt to completely assimilate the Belarussian population, the Belarussian language was finally banned and the use of names such as Belarussian, Belarusy, or White Russian was forbidden in the 1840s. Called the Northwestern Region by the czarist government, the Belarussian homeland was divided into several Russian provinces and all traces of a separate Belarussian culture were eradicated.

Serfdom, widespread in the region, was officially abolished in the empire in 1861. Promised lands of their own that were never forthcoming, the former Belarussian serfs rebelled in 1863. The rebellion rapidly spread to the upper classes and the free peasant farmers, taking on overtly nationalistic overtones. The revolt, brutally suppressed by czarist troops, virtually ended all economic activity in Belarus. Dependent on subsistence farming or work in the Russianized urban areas, the Belarussian provinces became a cheap labor pool for the czarist authorities. The grinding poverty sent a new wave of immigrants, including many of the region's Jews, to North America between the 1880s and the turn of the twentieth century. In the late 1880s an estimated 82 percent of the Belarussians were illiterate, retarding the ethnic revival that swept most of Europe in the latter half of the nineteenth century. Russian assimilation policies nearly succeeded in Belarus. By the late nineteenth century the majority of the Belarussians had no clear national identity, considering themselves as ethnic Russians or Poles, the distinction usually determined by religion, the Orthodox Belarussians being closer to the

Russians, and the Roman Catholic minority thinking of themselves as Poles. Only in the 1890s did a national revival begin to take hold among the Belarussians, much later than the cultural revivals experienced by neighboring ethnic groups. The revival, more modest than in most of Europe, was principally confined to the small urban population and was hindered by the backward condition of the rural majority of the Belarussian population.

## The Finnic Peoples of Northwestern Russia

### Karels

The Karels, the largest of the Finnic peoples in northwestern Russia, are closely related to the Finns, although religion determined the traditional boundaries between Finland and Karelia, the Finns having adopted the Lutheran faith of their Swedish rulers, whereas the Karels had mostly accepted Orthodoxy. Historically the Karel homeland was contested by Sweden and the Russian republic of Novgorod. When the Muscovites took control of Novgorod in 1478 many Karels came under Russian rule. The early Karelian folktales and songs of the medieval period are the source of the noted Finnish national epic, the *Kalevala,* considered a national heritage by both Karels and Finns. Orthodox Karels, fleeing Swedish rule and the imposition of Protestantism, participated in a migration of some 25,000 to 30,000 people into Russian territory in the late sixteenth century, a very large migration for the time. The Russian government supported the migration of the Orthodox Karels with financial assistance and land. The Russians took all of eastern Karelia from the Swedes during the Northern War in the early eighteenth century, and western Karelia and Finland were added to the Russian Empire during the Napoleonic Wars, in 1809. The two Karelian regions were kept separate as part of czarist policy. Eastern Karelia, poor and underdeveloped, was used as a place of exile for czarist political prisoners and common criminals. Western Karelia, lying between Finland and St. Petersburg, was more developed and was ruled as part of the autonomous Grand Duchy of Finland.

Influenced by the more advanced national sentiment of the Finns, the Karels experienced a national and cultural revival in the late nineteenth century. The czarist authorities, already faced with a growing national movement in neighboring Finland, cracked down on the Karel cultural movement in 1899. New restrictions were placed on publishing or education in the Karel language. Finnish nationalist literature, smuggled across the Finnish-Karelian border, supported the spread of a particular Karel nationalist movement that demanded linguistic, cultural, and national rights for all the Karels of the Russian Empire. The czarist authorities in the region countered the Karel nationalist demands with renewed pressure to assimilate into Russian culture.

## Ingrians

The Ingrians, whose homeland lay around the Gulf of Finland, mostly lived as farmers or fishermen. Although Christianized in the thirteenth century, the Ingrians adopted the Lutheran faith of their Swedish rulers in the seventeenth century. Brought under Russian rule following the Northern War between Sweden and Russia in the early eighteenth century, they remained relatively isolated until the beginning of the construction of the new Russian capital, St. Petersburg, on Ingrian territory in 1703. The construction of the new capital at the head of the Gulf of Finland brought a massive influx of Slavic workers that quickly outnumbered the indigenous Ingrians. In spite of the loss of much of their ancient territory, the Ingrians prospered by supplying the rapidly growing city of St. Petersburg with vegetables, grains, and building materials.

The official policy of assimilation succeeded with the urbanized Ingrians in the expanding urban area around St. Petersburg, but it met strong resistance among the rural Ingrians. A cultural revival, effected by the nationalism embraced by the neighboring Finns and Estonians, spread across the Ingrian territories north and south of the Gulf of Finland in the 1880s. As a result of the Ingrians' Lutheran faith and their close cultural ties, a feeling of unity with the Finns developed. The cultural revival spawned a modest national movement that aimed to separate the Ingrian homeland from direct Russian rule and to unite with Finland, then a semiautonomous grand duchy ruled separately from the Russian territories.

The smaller numbers of Finnic peoples populating the region of the great lakes just north of the Gulf of Finland were reduced to minorities in their homelands by the influx of Slavs in the eighteenth century. Under the rule of the Slavic Republic of Novgorod until the Muscovite conquest of that commercial state in 1478, the Finnic minorities were early targets of assimilation. Forcible conversion to Orthodoxy, education only in Russian, and the close proximity of Slavic settlements formed the foundation of the long process of assimilation of the Finnic Karels, Veps, Votes, and Ludians into Russian culture. The Finns of Finland, incorporated into the Russian Empire in 1809, acted as the champions of the related Finnic peoples within Russia proper. The policy of assimilation, legislated in 1899, brought great pressure on the surviving Finnic peoples to abandon their ancient cultures and to disappear into the surrounding Russian-speaking populations. Slavic ethnologists working in the northwestern provinces in the late nineteenth century were of the opinion that the small Finnic nations would shortly become extinct.

## The Baltic Peoples

The major national groups of the Baltic region—Estonians, Latvians, and Lithuanians—evolved somewhat differently from other groups in the Russian Empire, owing to their history of conquest by German crusaders and later control by more liberal Sweden in the north and rule by the Roman Catholic Poles in the south. Even though the Estonians are a Finnic people closely related to the Finns, and the Latvians and Lithuanians form the two branches of the Baltic peoples, they all share a history of contact and rule from the West rather than from Russia to the east. Baltic architecture, folk traditions, food, dress, and religion all tie them to the West rather than to Russia.

### Estonians

Sweden's expansion to the east brought the Scandinavian kingdom into open conflict with the Russian Empire. The conflict culminated in the long war called the Great Northern War, which began in 1700 and ended in 1721 with Swedish defeat. By the terms of the peace treaty, the Swedish kingdom ceded its Baltic territories, Estonia and Livonia (southern Estonia and northern Latvia), to the Russian Empire. Like the Swedes before them, the Russians allowed the German minority to retain its privileged status. The power of the German landed aristocracy was again strengthened over the land and the mostly rural Estonian population. By the 1740s serfdom was firmly established and the Estonian peasants were treated as property of the German estates.

Reforms introduced by the provincial governments of Estonia and Livonia in 1816 and 1819 gradually ended serfdom in the region. Counties were established as the basis of local government, and county schools, teaching in both Estonian and German, quickly raised the educational level of the Estonian peasantry. Laws adopted in 1849 and 1856 set aside a certain amount of land for the peasants. In 1866 the German manors lost their traditional control over the peasants' governing bodies. The new land laws in the provinces inhabited by Estonians marked a radical change in the social structure of the region.

The spread of education promoted the growth of Estonian national consciousness in the mid-nineteenth century. Estonian nationalism began as an anti-German mass movement, inspired by their near-feudal subjugation by the so-called Baltic Barons. The publication of their epic poem, *Kalevipoeg,* the story of their powerful, ancient hero, along with the mass folk festivals that began in the 1860s, accelerated the national revival in the later part of the nineteenth century. The rapid industrialization of the region aided the national movement. Industrialization fostered urbanization and the establishment, for the first time, of large Estonian middle and working classes. Education in the Estonian language expanded rapidly with the urbanization of the Estonian population. Czar Alexander III, crowned in 1881, sharply curtailed the privileges of the Baltic Germans but also stepped up the government program of assimilation in the 1880s in response to the growing nationalist sentiment among the Estonians. Russian replaced German as the official language in the Baltic provinces in 1885, censorship became stricter, education or publishing in the Estonian language was forbidden, and conversion to Russian Orthodoxy was encouraged. The assimilation policy was officially ended in 1897. The Estonian national movement, no longer suppressed, rapidly gained strength. A new generation of young educated, urban Estonians rapidly embraced national ideals.

## Latvians

The Swedish kingdom, which had controlled Estonia since 1521, won control of most of Latvia from the Poles in the early seventeenth century. Swedish rule reinforced the Protestant faith that spread among the Latvians, with most adopting the Lutheran creed of their Swedish rulers. Only in the Latgale region, which remained under Polish rule, did Roman Catholicism continue to be the dominant religion. Czarist Russia's long desire for the ice-free ports on the Baltic Sea precipitated several wars with the Swedes. The Northern War between Sweden and Russia devastated the region and ended with Russian control of most of Latvia, except for Roman Catholic Latgalia, which remained part of the Polish kingdom.

The imposition of Russian rule was welcomed by the Baltic German minority whose position as the ruling class, lost under Swedish rule, was rapidly restored. The return of feudalism and the official policy of assimilation of the Latvians into Russian culture marked the miserable existence of the majority during the first decades of Russian rule. Russian Orthodoxy was imposed as the state religion, and Lutheran churches were often closed. Oppressed by the German landowners and the Russian provincial governments, the Latvian culture and language were again relegated to rural curiosities. The Latvians were unable to express their identity politically or culturally. Only during the period of rapid change from a feudal agrarian society to capitalist industrialization at the end of the eighteenth century did the circumstances of life for the average Latvian begin to change. The abolition of serfdom in the Baltic region, in 1817–1819, decades before the abolition in the rest of Russia, stimulated the growth of industry, which began to develop rapidly. Industrialization absorbed the excess workers released from serfdom even though the population began to grow rapidly.

The development of the modern Latvian nation began only in the first decades of the nineteenth century, much later than most other European national groups. Education, available even in rural areas, including university education in the German language, fostered the formation of a Latvian national consciousness. By the mid-nineteenth century an educated elite demanded additional reforms, including education in the Latvian language and the right to acquire land. An urbanized middle class, emerging between the 1840s and 1860s, began to oppose the traditional centers of power in Latvia, the German aristocracy, and the Russian civil government of the province. The national movement developed out of a growing anti-German mobilization of the Latvian public. Nationalist sentiment spread as Latvian leaders demanded the same rights enjoyed by other European ethnic groups. In the 1880s the czarist government stepped up the policy of assimilation. Russian replaced German as the official language of the province in 1885, with Russian becoming the only language used in government and education. The imposition of the Russian language was paralleled by a crackdown on nationalist activities, including cultural events not sanctioned by local authorities. The suppression of the Latvian culture spurred the growth of radical political groups. Latvian worker movements, organized by radicalized leaders in heavily industrialized Latvia in the 1890s, espoused revolutionary ideals. Nationalism became the cause of a small, educated elite while the majority, particularly the growing number of industrial workers, rejected separation from Russia in favor of a worker's state that would replace the unjust and hated czarist system. The lifting of the more oppressive measures in 1897 allowed nationalist and revolutionary groups to become more active.

## Lithuanians

Farther south the Lithuanian elite had adopted Polish language and culture during the period of the joint Polish-Lithuanian commonwealth. Under Polish rule during the seventeenth and eighteenth centuries the Lithuanian language and traditions survived only as a rural peasant culture. Unlike the other Baltic national groups, the Estonians and Latvians, the Lithuanians remained staunchly Roman Catholic. Weakened by the expanding Russian power, the Polish-Lithuanian state declined rapidly in the late seventeenth century. Between 1772 and 1795 the Polish and Lithuanian territories were partitioned between their more powerful neighbors in a series of territorial annexations known as the Polish Partitions. Prussia, Austria, and Russia all took territories from the weakened Poland, which finally disappeared from the map of Europe. Russia's portion included territory in eastern and central Poland and all of Lithuania except for a small part in the southwest taken by Prussia.

The Roman Catholic Lithuanians, coming under intense Russian pressure to adopt the Russian language and culture and to abandon their Catholic religion for Russian Orthodoxy, attempted several times to throw off harsh Russian rule. Lithuanian uprisings were particularly serious in 1794 and 1830–1831. In 1832, in reprisal for the latest uprising, the Russian authorities closed the ancient university at Vilnius, the Lithuanian capital. In opposition to intense official pressure to assimilate, the Lithuanians began to embrace nationalist ideals seeping into the region from Western Europe in the mid-nineteenth century. The abolition of serfdom in Russia in 1861 freed many Lithuanians from their near-feudal existence and stimulated the growth of a market economy. Lithuanian farmers increasingly received some education, leading to the strong opposition of the government's oppressive policies. In 1863 the Lithuanians joined the neighboring Poles in open rebellion. One of the consequences of their defeat was the 1864 banning of all books and newspapers published in the traditional Lithuanian Latin alphabet. The first Lithuanian-language newspaper was founded in Memel, then controlled by the German Kingdom of Prussia, in 1883. Their Roman Catholic religion, closely tied to the growing Lithuanian nationalist movement, again came under attack in the 1890s. In 1894 all Roman Catholics were excluded from local government offices. The policy of Russification was terminated in 1897, allowing the nascent Lithuanian national movement to gain strength. Revolutionary activism during the upheavals of the 1905 Revolution accelerated the spread of nationalism. Reforms were introduced that allowed political opposition, trade unions, and language education reforms. Many Baltic activists supported radical revolutionary groups as a way of freeing their small nations from the double oppression of Czarist Russia and the Baltic German aristocracy.

## The Caucasus

The long rivalry between the Ottoman Turks and the Persians allowed the Russians to exert a growing influence in the lands to the south of the empire. The continuing wars with the Turks enabled the Russians to annex the Romanian-speaking Bessarabia, later known as Moldova, following the Russo-Turkish War of 1806–1812. In the Caucasus the Russian conquest of the remaining territories in the Transcaucasus followed the Russo-Persian Wars of 1804–1813 and 1826–1828. Armenians, Georgians, and the Muslim Azeris were brought under Russian authority by the treaties of Gulestan in 1813 and Turkmanchai in 1828. Further annexations followed, and by the mid-1860s, eastern Armenia, all of Georgia, and northern Azerbaijan were incorporated into the Russian Empire. Christian Russian rule was seen by many of the Georgians and Armenians as preferable to rule by the Muslim Turks or Persians. Active support for the expansion of the Russian Empire into the Caucasus gave the native Christians an often-privileged position in regards to the Muslim tribes.

Resistance to Russian rule was particularly intense in the Muslim eastern regions of the North Caucasus, among the fierce Dagestani tribes and the Chechens, who looked to the Ottoman Turks for support. Long after the official Russian annexation, the Muslim peoples of this rugged territory, seeing themselves as part of a larger Muslim nation, continued to resist Russian control. Muslim solidarity was the supreme loyalty of the many small Turkic and Caucasian tribes living in the isolated valleys and highlands of the Caucasus Mountains. The most sustained anti-Russian rebellion—the Murid Uprising—lasted for more than thirty years, from 1828 to 1859, part of the so-called Caucasian War that continued from 1817 to 1864. The uprising was led by a Muslim cleric, Imam Shamil, who declared a holy war against the Christian Russian invaders. The North Caucasus was covered in beech and oak forests, and the Muslims of the region were particularly skilled at forest warfare, so the Russians completely deforested the foothills of the Caucasus Mountains. In 1865 tens of thousands of Muslims died in the final Russian drive into the region; many thousands more fled or were expelled to Turkish territory. Revolts periodically flared up in the region over the remaining decades of the nineteenth century.

The Russian expansion to the south, into the strategically important Caucasus, was achieved by varied methods. In 1723 the Russians took control of the plains south to the Terek River in the North Caucasus. The last king of Georgia, pressed by the powerful Muslim Ottoman Empire and Persia, abdicated in 1801 after placing his kingdom in central Georgia under Russian protection. The Russian Empire acquired the remainder of the Georgian-speaking lands between 1803 and 1829. The neighboring Armenians also welcomed Russia's advance into the region. The Persian conquest of eastern Armenia had effectively partitioned the ancient nation between the Ottoman Turks and the Persians. In 1828 the Russians took control of eastern Armenia from Persia, setting off a wave of pro-Russian sentiment among the oppressed Christian Armenians still living under harsh Turkish rule. In Russian Armenia and Georgia, the Russians, although resented as newcomers to the region, were often seen as protectors against the surrounding Muslims.

## Armenians

The Armenians of the Transcaucasus, who form a distinct branch of the Caucasian peoples, are the heirs of an ancient culture that combines both Oriental and Occidental influences. Their culture and their independent Armenian Orthodox Church are closely intertwined. Until the nineteenth century the church played the role of the guardian and perpetuator of the Armenian culture. The location of the Armenian homeland, a frontier region between the Russians, Turks, and Persians, meant that the culture developed in a region of near constant conflict. Russian interest in Armenia set off a period of repression and persecution of the Armenians in the Ottoman Empire in the latter half of the nineteenth century. The focus of nineteenth-century Armenian culture, owing to increased repression in the Ottoman territories, lay outside the Armenian heartland regions of eastern Anatolia and the Transcaucasus, in Russian Armenia, in Constantinople, and in Tbilisi, the capital of the neighboring Georgians.

The major European states, uncomfortable with the Ottoman persecution of Christians, demanded political and social reforms in the Ottoman Empire in 1878 and again in 1883, but demands by the European Christian nations only increased Turkish distrust of their Christian subjects. A small number of educated Armenians founded the Armenian national movement in the relatively more liberal Russian Armenia in 1840. National sentiment fueled a cultural revival, which rapidly spread through the Armenian populations in Russia, Ottoman Turkey, and Persia. Armenian leaders, persecuted in Ottoman Turkey, often fled to Russian Armenia, adding fuel to the growing national movement. The growth of Armenian national sentiment was accompanied by a parallel cultural movement. The cultural revival rapidly spread through the Armenian communities in Russia, Turkey, and Persia.

Determined to crush the perceived Christian threat to Ottoman rule, the Turkish authorities, beginning in 1890, encouraged attacks on defenseless Armenian towns and villages, leading to horrible massacres by rampaging Muslim mobs. By 1895 more than 300,000 Armenians and other Christians had died in attacks and massacres. In the late 1890s Armenian nationalists organized the Armenian Revolutionary Federation, the Dashnaktsutiun, popularly called the Dashnaks, which soon had underground cells in most Armenian towns and villages in both Russian and Turkish Armenia. The nationalists, following Dashnak leaders, openly opposed both the ongoing Turkish oppression and the Russian government policy of assimilation.

## Georgians

The Georgians, perhaps the most ancient nation in the Caucasus, developed a unique culture that combined influences from many neighboring peoples. By the eighteenth century the Georgians had adopted many European traditions, such as clothing styles, as a reaction against centuries of conquest or threats by the Turks and Persians to the south. The devoutly Christian Georgians increasingly looked to their fellow Christians, the Russians, as protectors against the Muslims. The Georgian kingdom became a pawn in the explosive Russian-Turkish rivalry in the Caucasus territories. The Russian annexation of the Georgian territories, which began with a protectorate agreement soon abrogated by the Russian authorities, was accompanied by the policy of assimilation. In 1811 the Georgian Orthodox Church was incorporated into the official Orthodox Church as part of the Russian government's assimilation policy. The large Russified Georgian aristocracy, famed for wealth and extravagance, became part of the political and cultural elite of the empire, numbering about one in every seven Georgians. The incorporation of the Georgian elite facilitated the extension of Russian and European ideas.

Under Russian rule European ideas came to influence not only the elite, but also the educated classes. Forbidden their language, and with their cherished national church absorbed into the Russian Orthodox Church, a small number of Georgian nationalists began to organize in the mid-nineteenth century. A modest cultural revival that began to take hold in the 1840s started as a reaction to Russian attempts to assimilate the Georgian culture. The Georgian cultural and linguistic revival that began in the mid-nineteenth century inspired the growth of nationalist sentiment in the 1880s and 1890s, particularly among a minority seeking to return to the independence and cultural flowering of medieval Georgia. The national movement increasingly looked to the liberal ideals of Western Europe for inspiration, ideals embraced by the Social Revolutionary Party, the largest of Georgia's fledgling political groups. Nationalists demanded linguistic and cultural freedom, a democratic Georgian government, and a free enterprise economic system modeled on those of the United Kingdom and France. Many Georgians rejected parochial nationalism and joined the wider Russian revolutionary circles seeking social justice and reforms across the Russian Empire.

### Azeris

The Russian Empire, expanding south into the Caucasus region, annexed northern Azerbaijan piecemeal from the weakened Persians between 1805 and 1813. Baku came under Russian rule in 1806. The Azeri territories taken by the Russians were formally ceded by Persia in the treaty of Gulistan in 1813, which divided historical Azerbaijan into Russian and Persian halves. A second treaty, the Treaty of Turkmanchai, signed in 1828, formally ceded the western Azeri territory of Nakhichevan to Russia. Southern or Persian Azerbaijan remained part of the Persian state as a separate satrapy with its capital at Tabriz. Russian attempts to extend their influence into Persian Azerbaijan were blocked by the Persian authorities but continued well into the twentieth century.

The Muslim religion formed the most basic identity of the Azeris, but by the nineteenth century a nationalist ideal had gained support. The discovery of oil at Baku, a small and dusty town in the Azeri-speaking region on the Caspian Sea spurred the growth of a distinct Azeri nationality. Azerbaijan's oil industry, then the largest in Europe, was established in 1872 and was tremendously important to the industrializing Russian Empire. Baku's oil fields were producing half the world's oil by 1900. The oil industry brought an influx of Slavic oil and industrial workers. The sudden economic importance of the region exposed the Azeris to urbanization, education, and technology. Resentment of Slavic privileges sparked an Azeri cultural and religious revival in the late nineteenth century, the revival provoked by Russian government programs aimed at the Christianization and assimilation of the Azeri population of the Russian Empire. The Slavic influx also brought nationalist and revolutionary ideas, setting off a cultural and religious revival among the Azeris. Linguistically close to the Turks but with the majority practicing the Shia Islam dominant in neighboring Persia, the Azeris were slow to develop a national sentiment beyond their Muslim religion. The Azeris' cultural-national movement gradually united the many closely related linguistic and cultural groups in a larger political and cultural entity. The numbers of Azeri-speaking inhabitants and the economic importance of their homeland made them the largest and most important of the Muslim groups in the Caucasus.

## Chechens and Ingush

Azeri nationalist ideas slowly spread to the less-populous Caucasian Muslim peoples, particularly the still violently anti-Russian groups just to the north of Azerbaijan, the Chechens and their allies, the Ingush and the various Dagestani groups. These groups had participated in revolts against Russian rule on several occasions since the defeat of their leader Imam Shamil in 1859. The most serious of the revolts occurred in 1863, 1867, and 1877, mostly in reaction to Russian attempts to spread Orthodox Christianity and the official government policy of assimilation. Driven from their most fertile lands in the valley of the Terek River, the Chechens remained the most anti-Russian ethnic group in the Russian Empire.

The Chechens of the eastern Caucasus were the backbone of the guerrilla war led by Imam Shamil from 1834 to 1859. Following the final Russian drive against the Muslim strongholds, the surviving Chechens were driven from their fertile lowlands along the Terek River. Forced to take refuge in the mountains, they lived in abject poverty. Hatred of the Slavs, particularly the Cossack colonists settled on their confiscated lands, provoked repeated revolts in the 1860s and 1870s. In 1865, in reprisal for a particularly violent uprising, the Russian authorities forcibly deported nearly 40,000 Chechens to Ottoman Turkish territory. The Chechen homeland was given added importance following the discovery of oil near Grozny in 1893. By 1900 the Grozny oil fields were the second largest oil producers in czarist Russia.

## Kalmyks

In addition to the Caucasian and Turkic peoples of the North Caucasus there is another small but important ethnic group, the Mongol Kalmyks. A branch of the Oirot (Altai) peoples of Mongolia and southern Siberia, they left their Asian homeland in the Altai Mountains in 1636, fleeing the disintegration of the Mongol Empire and political and economic pressure from surrounding Chinese, Kazakhs, and other Mongol groups. The Oirot clans migrated west, displacing the nomadic tribes in their path. According to Kalmyk tradition, the migration lasted for thirty-two years before their ancestors finally settled in the lower Volga River basin west of the Caspian Sea. Their new homeland, which had once formed part of the Tatar khanate of Astrakhan, had been incorporated into the Muscovite Empire in 1556. The Oirot migrants created an independent khanate in the region, a confederation of the various tribes. In 1608 the clan leaders petitioned the czar, Vasily Shuysky, for military protection against the ravages of nomadic tribes. In 1646 the confederation signed a treaty of allegiance to the Russian czar, who charged them with the protection of Russia's new frontier in the North Caucasus. Russian protection saved the Oirots from further attacks, allowing for the flowering of their distinctive Mongol culture. From 1664 to 1771 the khanate formed a semi-independent state in personal allegiance to the Russian czars. In the eighteenth century the Mongol Oirots adopted the Lamaism brought to their North Caucasus homeland by missionary monks from far-off Mongolia and Tibet. The Dalai Lama, the religious and secular ruler of Tibet, thereafter appointed the Oirot confederation's khans, or rulers.

News that their ethnic cousins in China and Mongolia were suffering intense persecutions under Chinese rule rallied the clans in 1769–1770. Catherine the Great, in the winter of 1771, put aside the 1646 treaty of personal loyalty and attempted to impose direct Russian rule on the Oirot confederation. Refusing to accept Christian domination and determined to rescue their ethnic kin in China, the Mongol clans east of the Volga River suddenly undertook an epic journey back to their original homeland, more than 2,000 miles (3,218 km.) to the east. Of the 300,000 Oirots that undertook the journey, only about a third survived. The majority died of cold, heat, hunger, and attacks by hostile tribes. The Volga River did not freeze as usual in the winter of 1771, stranding the 60,000 Oirots living west of the river. Those that were left behind came to be called Kalmyk, derived from a Turkic word for remnant. The Kalmyks left in the North Caucasus formed close military and cultural ties to the Cossacks living in the frontier districts, taking on many of the Cossack military and social traditions. Like the Cossack peoples, in return for military service and an oath of personal loyalty to the Russian czar, the Kalmyks were mostly left to govern themselves.

Immigration, supported by the czarist government, began to change the situation in the Kalmyk homeland in the early nineteenth century. Limits were placed on grazing lands and their nomadic way of life. The Kalmyk herds, the basis of their culture, declined from about 2.5 million in 1803 to about 1 million in 1863, and again dropped to just 450,000 at the turn of the twentieth century. Deprived of their traditional way of life, many Kalmyks were forced off the land to find work as fishermen on the Volga River or the Caspian Sea or as miners in the salt and mineral mines established in the North Caucasus.

## The Crimean Tatars

The decline of the Turkish Ottoman Empire in the seventeenth century provided the Russians the opportunity to push south into the steppe lands of southern Ukraine. The powerful khanate centered on the Crimean Peninsula remained a major impediment to Russian expansion to the south. Russian attempts to invade the Crimean Peninsula in 1687 and 1689 failed, but in 1696, Peter the Great captured Azov, on the mainland opposite the peninsula. Russian control of Azov gave the empire access to the Black Sea. The Crimean Tatar khanate, rich on Black Sea trade, developed a brilliant and sophisticated civilization even as its northern provinces fell to the expanding Russian Empire. In 1736 the Russians again attacked the Crimean khanate. Advancing imperial troops quickly overran all Crimean Tatar territory except the heartland, the Crimean Peninsula, and the adjoining mainland territory of Tauria.

The problems presented by the Crimean Tatars were twofold. They blocked easy Russian access to the Mediterranean through the Black Sea—and thereby reduced Russia's role in European politics—and their raids destabilized the empire's southern frontier, thus making it impossible for the Russians to turn their full attention to the threat presented by Poles to the west. Russian Empress Catherine the Great forced the weakened Ottoman Turks to recognize the independence of the Crimean khanate, allowing Russia to proclaim the annexation of the Crimean khanate in 1783. The annexation allowed the Russians to conquer the remaining Crimean Tatar territories in 1792–1793, but without the risk of war with the still powerful Ottoman Empire (Olson 1994).

Centuries of slave raids and incursions by the Crimean Tatars into Slavic territory had left the Russians with a deep hostility toward the newly conquered Crimean Tatars. Deportations and expropriation of the best and most productive lands, especially in the 1850s and 1860s, forced an estimated 1 million Crimean Tatars to seek refuge in Turkish territory. The deportations left parts of the peninsula practically depopulated. Government-sponsored settlement plans brought a mass influx of Slavs to mainland Tauria. During the nineteenth century an official policy of Russification went forward in the Crimea. Although the Muslim religion was allowed, Crimean Tatar architecture and other ancient cultural monuments were wantonly destroyed. Large-scale immigration of Russian Slavs to the peninsula was encouraged, and Slavic political and administrative institutions were imposed. The Crimean War in the 1850s and the Russo-Turkish War of 1879 accelerated the emigration of Crimean Tatars. The Tatars accounted for 98 percent of the region's population in 1800, but by 1900 the devastated nation formed only 34 percent of the population of Taurida province, made up of the Crimean Peninsula and the mainland region of Tauria.

Late in the nineteenth century, partly as a reaction to forced assimilation and Russian oppression, a Crimean Tatar national awakening began to take hold. After 1860 the Russian government enrolled Crimean Tatar children in Russian-language schools. Eventually a Russian-speaking Tatar intelligentsia emerged, separate from the traditional Muslim hierarchy of Tatar society. Education, which fostered modernization, sparked the growth of national consciousness and fueled demands for linguistic and cultural rights for the Crimean Tatars of the Russian Empire. The opening of a Crimean Tatar press in 1883 stimulated the spread of a Tatar cultural revival and the growth of Crimean Tatar national sentiment. The national elite that had developed since the mid-nineteenth century had increasing access to education. Modernization and the lure of pan-Turkish nationalism stimulated the growth of underground movements. Several nationalist groups emerged, the more radical calling for the restoration of Crimean Tatar independence. The revival was suppressed as antigovernment activity in 1891, forcing cultural activities underground and obliging many nationalist leaders to flee to Turkish territory.

### The Peoples of the Volga Basin

The immense valley of the Volga River, conquered by the Russians following the capture of the khanate of Kazan' in 1552–1553, remained a center of non-Slavic cultures in eastern European Russia. In 1708 Kazan' was made the center of Slavic colonization of the Volga basin. Thousands of Slav settlers, supported by the imperial government, colonized the region over the next century. The Volga Tatars constituted the largest of the region's ethnic groups, but by the mid-nineteenth century Russians and other Slavs outnumbered the other important regional ethnic groups, including the Muslim Bashkorts, the Finnic peoples—the Udmurts, Maris, and Mordvins—and the Chavash, like the Tatars, claiming descent from the region's ancient Bulgar tribes.

Russian attempts to assimilate the non-Slavic population, particularly the suppression of the Islamic religion of the Tatars and Bashkorts, led to widespread resistance and several serious rebellions between the mid-sixteenth century and the mid-eighteenth century. Savage reprisals against the entire population following each uprising destroyed much of the earlier cultural institutions of each group. By the early nineteenth century most of the non-Slavic population formed impoverished minorities, with many held as serfs on the estates of Russian absentee landlords. The freeing of the serfs in 1861 ended the worst of the oppression but brought an even greater influx of freed Russian serfs seeking free government lands in the minority regions. The construction of the Trans-Siberian Railroad, completed in the early 1900s, facilitated the Slavic colonization of the region.

## Tatars

The most advanced of the Muslim peoples of the Russian Empire, the Tatars were useful as middlemen between the distant imperial government and the newly conquered Turkic peoples of Central Asia and Siberia. Their Islamic religion was ruthlessly suppressed from the conquest of Kazan' in 1552 even though the family of the last Tatar khan and the Tatar aristocracy were absorbed into the czarist nobility, greatly facilitating the colonization of the immense Volga region. The best of their land went to Russian nobles, immigrating Russian peasants, and Russian Orthodox monasteries. Early in the eighteenth century, Peter the Great added new coercive measures, exempting Tatar converts to Orthodox Christianity from certain taxes and military service. Finally, in the mid-eighteenth century, the Russian government launched an attack on Muslim mosques in the Middle Volga region, destroying 418 of 536 mosques in the region between 1740 and 1743 (Olson, 1994).

The reign of Catherine II (the Great) brought a temporary respite. Catherine looked for new conquests in the Kazakh steppes and Central Asia. She decided that the Tatars of the Volga region could be useful to the Russian state in its expansion. The Tatars, as an enterprising people with extensive trade and cultural ties throughout the Muslim world, had relationships with the peoples of the Kazakh steppe and Central Asia that Catherine

*Volga Region, c. 1750*

wished to exploit. Catherine's ministers put an end to the heavy-handed attempts to convert the Tatars to Orthodoxy and allowed limited linguistic and cultural freedoms. Catherine's liberal ideas ended when Nicholas I came to the Russian throne in 1825, when the conversion campaigns were renewed and cultural and linguistic assimilation again became official policy.

During the mid-nineteenth century, despite renewed pressure to adopt Russian culture and the Orthodox religion, a Tatar cultural revival took hold. New economic associations reinforced the growth of a middle class in the 1880s, the first among the Muslim ethnic groups in Russia. Literary and historical societies appeared, supporting the publication of books, newspapers, and magazines in the Tatar language. Political activity, paralleling the cultural revival, also involved the growing middle class. A progressive religious outlook, renewed emphasis on modern education, an increase in publication, and general political and cultural activity incited the growth of a national consciousness. The Tatars' high literacy rate and their well-developed national culture stimulated a widespread national revival in the late nineteenth century.

### Bashkorts

The Bashkorts, called Bashkirs by the Russians, whose traditional homeland lies in the eastern Volga region and western Ural Mountains, are religiously, linguistically, and historically related to the Tatars. Brought under Russian rule with the fall of the Tatar khanates in the sixteenth century, the Bashkorts became virtual slaves on Russian estates or in Russian mines. Their best lands were seized, heavy taxes were imposed, and most lived in humiliating poverty. The city of Ufa was founded as the center of the Slavic colonization of the Bashkort territory in 1574, the first of a string of forts that allowed the Slavs to take control of the region. Serious revolts broke out among the Bashkorts in the eighteenth century, the most serious in 1773, but all were ruthlessly suppressed. Revolts were so frequent that Bashkort smiths were forbidden to practice their trade in order to prevent the fabrication of weapons. To control the volatile Bashkorts the Russian authorities established Cossack military colonies in the southern part of Bashkort territory. The Cossack colonists took as their name the name of the most important fortified outpost, calling themselves the Orenburg Cossacks.

In the late eighteenth and early nineteenth centuries a great influx of Russians, Ukrainians, Tatars, and other ethnic groups completely changed the population of the Bashkort homeland. The colonists seized or bought vast tracts of Bashkort pastoral lands, leaving the former nomads impoverished and dispossessed of their traditional lands. Most Bashkorts were forced to settle in agricultural villages or to seek work in the towns that grew up around the original forts. The majority, even in the towns and villages, retained their ties to their clan and tribal groups. The abolition of serfdom in Russia in 1861 brought a new influx of land-hungry colonists to the region. The migration of freed serfs, seen by the Bashkorts as a serious threat to their cultural survival, stimulated a national revival in the late nineteenth century. A small national movement, led by Bashkorts educated in the Russian language, adopted many of the demands of revolutionary groups across Russia, including the right to reclaim their traditional lands.

## Chavash

The Chavash, called Chuvash by the Russians, claim, as do the Tatars, descent from the medieval Black Bulgars. Their language, which forms a separate branch of the Turkic languages, is unlike any other spoken language, showing influences from the early Bulgars, the Mongols, Tungusic dialects, and many loan words from the Slavic and Finnic languages. Like the other Volga nations the Chavash came under Slavic rule with the conquest of the Tatar khanates. Although they had been converted from Islam to Orthodox Christianity by Russian monks in the fourteenth century, the common religion, which could have formed a bond between them and their new Slavic rulers, was seriously undermined by government policies aimed at total assimilation. The Chavash participated in several serious revolts in the eighteenth century, suffering savage reprisals when defeated. By 1750 the traditional Chavash lands had been divided between two Russian provinces, Kazan' and Simbirsk. During the period of cultural suppression, from the mid-eighteenth century to the early nineteenth century, the remaining Muslim Chavash were forcibly converted to Orthodoxy.

The consolidation of the Chavash as a distinct nation was advanced by the spread of education and literacy during the same period, from the mid-eighteenth to the mid-nineteenth centuries. The first Chavash grammar was published during this period, in 1769. A more complete primary grammar and a Chavash dictionary appeared in 1836. The first Chavash secondary school was opened in the city of Simbirsk in 1868. The development, during this period of cultural consolidation, of a written form of the Chavash language contributed greatly to the strengthening of the Chavash culture to survive despite official government policies of assimilation. The impoverished Chavash, although dominated by Russian landlords, stubbornly clung to their culture and language. Serfdom, extended to most parts of the Russian Empire, failed in the Chavash region. Russian attempts to impose serfdom or to conscript Chavash men for military duty led to several serious confrontations in the mid-nineteenth century. The Chavash culture, due to widespread poverty and illiteracy, only began to revive in the latter half of the 1800s with the opening of more educational institutions using the Chavash language.

## The Volga Finnic Peoples

The Finnic peoples of the Volga basin comprise several traditional groups that evolved from the early tribal formations. Thought to be the original homeland of all the Finnic peoples, the Volga basin also remained an important center of Finnic culture. The migrations that eventually moved as far west as Finland and Estonia also included the Permian Finnic peoples who turned north to settle the fertile river valleys north of the Volga. By the seventeenth century the majority of the eastern Finnic ethnic groups had been converted to Russian Orthodoxy, but a portion of the population, particularly strong among the Maris, retained their traditional religious beliefs, which revolved around spirits and ancestor worship.

Russian colonial expansion into the region was accompanied by a harsh regime of serfdom and the loss of most traditional lands. Kept in near slavery as unpaid agricultural workers, the majority of the Finnic peoples lived in ignorance and poverty. Isolated from the European influences farther west, few were literate or had any concept of a national identity beyond the village level, although the ties of their traditional peasant cultures and languages were vaguely recognized. Official efforts to eradicate their languages and cultures provoked several serious revolts in the seventeenth and eighteenth centuries. Their lands were partitioned among several Russian provinces, and their languages and cultures were officially banned.

Efforts by a few poorly educated priests and the educated sons of local officials to preserve ancient traditions stimulated the growth of small anti-Russian movements in the latter half of the nineteenth century. Assimilation into Russian culture, most advanced among the Mordvins (whose lands had been largely colonized by Slavs), accelerated following the freeing of the serfs in 1861 and the government's support for a massive influx of freed Slavic serfs to colonize the region. By the 1880s only a small, educated elite had begun to embrace the idea of the national culture as opposed to the traditional idea espoused by the imperial government of numerous peasant cultures that would eventually disappear as assimilation progressed.

## Maris

Significant Slavic economic and cultural contact with the Maris began as early as the twelfth century, but political influence began only with the penetration of the Tatar khanate of Kazan' in the fifteenth century. Many of the Finnic Maris were converted to Orthodox Christianity, although many rural or more isolated communities retained their traditional animist beliefs. Following the conquest of Kazan' and the beginning of the Slavic colonization of the Volga River region, the Maris set up a stiff resistance. A series of devastating conflicts known as the Cheremiss Wars ended with defeat and massacres. Thousands of Maris fled their homeland while the Slavic colonization accelerated in the early seventeenth century. Even though more blond and Nordic than the Russian colonizers, the Maris were relegated to virtual slavery as serfs on Russian estates established on Mari lands. Mari assimilation into Russian culture, the official policy of the local authorities, accelerated during the seventeenth century. Slavic social and economic pressure was often countered by nativistic movements supported by the Mari. Pressure to abandon their traditional religious practices for Orthodox Christianity became particularly intense in the early 1800s. The Mari resistance to Russian Orthodoxy resulted in severe persecution and intense assimilation efforts that were often led by Orthodox missionaries. Believing that Christianity and education were closely related, Orthodox missionaries worked to develop a Mari literary language; it was produced in 1803, the same year that a catechism was published in one of the Mari dialects.

The majority of the Maris, living in conditions of poverty, ignorance, and cruelty, stubbornly clung to their shamanistic beliefs, which began to play an important part in the development of a distinct Mari identity. Even the Christian converts incorporated portions of their earlier beliefs in their services. The effort to preserve animist beliefs activated a strong religious and cultural resurgence in the late nineteenth century, a mass anti-Russian movement that stimulated the growth of nationalist and revolutionary ideas. In the 1870s, when a number of Mari leaders openly resisted further attempts at religious conversion and assimilation, the various traditional religious beliefs were formalized in a nationalistic religious sect called Kugu Sorta (Great Candle), incorporating intense anti-Russian and anti-Orthodox influences with efforts to spread education and literacy among the Mari population, in the late nineteenth century more than 90 percent illiterate.

## Mordvins (Mordvinians)

Like the Maris, the Mordvins are a Finnic people, made up of five regional groups, of which the largest are the Erzyas and Mokshas. In the wake of the conquest of the Volga region by the Slavs in the mid-sixteenth century Slavic colonization became government policy. The Mordvins, whose traditional religious beliefs revolved around ancestor veneration, were forcibly converted to Orthodoxy between the sixteenth and eighteenth centuries. The Russians built a string of strong military fortifications and settlements to provide a line of defense against the rebellious Mordvin groups. Several widespread rebellions, involving a cooperative leadership of Mordvins, Chavash, and Maris, threatened the Russian hold on the western part of the Volga region in the seventeenth and eighteenth centuries. Gradually reduced to serfdom on Russian estates, the Mordvin population was pushed into ethnic pockets surrounded by Slavic colonies. Colonization advanced rapidly following the abolition of serfdom in Russia in 1861. Living in scattered ethnic communities surrounded by Slavs, the Mordvins began to succumb to assimilation even as nationalist ideals began to influence the small, educated Mordvin elite. The completion of a major railroad across Mordvin territory in the 1890s hastened the Slavic colonization and the isolation of the Mordvins in remote ethnic enclaves.

## The Permian Peoples

During the Finnic migrations from the Volga basin north and northwest over a long period of time, some of the Finnic groups left the major migrations to turn north and settle the basin of the Kama River. During the first millennium before the Christian era, these settlers, called the Permians, split into two major groups, the Komis and the Udmurts. Around A.D. 500, the Komis again split when several major Komi clans moved farther north to the Vychegda basin. The smaller Komi clans left behind in the Kama region became known by the name Permyaks or Komi-Permyaks.

## Komis

The Komi, the farthest north of the Permian peoples, came under the rule of the Slavic Republic of Great Novgorod in the thirteenth century. Called Perms by the Slavs, they formed a vital link in the Novgorodian fur trade.

When overhunting diminished the regional wealth of furs and easier routes to the Siberian fur fields were discovered, the Komi area declined in economic importance. Originally the Komis practiced the traditional religion of the Finnic ethnic groups, a form of ancestor worship. Orthodox Christianity, introduced by Saint Stephen of Perm in the 1360s and 1370s, began the opening of the Komi homeland to the larger world. Saint Stephen, called the "Enlightener of the Komi," is revered not only for converting the majority to Orthodoxy but also for his invention of a Komi alphabet into which he translated parts of the Bible.

The conquest of Novgorod by the Muscovites in 1478 brought a new and much harsher Slavic rule. The Muscovites suppressed the Komi language and culture and pressed assimilation. Many Komi clans, seeking to escape Slavic persecution, moved deeper into the upper Vychegda and Pechora River basins. In the eighteenth century the Russian authorities opened the southern part of the Komi homeland to Slavic colonization. Exploitation of the region's rich forest and mineral resources accelerated the influx of Slavs. The abolition of serfdom brought even more land-hungry colonists. The northern Komi clans took to reindeer breeding in the nineteenth century in an effort to survive. Komi resentment provoked several violent confrontations with the czarist authorities in the 1870s and 1880s. Their treatment by the czarist government and their yearning for their former freedoms stimulated a cultural and national revival in the late nineteenth century that emphasized their cultural and linguistic heritage, particularly the distinguished tradition of oral epics. The Komi national revival, which grew as an anti-Russian and antigovernment movement, began to reverse centuries of forced assimilation.

### Permyaks (Komi-Permyaks)

Russian colonists began to settle the Permyak homeland in the sixteenth century. Serving as an important part of the Russian trade in salt and minerals with areas of Siberia, the Permyaks were early subjected to the Russian language and culture and efforts to convert them to Orthodoxy. Forced to work on Russian estates or in the important mines in near-slave conditions the Permyaks began to lose their traditional culture and way of life. The influx of Slavs following the abolition of serfdom in the mid-nineteenth century further threatened their culture and language. Land shortages and growing discrimination forced many Permyaks to migrate further east to escape the harsh conditions. Permyak resentment of the Slavic colonists, who took control of the best and most fertile lands, led to violent uprisings in the 1870s and 1880s. Permyak resentment of their treatment by the growing number of government-sponsored colonists triggered a nationalist backlash built on ideas brought to the region by exiled revolutionaries and political prisoners. A Permyak cultural movement in the late nineteenth century emphasized the use of their language and their cultural traditions.

## Udmurts

The Udmurt homeland, south of the territories of the Komis and Permyaks, also came under the rule of the Kazan' khanate, the Novgorodians, or the rival Slavic Republic of Vyatka following the breakup of the Golden Horde. By the late fourteenth century most of the Udmurts had adopted the Christian religion, although most also retained their traditional beliefs, including ancestor veneration, or adopted Islamic customs from their southern neighbors. They were united under Muscovite rule in the late fifteenth century, although the Udmurts of the Kama River region continued to resist Russian rule for another half century. Forced conversion to Orthodox Christianity was spread to even the more remote areas, and assimilation was imposed.

The best lands were taken by the Slavic colonists, forcing many Udmurts to move away from the rivers, the means of transport, which increasingly became Slavic strongholds. By the late seventeenth century most ethnic Udmurts were tied to the large Russian estates established in the region as serfs. Kept in ignorance and poverty, the Udmurts' only escape was the lower ranks of the Orthodox religious hierarchy. The latter half of the nineteenth century was marked by the rapid development of industry in the region. New regional enterprises began to draw in large numbers of Udmurt workers, who formed an urbanized working class. In 1899 the construction of rail lines added to the rapid industrialization of the region. The small Udmurt population in the Kama River region produced the first educated minority, mostly drawn from the clergy, that led the movement that began an Udmurt cultural revival in the late nineteenth century.

## Moldovans

The Moldovans represent one of the three divisions of the Romanian peoples. Their homeland, lying between Romania and Ukraine, has long been a frontier region. Early inhabitants included the Romanized tribes that developed into the Romanian peoples and Slavic tribes, particularly the Bessi, who gave their name to the region as Bessarabia. The region fell to the Ottoman Turks in the early sixteenth century, marking the northern limit of Turkish conquest. The Austrians wrested the western districts from the Turks in 1774, bringing some Moldovans under Austrian rule in the province of Bukovina. The expanding Russians contested Turkish control of Moldova, historically called Moldavia, from the early eighteenth century, finally annexing Bessarabia following the Russo-Turkish War of 1806–1812. The population of the region, 86 percent Romanian-speaking, came under intense assimilation pressure. In an effort to dilute the Romanian population the czarist government opened the territory to settlement by non-Romanian colonists. Thousands of Gagauz, Bulgarians, Ukrainians, Poles, and Russians settled in the territory, often receiving government assistance for resettlement. In 1818 Moldova was granted the status of an autonomous area, with Romanian as its second official language, after Russian.

The reactionary Russian administration that took control in 1825, under Czar Nicholas I, began to dismantle the Moldovan privileges. In 1828 the autonomy statute was revoked and all Moldovans holding official offices were replaced with ethnic Slavs. The Russian legal and administrative systems were introduced, including the closure of most Romanian-languages schools. The increasingly oppressive Russian rule incited the first revolutionary groups to form in the 1840s. Nationalism and irredentist claims for union with Romania gained much support until they were suppressed during the severe outbreaks that erupted in Moldovan in 1848. Nationalist ideas again emerged in the 1870s and 1880s, often supported by the government of neighboring Romania. The Romanians, seeking to recover territory they claimed as part of the historic Romanian homeland, covertly supported the growth of Moldovan nationalism as an anti-Russian and anti-Slav movement. Nationalist and antigovernment activities, suppressed in Russian Moldova, were permitted in Austrian Bukovina, but only as anti-Russian movements. Political tracts and newspapers, smuggled into Russian territory from Bukovina, aided the spread of nationalist and revolutionary ideas in the last decades of the nineteenth century.

## Nonterritorial Ethnic Groups

The continued expansion of the Russian Empire brought numerous ethnic, linguistic, and religious groups under Russian rule. Of these many subject peoples, several were spread across large territories without having homelands of their own, although they often played an important part in the future political development of the empire.

## Jews

The Jews of Russia, probably the scattered descendants of the Khazars, were few in number until the partitions of Poland by Russia, Austria, and Prussia in the eighteenth century. Although they endured the hostility of the Christian clergy, the Jews encountered fewer restraints in Kievan Rus' and Tatar-controlled Russia than did Jews elsewhere in Europe. That changed radically with the so-called Judaizer Heresy, which reputedly attempted to introduce certain Jewish practices into the Russian Orthodox service. By the early sixteenth century Jews were barred from entering Russia. When Russia took control of Ukraine in the 1670s, Jews living in the territory were allowed to remain, with some even moving to Moscow, where they established the nucleus of Moscow's Jewish population.

In 1727, Catherine I, pressured by Christian religious leaders, anti-Semitic ministers, and Slavic merchants, threatened by Jewish commerce, ordered all Jews to leave Russia without their possessions. The Jews of Little Russia (Ukraine) were expelled in 1739. The official ban on Jews entering Russia remained until the first partition of Poland in 1772, with ever-increasing persecutions. The three partitions of Poland brought a Jewish population of around 1 million into the empire. At first the Jews were allowed the same privileges they had enjoyed in the Polish state, but the well-intentioned attitude was put aside within two decades. Faced with Jewish competition, many influential Russian merchants complained to empress Catherine II (the Great), resulting in many new restrictions. The Jewish Pale of Settlement, established in 1791, limited Jewish habitation to the territories newly acquired in the Polish Partitions. The decree that established the Pale also prohibited Jewish settlement in the territories of prepartition Russia.

The situation of the Jews deteriorated during the first decades of the nineteenth century. In 1827, an imperial decree ended the Jewish exemption from military service, with many Jews forcibly conscripted into the army for periods of twenty-five years. The conscripts often came under intense pressure to convert to Orthodoxy. The Pale of Settlement was reduced in the late 1820s with the expulsion of all Jews from Kiev. Laws were passed forbidding conventional Jewish styles of dress, against the tradition of women shaving their heads before marriage, and against the historic hair lock worn by Jewish men. During the reign of the relatively more liberal Alexander II, in the mid-nineteenth century, conditions eased and privileged Jews were allowed to live in St. Petersburg, Moscow, and Kiev. Restrictions on Jewish academics, artists, and others were lifted, allowing them to live where they wished. Jewish merchants, freed from the anti-Semitic laws, played an important part in the development of the Baku oil fields in the late nineteenth century.

The situation of the Jews deteriorated once again in the last decades of the nineteenth century. In 1887, the Russian government introduced strict limits on Jewish educational opportunities and began enforcing residency requirements for Jews living outside the Pale. Tens of thousands of Jews were expelled from Moscow and other large cities. Pogroms, beatings, and anti-Semitic riots took on serious dimensions from the early 1880s. Led by officially sanctioned reactionary groups composed largely of lower level civil servants, the pogroms, by the end of the nineteenth century, had become institutionalized. In spite of the difficulties of life in the Russian Empire and the emigration of large numbers, the Jewish population grew from about 1 million in 1800 to around 5.7 million in 1897. Over 93 percent of all Jews lived in the Pale of Settlement, encompassing Belarus, Ukraine, Bessarabia, Russian Poland, and Lithuania.

## Germans

Catherine the Great, born in the southern German state of Anhalt-Zerbst, eager to replace the Turkic peoples of the newly conquered territories in southern Ukraine and the North Caucasus with more reliable European settlers, invited immigrants from her native Germany. The effects of the fierce religious wars that devastated Germany following the Reformation remained well into the eighteenth century. The inhabitants of the southern German states, suffering overpopulation, religious conflicts, and crop failures, responded in large numbers. The industrious Germans were welcomed as immigrants to many areas of North America; however, the passage to the Americas was expensive. Catherine's invitation opened new lands for settlement in much the same way as in the United States and Canada, but offered a less-costly alternative. Between 1764 and 1768 thousands of German colonists were settled in the frontier districts in southern Russia, the Volga region, and around the northern and eastern shores of the Black Sea. Catherine's manifesto of 1763 guaranteed the colonists and their descendants free farmland, exemption from military service, freedom of religion, use of their own languages, local political autonomy, local control of education and schools, and many other incentives.

The German colonists, isolated and self-sufficient, after initial problems prospered as farmers and merchants in close-knit communities having little to do with surrounding Slavic populations. Folk cultures, dialects, and traditions that gradually evolved or disappeared in Germany continued to thrive among the Russian Germans to eventually form part of a distinctive Slav-influenced German culture. The settlers, spreading out across the flat steppe lands, suffered great hardships in southern Russia and Ukraine. The lack of trees evolved a unique type of dwelling, the sod house, similar to those later constructed on the North American plains. The Russian government determined that the settlers should produce much-needed grain. This determination was embodied in a 1767 decree prohibiting the German colonists from engaging in any occupation except farming. The decree openly violated Catherine's 1763 manifesto and reduced the immigrants to imperial serfs in all but name. Frequent crop failures and poor harvests in the early years were worsened by the inability of the Russian authorities to deliver the required seed grain on time each spring. The mixture of privations, raids by nomadic tribes and bandits, and above all, government interference, took a toll on the immigrant population. Some returned to Germany, others fled to Russia's German-dominated Baltic provinces, while others chose to immigrate once again to North American, where they settled on the Great Plains of the United States and Canada. Those that persevered celebrated their first good harvest in 1775. Production thereafter improved rapidly with the introduction of farming equipment imported from Germany.

Catherine's successors progressively abolished the Germans' privileges. By 1870 nearly all of Catherine's guarantees had disappeared. Assimilation and the official policy of Russification closed German-language publications, institutions, and schools. The promise of exemption from military conscription was revoked. Resistance to Russification and to the forced conscription of young German men into the Russian military stirred the growth of a particular national sentiment in the 1880s and 1890s based on the German dialects and cultures. A modest national movement, based in the Volga region, demanded the autonomy and other rights promised by Catherine the Great as a basis for German self-government and autonomy within the Russian Empire.

## Rom (Gypsies)

The Rom, or Gypsies, as they are popularly called, are a unique ethnic group without ties to a particular territory. Although their origins are still debated, they are believed to have originated in south Asia. They spread from there to the west and north, eventually migrating into Europe in the fourteenth century. Often called Tsiganes in Russia, they have been known by many names depending on which part of the world they settled. The earliest records comment on the powerful sense of ethnic identity that the Rom maintain, as well as their sense of self-protection and self-preservation as a cultural group.

Although the majority of the Roms were traditionally nomadic, by the late nineteenth century many had settled in urban areas, often in separate quarters in the larger cities and towns. They tended to adopt the language and religion of the surrounding population, but most maintain their group language and the complex Rom folk culture. Socially, the Rom remained divided into tribal groups, often with distinct dialects and localized identities. At the end of the nineteenth century there were Rom communities across the European provinces of the Russian Empire and a sizable historical group of Rom in Central Asia, where they continued their nomadic ways. Most Rom made their living by peddling, fortune-telling, begging, singing and dancing, and other forms of entertainment. Rom music and entertainers had considerable influence on the popular music and culture of the prerevolutionary Russian Empire.

## The Central Asians

An alliance between the Russian Empire and one of the hordes of the Kazakh nation began the Russian expansion into Central Asia. The Russians aided the allied Kazakhs against their enemies, but at the same time the Russians began to extend their authority, eventually taking control of the enormous Kazakh Steppe. The czarist government established a string of forts at key locations and encouraged European and Russian immigration to Kazakhstan. These groups expelled the native Kazakhs and competed for the most productive lands.

Beginning in the early 1800s, Russian influence spread from the steppe lands of northern Kazakhstan to Turkestan, the heart of Central Asia. By the middle of the nineteenth century the Russian government had embarked on a program of military conquest in Central Asia. In the 1860s Russian troops moved into the territory, taking control of the great centers of the Turkestani Muslim peoples. By 1884 all of the major urban centers were under Russian control. In the late 1800s, Russian Turkestan included all of the land between Chinese territory on the east and the Caspian Sea, except for a pair of small protectorates, the Uzbek-dominated states of Bukhara and Khiva. The Russians brought with them a more advanced infrastructure, including railroads, but the Islamic institutions were not abolished or persecuted. The Russian Orthodox Church was allowed to pursue prospective converts among the subject peoples but found few willing to renounce Islam even for the benefits of Russian citizenship that accompanied conversion to Orthodox Christianity.

## Kazakhs

The Kazakhs are the most northerly of the Central Asian peoples, inhabiting a large expanse of territory in northern Central Asia and southern Siberia known as the Kazakh Steppe. They are a formerly nomadic people of mixed Turkic and Mongol ancestry. Physically the majority of the Kazakhs resemble the Mongols, but culturally and linguistically they are closer to the nomadic Turkic tribes that settled the region in the eighth century. The tribal groups formed a powerful confederation that grew wealthy on the trade passing through the steppe lands along the fabled Silk Road. Invading Mongols conquered the vast region in the thirteenth century, destroying the sophisticated cities and the important irrigation systems. The Turkic inhabitants were scattered across the steppe as refugees. A division of the invading Mongols, known as the White Horde, began to settle the depopulated areas in 1456, slowly absorbing the surviving Turkic peoples. Taking the culture and language of the Turkic groups, the Kazakhs, as they came to be called, formed three new hordes, or ordas, under local khans.

Russian explorers made contact with the nomadic Kazakhs in the early sixteenth century, beginning a long period of gradually increasing encroachment. The first organized Russian expedition entered Kazakh territory in 1715, during a time of turmoil. The Kazakhs, under attack from the Oirots, an Altai tribe, saw the Russians as possible allies. Between 1731 and 1742 the three hordes accepted Russian protection. The Russians gradually extended their influence until the tribal confederations, the hordes, were finally abolished and direct rule begun. Serious Kazakh revolts erupted between the 1820s and 1840s. By the middle of the nineteenth century nearly all of Kazakhstan was directly administered by the Russian authorities. The huge territory was organized, in 1868, as three governments: the Steppe Provinces, Tugai Province, and Ural Province. Probably as a reaction to Russian attempts to convert the Kazakhs to Orthodox Christianity, the Kazakhs adopted the Muslim religion of their southern neighbors, making them the only nation to embrace Islam after their conquest by the Russians.

## Uzbeks

The most numerous of the Central Asian nations, the Uzbeks are of mixed Turkic, Caucasian, and Mongol origins. Traditionally the Uzbeks were divided into ninety-two tribal groups spread across the area known as Turkestan. Although their language and culture are Turkic, the Uzbeks have adopted many traits and customs from the other Central Asian peoples and from the Arabs and other Muslim peoples farther south. The Uzbek homeland is traversed by the ancient trade routes known as the Silk Road, the reason that civilizations flourished in the region as early as 3000 B.C. The wealth brought to the region along the legendary trade routes that connected the Mediterranean and China supported sophisticated cities and a flourishing agriculture based on a complex irrigation system. Converted to Islam by Arabs in the seventh and eighth centuries, the Uzbek cities became great centers of Islamic learning and culture. The Seljuk Turks conquered the region in the eleventh and twelfth centuries, but maintained the ancient trade routes and irrigation systems. The Turkic conquerors mixed with the Persianized oasis dwellers, imposing their language and much of their culture.

The Mongol invasion of the thirteenth century devastated Turkestan. The Mongols destroyed everything they couldn't carry away, including the irrigation system. Turkestan quickly declined and later came under the rule of several successor states following the breakup of the Golden Horde. The destruction of irrigated farming had a profound influence on the Turkestani decline. Late in the fourteenth century, after trade had resumed along the historical routes, the Uzbek cities again flourished under the rule of Tamerlane, who made fabled Samarkand the capital of his conquests, which included territories as far west as southern Europe. A remnant of the Golden Horde conquered Central Asia between 1490 and 1505. Taking the name Uzbeks from a mythical ancestor, they extended their empire to include parts of Afghanistan, Iran, and China.

Internal conflicts split the extensive Uzbek Empire in the seventeenth century. Two small Uzbek states, Bukhara and Khiva (Khorezm), emerged as regional powers with large Uzbek-dominated multiethnic populations. A Russian expedition reached Khiva and established diplomatic ties with Bukhara in 1619–1621. A military expedition to Khiva in 1717 ended with the Uzbek massacre of the Russian column. The massacre of the Russian troops ended all Russian contacts with the Turkestan region for several decades. The Uzbeks remained the dominant ethnic group in the Turkestan region throughout the eighteenth century. Uzbek dynasties ruled in Bukhara and Khiva, and after 1798 in Kokand, a third Uzbek state created in Turkestan.

Russian troops invaded Turkestan in 1865, quickly taking control of the important stronghold of Tashkent. In 1867 the Slavic conquerors established a colonial government for the region, the Governorate-General of Turkestan, with Tashkent as its capital. The next year they took control of the city of Samarkand and regions farther west. The independent Uzbek-dominated states were forced to accept the status of Russian protectorates although the colonial authorities annexed the khanate of Kokand outright in 1876. Slavic colonists, with government assistance, were settled in the Turkestan region, often enjoying special privileges as the administrators of the harsh colonial administration. In 1884, in an effort to make their Central Asian colonies economically viable, the Russian authorities introduced American cotton as a major cash crop. Fired by Uzbek calls to Muslim solidarity, the Turkestani peoples rebelled several times in the late nineteenth century, particularly serious uprisings taking place in 1885 and 1898.

## Turkmen (Turkomen)

The Turkmen, also known as Turkomen or Turcomen, are the descendants of early Caucasian tribes and later Turkic migrants. Considered the most traditional of the Central Asian peoples, the Turkmen are divided along tribal, clan, and extended family groups. As devoted followers of Tamerlane in the fourteenth century, Turkmen populations were deposited throughout his conquests as far west as northern Iraq and Turkey. Often forming part of ancient Persian Empires, the Turkmen homeland developed a mostly rural society with several important trading centers at the larger oasis. Converted to Islam by invading Arabs in the mid-seventh century, the Turkmen took on much of the Muslim organization as a powerful tribal confederation. The oasis cities on the Silk Road became centers of Muslim culture and scholarship. The tribal homeland was conquered by the migrating Seljuk Turks in the twelfth century, becoming primarily Turkic in language and culture. The Mongol invasion destroyed the Turkmen homeland, leaving only ruins and death in its wake. The survivors gathered in tribal groups that spread across the region as nomadic herders. Although later known as horsemen and warriors, the Turkmen began to come under the domination of the Uzbeks in the sixteenth century. The last Turkmen tribes didn't come under the rule of the Uzbek Khiva state until the early nineteenth century.

The first Russian expedition to reach the Turkmen territory traveled east in the early eighteenth century. The members of the Russian expedition, seeking a trade route with southern Asia and the Middle East, were murdered by Turkmen tribesmen in 1716. Several Turkmen tribes became Russian subjects in 1802 as part of the Uzbek states. During the nineteenth century the Turkmen tribes often accepted Russian military aid in their frequent rebellions against the Uzbek rulers of Khiva and Bukhara. The khanate of Khiva, seriously weakened by ethnic disputes and Russian encroachments, lost control of the Turkmen territory in the mid-nineteenth century. The tribes began to create an independent Turkmen state in the Transcaspia region, but a Russian army invasion ended the attempt in 1869. Some Turkmen tribes, fearing a return of Uzbek rule, accepted Russian protection; others inflicted the most serious losses ever suffered by the Russian military in Central Asia before their final defeat in the 1880s. Some Turkmen continued to resist Russian rule until 1895. The turbulent Turkmen territories, administratively added to the province of Turkestan, remained the least developed, poorest, and most backward of Central Asia.

## Tajiks

Ethnically, the Tajiks form a kind of bridge between the Turkic and Iranian worlds. Although linguistically the Tajiks are related to the Iranians, their culture has evolved in a manner similar to their Turkic Central Asian neighbors. Thought to descend from Central Asia's pre-Turkic population, the Tajiks are divided into regional, tribal, and clan affiliations. The majority are Sunni Muslims, with Shia and Ismaili minorities in the Pamir Mountains. Islam was introduced by invading Arabs about A.D. 710, quickly replacing the earlier Persian religion, Zoroastrianism. The merging of the Arab and Persian cultures produced a great flowering of Tajik Muslim culture in the ninth and tenth centuries. The Mongol invasion of the thirteenth century ended the brilliant Tajik civilization. Ruled by Turkic successors to the Golden Horde, the Tajiks had degenerated to a backward, tribal existence when the Uzbeks conquered Turkestan in the sixteenth century and divided the territory between the various Uzbek khanates.

Russian explorers passed through the Tajik lands in the sixteenth century, but little contact was made with the tribal rulers. Distanced from Russia's colonial expansion, the Tajiks were first confronted with the Russian invaders in 1865. The tribal territories were eventually divided between the Uzbek protectorates and the Russian government of Turkestan. The Tajiks remained poor, economically backward, and dominated by religious leaders. Considered the most conservative of the Turkestani peoples, the Tajiks were mostly ignored by the Russian authorities as troublesome and backward tribal peoples to be exploited. The Uzbeks dominated trade and the urban centers, while the Tajiks were still nomadic herdsmen.

## Kyrgyz

The Kyrgyz tribes, conquered by the Mongols in the late thirteenth century, had migrated south from the Yenisei region of Siberia. Under pressure from neighboring tribal groups, they migrated south from central Siberia to the mountainous areas of northeastern Central Asia probably between the fourteenth and sixteenth centuries. Conquered by the tribes of the Altai federation from the Altai Mountains, the Kyrgyz finally regained their freedom with the disintegration of the federation in the 1750s. In the early nineteenth century the tribes came under the rule of the Uzbek khanate of Kokand. The Muslim religion and the Persianized Uzbek culture were introduced by ethnic Uzbeks who settled in the tribal areas as administrators, soldiers, or colonists in the fertile regions of the Fergana Valley. The Uzbeks, with their long urban tradition, established small trading towns that grew into important cities as centers of regional trade and Muslim learning. The more rural Kyrgyz began to urbanize in the early nineteenth century, about the same time that Russian explorers began to visit the area.

The Russian military expansion into Central Asia in the mid-nineteenth century took control of the northern Kyrgyz lands in 1855. The remaining tribes were brought under Russian authority following the annexation of the Kokand khanate to the Russian Empire in 1876. Slavic settlers moved into the region, often taking the most fertile lands. The Kyrgyz generally moved their herds into the higher altitudes, away from the Slavic colonies. In their isolation, the Kyrgyz remained feudal and backward, economically exploited by the colonial administration, and dominated by Islamic clerics.

## Karakalpaks

The Karakalpak (the Black Caps) homeland, lying around the Aral Sea, was originally populated by Caucasian peoples but came under the domination of Turkic groups in the seventh century. The Turkic peoples absorbed the earlier inhabitants, and their language and culture became dominant in the region. Arab invaders introduced Islam, which was reinforced by the migrating Seljuk Turks. In the thirteenth century the region was brought under Mongol rule. According to their national tradition the Karakalpaks split from the Golden Horde as a distinct national group in the fifteenth century.

The Karakalpaks encountered the first Russian and Cossack explorers that traveled through the Uzbek states in the seventeenth century. The Russian onslaught in the nineteenth century eventually divided the Karakalpak tribes. Their territory west of the Aral Sea was annexed outright to the Russian Empire in 1873, while the eastern districts remained under the Uzbek rulers of Khiva, the nominally independent Russian protectorate.

## Siberia and the Far East

The Muscovite state had acquired territory in Siberia west of the Ob' and Irtysh Rivers, but by the seventeenth century large numbers of Slavic traders, merchants, and explorers pushed farther east. By the late seventeenth century Russians had reached the Amur River Valley, long considered part of the Chinese Empire. Although a later treaty recognized Chinese claims to the Amur region, the expansion to the east during the seventeenth century gave the Russians nominal control of a territory that extended from Europe almost to the Pacific Ocean. Other than the furs that the tribal peoples paid as taxes the region was believed to contain little but ice and snow, and colonization was not pursued.

In the mid-nineteenth century, Russian expansion in northern Asia began again. The Opium War of 1839–1842 between the British and China renewed Russian interest in the Far East. The British victory and the annexation of Hong Kong spurred renewed Russian efforts to gain a foothold on the Pacific. In 1858, the Russian government signed a treaty with China that provided for Russian control of part of the Amur region, and Russia and China, to forestall British expansion, agreed to joint sovereignty over the territory all the way to the Amur's outlet on the Pacific Ocean. In 1860 Vladivostok was established on the coast near the Korean border. Later in 1860 Russia gained control of the entire Amur region. Due to the cost of the new acquisitions in the Far East, the czar sold Russian Alaska to the United States for $7 million in 1867.

The Russians had no organized colonization of the huge Siberian territories until the mid-nineteenth century, partly owing to the resistance of the indigenous peoples east of the Ural Mountains. The abolition of serfdom in 1861 freed tens of thousands of land-hungry peasants. Offered free land in the underpopulated Siberian territories, many crossed the Urals to settle the valleys of western Siberia. The completion of the Trans-Siberian Railroad in 1891–1892 allowed for the efficient transfer of excess population from Europe to the Siberian territories. Although organized as an imperial province in 1710, Siberia mostly remained a place of exile, a dumping ground for political prisoners, ethnic deportees, rebellious serfs turned over for deportation by landlords, Jews who failed to pay their heavy taxes, and convicted prostitutes. The attitudes and ideals of the often well-educated deportees spread throughout Siberian society, becoming a part of the political culture. By 1890 Siberia, along with the more than 2 million colonists and the scattered tribal peoples, was inhabited by an estimated 100,000 Poles, deported following the defeat of several rebellions, 50,000 political prisoners, 40,000 common criminals and prostitutes, and more than 5,000 wives who chose to join their prisoner-husbands in exile, often taking their children with them.

Just south of Russia's Pacific territories lay the rich Chinese-controlled region of Manchuria. As the powers of the Manchu rulers of China waned the Russians increased their influence over the Manchu's ancient homeland in northwestern China. In 1896 Russian troops were ordered to move across the border and to take control of the major cities, mines, and industrial areas of Manchuria. The weakened Manchu dynasty was unable to counter the Russian encroachment, allowing the Russians to establish a virtual protectorate in Manchuria and to begin exerting influence in Korea. The Japanese, having defeated Manchu China in a brief war in 1895, also sought to assert influence in the mineral-rich region, setting the stage for a serious clash between the Russian and Japanese Empires.

### The Russian Empire in 1900

By the end of the nineteenth century, Russian territorial expansion had brought a sixth of the world's land mass into the empire. The territorial extension of the Russian Empire stretched across two continents, from the western borders of Finland, Russian Poland, and Ukraine on the west to the Pacific Ocean on the east, and from Central Asia, the Caucasus, and Mongolia on the south to the Arctic Ocean on the north. Scholars at the time disagreed on the exact number of ethnic and national groups included in the Russian Empire, with the numbers ranging from about 100 up to 300. Most ethnic designations were inventions of the small, educated Russian elite, who also decided which local Slavic groups were to be included as ethnic Russians. For most of the inhabitants of the enormous and growing empire the question of ethnic or national affiliation would have been answered with allusion to religion, such as Orthodox, Roman Catholic, Protestant, Muslim, Buddhist, and so on; or would be referenced by local areas, provinces, or towns; or by kinship, clan, and tribal ties.

## Timeline

| | |
|---|---|
| 1735–1774 | Wars with Ottoman Turkey allow Russian expansion into the North Caucasus. |
| 1772–1795 | The three partitions of Poland give Russia new territories in the west, including the Baltic region and the western parts of Belarus and Ukraine. Along with a large Eastern Slav population, Russia gains a Jewish population of more than 1 million. |
| 1783 | Russia annexes the Crimea and overthrows the Crimean Tatar khanate. |
| 1787–1791 | War again breaks out between Russia and the Ottoman Empire. |
| 1806–1812 | Another Russo-Turkish war ends with Russian territorial expansion in Moldova. |
| 1813 | Russia annexes territory taken from Persia in Transcaucasia. |
| 1828 | Wars with Persia and the Ottoman Empire end, with the Russian annexation of part of Armenia, Azerbaijan, and additional territories in the North Caucasus. |
| 1834 | The Muslim rebellion led by Imam Shamil begins in the North Caucasus. |
| 1846 | Russian expansion occurs into additional territories in Central Asia, called Turkestan by the Russian authorities. |
| 1858 | The rebellion led by Imam Shamil begins in the eastern Caucasus region. |
| 1859 | Imam Shamil surrenders. The Russian conquest of the Caucasus is complete. |
| 1861 | Serfdom is abolished in the Russian Empire. |
| 1864–1880 | The conquest of Central Asia takes place. |
| 1867 | The Russian authorities establish a colonial government in Turkestan. |

| | |
|---|---|
| 1880–1885 | The Russians complete the conquest of Central Asia. |
| 1894 | Alexander III dies. The last Russian czar, Nicholas II, takes the throne. |
| 1894–1896 | Massacres of Armenians spread across the region of eastern Anatolia, also known as Turkish Armenia. The massacres, accompanied by the destruction of churches and other Armenian cultural institutions, were often carried out on the orders of local Turkish military commanders. |
| 1896 | Russian troops move into Manchuria, setting the stage for conflict with expanding Japan. |

## Significant People, Places, and Events

ALEXANDER I Czar of Russia from 1801 to 1825. The first years of his reign were marked by a more liberal stance. He lifted the ban on books and foreign travel, suppressed the powerful secret police, and attempted to improve the position of the serfs. During this period Russia gained control of Georgia and other parts of the Caucasus region.

ALEXANDER III Czar of Russia from 1881 to 1894. Alexander's reactionary policies led to an increase in the oppression of the subject peoples, including pressure to assimilate. Measures included increased powers for the police, tightened censorship, and greater control of education. Persecution of national and religious minorities became government policy.

ARMENIAN REVOLUTIONARY FEDERATION Popularly called the Dashnaktsutiun. The first openly nationalist Armenian organization. It was formed in Russian Armenia in the late 1890s and soon had cells in towns and villages in both Russian and Turkish Armenia.

AZERIS The Azeris are a people of mixed Turkic and Caucasian background. They are the largest and most important of the many Muslim peoples of the Caucasus region. The discovery of oil in the late nineteenth century brought rapid modernization and the European idea of nation.

BALTIC PEOPLES The Baltic Peoples include the three small nations living on the eastern shore of the Baltic Sea, the Finnic Estonians and the two surviving representatives of the ancient Baltic group, the Lithuanians and Latvians.

BASHKORTS Called Bashkirs by the Russians. The Bashkorts are of mixed Finnic, Turkic, and Mongol ancestry, speaking a Turkic language. They are the second largest, after the Tatars, of the Muslim peoples of the Volga River basin.

**Bukhara** A powerful emirate in Central Asia dominated by the Uzbeks but with a multiethnic and multilingual population. It was a trade, transport, and cultural center of the Muslim world.

**Catherine II (Catherine the Great)** Czarina of Russia from 1762 to 1796. A German princess, she married the Russian heir and eventually became sole ruler of the Russian Empire. Her policies began a series of wars with the Ottoman Empire and the rapid expansion of the empire.

**Caucasus** Region at the confluence of Europe and Asia between the Black and Caspian Seas. The rugged highland territory, over thousands of years, had become the home of many varied peoples. Russian colonial expansion met its most vehement opposition among the fierce Muslim tribes of the Caucasus Mountains.

**Chavash** The descendants of the medieval Bulgars, who later split with one branch moving into the Balkans. Calling themselves Chavash, they speak a unique language that forms a separate branch of the Turkic languages. They have proved less susceptible to assimilation than many of the larger ethnic groups in Russia.

**Chechens** The Chechens are a Caucasian Muslim people with a long history of opposition to Russian rule. They were the chief supporters of Imam Shamil, who led the Muslim opposition to Russia's colonial expansion into the Caucasus in the mid-nineteenth century.

**Dagestani Peoples** The Dagestanis are a group of closely related Caucasian peoples living in the eastern Caucasus region. The largest of the Dagestani groups are the Avar, Lezgin, Dargin, Lak, and Tabasaran. They, like the Chechens and Ingush, were followers of Shamil during the mid-nineteenth century.

**Far East** Also known as the Far Eastern Region or Far Eastern Territory. The region, lying in eastern Siberia on the Pacific Ocean, stretches from the Arctic Ocean to the Chinese border and includes a number of provinces and the Republic of Sakha, one of the constituent republics of the Russian Federation.

**Ingush** A Caucasian people linguistically and culturally closely related to the Chechens. They were among the most ardent supporters of the anti-Russian war led by Shamil in the mid-nineteenth century.

**Karakalpaks** The smallest of the Turkic ethnic groups of Central Asia. Although closely related to the Kazakhs, they are physically more Turkic. They developed as a separate tribal people in the fifteenth century.

**Kazakhs** A people of mixed Turkic and Mongol ancestry, although the majority physically resemble the Mongols. They speak a Turkic language and are mostly Sunni Muslims. They are the only major ethnic group to adopt

Islam after their conquest by the Russians.

**KHIVA** An ancient khanate in Central Asia dominated by an Uzbek dynasty. From the sixth to the early twentieth century Khiva served as the capital of an ancient kingdom, which became a khanate following the Muslim conquest in the seventh century. It came under Russian authority in 1873.

**KOKAND** An Uzbek khanate that separated from Bukhara in the late eighteenth century. The khanate flourished in the 1820s and 1830s. In 1876 the khanate was taken by the Russians and formed the heartland of the Russian province of Turkestan.

**KYRGYZ** Also called Kirghiz. A Central Asian people of mixed Turkic and Mongol descent, but with the Mongol strain predominate. They speak a Turkic language and are mostly Sunni Muslims. They were formerly nomads before coming under Russian rule between 1855 and 1876.

**PALE OF SETTLEMENT** A region of western Russia and Ukraine and eastern Poland occupying part of the territories taken from Poland during the Polish Partitions of 1792 and 1795. Resulting from a 1791 decree, the Pale of Settlement restricted Jewish settlement to the newly acquired territories and barred them from historical Russian territory. The Jewish population was subjected to many restrictions, most of which remained in force until the Russian Revolution of 1917.

**PERMIAN PEOPLES** The Permian peoples are Finnic groups that turned north to settle the fertile river valleys while the majority of the Finnic migrants continued on to the Baltic Sea region. They include the Udmurts of the northern Volga River basin, and the Komi and Permyaks (Komi-Permyaks) in northeastern European Russia.

**RUSSIAN REVOLUTION OF 1905** The name given the upheavals that followed Russia's defeat in the Russo-Japanese War. It began when troops fired on a defenseless crowd of marching workers in St. Petersburg. This massacre was followed by months of strikes, riots, assassinations, naval mutinies, and peasant outbreaks. These disorders, coupled with the military defeat, forced the Russian government to promise reforms, including a parliament, or duma.

**RUSSIFICATION** The official Russian government policy of assimilation of the many national, folk, and peasant cultures that existed in the Russian Empire in the nineteenth century. The policy pressed for the homogenization of the multiethnic population in culture, language, and religion.

**SERFDOM** The government policy of tying peasants to the land in a system of near-slavery. Serfs could be sold or mortgaged and runaway serfs were often executed. Serfdom was officially abolished in Russia in 1861, although the practice had been abandoned in the Baltic provinces even earlier. The abolition allowed millions of freed peasants to migrate to less-developed territories, often the homelands of the national minorities.

TAJIKS The Tajiks are an Iranian people believed to be the descendants of Central Asia's pre-Turkic inhabitants. Their language is closely related to modern Iranian; however, they are mostly Sunni Muslims like their Turkic neighbors.

TATARS The largest of the ethnic groups of the Volga River basin and one of the most numerous of the Muslim peoples of the former Russian and Soviet Empires. They are concentrated in the Volga Valley, which was conquered by the Russians in the mid-sixteenth century, but historically they dispersed as administrators to newly conquered Muslim regions during the eighteenth and nineteenth centuries.

TURKESTAN The name given the conquered parts of Central Asia by the Russian government in the nineteenth century. A colonial government, called the Governorate-General of Turkestan, was established in 1867 with Tashkent as its capital.

TURKMEN Also called Turkomen. They are the descendants of early Caucasian tribes and later Turkic conquerors. They are the most traditional of the Central Asian people. They retained their tribal structure well into the twentieth century.

UZBEKS The largest group of Turkic peoples of Central Asia. Historically they were the descendants of the original Caucasian oasis dwellers and the later Turkic conquerors. Living in the more fertile regions they historically dominated the other peoples of Central Asia.

VOLGA FINNIC PEOPLES The peoples of the original homeland of the Finnic peoples are often referred to as the Volga Finnic Peoples, or Volga Finns. They include the Mari and the Mordvins. Although the Mari have successfully resisted assimilation, the Mordvins, who live in scattered groups surrounded by Slavs, have suffered more from the Russification policies of the former Russian and Soviet governments. The Udmurts, although historically and linguistically they form part of the Permian group farther north, are sometimes included as a Volga Finnic nation because their homeland lies in the northern part of the Volga River basin.

## Bibliography

Adshead, Samuel Adrian M. *Central Asia in World History.* New York: St. Martin's Press, 1993.

Allen, W. E. D., and Paul Muratoff. *Caucasian Battlefields: A History of the Wars on* the *Turco-Caucasian Border, 1828–1921*. Cambridge, MA: Harvard University Press, 1953.

Armstrong, John A. *Ukrainian Nationalism*. New York: Columbia University Press, 1963.

Baron, Salo W. *The Russian Jew under Tsars and Soviets*. New York: Macmillan, 1964.

Bushkovich, Paul. *Religion and Society in Russia: The Sixteenth and Seventeenth Centuries*. New York: Oxford University Press, 1992.

Diuk, Nadia, and Adrian Karatnycky. *The Hidden Nations: The People Challenge the Soviet Union*. New York: William Morrow, 1990.

Forsberg, Tuomas, ed. *Contested Territory: Border Disputes at the Edge of the Former Soviet Empire*. Aldershot, UK: Edward Elgar, 1995.

Gammer, Moshe. *Muslim Resistance to the Tsar: Shamyl and the Conquest of Chechnia and Dagestan*. London: Frank Cass, 1994.

Olson, James S. *An Ethnohistorical Dictionary of the Russian and Soviet Empires*. Westport, CT: Greenwood Press, 1994.

Pierce, Richard A. *Russian Central Asia, 1867–1917: A Study in Colonial Rule*. Berkeley: University of California Press, 1960.

Rieber, Alfred J. *Nicholas I and Official Nationality in Russia, 1825–1855*. Berkeley: University of California Press, 1959.

Thaden, Edward C., ed. *Russification of the Baltic Provinces and Finland, 1855–1914*. Princeton, NJ: Princeton University Press, 1981.

# Ethnic Consolidation
## and Ethnic Suppression

## CHAPTER FOUR

# Upheavals and Revolution, 1900–1921

THE INTENT, ON THE PART OF RUSSIA'S MORE ENLIGHTENED RULERS, to Westernize and modernize by importing technology, artisans, and ideas from Western Europe also introduced many unwanted influences. The idea of nationality, an offshoot of the eighteenth-century doctrine of popular sovereignty, resonated across the huge, feudal Russian Empire. Invigorated by the principles of the American and French Revolutions, many clan, tribal, and regional groups adopted the idea of nation and nationhood and began ethnic consolidation. Identification with religion, local area, or traditional leaders gave way to the idea of a cultural or linguistic affinity beyond the local level. Tribes became nations. Small groups, once isolated and vulnerable, took great pride in belonging to a larger political entity based on language, culture, or historical affiliations. The basis of the new national sentiments, the historical religious and geographical identities, remained a strong element in the new national equation.

Most of the languages spoken in the Russian Empire remained local peasant dialects. The very small numbers that had access to education learned in the language of the empire, Russian, or, in the Baltic provinces, in the traditional language of the ruling class, German. Even the Georgians and Armenians, with their ancient languages and cultures, were forced to adopt Russian as the language of administration and government. The official Russian policy of the assimilation of all the varied languages and cultures of the empire into a single Russian culture was widely resisted, reinforcing local cultures and languages at a time when revolutionary ideals were gaining adherents across the empire. The first chink in Russia's seemingly invincible armor would come with the empire's defeat by Japan in the Russo-Japanese War of 1904–1905. The shocking defeat highlighted the feudal nature of the immense empire and ended the myth of the Russians' God-given right to rule over all the other groups living within the imperial boundaries.

The growth of nationalist ideals that animated Europe's cultural and ethnic revival in the nineteenth century clearly threatened the feudal Russian

Empire, where nationalist sentiment was abhorrent to the supporters of the autocratic Romanov dynasty. Ancient nations, such as the Armenians and Georgians, revived the myths of their particular histories, and newer ethnic groups, as part of their cultural and ethnic revivals, developed a definite sense of identity separate from the dominant Russians. Before the late-nineteenth-century growth of national sentiment many of the inhabitants of the Russian Empire had identified with their religion, home village, or region, or with the traditional tribal structures, but by the late nineteenth century the majority had begun to view themselves as distinct ethnic groups or nations with their own histories, languages, and cultures. The development of national sentiment among the numerous ethnic and religious minorities was in direct opposition to the traditional Russian subservience to the empire and the ruling dynasty and the long-held assumption that official policies of assimilation would eventually homogenize the population.

Tensions between the increasingly militant revolutionaries and the nationalist ethnic minorities, on one hand, and the czarist regime, on the other, heightened as the Russian government again embraced reactionary policies as the twentieth century began. The period of limited reforms adopted following the upheaval of the 1905 Russian Revolution was brief. The reforms were renounced, and the harsh czarist policies were quickly reinstated. The years before World War I were marked by increasingly radicalized dissidence, widespread poverty, and brutal repression. Nationalist upheavals in the non-Russian territories of the empire frightened the czar's army of bureaucrats. The outbreak of World War I, in 1914, initially submerged the empire's growing nationality problems. The war dragged on, casualties mounted, and the non-Russian nationalities were forced to participate. By late 1915 the unrest returned, more widespread and much more radical than before.

### The Prelude to Revolution

At the turn of the twentieth century, the Russian authorities carried out the first all-Russian census, counting 128,907,692 inhabitants of the empire, making it by far the largest European power. Although rivals in Europe and Asia were modernizing and upgrading their military capabilities, Russia's government counted on numbers to overcome a serious lack of modern armament. The arrogant Russian generals, never having fought a serious modern war, blundered into the disastrous conflict with Japan in 1904–1905. Imperial rivalries in Manchuria and Korea had been building for more than a decade. Russia's refusal to withdraw from Manchuria and Russian penetration into northern Korea were countered by Japanese attempts to negotiate a division of the regions into spheres of influence. The Russian government remained inflexible, willing to risk an armed conflict in the belief that the Japanese were bound to be quickly defeated. The czarist authorities also believed that a resounding Russian victory in the Far East would head off the growing threat of internal revolution in the Russian Empire. When the negotiations broke down, the Japanese attacked Russian positions in Manchuria. A series of important Japanese victories culminated in the destruction of the huge, but antiquated, Russian fleet sent from Europe.

The disastrous Russo-Japanese War, which precipitated the Russian Revolution of 1905, led to the loss of southern Sakhalin Island and the expulsion of the Russians from port concessions they had controlled in Manchuria. The war ended Russian attempts to expand into Manchuria and Korea and concentrated official focus in the region on the colonization of the potentially rich agricultural lands in the southern parts of the enormous region of Siberia. The increase in colonization greatly affected the mainly tribal groups, who, like the non-Slavs of European Russia, lost their lands and were subjected to the official policy of assimilation and the eradication of local cultures.

## The 1905 Russian Revolution

In the first years of the twentieth century the Russian Empire was divided into several distinct political camps. The autocracy was supported by the landed nobility and the Orthodox religious leaders, but other groups upheld the ideals of a constitutional monarchy and democratic reforms or supported radical revolutionary groups dedicated to the removal of the hated Romanov dynasty and the creation of a new kind of Russian state. The majority of the non-Russian nationalities were divided, with many leaders supporting the revolutionaries in hopes of bettering the situation of their national group, and others seeking to win cultural and linguistic concessions in a more democratic Russia. The 1905 Russian Revolution began in St. Petersburg when imperial troops fired on a peaceful demonstration of workers marching to the winter palace to petition Czar Nicholas II. The massacre was followed by a series of strikes, riots, assassinations, mutinies, and widespread peasant and nationalist outbreaks. These disorders, following the disaster of the military defeat in the Far East, forced the government to promise reforms, including a consultative assembly with representation for the major national minorities. Unsatisfied popular demands provoked a general strike and renewed disorders. A more democratic assembly was granted

*The front page of the* New York Times *announces the success of the Russian Revolution and the abdication of Czar Nicholas II on March 16, 1917. (Hulton Archives)*

along with other reforms, including a reversal in the historic policy of assimilation, but as soon as order was restored most of the reforms were revoked, leaving widespread discontent, growing revolutionary activity, and the leaders of the non-Russian ethnic groups more and more inclined toward the radical manifesto of the revolutionaries, to win freedom by removing the major impediment, the czarist autocracy.

## World War I

The outbreak of World War I changed the face of czarist Russia. The nationalist ideals that accompanied the growth of revolutionary organizations up to 1914 were at first suppressed in the heady rush to overcome Russia's European enemies. Shaken by their defeat by the Japanese ten years before, the czarist authorities mobilized the world's largest army, still believing that numbers not technology would win the war. As the war dragged on and conditions worsened across the tottering empire, the various ethnic groups mobilized in support of a vague idea—revolution. The overthrow of 300 years of autocratic Romanov rule, along with the feudal ideals and traditions that underpinned the empire, gave the diverse ethnic groups of the empire their

*Russian Empire, c. 1914*

first opportunity to take control of their own destinies. When revolution swept the faltering Russian Empire in early 1917, most of the non-Russian national groups favored greater cultural, linguistic, and political autonomy in a reformed, democratic Russia. The overthrow of the Romanov monarchy, the spreading chaos, and the takeover of the Russian government by the small, radical Bolshevik faction of the Social Revolutionary Party ended the hope of autonomous status in a democratic Russian state. The rapid collapse of civil government left most Russian provinces without effective government. While the dominant ethnic group, the Russians, divided into two groups, the Reds, or revolutionaries, and the Whites, the remnants of the czarist hierarchy, the majority of the leaderships of the minority ethnic groups rushed to fill the power vacuum with local ethnic governments, some of which attempted to secede from the collapsed empire and to win international recognition and the support of the Allied governments.

## The Caucasus

When World War I began in 1914, the ethnic and national movements in the Caucasus, except for the Armenians and Georgians, were still in their

early stages. The Armenians and Georgians, seeing themselves as more ancient and cultured than their Russian overlords, focused on self-rule and
cultural autonomy. The region, a battleground on the Turkish front, was
severely divided following the outbreak of World War I in 1914. The Muslims mostly supported the Muslim Turks, and the Christians favored the
Christian Russians. The Russian Revolution that ended the Russian Empire in 1917 brought renewed turmoil. The Allies, although supportive of
independence movements in the strategic region, favored the anti-Bolshevik Whites rather than direct intervention. The Whites, like the Soviets, or
Reds, were adamantly opposed to separatist movements anywhere in the
collapsed empire.

## Armenians

The Russification policy increased in parallel with the growth of Armenian
nationalism up to World War I. Attempts to incorporate the ancient Armenian Church into Russian Orthodoxy greatly increased tensions. In 1903
all of the holdings of the Armenian Church in Russia were confiscated and
turned over to the official state Russian Orthodox Church. The outraged Armenians joined the revolutionary activities that led to the 1905 Russian Revolution. Concessions agreed to by the government in order to end the uprising included the return of all church property to the Armenian authorities
and the retraction of the 1903 decree.

The Armenian leaders, although divided politically among several re-
formist, revolutionary, and social-nationalist organizations, agreed that the
Armenians of the Russian Empire should be granted self-rule and insisted
on reforms in the corrupt and violent Armenian provinces of the adjacent
Ottoman Empire. In an effort to deflect rising nationalist passions, the local
czarist authorities had instigated a violent conflict between the Christian Armenians and the Muslim Azeris. The Armenians formed a large minority in
Baku and other industrial cities in Azerbaijan and formed a majority in the
highland Karabakh region. The conflict, which raged from 1905 through
1907, focused Armenian nationalist energies on the Azeris and not on the
Russian government.

The Turkish sultan, Abdülhamid II, suspicious of Armenian nationalist
aims, had ordered massacres of Armenian populations in Turkish Armenia
in 1894–1896. Armenian hopes were raised following the overthrow of the
"bloody sultan" in 1908, but the promises of a state where all citizens were
equal were never realized. Pan-Turkish and Pan-Islamic sentiment, which

*A bread distribution center at an Armenian refugee and orphan center, June 17, 1920 (Bettmann/Corbis)*

embraced the Armenians' enemies, the Azeris in the Russian Empire, ended all attempts at cooperation between Armenians and Turks in the Ottoman Empire. The outbreak of war in 1914 increased the Turkish suspicion that the Armenians in the Ottoman Empire were pro-Russian. In April 1915 the Turkish government began the century's first genocide. The defeat of the Turkish army in the winter of 1914–1915 gave the Turkish authorities the excuse to rid the Turkish provinces in eastern Anatolia of their Armenian populations. Much of the population of Turkish Armenia was killed outright or died during brutal forced deportations into the Syrian Desert. Many Armenian men were murdered, and the women were raped and the children sold into slavery. Of the 2 million Armenians in the Ottoman Empire in early 1915, only about half a million, mostly women and children, escaped to Russian Armenia, Syria, or other areas of the Middle East.

The Russian Provisional Government, following the revolution in February 1917, gave the Armenian leadership in Russia vague promises of unification of all Armenian lands. The Bolshevik coup later the same year ended Armenian cooperation with the revolutionary government. The Armenians sought protection by joining neighboring Georgia and Azerbaijan in an independent Transcaucasian Federation. Tensions between the federation partners, particularly between the Armenians and Azeris, ended the attempt at shared sovereignty. The Armenian leaders declared a separate independent Armenian republic on 28 May 1918. The new state, although centered in Russian Armenia, claimed territories also claimed by Azerbaijan and the largely depopulated provinces of Turkish Armenia. In May 1919, taking advantage of Turkey's defeat by the Allied powers, the new Armenian government formally annexed the provinces of Turkish Armenia.

The Allies, over Turkish objections, prepared to recognize "Greater Armenia" as an independent state. The Armenians, threatened by the advancing Red Army and a resurgent, nationalist Turkey, appealed for protection to U.S. President Woodrow Wilson, a staunch advocate of Armenian independence. The Allies urged the United States to accept Armenia as a League of Nations mandate, but the U.S. Senate, having kept the United States out of the League, voted 52 to 23 against the mandate, thus sealing the fate of the beleaguered Armenians. The Soviets, emerging victorious from Russia's civil war, and the resurgent Turks agreed on the need to end the bothersome independent Armenian state. In September 1920 the Soviets attacked from the east while the Turks invaded from the west. The Turks easily overran the depopulated western provinces in Turkish Armenia and obliterated all signs of the historic Armenian presence. The renewed Turkish massacres sent the survivors fleeing to the scant protection of the eastern districts, the former Russian Armenia, then under attack by the Soviets. In December 1920 the Red Army defeated the starving, overcrowded remnant of the Armenian Republic. The defeated Armenians rebelled against Soviet rule in February 1921, while the Soviets were occupied with the conquest of the neighboring Georgians, but were again defeated.

## Georgians

The Georgian nationalist leaders began to demand linguistic and cultural rights in the 1890s. The political leadership mostly adhered to the Mencheviks, the more moderate wing of the Social Revolutionary Party. Spurred by the ideals of the 1905 revolutionary movement, many Georgians embraced the revolutionary ideals of the moderate Menchevik wing of the Social Revolutionary Party, the largest of the many fledgling political groups. When war began in 1914 the Georgians felt threatened by the Turks and initially supported the czarist government's war aims. Demoralized by hardship and the growing number of refugees in their homeland, the Georgians enthusiastically supported the revolution that overthrew the Romanov dynasty in February 1917. The Menchevik faction took control of Georgia as the czarist civil government disappeared. Seeking safety in numbers, the Georgian leadership joined their homeland in an independent Transcaucasian Federation with the neighboring Armenians and Azeris. When the federation collapsed because of internal disputes, the Georgians declared the independence of the Republic of Georgia on 26 May 1918.

The Red Army, victorious in the civil war in 1920, moved south into the Caucasus, intent on reconquering the wealthy region. By early 1921 the Soviets had overrun the neighboring territories, and the Georgians stood alone against the might of the new Soviet state. Less than nine months after Soviet Russia signed a treaty that recognized Georgian independence, the Soviet Red Army invaded. Their frantic appeals to the Allies ignored, the Georgians finally surrendered in April 1921. A new Soviet Transcaucasian Federation, under the personal direction of a local Georgian revolutionary named Joseph Stalin, was formed by the newly conquered states of Armenia, Azerbaijan, and Georgia.

## Azeris

The industrialization of Baku and the surrounding region brought great wealth to the region. The sudden economic importance of the region exposed the Azeris to Western-style education, urbanization, and modern technology. Oil millionaires financed a massive array of public institutions, schools, and fine buildings. In 1907 Baku boasted the first opera house in the Muslim world and the first Muslim opera, *Leila and Majnun,* by Uzeir Ghajibekov.

Resentment of Slavic privileges fueled the growth of the Azeri cultural movement and a religious revival in the late nineteenth century. Serious rioting swept the region in 1901 and 1904, culminating in the revolutionary activities that accompanied the Russian Revolution of 1905. During that period Azeri nationalists controlled the Baku oil region until routed by czarist troops. The cultural-religious movement increasingly incorporated nationalist ideals. The formation of specifically Azeri political parties between 1904 and 1911 included formations dedicated to revolution and other groups, such as Mussavat, which advocated a nationalist view.

The Azeris, led by the nationalist Mussavat Party, repeatedly demanded autonomy and Muslim religious freedom within the Russian Empire in the years before World War I. When fighting erupted in the region in 1914, the Azeris overwhelmingly supported their fellow Muslims, the Turks of the Ottoman Empire. Turkish overtures to the Turkic peoples of the Caucasus region stirred ethnic and religious conflicts in Baku and other cities with mixed populations. The Azeri nationalists took control of the region when revolution swept the empire in early 1917. Fearful of the growing chaos and Turkish territorial claims, the Azeris agreed to be integrated into the independent Transcaucasian Federation along with neighboring Armenia and Georgia. Even though threats to the region increased as the war continued, the federation collapsed because of severe ethnic and religious differences, particularly between the Christian Armenians and the Muslim Azeris, who had fought each other between 1905 and 1907. The Bolshevik coup ended all attempts to cooperate with the Russian government. Radicalized Russian soldiers, returning from the Turkish front, took control of Baku, where they encouraged the local Armenians to attack Azeris. More than 12,000 Azeris were killed, and the federation collapsed. Azerbaijan was declared a separate republic on 28 May 1918. Azeri rioters then turned on the Armenian minority in the new state, killing thousands before order was restored.

The agreement between nationalist Turkey and the Soviet government to end the inconvenient independence of the new Caucasian states gave the military forces of the two states virtually a free hand. The Western Allies, exhausted from the war, refused to provide direct aid and favored cooperation between the separatist states and the anti-Bolshevik White Russian forces. The Azeris, like the Armenians and Georgians, attempted to win support at the Paris Peace Conference that was called to reorganize the postwar order, but their pleas were also ignored. The Soviet defeat of the Whites in the North Caucasus brought the Red Army to Azerbaijan's northern border in early 1920. Ignoring earlier assurances to the Azeris, the Red Army invaded the north as the Turks occupied the south. In April 1920 the Azeri republic collapsed, and its leadership fled abroad or was imprisoned or killed. The victorious Red troops, in control of Baku, were allowed to "amuse" themselves with the city's upper and middle class inhabitants, whether Azeri, Armenian, or Russian. Hundreds died in the ensuing violence. The Bolsheviks reached an agreement with the departing Turks and on 1 May 1920 declared Azerbaijan a Soviet republic. As noted previously, under firm Soviet control the Azeri homeland was again joined with the Armenian and Georgian states to form a new Transcaucasian Federation, which became part of the new Union of Soviet Socialist Republics.

## North Caucasians

The Chechens, Ingush, and Dagestanis of the North Caucasus, having been defeated in 1859 and brought into the Russian Empire, had remained the most ardent opponents of Russian rule in the entire empire. Their best lands had been confiscated and settled by Russian settlers and Cossack military colonies, while they lived in abject poverty in the less-productive heights of the Caucasus Mountains. The nineteenth-century nationalism had activated their Muslim identity, although tribal differences remained important. The Muslim peoples clung to their traditional languages, partly owing to their contempt for Russians and Russian culture. The influx of colonists, particularly after the discovery of oil in 1893, continued to push the Muslims farther into the mountains. The drilling of oil wells and the completion of the railroad through the region from Russia to Baku brought even more Slavs.

Openly supportive of the Muslim Turks when war began in 1914, the Muslim peoples of the Caucasus suffered brutal suppression. When the revolution overthrew the hated Russian government in 1917, the Muslim Caucasians, led by the Chechens, took control of the local civil government and expelled all Slavic officials. An all-Muslim conference, convened in September 1917, was attended by delegates from most of the Muslim peoples of the North Caucasus. At first they attempted to negotiate autonomy within a proposed democratic Russia, but that ended with the Bolshevik coup in October 1917. Alarmed by the antireligious stance of the Bolsheviks, the Chechens formed a temporary alliance with the anti-Bolshevik Cossacks, but territorial disputes over traditional tribal lands cut short the alliance. The Muslims proclaimed a holy war and drove the Cossacks from the area. They established a Muslim theocracy, led by a Chechen emir, Sheikh Uzun Haji, which took the name Republic of North Caucasia. Violent confrontations continued as the Muslims attempted to expel the Slavs from lands they considered their own. The Muslims, believing Bolshevik promises of independence in a proposed federation of Soviet states, went over to the Reds in 1918. With the aid of Bolshevik forces, they drove thousands of Slavs from their traditional lands. In January 1920, despite earlier promises, the Soviet government attempted to incorporate the North Caucasus into their new Soviet state. The Muslim warriors turned on their Red allies but were defeated following a vicious war that lasted for two months.

## Abkhaz

The Abkhaz homeland lies in northwestern Georgia, a lush, subtropical region on the Black Sea. The Abkhaz adopted the Muslim religion from the Turks in the sixteenth and seventeenth centuries, but retained some autonomy under a local dynasty. In the eighteenth century the Turks attempted to annex Abkhazia. The Abkhaz rulers turned to the expanding Russians for help. In 1810 the Abkhaz leaders accepted Russian protection, maintaining a precarious semiautonomous existence until the conquest of the Caucasus was completed. In 1864 the last Abkhaz prince was exiled and the region was annexed to the Russian Empire. Czarist attempts to promote assimilation, particularly pressure to abandon their Muslim faith and convert to Ortho-dox Christianity, incited a widespread uprising in 1866. The Russian army quickly defeated the poorly armed Abkhaz rebels. The surviving Abkhaz were brutally suppressed, the majority reduced to serfdom on Russian and Geor-gian estates established in the region. More than 70,000 Abkhaz fled to Turk-ish territory to escape Russian rule between 1866 and 1878. The czarist au-thorities resettled the abandoned Abkhaz lands with ethnic Slavs and Georgians.

Health resorts along the Abkhaz coast became fashionable among the czarist nobility in the late nineteenth century, bringing economic prosper-ity and modernization. Increased education stimulated the growth of a lo-cal Abkhaz intelligentsia that led a national revival. By the early 1900s a strong national consciousness had developed. Although depleted by wartime hardships, the Abkhaz mobilized following the outbreak of revolution in February 1917. The breakdown of the local government allowed the leader-ship to organize. An Abkhaz National Council took control of the region and asserted the Abkhaz right to autonomy within the new revolutionary Rus-sia. Georgian troops moved into Abkhazia after the Bolshevik coup in Oc-tober 1917, setting off fighting with Abkhaz nationalists. In February 1918 the Abkhaz forces drove the last Georgian troops from the region. On 8 March 1918 the leaders proclaimed the independence of Abkhazia. The free Abkhaz state lasted just forty-two days before it was overthrown by invad-ing Bolshevik troops. In desperation, the Abkhaz turned to the Georgians for aid. A large Georgian force defeated the Bolsheviks, but stayed to incorpo-rate the region into the newly independent Georgian republic. The Abkhaz revolted in early 1921, providing a pretext for the Red Army's subsequent in-vasion and conquest of both Georgia and Abkhazia.

## The Crimean Tatars

When World War I broke out, the Russian Empire went to war against Ger-many, the Austro-Hungarian Empire, and the Turkish Ottoman Empire. His-toric antipathy to the Muslim Crimean Tatars became suspicions that the

Crimean Tatars favored Russia's enemies, particularly their fellow Muslims, the Turks. Russian suppression galvanized the growth of Crimean Tatar nationalism, partly as an act of self-defense. Many nationalist leaders fled to Turkish territory to escape arrest. In 1917, led by exile leaders in Turkey and Switzerland, a constituent assembly was convened and called for Crimean Tatar independence. Its program of national self-determination included a Crimean Tatar parliament and universal male suffrage.

When revolution swept Russia in February 1917, the Crimean Tatar nationalists had underground cells in most Tatar towns and villages. A Tatar congress, convened in September 1917, pressed for autonomy within a democratic Russia. The Bolshevik coup, in October 1917, stirred an uprising by local Bolsheviks. Fighting between Tatar nationalists and radical soldiers and sailors ended when Germans occupied the region in March 1918. Tatar leaders emerged from hiding to declare the complete independence of the Crimea. The invading Red Army took control of the peninsula in 1919. The majority of the Crimean Tatars saw the imposition of Communist rule as yet another form of Slavic oppression. Several national leaders were executed, and groups of guerrillas appeared in the more remote areas. The new Soviet government, unable to fully suppress the Crimean Tatar nationalist movement, decided in 1921 to allow the Crimean Tatars, like the other larger national groups, to have their own autonomous republic.

### The Baltic Peoples

The activism of the 1905 Russian Revolution accelerated the rapid spread of nationalist ideals in the Baltic region. Reforms were introduced following the upheaval that allowed political opposition, trade unions, and the use of local languages in education and publishing, but the reforms were later rescinded. Revolutionary activity and nationalist sentiment increased with the outbreak of World War I in 1914. Many Baltic activists supported radical revolutionary organizations as a way of freeing their small nations from the double oppression of czarist Russia and the Baltic German landlords. The Germans overran the southern Baltic territories in Latvia and Lithuania in 1915. Hope of autonomy within a more democratic Russia disposed most of the Baltic revolutionaries to support the revolution that overthrew the imperial government in 1917. Workers and Soldiers Soviets, newly formed political collectives that took power as civil and military authority disappeared, competed with nationalists for control of the provinces as civil governments collapsed. The German authorities allowed nationalist activities in their occupation zone, but following the Germans' defeat in 1918 the Bolsheviks mostly took control. A British squadron in the Baltic Sea supported the Baltic nationalists against the Bolsheviks and the Germans, but the chaos and confusion prevented a clear victory. In November 1918, with Germany defeated, the Estonians, Latvians, and Lithuanians declared their homelands independent. The Soviet government, reluctant to lose the ice-free ports on the Baltic Sea, aided local Bolshevik and worker's organizations, which undermined the stability of the new states. In mid-1919 the Baltic military forces were successful in defeating a Baltic German force that attempted to seize control of Estonia. In 1920, the Soviet government reluctantly signed peace treaties with the three Baltic republics, recognizing their independent status.

## The Volga Peoples

The emergence of a large middle class among the Tatars by the 1880s, the first middle class to develop in a Muslim community in Russia, as discussed previously, was a decisive event in the Volga region. A progressive religious outlook, emphasis on modern education, and an increase in local publishing stimulated the growth of Tatar nationalism up until World War I. The high Tatar literacy rate and well-developed sense of national consciousness aided the cultural revival that swept the region in the late nineteenth century. The first openly nationalist Tatar organization formed in 1906, with affiliates among the other Volga ethnic groups. Radical groups supported revolutionary ideas of independence, socialism, and the expulsion of the Slavic colonists from the Volga region.

The non-Russian minorities were generally exempted from military conscription when Russia declared war in 1914. However, as Russia's armies were decimated owing to poor arms and organization, conscription was ordered in 1916. Resistance to military conscription continued until revolution swept the empire in February 1917. Tatar nationalists and moderate Slav Mencheviks took control of the Volga region as the czarist provincial governments disappeared. Threatened by the Bolshevik takeover of the Russian government in October 1917, the Volga nationalities sent delegates to a conference of the non-Russian peoples of the Volga-Ural region. The delegates, led by the Tatars, declared the autonomy of the region that they called Idel-Ural, an older form of Volga-Ural.

Bolshevik forces, supported by some revolutionary militants, overran the region in April 1918. The Volga peoples rebelled and, with the aid of the Czech Legion—a strong fighting force comprising Czech and Slovak pris-

oners of war—they routed the Bolsheviks. Joined by most of the ethnic nationalist organizations of the Volga region, the regional leaders declared the
independence of the Idel-Ural Federation on 30 September 1918. A majority of the Volga peoples supported the federation, although a minority of the
Orthodox Christians favored a smaller federation of just the Christian nations. In 1920, the Reds, having defeated the last of the White forces and the
nationalist rebels in the region, took control of the Volga basin. A massive
famine followed the widespread destruction of the civil war and the inept
introduction of communism. More than one-third of the pre–World War I
population of the Volga region perished by late 1921. Nominally autonomous republics were formed for the various national groups of the
Volga, even though, in reality, all-important posts were held by reliable ethnic Slav members of the Communist Party.

The Muslim Bashkorts in the eastern Volga region were largely untouched
by World War I, fought far to the west on Russia's European borders.
Bashkort leaders convened a national congress following the revolution of
February 1917. They adopted a program of autonomy within a new, democratic Russia and expulsion of the Slavs from their traditional territories. The
Bashkorts adamantly refused to join the other Volga peoples in the Volga-
Ural Federation, which they saw as dominated by the Tatars. The Bashkort
leaders embraced a nationalist platform when it became clear that the revolution had failed to secure their lost lands. The threat posed by the Bolshevik coup in October 1917 forced the Muslim Bashkorts into an alliance
with their old enemies, the Orenburg Cossacks, who controlled the southern part of traditional Bashkort territory. The Bashkir Revolutionary Committee, the Bashrevkom, declared their homeland an autonomous state on
29 November 1917. They laid claim to the provinces of Ufa and Orenburg,
although Orenburg was held by Cossack military units allied to the anti-Bolshevik White forces. The claim to Orenburg ended the shaky alliance between
the Bashkorts and the Orenburg Cossacks, who fought and defeated the
Bashkorts for control of the province. The fighting weakened the anti-Bolshevik forces in the region, and in February 1918 the Bolsheviks occupied
the Bashkort homeland.

The alliance with the Whites, including the Cossacks, completely broke
down over White opposition to Bashkort separatism. Spurned by the Whites,
the Bashkorts accepted a Soviet offer of independence within a Soviet federation of sovereign states. They went over to the Reds in March 1919. The
Bashkort leaders prepared to send ambassadors to Moscow to represent their
new republic within the Soviet federation, but were outraged to find themselves treated as a conquered people rather than as allies. Denied the prom-

ised independence within a Soviet federation, the Bashkorts rebelled against the new Bolshevik government. At first the Bashkorts advanced, but the Red Army, after its victory over the Whites in 1920, concentrated troops against the Bashkort forces, which were quickly forced to retreat.

## Siberia and the Siberians

More than 3 million Slavs had settled in Siberia by 1914, their transfer from Europe facilitated by the completion of the Trans-Siberian Railroad. Most of the colonists settled along the rivers, the main transport links for huge tracts of territory. The best and most fertile lands, mines, and natural resources were taken from the indigenous Siberian ethnic groups and set aside for colonization or government exploitation. The new arrivals from European Russia often adopted the speech and antigovernment attitudes of the earlier European settlers, mostly political and criminal exiles. The society that formed east of the Ural Mountains in many ways was more similar to the frontier regions of North America than European Russia. The Siberian ethnic groups, often pushed aside or driven away from the best and most fertile lands, at first welcomed the news that the hated autocracy had been overthrown in far-away Europe.

## Altai

The Altai tribes, traditionally nomadic, were often forcibly settled in permanent villages by the Russian government. Although the majority were officially converted to Russian Orthodoxy, Burkhanism, a distinctly nationalistic, anti-Russian messianic religion, spread through the tribes in 1904. The center of the new religion was the figure of the mythical Oryot Khan, who promised to restore the Altai to their historic greatness. Burkhanism served as the foundation of a new nationalist liberation movement in the first decades of the new century. Continued Russian colonization further heightened ethnic tensions in the region. The Japanese defeat of the mighty Russians in 1905 also affected the region, giving Altai Burkhanism a decidedly pro-Japanese orientation. In 1911, when the related Tuvans declared their independence during the Chinese Revolution, nationalism became a serious factor. The first determined attempts to unite the fractious Altai tribes as a viable nation were undertaken, with Burkhanism at its core, in the years leading up to World War I.

The Altai were left effectively independent when the provincial government disappeared following the overthrow of the Russian imperial government in early 1917. More secular nationalists emerged with demands for the creation of an independent Altai state based on their historic homeland and distinct culture, possibly in federation with the related Khakass to the north. United for the first time, the Altai tribes mobilized to resist attempts by local Bolsheviks to take power as the chaos of the Bolshevik takeover and the spreading civil war reached the remote region. The victorious Altai declared the independence of their homeland in January 1918, laying claim to historical Altai lands, including the huge Altai Steppe to the west. Allied to the White anti-Bolshevik forces in western Siberia, the Altai participated in some of the most ferocious battles of the Russian Civil War. The Red Army, in 1920, finally defeated the last White troops and moved into the Altai Mountains.

## Buryats

The Trans-Siberian Railroad reached the Buryat heartland in southern Siberia in 1898, bringing an influx of Slavic colonists in the first years of the twentieth century. The colonial onslaught finally united the historically passive Buddhist peoples in opposition to the increasingly discriminatory land laws. Serious uprisings by the Buryats spread across the region in 1903 and 1905, countered by Russian threats to completely destroy the Buryat culture. During the Russo-Japanese War in 1904–1905, the Japanese embraced an official policy of "pan-Mongolism," seeking the support of the Mongol peoples of Asia. Nationalism mostly took the form of demands for greater religious, cultural, and linguistic freedoms. A Buryat congress, held in 1905, issued demands for linguistic freedom and self-government for the Buryats in the Russian Empire, but the movement was quickly suppressed. Even though the Japanese courted the Buryats, secret treaties between Japan and Russia, signed between 1907 and 1912, recognized the Buryats as falling within Russia's sphere of influence.

Buryat life remained largely untouched by World War I until the Russian Revolution of 1917. The Buryats, effectively independent as the czarist civil government collapsed, put aside their remaining tribal differences and united to drive all Russian officials from their homeland around Lake Baikal. A Buryat congress in April 1917 voted for independence from Russia and closer cultural and political ties to neighboring Mongolia. In an ironic twist, Buryat Buddhist monks were the first to divest the many monasteries of their extensive land holdings. The lands were distributed to Buryat peasants in an attempt to return the Buryat Buddhist religion to a more traditional form.

A Japanese intervention force, dispatched to keep eastern Siberia from falling to the Bolsheviks, occupied the Buryat territories in early 1918. Encouraged by the Japanese officials, who envisaged a renewed Mongol federation under Japanese control, the Buryats formed a national government. The new government participated in a pan-Mongol conference that endorsed a Buryat demand for the expulsion of all Slav colonists east of Lake Baikal. Threatened by the spreading violence of the Russian Civil War, the Buryat leadership declared their homeland independent of Russia in February 1919. They set about creating a state administered according to historic Buddhist teachings, but the Lake Baikal region remained chaotic and the new Buryat government was unable to assert its authority. Even though they attempted to maintain their neutrality during the Russian Civil War, the Buryats were overrun by invading Bolshevik troops in 1920. Their region was included in a new Far Eastern Republic, set up by the Soviets as a Communist-dominated buffer state between the new Soviet state and Chinese and Japanese territory.

## Sakhas

Gold deposits, found in Sakha territory in the mid-nineteenth century, brought a new influx of Slavic settlers. The ongoing transfer of Slavs to the region was facilitated by the construction of rail links in the late nineteenth century. The region remained an important place of exile, with many educated scholars and scientists who dedicated their time in exile to the study of the Sakha culture and language. A Sakha museum was opened by exiles in 1891, and a political exile compiled the first dictionary of the Sakha language. Primary schools opened by political deportees and the Russian Orthodox Church helped the development of a Sakha literary language and an educated Sakha minority before World War I. The revolutionary ideas of the political exiles, including freedom and self-determination, resounded in the region, where poverty and malnutrition were endemic. A nationalist organization, formed in 1906, demanded the complete rejuvenation of the Sakha homeland, including the return of all confiscated lands and wealth. The czarist authorities reacted by arresting the local leadership, which encouraged the growth of antigovernment sentiment.

The Sakhas, as a non-European national group, were initially exempted from military service when war began in 1914, but desperate for manpower the authorities began to conscript Sakhas for labor battalions in 1916. Resistance to the conscription strengthened the small nationalist movement that mobilized following the overthrow of the czar in early 1917. An alliance of liberal political parties took control of the region following the breakdown of civil authority. The Bolshevik coup, later in 1917, pushed the majority of the Sakhas to form an alliance with the Whites, the anti-Bolshevik forces formed by the remnants of the czarist military. Allied to the Whites, the Sakhas created an autonomous government and turned their homeland into an anti-Bolshevik bastion. Over vehement White opposition, the Sakha leaders declared the region, taking the name Sakha Omuk, independent of Russia in February 1918. A minority of the Sakhas joined the Bolsheviks, believing promises of independence within a federation of Soviet states. Too far from the Russian heartland to feel the full effects of the Russian Civil War, the Sakhas escaped the spreading devastation until the region fell to the invading Bolshevik forces following the final defeat of the Whites in 1920.

## Tuvans

Cossack explorers made contact with the Tuvans around 1860, after the Treaty of Peking between China and Russia opened the territories in Chinese Mongolia to Russian trade. Russian influence increased as Manchu power waned in the next decades. By 1900 more than 7,000 Russian colonists had settled in the fertile river valleys of the Tuvan region. Supported by the local Russians, Tuvan leaders organized a national government during the 1911 Chinese Revolution, which overthrew the Manchu dynasty. On 18 December 1911 the Tuvans declared the independence of their homeland, called Tannu Tuva, from China. When war broke out in Europe in 1914, they accepted Russian protection against renewed Chinese or Mongol claims to the region. Proclaimed a Russian protected state, Russia took responsibility for Tannu Tuva's foreign relations and defense. To most of the Tuvans, who lived in remote villages, often working for members of the small aristocratic class or the Russian colonists, life remained as always, ordained by religion and a feudal system of local loyalties.

News of the Russian Revolution was followed by the gradual breakdown of authority in the region. The Tuvans, freed of oppressive Russian control, asserted their independence, but in early 1918 local Bolsheviks, supported by many Russians in the region, rebelled against the traditional ruling class. The Bolshevik uprising weakened the Tuvans just as the violence of the Russian civil war spilled into southern Siberia. The Chinese attempted to reassert their claim to the region, but the White defeat and the Bolshevik occupation of neighboring Mongolia brought the Tuvans under Bolshevik authority. The feudal Tuvan lords were overthrown, and an independent people's republic was proclaimed in August 1921. Although organized along traditional lines, the new state had a functioning parliament with popular participation. The establishment of the autonomous Tuvan state aided the Tuvans to resist renewed attempts by the Mongolian republic to gain control of the mountainous region.

### The Tribal Peoples of Northeastern Siberia

The Chukots, Koryaks, and other small tribal peoples of northeastern Siberia were mostly left to their traditional way of life by the Russian authorities. Orthodox missionaries introduced a system of education in the nineteenth century, which, although usually limited to chief's sons, gradually produced a core of educated, modern tribal leaders in the early twentieth century. Contact with educated political prisoners exiled to their frozen homeland introduced many new ideas. In the early twentieth century the tribal peoples began to demand redress of past injuries. In the wake of the 1905 Russian Revolution, the small national movements focused on land, culture, and hunting and fishing rights restricted under colonial rule. Virtually untouched by the war in Europe until the revolution that swept the Russian Empire in early 1917, the tribal peoples were slow to react. They began to mobilize as the colonial authorities disappeared. They were pushed aside or ignored as rival Russian factions sought to win control of the strategic region during the Russian Civil War and remained unsure how to counter the chaos as the civil war spread to even the most remote corners of their homelands. In 1920 the victorious Red Army expelled the last of the White troops and established Soviet rule in the remote territories. Outraged by clumsy Soviet attempts to collectivize reindeer herds and fishing communities, the tribal peoples began to resist. Attempts by the new Soviet authorities to break the traditional power of the shamans provoked violent resistance in early 1921.

### Jews

During the 1890s the Russian government began enforcing educational quotas and residency requirements that further curtailed Jewish access to education and tightened the regulations on the small Jewish minority living outside the Pale of Settlement. In 1891, the government expelled the 20,000 to 30,000 Jews living in Moscow. By 1900 an estimated 650 restrictive laws directed against the Jews were part of the Russian code. These laws made the life of the majority of Jews in Russia extremely onerous. In the decades after 1881 a series of vicious pogroms—beatings, rioting, murder, and rape directed against the Jews and Jewish properties—were partly sponsored by local officials in an attempt to divert popular anger against the inept government. Hundreds of riots and pogroms swept various parts of Russia between 1881 and the outbreak of war in 1914.

The Jewish population of the Russian Empire had grown to more than 5 million by 1900. The harsh conditions, officially sponsored violence, and anti-Semitic laws drove many Jews to emigrate; between 1881 and 1914 more than 1.5 million Jews left the empire, mostly to the United States, Canada, Argentina, and South Africa. The increasingly violent pogroms, often carried out by Cossacks under the orders of government officials, continued after the outbreak of war in 1914, but the worst pogroms came during the civil war in the period 1918–1921. Historians estimate that between 180,000 and 200,000 Jews were killed in riots, pogroms, and actions carried out by local populations and by factions of both the Reds and Whites.

World War I and the Russian Civil War were disastrous for the Jews of Russia. Most of the fighting on the Russian front took place in the historic Pale of Settlement. Jews were often targeted by the Russian military, or were killed indiscriminately by Cossacks, anti-Bolshevik Whites, Ukrainian nationalists, peasants, and armed groups of many ideologies. Only the Red Army officially prohibited anti-Semitic attacks. Even though many Jews opted for emigration, others responded to oppression by remaining and participating in the growing revolutionary movement. Jews played an important role in the movement and had a prominent part in the Bolshevik movement that overthrew the imperial government in 1917. Although none of the revolutionary Jewish leaders were religious, they actively pressed for the lifting of czarist restrictions on Jewish life. Jews played an important part in the early years of the Soviet state, but attacks on Jewish life and religion later resumed.

The breakup of the Russian Empire was yet another calamity for the Jews. The emergence of independent states in Poland, Lithuania, Estonia, and Latvia, and the annexation of Bessarabia by neighboring Romania left large numbers of Russian Jews outside the borders of the new Soviet state. By 1921, the Jewish population of the Soviet Union was less than half of what it had been in the former Russian Empire. Jewish life in the newly independent states was often more precarious and more restricted than under the new Soviet authorities.

## Germans

The Russian government suspected the large German-speaking population in the western provinces of pro-German sentiment when war began in 1914. Harsh restrictions were imposed on the Germans, including restrictions on their dialects. In 1916 the Russian government issued a decree for the deportation of all Germans to the east, to be implemented in April 1917. The order, at first suspended when revolution erupted in February 1917, was later rescinded by the Bolsheviks, along with all other czarist decrees. The Bolshevik coup in October 1917 further divided the Germans of Russia. The Germans of the Russian Empire were unsure as to whether to support the Whites or the Reds. In the western provinces they generally supported the anti-Bolshevik White forces, but in the eastern European provinces, particularly in the Volga region and Ukraine, the Germans often supported the Reds, partly because of Soviet promises of cultural autonomy, self-government, and land.

The Germans of the Volga region organized an autonomous government as the civil administration ceased to function. Nationalists prepared to declare independence and to seek assistance from the German military units that had occupied Russian provinces farther west, but events in Russia intervened. The Bolshevik coup in October 1917 and the rapid occupation of the Volga region by Bolshevik supporters ended the nationalist movement. The Volga Germans were the first non-Russian ethnic group to be organized under Lenin's nationality policy. The Volga German autonomous region was authorized and raised to the status of an autonomous republic in 1919. In an effort to encourage the spread of communism in Germany, the Volga Republic was made a model showcase for communism. Outside the republic the Soviet government organized seventeen autonomous districts for the scattered German-speaking territories. The Volga German showcase continued as a privileged region until the collapse of the post–World War I Communist uprisings in Germany.

## Central Asians

The Russian government completed the Orenburg–Tashkent Railroad in 1906, linking Turkestan to European Russia. The railroad brought Slav set-

tlers and European technology to the region, but, more importantly, it allowed the government to quickly move soldiers into areas of unrest. Revolutionary ideals had spread to the region in the wake of the 1905 upheavals,
affecting principally the Muslim religious elite. The Turkestani Muslims were
not directly involved in the war effort following the declaration of hostilities in 1914, but by 1916 the need for manpower persuaded the imperial government to extend conscription. The local czarist authorities attempted to
conscript 250,000 Central Asians for labor battalions. The conscription was
resisted, setting off a rebellion that spread from the Kazakhs to the Uzbek
heartland of Central Asia. The rebels defeated the few soldiers in the region,
and in many areas they turned on the Slav colonists. Thousands were slaugh-
tered, and the survivors fled to military outposts or attempted to return to
Europe. Troops, hastily withdrawn from the front, were sent against the rebel
groups, often attacking peaceful villages or unarmed civilians.

The rebellion was overtaken by the Russian Revolution, leading to the
gradual collapse of Russian control of Central Asia. The scattered Kazakh
clans in the north formed an ethnic government, but most of the Central
Asians participated in a unified Muslim government formed at Tashkent. A
rival Russian-dominated organization, the Tashkent Soviet Workers' and
Peasants' Deputies, supported the more radical revolutionary leaders. The
Muslim government demanded an end to Russian colonization and the re-
turn of stolen lands. The Bolshevik coup in St. Petersburg spread to Central
Asia in late 1917. Bolsheviks seized control of Tashkent and overthrew the
Muslim government. They then voted to exclude Muslims from local ad-
ministrations. The Muslims formed a Muslim Provisional Government of
Autonomous Turkestan at Kokand. Outraged by the Bolshevik's antireligious
stance and threatened by the arrival of Bolshevik troops from Europe, the
Muslim leaders declared Turkestan independent in December 1917. The
Kazakhs also declared their immense homeland independent of Russia. The
declarations were echoed by declarations of independence by the rulers of
the protectorates of Bukhara and Khiva.

In January 1918, following the declared secession of the Muslim Central
Asians, fighting broke out. The Kazakhs allied with the White anti-Bolshevik Russian forces in neighboring Siberia, but the ill-equipped Turkestan
forces were quickly defeated by the Bolshevik troops. In February the Bolsheviks took control of the Muslim capital at Kokand. Allowed to loot the
city by their elected military leaders, the Bolshevik troops wantonly destroyed
ancient Muslim monuments and historic buildings. The city's 120,000 inhabitants were either killed or driven from their homes. In April 1918 the
Bolsheviks established the Turkestan Autonomous Soviet Socialist Republic.

Although a minority of the Muslim Turkestani population supported the Bolshevik cause, a ruling adopted in July 1919 excluded Muslims from government posts and a harsh antireligious stance was adopted. Many Central Asian Muslims joined rebel groups, called Basmachi. In 1920 the Bolsheviks took control of Kazakhstan and overthrew the governments of Khiva and Bukhara, thus completing the Communist takeover of Central Asia.

## Ukrainians and Belarussians

Millions of Ukrainians and Belarussians joined or were conscripted to fight in the czarist armies when war began in 1914. Lying on the front lines between the Russian and German/Austrian armies, parts of the region were devastated. The poorly equipped military units drawn from the non-Russian Slavs suffered massive losses. Tens of thousands were forced from their homes as fighting raged across the region. When revolution swept the Russian Empire, the Ukrainians formed an independent parliament, the Rada, at Kiev and demanded the status promised Poland and Finland—wide autonomy within a restructured, democratic Russia. The revolutionary government rejected their demand for autonomy, because it was believed that the war effort would collapse without Ukraine's grain, coal, and other important resources. The overthrow of the Russian Provisional Government by the small Bolshevik faction in October 1917 ended Ukrainian efforts to win autonomy within a reconstituted Russia.

The new Bolshevik government of Russia, desperate for peace in the west while fighting the anti-Bolshevik White Russian forces in the spreading Russian Civil War, signed the Treaty of Breast-Litovsk that surrendered control of Poland, Lithuania, Latvia, Estonia, Ukraine, Belarus, and parts of the Caucasus. Nationalists in both Ukraine and Belarus organized and in early 1918 declared the independence of Ukrainian and Belarussian republics. Rival Bolshevik governments, supported by many local revolutionaries, were erected to offset the attraction of the nationalists. The Poles, having won their independence from the Russians and Austrians, also put forward claims to the western provinces of Ukraine and Belarus. Armies and guerrilla bands of every political stripe plundered the territories. By 1919 the Bolsheviks had defeated the nationalist forces in Ukraine and Belarus and had set up Soviet governments in both areas. Following the end of the war and the German-Austrian withdrawal, the Poles declared war on the new Soviet government. Polish forces stopped the Bolshevik advance and occupied western Belarus and the Ukrainian majority provinces of the defeated

Austro-Hungarian Empire. With the Soviet victory over the Whites in 1920 troops were freed for the Polish front. In July 1920 the Red Army began an offensive, retaking much territory. The Treaty of Riga, signed in March 1921, partitioned Belarus and Ukraine between the Polish and Soviet states, giving the Poles control of the mostly Roman Catholic provinces and allowing the Soviets to retain control of the majority Orthodox eastern regions. The new state of Czechoslovakia, formed from territory formerly part of the Austro-Hungarian Empire, incorporated Transcarpathian Ukraine as the province of Ruthenia.

## Finns and Karels

Finland, taken from Sweden in the early nineteenth century, and Karelia, long held by the Russians, formed the two most important Finnic territories in the northwestern part of the Russian Empire. Finland was granted the status of a semi-independent grand duchy in 1809. The Lutheran Finns, among the most advanced nations in the empire, had progressively lost the autonomy they had initially enjoyed under Russian rule. By the end of the nineteenth century, the czarist authorities had abolished the separate Finnish army, drafted Finns into the imperial forces, tried to impose Russian as the official language as in Karelia, and persecuted the Lutheran Church as part of the assimilation policy that stressed Russian Orthodoxy. Czar Nicholas II eliminated all meaningful power from the Finnish legislature in 1899. The Russian governor of Finland became a virtual dictator in the first decades of the twentieth century. The Karels, along with the smaller groups of Finnic peoples living in the region just east of Finland, although historically heavily influenced by Russian culture, looked to the more numerous Finns for protection, cultural support, and brotherhood. In 1899, as part of its crackdown on the Finnic peoples, new restrictions were placed on Karel culture and on cross-border ties to the Finns, including the smuggling of Finnish nationalist material.

Although estimated at 90 percent illiterate in 1905, the Finnic peoples had a long list of grievances that were increasingly voiced by the educated minority. When revolutionary activities spilled into the region in 1905, thousands rose to attack and burn Russian estates. Many rebels fled into the forests following a number of skirmishes with government troops. The last rebel bands held out for nearly two years. The reforms that accompanied the end of the 1905 revolution somewhat eased conditions. The first books were published in the local Finnic languages, accelerating the cultural rebirth that accompanied the national awakening of the various peoples.

Finns and Karels fought in the Russian Army during World War I, but many returned to their homes following the overthrow of the czarist autocracy in February 1917. The collapse of provincial governments threw the northwest into chaos; criminals and political exiles were freed in Karelia, and Finnish nationalists attempted to take control of both Finland and Karelia. Local Bolsheviks, following the coup in Russia in October 1917, fought nationalists for control. Civil war broke out in Finland, an offshoot of the spreading civil conflict in the rest of Russia. Protected by Finnish troops and British interventionist forces that landed to support the anti-Bolshevik Whites in the region; the Karels declared their homeland an autonomous state in May 1919. Following the Finns' declaration of independence on 17 June 1919, the Karels voted for union with the new Finnish state. When their attempts to join Finland were blocked, the Karels rebelled. A Karel congress voted for secession and independence from Russia. The Red Army moved into Karelia to suppress the secession movement, forcing many Karels to flee to Finland. The Karel region also became a Communist refuge for the many Finnish Bolsheviks who left Finland following their defeat in the Finnish civil war. In early 1921, the Karels rebelled and drove the Soviets from their region. The Karel leaders declared the independence of the Republic of Eastern Karelia on 21 April 1921. The Finns, exhausted by civil war and attempting to maintain a fragile peace with their aggressive Soviet neighbor, were unable to respond to the Karels' frantic pleas as the Red Army returned.

### Moldovans

The Moldovans remained Romanian in culture and language, closely related to the neighboring Romanians; however, Russian policy was to establish a Moldovan nationality separate from the Romanians. In the nineteenth century, immigration was sponsored by the Russian government as a policy to dilute the Romanian majority. Immigration nearly succeeded in submerging Romanian culture in the region. By the end of the nineteenth century, the Moldovan population of the Russian territory of Bessarabia had fallen from about 87 percent of the total in 1815 to less than 49 percent in 1900.

Bessarabia, at the turn of the twentieth century, was one of the most backward provinces in the Russian Empire, with a population that had the highest mortality rate in Europe. Ethnic tensions, exacerbated by the settlement of many non-Moldovans in the region, increased Moldovan support for nationalist calls for cultural and linguistic autonomy. The Romanian government, seeking to recover lands they claimed as part of the historic Romanian homeland, supported the growth of Moldovan nationalism as an anti-Russian movement. More militant groups called for the forced removal of all non-Moldovans without historic ties to the region. Russian government attempts to channel the growing nationalist sentiment in Moldova into the region's traditional anti-Semitism incited reoccurring violence. The worst example of the government-condoned pogroms took place in Kishinev, the regional capital, in 1903. Rioters, enflamed by government agents, tore into the city's Jewish quarter, killing and wounding hundreds. Anti-Semitism proved only a temporary distraction. Moldovan nationalism continued to gain strength, culminating in widespread disturbances during the Russian Revolution of 1905. A Moldovan uprising in early 1907 was cruelly crushed by czarist troops, who stayed to drive the nationalist movement underground.

The Russian Revolution of 1917 stirred long-dormant nationalist sentiment among the Moldovans. Although there was considerable sentiment for unification with Romania, the nationalists, seeing little attraction in backward, feudal Romania, established a national committee and called for autonomy, land reform, and the use of the Romanian language in the province within a projected democratic Russia. The turmoil of the Bolshevik takeover in October 1917 allowed nationalists to take control of the province, which was declared independent on 24 January 1918. Threatened by advancing Bolshevik troops, the nationalists changed their strategy and voted for a provisional unification with Romania in April 1918. In November 1918 the territory held by Moldovan and Romanian troops was formally joined to the Kingdom of Romania. The Austrian province of Bukovina, although with a mixed Ukrainian and Moldovan population, was also eventually turned over to Romania. At the Paris Peace Conference in 1920, the Allied powers recognized Romanian control of the Moldovan territories.

## Cossacks

The Cossacks, of mixed ethnic backgrounds, after three centuries of guarding Russia's frontiers, had emerged as a culturally distinct mobile military force personally loyal to the czar but not the Russian state. Often dispatched to crush rebellions in other parts of the vast empire, the Cossacks had become the feared "fist" of the czar. Decimated as elite military units during World War I, the Cossacks were increasingly used to control a restive civilian population. Freed of their oath of loyalty by the overthrow of the czar in early 1917, the Cossacks, particularly the three groups, or hordes, in the northern Caucasus region, the Don, Kuban, and Terek Cossacks, formed military governments under their own elected leaders. Virtually independent as Russia collapsed, the Cossack military units ensured that their territories, including the rich agricultural lands held in common but worked by non-Cossack tenants, remained calm amid the spreading chaos of the Russian Revolution and civil war.

The new Bolshevik government, after taking power in October 1917, as part of their land redistribution program, proclaimed the expropriation of the extensive Cossack holdings. The Cossacks reacted by declaring war on the Bolshevik government and forming alliances with the anti-Bolshevik White forces. Although the different Cossack hordes represented distinct ethnic backgrounds, usually Slav and influences from local ethnic groups, they historically identified with the Romanov dynasty as ethnic Russians. The events of 1917 emphasized the differences between the Cossacks and the Russians, particularly in language, with the mixed Cossack dialects being declared official in their homelands and in their civil and military structure. In early 1918 the three Cossack groups in the North Caucasus declared the independence of their territorial republics until such time as the Romanov dynasty should be restored. In 1919 the Cossack republics sent delegations to the Paris Peace Conference seeking recognition, but they failed to win Allied support. Close to victory in late 1919, the White offensive then faltered and began to collapse. In 1920 the Red Army overran the Don, Kuban, and Terek Cossack states. Determined to end the Cossack threat to Soviet control, the new rulers ended all traditional Cossack privileges, prohibited military training, banned the use of the Cossack language, and forbade all references to Cossack history or culture. The Cossacks officially disappeared, having been reclassified as ethnic Russians or Ukrainians.

## Soviet Consolidation

The Russian Empire, as the self-proclaimed protector of Europe's Slavic peoples, supported the Serbs against the Austrians following the assassination of the Austrian heir by a Serbian nationalist in 1914. Serbian defiance of Austrian demands set off a continental conflict that soon drew in all the major European powers. The Russian Empire, poorly prepared and cut off from its allies in the West, suffered calamitous military defeats and thousands of deaths. Corruption, inflation, growing shortages, an exhausted and restive population, and poor morale among the front-line troops eventually led to revolution in February 1917, the overthrow of the czar, and the splintering of the Russian Empire. The disastrous civil war that followed the downfall of the monarchy ended with the victory of the Soviet forces, but during the upheavals many of the ethnic groups of the empire, taking advantage of the chaos, attempted to create independent states.

In 1920 the new Soviet state signed treaties recognizing the independence of the Baltic States, Estonia, Latvia, and Lithuania and the Transcaucasian states of Armenia, Georgia, and Azerbaijan. Of the other breakaway states established on the territory of the former Russian Empire, Finland and Poland, like the Baltic and Transcaucasian states, were recognized as independent nations. Ukraine, Belarus, the various republics established by Cossack groups, and breakaway states in Siberia, the Far East, and the North Caucasus had been overcome and their territories incorporated into the new Soviet Union. Moldova had been annexed by the neighboring Kingdom of Romania. The Bolsheviks established a new centralized state controlled by the Communist Party that was as tightly controlled and increasingly as oppressive as the former Russian Empire.

The growth of the nationalist ideal in Europe in the mid-nineteenth century resonated in the multinational Russian Empire. The various non-Russian ethnic groups, particularly those in the European territories of the empire, embraced nationalism as a means of saving threatened cultures and languages and of maintaining the dream of independence from Russia's harsh rule. World War I and its offshoot, the Russian Revolution, allowed many of these ethnic groups to briefly throw off hated Russian authority and to sample independence, although all but the Baltic states were reconquered by the Bolsheviks at the end of the Russian Civil War.

## Timeline

| | |
|---|---|
| 1900 | By the turn of the twentieth century Baku's oil fields are producing half the world's oil. |
| 1903 | The Trans-Siberian Railroad is finished, bringing a massive influx of colonists from central Russia to the Volga River basin and on into Siberia. |
| 1904–1905 | The Russo-Japanese War takes place. Russian defeat leads to revolution. |
| 1905 | The Russian Revolution of 1905 erupts. Disorder spreads across European Russia, particularly to the territories of the ethnic minorities. |

| | |
|---|---|
| 1907 | The first opera house in the Muslim world opens in Baku. |
| 1914 | World War I begins in Europe. Universal conscription is begun, with exemptions for many of the national minorities, particularly the Muslim peoples suspected of sympathy with the Turkish Ottoman Empire. |
| 1916 | Anti-Russian rebellions, inspired by the attempted conscription into labor battalions of thousands of Muslims, spread across Central Asia. |
| 1917 | The February Revolution overthrows the czarist government. In October the Bolsheviks take control of the Russian state and withdraw from the war. Lenin becomes the leading political figure in Russia. A Ukrainian Soviet Republic is proclaimed to counter the claims to independence by Ukrainian nationalists. |
| 1918 | World War I ends. The Bolsheviks murder the last Romanov czar and his family. The Ukrainians, Armenians, Azeris, Estonians, Latvians, Georgians, Lithuanians, North Caucasians, Moldovans, and many other national groups declare their autonomy or even complete independence from Russia. Civil war sweeps across the former Russian Empire. The Transcaucasian Federation is proclaimed. |
| 1919 | The Soviet Union, desperate for peace, signs the peace treaties that formally end World War I. Russia loses its Polish territories, Finland, Estonia, Latvia, and Lithuania. Belarus and Ukraine are recognized as independent republics. The anti-Bolshevik Basmachi groups gain support across Central Asia. |
| 1920 | The Soviet Union recognizes the independence of Estonia, Latvia, Lithuania, Armenia, Azerbaijan, and Georgia, but with the defeat of the last White forces the Red Army reconquers the Caucasus. Numerous autonomous provinces, districts, and republics are established for the national groups within the new Soviet Union. |
| 1921 | The civil war in Russia ends with the consolidation of political power by the Bolsheviks. |

## Significant People, Places, and Events

ABKHAZ (ABKHAZIANS) Also known as Abkhazi or Apsua. A Caucasian nation whose homeland lies between the southern reaches of the Caucasus

Mountains and the Black Sea coast in the northwestern extension of the Republic of Georgia. The majority of the Abkhaz are Sunni Muslims, although a minority has adopted Christianity.

**AUTOCRACY** The system that evolved in czarist Russia under the Romanov dynasty. The Romanov czars, called autocrats, were absolute rulers, controlling the vast empire without the impediments of a constitution or parliament. Therefore the system was one of absolute power vested in the czar, the autocrat.

**BASMACHI** Members of guerrilla groups that formed in Central Asia following the Bolshevik coup in late 1917. Unreconciled to the Bolshevik's antireligious policies and harsh rule, thousands of Muslims joined the groups to fight the new government. Some of the Basmachi groups continued to fight until they were liquidated during the mid-1920s.

**BOLSHEVIKS** The more radical wing of the Social Revolutionary Party, although they formed only a small minority. The Bolsheviks were able to take control of the Russian government and to depose the Russian Provisional Government in October 1917. They later changed their name from Bolsheviks to Communists.

**COSSACKS** Various geographically distinct groups historically formed from runaway serfs, local tribal warriors, and military deserters. By the mid-nineteenth century Cossack hordes across the Russian Empire traded their military skills, often used to suppress national minorities, for autonomous rule. They swore loyalty to the czar, not the Russian state. Following the Russian Revolution and the overthrow of the czar, several of the Cossack hordes declared their independence and attempted to secede from the new Soviet state.

**FINLAND** A republic lying between Russia and Sweden on the Baltic Sea in northern Europe. Conquered by the medieval Swedes, Finland was taken by Russia and was established as a semi-independent grand duchy with the Russian czar carrying the title Grand Duke of Finland. During the revolution and civil war the Finns declared their independence, which was supported by the Allied powers.

**IDEL-URAL** The local name of the Volga-Ural region. Following the overthrow of the Russian Empire in 1917, the nationalities of the Volga region united in a shared autonomy, which they called Idel-Ural.

**KARELIA** The territory in northwestern Russia adjacent to Finland. The ancient inhabitants of Karelia, the Karels, are closely related to the Finns linguistically and culturally, but are mostly Russian Orthodox, whereas the Finns are overwhelmingly Protestant Lutherans.

**LEAGUE OF NATIONS** An international organization established by the treaties that ended World War I. Like its modern successor, the United

Nations, the League of Nations was founded to promote international peace and security.

**LENIN, VLADIMIR ILYICH** The first and most important of the revolutionary rulers of Russia following the 1917 revolution and the overthrow of the Romanov dynasty. Many of the ideals of the first years of the revolution were Lenin's, but his death in 1924 radically changed the direction of the leadership and brought Joseph Stalin to power.

**MENCHEVIKS** The more moderate and the most numerous of the adherents of the Social Revolutionary Party, the largest at the time of the Russian Revolution in February 1917. The Mencheviks were active in many areas, including the Caucasus and the Volga, until they were superseded and later destroyed by the Bolsheviks.

**MOLDOVA** The territory lying between Ukraine and Romania mostly lying between the Pruth and Dniester Rivers. Often referred to as Moldavia or Bessarabia, the territory formed a province of the Russian Empire from 1812 until the Russian Revolution in 1917.

**MOLDOVANS** Formerly called Moldavians. The Romanian-speaking inhabitants of the historic province of Bessarabia, now mostly included in the Moldovan republic. The dialectical and historical differences between the Moldovans and Romanians are mostly a fabrication of the former Soviet government.

**ORENBURG COSSACKS** The Cossack horde based in the southern part of traditional Bashkort territory in the province of Orenburg. During the Russian Revolution and the civil war that followed, the Orenburg Cossacks provided the majority of the troops to the anti-Bolshevik White forces in the region of the southern Urals and northern Kazakhstan.

**PARIS PEACE CONFERENCE** The international conference convened in Paris in 1919 to settle the outstanding disputes and demands that resulted from the various treaties signed between the Allies and the Central Powers.

**REDS** The supporters of the Russian Revolution often carried red flags, copied from the Paris Commune of 1871. The flags were later adopted as the official symbol of the new Soviet state, and red became the official color. The name was later applied to many Soviet institutions and places, such as the Red Army and Red Square.

**RUSSIAN PROVISIONAL GOVERNMENT** The first revolutionary government following the overthrow of the Romanov dynasty. The government continued to pursue the war against Germany and Austria, but lost support owing to factionalism and corruption. The government was overthrown and replaced by the Bolsheviks some eight months after its creation.

**RUSSO-JAPANESE WAR OF 1904–1905** An imperialistic conflict that grew out of the rivalry between the Russian and Japanese Empires in Korea and Manchuria. Russian belief that its armed forces were invincible led to an inflexible policy and assurances to the czar that a victory would head off the growing revolutionary threat in Russia. Russia's decisive defeat set off the events later called the Russian Revolution of 1905.

**SOVIET** A system of local councils elected from among workers and soldiers following the outbreak of the Russian Revolution in 1917. Local Soviets often competed with nationalist groups or rival political organizations for power as civil administration collapsed in many areas.

**STALIN, JOSEPH** Popularly called Stalin, meaning steel, he was one of the original revolutionary leaders in 1917. He was one of Lenin's trusted lieutenants and for a time was given responsibility for national minorities. In 1924, following Lenin's death, Stalin defeated all rivals and took control of the Communist Party and the Soviet Union.

**TRANSCAUCASIAN FEDERATION** A federation of the three Transcaucasian states of Armenia, Azerbaijan, and Georgia, formed for mutual protection following the Bolshevik coup in late 1917. The federation collapsed soon after because of the ongoing enmity between the Christians and Muslims, particularly the Armenians and Azeris. A second Soviet federation was formed from the same three territories following the Bolshevik conquest of the region in 1920–1921.

**WHITES** The anti-Bolshevik opposition, mostly made up of the persecuted middle and upper classes, Cossacks, and part of the Russian military, took the name Whites during the Russian Civil War of 1918–1920 in opposition to the Bolshevik Reds.

## Bibliography

Allsworth, Edward, ed. *Central Asia: One Hundred Thirty Years of Russian Dominance: A Historical Overview.* Durham: Duke University Press, 1994.

Bacon, Elizabeth E. *Central Asians under Russian Rule: A Study in Cultural Change.* Ithaca, NY: Cornell University Press, 1980.

Baron, Salo W. *The Russian Jew under Tsars and Soviets.* New York: Macmillan, 1964.

Bradley, J. F. N. *Civil War in Russia, 1917–1920.* London: Batsford, 1975.

Bremmer, Ian, and Ray Taras, eds. *Nations and Politics in the Soviet Successor States.* New York: Cambridge University Press, 1993.

Hiden, John, and Patrick Salmon. *The Baltic Nations and Europe: Estonia, Latvia and Lithuania in the Twentieth Century.* New York: Longman, 1994.

Magocsi, Paul Robert. *A History of Ukraine.* Toronto: University of Toronto Press, 1996.

Pipes, Richard. *The Formation of the Soviet Union: Communism and Nationalism, 1917–1923.* Cambridge, MA: Harvard University Press, 1964.

Wolfson, Zeyev. *The Geography of Survival.* London: M. E. Sharpe, 1994.

Zaprudnik, Jan. *Historical Dictionary of Belarus.* Westport, CT: Greenwood, 1998.

# CHAPTER FIVE

# Consolidation of Soviet Power, 1920–1938

THE ONSET OF WORLD WAR I IN 1914 exposed the feudal nature and the widespread discontent that undermined the Russian Empire. As the war dragged on and hardships mounted, many political organizations emerged throughout the empire. The organizations represented a wide range of political opinion, from moderate reformists to radical leftists, with openly nationalist groups agitating for greater rights for the non-Russian peoples of the tottering empire. Opposition to conscription, widespread corruption, inept leadership, and military setbacks further enflamed opposition to the Romanov dynasty. In February 1917 revolution broke out, leading to the abdication of the last Romanov czar. The establishment of a weak democratic regime stirred the growth of political factions, including a small, radical group known as the Bolsheviks. In October 1917, the Bolsheviks led a coup against the Russian government and in the confusion that followed attempted to take control of the country. Desperate to consolidate their hold on the vast territories of the Russian Empire, the Bolsheviks withdrew Russia from the war and signed peace treaties with the Central Powers that recognized Russia's loss of many of the western provinces. Across the enormous territory of the collapsing Russian state ethnic and national groups established governments to fill the vacuum left by the disappearing civil authorities. As chaos spread, a number of national groups declared their homelands independent of Russia.

The Russian Civil War, pitting the Bolsheviks, called the Reds, against the forces of the former Russian Empire, the Whites, continued in many parts of the collapsed empire from 1918 to 1920. The non-Russian ethnic and national groups were often courted as military allies by both sides, including promises by the Reds of independence in a federation of independent Soviet states. By 1921 the last White units had been defeated and the power of Lenin and his Bolshevik faction had been consolidated. The breakaway states in the Caucasus, the western provinces, and Siberia were reconquered, with the exception of the Polish and western Ukrainian territories, which became part of the new Polish republic, Moldova, annexed by Romania, and Finland and the Baltic republics that managed to retain their independence. Uprising by national groups demanding the promised independence or opposed to the Bolsheviks' antireligious stance continued in many areas. Under Lenin's nationalities program the many non-Russian ethnic groups of the former Russian Empire were to be under central government control but were to be allowed considerable autonomy within national territories, designated as autonomous republics, provinces, regions, and districts.

## Soviet Consolidation

The Bolshevik revolution and the establishment of Soviet power brought even greater changes to the Slav and non-Slav ethnic groups of the new Soviet Union. Although the new leaders talked about self-determination for the non-Russian peoples, their real concerns were with class divisions, not with ethnic affairs, so even the most liberal of the new leaders viewed ethnic self-government as only a transitional stage toward Soviet assimilation. Russian colonization, during the nineteenth century, had spread Russian populations and culture throughout the vast expanse of the Russian Empire. The Soviet government believed the spread of the Russian culture and language made assimilation inevitable.

Lenin's proposal for a mosaic of self-governing territories as the way to involve the non-Russian peoples in the creation of the new Soviet state was the ideal followed during the first years of Bolshevik rule. The consolidation of Soviet power was accompanied by the creation of numerous autonomous districts, regions, and republics that, in theory, offered the numerous non-Russian peoples of the new Soviet Union a considerable degree of autonomy. Republics like Ukraine were initially treated as sovereign Soviet republics, with several treaties regulating relations between them and the Soviet Russian state. Lenin envisioned benign, local nationalisms as the cornerstone of a multinational, multiethnic, and multireligious Soviet state. Lenin's nationalities policies were particularly generous to the larger national groups on the fringes of Soviet territory. The new Soviet government, recognizing the loss of territory in the west, signed peace agreements with Poland, Lithuania, Latvia, Estonia, and Finland, similar to those granting Soviet recognition to the Transcaucasian states of Armenia, Azerbaijan, and Georgia. Efforts to regain control of the breakaway republics were ultimately successful in the Caucasus, but Poland, Finland, and the Baltic republics retained their newly won independence. Under Lenin's leadership, a union of the

*A leading member of the Bolshevik Party during the Russian Revolution, Joseph Stalin became the successor to Vladimir Lenin as the leader of the Soviet Union. Stalin led his country through the formative years of its existence, through World War II, and finally through the early years of the Cold War. (Library of Congress)*

nominally independent states, the Russian Federation, Ukraine, Belarus, and the Transcaucasian Federation, made up of Armenia, Azerbaijan, and Georgia, was formed through a series of interstate treaties in 1922. The new union, called the Union of Soviet Socialist Republics (USSR), although theoretically a union of four equal states, increasingly developed as a dictatorship dominated by the ethnic Russian leadership of the Communist Party. Joseph Stalin, named people's commissar for nationalities in the Soviet cabinet, became increasingly powerful in the early 1920s. Although suspicious of national sentiment and local loyalties, he oversaw Lenin's national policies, which established dozens of autonomous national territories for the major ethnic groups. Initially activists organized literacy classes, invented alphabets for nonliterary peoples, and fostered cultural development.

Lenin's lingering illness, which began in 1922, allowed Stalin, elected general secretary of the central committee of the Communist Party, to control the membership of the party and to construct an apparatus within the party loyal to him. When Lenin died in 1924 Stalin battled for power against the other leaders of the Communist Party, finally consolidating his hold after ruthlessly eliminating his rivals. Stalin quickly dismantled Lenin's creation. Despite the trappings of local autonomy at republic, regional, or district levels, by the early 1920s only limited cultural and linguistic freedoms were allowed and all positions of power in the minority areas were held by reliable members of the Communist Party, mostly ethnic Russians. Following the death of Lenin in 1924 even this limited autonomy was abrogated. The new leader of the Soviet Union, Joseph Stalin, as he was known in the West, remained highly suspicious of the loyalties of the many nationalities of the Soviet state and attempted, by often brutal methods, to eliminate all loyalties except to the Soviet state and the Communist Party. His efforts to replace national loyalties with a homogenous Soviet nationality cost the lives of millions of Soviet citizens.

Stalin's hold on power was accompanied by shifts in national policy and a cynical manipulation of the aspirations of the country's many national groups for his own purposes. Like the leadership of the former Russian Empire, the leaders of the new Soviet government were drawn from the traditional center of power, the ethnic Russian heartland in European Russia. The many national minorities, although often benefiting from early Soviet cultural and educational policies, were again politically suppressed. Assimilation policies similar to those of the czarist regime stressed the homogenization of the population of the new Soviet Empire and the disappearance of all ethnic and national identifications except that of the government's newly fabricated Soviet identity. Soviet culture, based on the Russian language and culture, was glorified, and traditional national cultures were vilified as anti-Communist and revisionist. Periodic purges of the party leaders in Moscow and the leaderships of the autonomous territories ensured that no power centers would develop that could oppose Stalin's authority.

## Ukrainians

Lenin's attempt to moderate Ukrainian nationalist sentiment through a measure of cultural and political autonomy was abandoned following his death and Stalin's rise to power. Stalin was suspicious of the Ukrainians' continued opposition to assimilation, viewing it as an affront to his ideal of the new Soviet man, and he determined to crush the rebellious Ukrainians for all time. He imposed strict controls, eliminated the national leadership, and forced collectivization of the rich Ukrainian agricultural sector. The policy of collectivization instituted by Stalin in 1929 to finance industrialization had a cataclysmic effect on agricultural productivity. Nevertheless, in 1932 Stalin raised Ukraine's grain procurement quotas by 44 percent. This meant that there would not be enough grain to feed the peasants, since agricultural law required that no grain from a collective farm could be given to the members until the government's quota was met. Stalin's decision and the brutal methods used to implement it condemned millions of Ukrainian peasants to death by starvation. Party officials, with the aid of regular troops and secret police units, waged an unrelenting war of attrition against peasants who refused to give up their grain. Even indispensable seed grain was forcibly confiscated from peasant households. Any man, woman, or child caught taking even a handful of grain from a collective farm could be executed or deported along with all family members. Those who did not appear to be starving were often suspected of hoarding grain. Peasants were prevented from leaving their villages by the secret police and a strict system of internal passports. An estimated 3 million people died during the brutal collectivization program between 1929 and 1932. Another 6 to 7 million perished as the result of Stalin's order to requisition all grain for export. The planned famine in Ukraine virtually depopulated whole districts. Millions more died in mass executions and in labor camps. Periodic purges between 1932 and 1937 eliminated the Ukrainian party leadership and all remaining opposition suspected of opposing the Stalinist policies. The purges decimated the political, cultural, and artistic elite of the Ukrainian nation.

In the western parts of historic Ukraine, incorporated into the new Polish republic in 1920, conditions were considerably less severe. Although denied the autonomy promised in the postwar treaties and settlements and under pressure to assimilate into Polish society, the western Ukrainians experienced material advances as Europe recovered from World War I in the 1920s. In 1922 the Polish government granted some limited autonomy, but agitation for separation of the Ukrainian territories from the Polish state continued. In 1932 the government disbanded the largest Ukrainian political party for advocating separatism. The Ukrainian problem in Poland was referred to the League of Nations, but without conclusive results. In the late 1930s periodic demonstrations were held in the Ukrainian provinces to support demands for the promised autonomy.

In 1920, the Paris Peace Conference recognized Ruthenia (Transcarpathian Ukraine) as part of Czechoslovakia on the condition that the inhabitants, who call themselves Carpatho-Rusyns, be granted broad autonomy. The terms of the autonomy agreement were quickly abrogated. Czechoslovakia's highly centralized government took direct control of most administrative functions and gave most local government positions to ethnic Czechs. The Carpatho-Rusyns suffered much less oppression than their Ukrainian kin in other states, particularly in the Soviet Union, but the promised autonomy was never delivered.

## Belarussians

The Belarussians, although with a weaker sense of nationhood than the neighboring Ukrainians, mobilized to oppose the occupation of their territory by various armies and factions during World War I and the subsequent civil war in Russia. Belarus was devastated during the long Russian Civil War of 1918–1920 and the Soviet-Polish War of 1919–1920, which left the western Belarussian provinces under Polish control. In 1921 the eastern provinces constituted the Belarussian Soviet Socialist Republic, which became one of the constituent republics of the newly formed Union of Soviet Socialist Republics.

The forced collectivization of agriculture, as in Ukraine, resulted in the deaths of between 3 and 5 percent of the Belarussian population of the Soviet Union. The purges of the Stalinist era, especially devastating in 1929–1930 and 1933–1934, destroyed the surviving national and cultural leadership of the smallest of the eastern Slav nations. Belarussian nationalism, although brutally suppressed, continued as an underground ideal. In 1937 Stalin ordered the entire Belarussian government, including the president of the Belarussian Soviet Central Committee, to be liquidated on the suspicion that they supported the establishment of a united Belarussian republic to comprise both the Soviet and Polish zones. The victims of the ongoing Stalinist purges were buried in mass graves, which were later claimed by the Soviet government to be victims of World War II Nazi atrocities.

The Belarussians living in the Polish state, although free of the fear and panic of their Soviet kin, were also deprived of their national rights. Language and cultural restrictions closed Belarussian schools, and the language was forbidden in all Roman Catholic churches. In 1927 the Polish government cracked down on suspected Belarussian nationalists. Many were arrested and imprisoned. Despite earlier agreements to allow broad autonomy, a program of assimilation into Polish society was instituted.

## The Caucasus

Caught between Russian and Turkish forces during World War I, the Caucasian peoples had organized self-defense groups, often with nationalist orientation. The war in the region, seen as a war between Muslims and Christians, divided the Caucasian peoples into two loose groups, the pro-Turkish groups, mostly the Muslim peoples of the region, and the pro-Russians made up of the Christian nations, particularly the Armenians, Georgians, and Ossetians. By 1920 the Caucasian territories had been conquered by the advancing Red Army and their homelands incorporated into the new Soviet Union.

### Armenians

The victorious Soviets overran the eastern part of the Republic of Armenia in December 1920, proclaiming the region a Soviet republic. Soviet Armenia was joined to newly conquered Georgia and Azerbaijan in the Soviet Transcaucasian Federation, which joined the new USSR in December 1922. The defeated Armenians rebelled against the new Communist government in February 1921, while the Red Army was occupied with the conquest of neighboring Georgia. The rebels were soon defeated and a purge of all suspected anti-Soviet Armenians was begun. In 1923, Stalin, then commissar of nationalities, placed the largely Armenian-populated territory of Nagorno-Karabakh under the control of the Soviet government of Azerbaijan.

The Soviet task in Armenia was to build a Socialist Armenian state to attract immigrants and to compete with the powerful Armenian diaspora. Russian Armenia, under Soviet rule, was transformed from a largely agricultural economy into an industrial region. The Armenian national church, so much a part of Armenian culture, was persecuted, and antireligious propaganda proliferated. Literacy and education were advanced, and women were encouraged to break the traditional domination of men. National culture was encouraged by Lenin and continued as the official policy after his death. Communist Armenian leaders defended the Armenian language, literature, and history. Diaspora Armenians were invited to "repatriate," and thousands responded. Some were immediately imprisoned as spies, but most were given homes and jobs, although many later left the Soviet Union at the first opportunity. The Soviet government encouraged local Armenian culture until Stalin reversed the policy in 1934.

The Soviet government, particularly following the ascension of Stalin as the supreme leader in 1924, remained acutely suspicious of the Armenians and their ties to the large Armenian diaspora in Europe, the Americas, and the Middle East. Men loyal to Stalin and his minions were installed in the Armenian capital, Yerevan, and effectively ruled until 1953. Periodic purges, ordered by Stalin and the Soviet leadership during the 1920s and 1930s, eliminated all potential leaders along with influential writers, intellectuals, and professionals. Armenian leaders acceptable to Stalin gradually began to convince the Armenians of the benefits of communism. The Transcaucasian Federation was dissolved in 1936, and Armenia became a separate member state of the Soviet Union. The Armenian national leadership, suspected of deviation from Stalin's wishes, was again purged in 1936–1938. Russians from the central Soviet bureaucracy were imported to replace the Armenians.

### Georgians

The new Georgian republic signed a peace treaty with Soviet Russia in May 1920. This treaty was quickly set aside as the Red Army, having conquered neighboring Armenia and Azerbaijan, crossed the border into Georgia in February 1921. The Georgians' frantic pleas for military aid were ignored by the Allies. In April 1921 the Georgians surrendered and a Soviet Republic of Georgia was proclaimed. In 1922 Soviet Georgia joined Armenia and Azerbaijan in the Transcaucasian Soviet Federated Socialist Republic, which was incorporated into the USSR as a constituent republic.

Many of the fiercely anti-Soviet Georgians, particularly following the repression of their ancient Christian religion, continued to resist Soviet power. In 1924 the last rebel groups were liquidated, with as many as 4,000 executed and many more deported or imprisoned. The ascension of Stalin as leader of the Soviet Union in 1924, himself an ethnic Georgian, might have given some Georgians the hope of lenient treatment or even special status within the new Soviet Union, but the more Stalin supported the ideal of the homogenization of the nations into the new Soviet identity the less he identified with his Georgian roots. The Stalinist purges of the late 1920s and the 1930s took as high a toll in Georgia as elsewhere. Stalin dissolved the Transcaucasian Federation in 1936, making Georgia a constituent republic of the

USSR. From 1936 until Stalin's death in 1953, Soviet Georgia was under the personal domination of Lavrenty Beria, one of Stalin's most trusted allies. Under Beria's firm grip, the Georgians were as tightly controlled by Moscow as any other national group in the Soviet Union.

Under Soviet rule, the Georgians experienced rapid industrialization and urbanization. The largest of the republic's non-Georgian nations were given autonomous territories as in other parts of the USSR. The Muslim majority Abkhaz and Ajars, culturally and historically more closely related to the neighboring Caucasian peoples than to the Christian Georgians, and the Ossetians, part of the larger Ossetian population of Iranian origin in the Russian Federation, were given autonomous status over Georgian objections. Stalin's suspicion that the Muslim populations of the Soviet Union continued to revere their Islamic religion more than the official Soviet ideal meant that they often suffered proportionally higher losses from the periodic purges than did the non-Muslim ethnic groups.

## Azeris

The economic importance of Azerbaijan prior to World War I had exposed the Azeris to urbanization and Western education, with an accompanying growth of Azeri national consciousness, which gained support during the chaos and violence of the civil war. Under Soviet control Azerbaijan was the third partner in the Soviet Transcaucasian Federation, which joined the new Soviet Union in 1922. Oil from the region began to flow to Soviet Russia to pay for war damage and the planned industrialization.

Azeri nationalism, severely suppressed under Soviet rule, shifted to the large Azeri population of neighboring Persian Azerbaijan. Many Azeri nationalists fled across the border to escape the Red Army but were later hounded by Iranian forces. Periodic purges eliminated all potential opposition to the consolidation of Soviet power in Soviet Azerbaijan in the early 1920s. Stalin viewed boundaries based on ethnic lines as too nationalist, therefore he established Nagorno-Karabakh, which was 80 percent Armenian and a center of Armenian resistance to Soviet rule, as an autonomous province of Azerbaijan and formed Nakhichevan, which lay along the Iranian border separated from Azerbaijan by a strip of Armenian territory, as an autonomous republic within Azerbaijan. These divisions formed the basis of an ongoing conflict between the Azeris and the Armenians that continues to the present. Once Soviet control was firmly established, a policy of Slavic colonization was begun. The region, rich in oil and natural gas and predominately Muslim, was treated differently from Armenia or Georgia. Resistance to Soviet polity resulted in the first purge of a local leadership in the Caucasus in 1921. A widespread purge of the Azeri national elite followed an uprising in 1924. Another purge decimated the region in 1930 when Stalin accused the Azeri leadership of supporting "bourgeois-nationalist" elements within the local party structure.

According to Soviet planning, the Azeris were to be the means for spreading communism to the neighboring Muslim states of the Middle East. Under Soviet rule an extensive and successful literacy program was begun. As literacy increased, religious influence decreased. Islamic influence was gradually reduced through educational and cultural programs until 1928, when a more direct attack was launched. Stalin dissolved the Transcaucasian Federation in 1936, making Azerbaijan a separate republic of the USSR. A series of purges at the same time culminated in 1937 with the elimination of all the religious-cultural leadership as well as many of the top Azeri Soviet officials.

The Soviet policy of atheism prohibited public manifestations of the Islamic religion. Of the "five pillars" of Islam, four were forbidden. Thousands of mosques and religious schools were closed. The month of fasting (Ramadan) was no longer possible owing to official suppression and the emphasis on work schedules. Only a token number of pilgrims were allowed to make the annual visit to Mecca. Although the Soviet authorities believed that they had eradicated Islam, the persistence of many Islamic traditions indicated that a strong underground belief system remained. An unwanted byproduct of the Soviet suppression of the Muslim religion in the region was the strengthening of the secular Azeri nationalist sentiment even as their Muslim identity was prohibited.

## The North Caucasians

The Soviet victory in the civil war brought the Red Army into the North Caucasus, where the Soviets' antireligious stance was particularly resented. Banditry and sporadic murders of ethnic Russians continued in the early 1920s, often blamed on Muslim fanatics. Lenin's nationalities policies dictated the formation of the Mountain Autonomous Republic soon after the Russian Revolution, with Arabic as the official language. Ethnic tensions among the many small Caucasian groups quickly brought the end of the autonomous republic, which was replaced by various autonomous provinces in 1921–1922.

Islam remained an important part of most North Caucasian cultures even after the imposition of Soviet rule. At first the Soviets tolerated the Muslim religion as necessary during the period of Communist consolidation. In 1925 the government, feeling that its control was firm, launched an intensive anti-Islamic campaign. The campaign closed all Islamic schools, ended the use of the Arabic language, and summarily executed many local religious leaders. Resistance to the regime's abolition of organized religion and the policy of Russification instituted by Stalin in the late 1920s was widespread, with the most militant being the Chechens, Ingush, and the Dagestani peoples. In the late 1920s, the Soviets conducted a concentrated anti-Islamic campaign, including widespread imprisonment and execution of Caucasian religious leaders. During the 1930s a cult was formed with cells across the Muslim regions of the Caucasus, based on the belief that Kunta Haji, a legendary Chechen leader, would return to earth to usher in an era of Islamic righteousness and Sharia law.

The Soviet effort to separate the Caucasian Muslim peoples from the large Muslim population in the Middle East included manipulation of education and literary systems. Attempts were made to Latinize the local Caucasian languages in the early 1930s, but the languages were then switched to the Russian Cyrillic alphabet in 1938. At the same time, Russian became the only language of instruction in all public schools. In addition to trying to Sovietize the Caucasian cultures, the Soviet government also manipulated the local economies. Traditionally, the Caucasian peoples worked the land as farmers or lived as communal livestock herders. The Soviet authorities converted the communities and communal groups into economic collectives, with the government owning all the land and the herds.

Stalin was particularly suspicious of the loyalties of the small Muslim nations of the Caucasus region. Collectivization of agriculture and animal herds provoked sporadic uprisings during the early 1930s. Owing to Stalin's antipathy, the reprisals and purges that followed each confrontation were often brutal. Whole families were executed, others were arrested and deported to remote parts of Siberia or Central Asia. In the late 1930s ethnic boundaries were redrawn, with the official territories set aside for the Muslim peoples often surrounded by lands with Slavic majorities.

## The Crimean Tatars

Crimean Tatar resistance to Soviet authority became a serious threat in 1920–1921. The Soviet leaders decided to reach an accommodation with the nationalists in 1921. A general amnesty was extended to the anti-Soviet Crimean Tatars, and the peninsula was organized as an autonomous republic within the Russian Federation. Initially the Crimean Tatars benefited from the autonomy offered under Lenin's policies. Education and cultural affairs were encouraged, and the Latin alphabet was adopted for the Crimean Tatar language, facilitating cultural exchanges with the Turks and Tatars living in Turkey. In spite of Soviet concessions, continued resistance to Soviet rule brought charges of "bourgeois nationalism" and revisionist crimes. Many Crimean Tatar leaders were executed or imprisoned, others fled to Turkey.

The initial collectivization of Crimean Tatar agriculture in 1921 led to mass starvation. The situation became even more devastating after the Crimea's food supplies were confiscated and shipped to central Russia. More than 100,000 Crimean Tatars starved to death, and tens of thousands fled abroad. During the collectivization campaign of 1928–1929, thousands more were deported or executed. The collectivization of agriculture led to another famine in the early 1930s. Between 1917 and 1933, an estimated 150,000 Crimean Tatars—about half the ethnic population—had been killed, deported, or fled. Increased oppression followed the famine, with many Crimean Tatar leaders purged for protesting the slaughter. In 1938, in yet another attempt to accelerate the assimilation of the surviving Crimean Tatars, the Soviets replaced the Latin alphabet with a Cyrillic script. At the same time most Crimean Tatar literature was completely banned. The Crimean Tatars suffered proportionally greater population losses than any other Soviet national group during the first decades of Soviet rule.

## The Baltic Peoples

The Soviet government recognized the independence of the Baltic states of Estonia, Latvia, and Lithuania in 1920, but continued to meddle in the internal politics of the three small states. During the 1920s the Baltic peoples increasingly supported right-wing political parties, often because of their fears of their giant Soviet neighbor. In spite of continued political instability the three states prospered. The Baltic peoples attempted to steer a course between the powerful Soviet Union and a resurgent Germany during the 1930s. The devastation of World War I had made the Russians wary of Germany, particularly under the militant Nazis. Soviet policy was to create a buffer in eastern and northeastern Europe between the Soviet homeland and the resurgent Germans. The small Baltic states, with their valuable ports and their historic ties to Russia, were seen as prime candidates for incorporation into the Soviet state.

## Estonians

During the 1920s, right-wing political parties gained support at the expense of the centrists who led Estonia to independence. The illegal Communist Party, aided by the Soviet government, attempted a coup in late 1924, further complicating the political life of the republic. Following the failure of the Communist coup, the left lost even more support and the right-wing parties gained support. However, despite political uncertainties, tiny Estonia prospered. Education was near universal, the economy flourished, and the standard of living soon equaled that of prosperous Finland.

The worldwide depression further destabilized the country. In an effort to steady the economy and calm political upheavals, authoritarian rule was instituted. The orientation toward Great Britain, a mainstay since 1920, was abandoned in 1935 following a treaty between the British and Nazi Germany that placed the Baltic Sea region in Germany's sphere of influence. Isolated from the West, the Estonians turned to Nazi Germany in an effort to offset growing Soviet pressure. In December 1938 the Estonian government declared the republic officially neutral.

## Latvians

The Soviet Union grudgingly recognized the independence of Latvia in 1920, but instituted a policy of rejecting all contacts and trade with non-Communist Latvians. Cut off from Soviet raw materials, highly industrialized Latvia quickly reverted to an essentially agrarian economy. New property rights and laws and effective agrarian reform aided the growth of the Latvian economy based on agriculture and light manufacturing. By the early 1930s the Latvians enjoyed a prosperous lifestyle compared with the inhabitants of neighboring Soviet territory; however, with a mixed population and dozens of political parties, political stability eluded the new republic. The situation was aggravated by Latvia's position between the two spheres of power in 1930s Europe, the Soviet Union, and Nazi Germany.

In 1934, in an attempt to strengthen the government and put an end to the ongoing communal disputes, Latvia's president, Karlis Ulmanis, suspended the parliament and assumed dictatorial powers. He quickly banned all political parties and limited political activities. The slogan of his government, "Latvia for the Latvians," emphasized the exclusion of the important Baltic German and Russian minorities from Latvian society. The population of the Latvian state in 1935 included a very mixed population with large Russian, Jewish, and German communities and smaller Polish, Belarussian, and Lithuanian minorities.

## Lithuanians

Lithuania was recognized as an independent state in July 1920, but the small republic was immediately enmeshed in territorial disputes. In October 1920, Polish troops took control of the historically and economically important region that included Vilnius, the Lithuanian's ancient capital. The Lithuanian government, transferred to the second city, Kaunas, continued to lay claim to Vilnius, with renewed fighting between Lithuanian and Polish troops in 1922. The territorial dispute, taken to the League of Nations, was finally settled in Poland's favor. The disappointed Lithuanians then turned to Memel, called Klaipeda in Lithuanian, an area long claimed as Lithuanian territory that had formed part of German East Prussia until the end of World War I. The Lithuanians expelled the French occupation troops and annexed Memel and the surrounding area to the Lithuanian state.

By the mid-1920s the majority of the international community had recognized the independence and territorial extent of the Lithuanian state. Political turmoil continued to undermine stability. In December 1926 a military coup overthrew the government. The leader of the coup, Antanas Smetona, was proclaimed president and gradually introduced a highly authoritarian government. Like their Baltic neighbors, the Lithuanians remained isolated between the Soviet Union and Nazi Germany in the 1930s. The ongoing territorial dispute with Poland that continued throughout the 1930s further impaired attempts to create a stable, independent state.

## Jews

The Soviet victory in the civil war finally removed the harsh czarist restrictions on Jewish life. The new Soviet Union, with many of its Bolshevik leaders of Jewish origin, encouraged the Jews to participate in society. The Jews, recognized as a Soviet nationality rather than as a religious minority, gained cultural and linguistic support from the new state even though the Bolsheviks suppressed the Jewish religion. Lenin opposed the Jewish religion and was against Zionism but supported cultural autonomy as part of his concept of Soviet internationalism. The revolution ended the Pale of Settlement and permitted Jews to live anywhere they wished, although the majority of the Jews remained in their traditional regions. The Jews were particularly interested in higher education as a means to advance in the new Soviet state. The czarist authorities had greatly hindered educational access for Jews, and quotas had limited their access to the best universities.

The nonreligious autonomy allowed the Jews under Soviet rule extended to the use of the Yiddish language. An estimated 97 percent of the Jewish population spoke Yiddish in 1897. By 1930, more than half of all Jewish children were studying in Yiddish-language schools. This led to a flowering of Yiddish-language publications and arts, including state-supported Yiddish theater. Until the Stalinist purges of the 1930s, Jews were represented in the Communist Party in disproportionate numbers, particularly in the higher echelons. When anti-Semitic Stalin took control of the Soviet government, things began to change once again for the Soviet Jews. In an effort to gather all Jews in one area, a resettlement region was set aside in the Soviet Far East. The regime encouraged Jews to settle there, but it never developed as an important Jewish center, because it was far from the major Jewish population centers in European Russia. The territory was established as the Jewish Autonomous Region in 1934 although no mass Jewish migration was undertaken. Birobidzhan, the so-called Jerusalem on the Amur, had a population mostly of Russians and Ukrainians. After 1930, renewed repression ended the attempt to lure overseas Jews to the official homeland. Foreign Jews were arrested as spies and many were deported. The Jewish schools, the synagogues, and the Jewish libraries were closed, and Hebrew and Yiddish publications were banned. The initial cultural autonomy granted the Jews had mostly been rescinded by the early 1930s. The Stalinist purges greatly reduced the participation of the Jewish intelligentsia in the political life of the Soviet Union.

## The Volga Nations

In the aftermath of the Russian civil war and the establishment of Soviet power in the Volga region, many nationalists in the region supported the creation of a single, autonomous Soviet Volga-Ural state. The state idea, which would have included the Tatars, Bashkorts, Chuvash, Maris, and Mordvins, was never accepted by the Soviet authorities because of suspect local nationalisms and Bashkort opposition to inclusion in a Tatar-dominated government. Instead various autonomous provinces and republics were established, although their boundaries were often manipulated to include large Slav, mostly Russian, populations. During the 1920s, the local national leaders, under the guise of communism, worked to build local nationalisms with underground societies and campaigns for political autonomy. Manifestations of nationalism throughout the region were finally ended with an extensive purge of the national leaderships during the late 1920s and 1930s, at the same time as collectivization was instituted. Local cultural organizations, publishing houses, and educational institutions were shut down. As part of its assimilation policy, accompanied by rapid industrialization and an influx of ethnic Slavs, Russian was made the only medium of instruction in the late 1930s.

### Bashkorts

The Bashkorts, promised independence within a Soviet federation of sovereign states, went over to the Reds during the civil war in March 1918. Treated as a conquered people following the Soviet advance into the Volga region, they eventually rebelled. The Red Army attacked the rebels in 1920 but was unable to conquer the fierce Bashkort warriors. A policy of burning crops and farms to deny the rebels finally took its toll. The starving Bashkort rebels surrendered in 1922. The Bashkort nation lost about a third of its prewar population in the suppression of the breakaway republic, the chaos of the Russian Civil War, and the imposition of Soviet rule. Crop failure and famine in 1920–1921 added to the rising death toll. Many Bashkorts remained nomadic until forced collectivization in the early 1930s. Thousands died resisting the end of their traditional way of life. Former nomads were forced to settle in permanent villages or were transported to towns with new industries and large Slavic populations. Oil was discovered in the region in 1932, making the Bashkort homeland the leading petroleum producer for the struggling Soviet Union.

The northern part of their traditional homeland, known as Little Bashkiria, comprising the province of Ufa, was formed as an autonomous republic within the Russian Federation in March 1922, the first erected for an ethnic group within the Soviet Russian Federation. The southern part of historic Bashkiria, the province of Orenburg, was left out of the new autonomous republic over vehement Bashkort protests. The new government of the Bashkort republic as constituted by the Soviet authorities lacked even one ethnic Bashkort in a position of authority. The Bashkorts increasingly aligned themselves with the more numerous Tatars during the 1930s, and many began to assimilate into the related Tatar culture.

## Tatars

After the Bolshevik Revolution, the Tatars played an important roll in establishing communism in the Volga region; however, the positive relationship between the Volga Tatars and the new Soviet government was not to last. During the 1920s, local leaders, although nominally loyal to the Soviet regime, worked to build Tatar nationalism. The so-called Tatar Communist national movement worked for the creation of an independent Turkic state to be called Turin, with territory stretching from the middle Volga to Azerbaijan and the North Caucasus. The suppression of the Islamic religion became an important task of the loyal party members sent to the region to root out all cultural and religious manifestations.

Although the Tatars constituted one of the largest non-Russian ethnic groups in the new Soviet Union, they were not granted the status of a union republic like those of the other large nationalities. Feared and hated since the Mongol-Tatar conquest of Russia, the Tatars were not trusted by the new Soviet rulers. Joseph Stalin reportedly quipped that the Tatars had as much chance of achieving union republic status as of seeing their ears. The Tatar homeland, its boundaries manipulated to include large Slav populations and only about a third of the ethnic Tatars, was made an autonomous republic within the Russian Federation with only limited powers of self-government. Mass purges periodically eliminated any potential leaders and most of the intelligentsia during the 1920s and 1930s.

## Germans

The Germans of the Soviet Union, initially held up as a model for the spread of communism to Germany, suffered harsh suppression in the early 1920s. The showcase Volga German Autonomous Republic, established within the Russian Federation, was the home of more than one-quarter of all Germans in the Soviet Union and the focus of much of the German cultural and intellectual life. The establishment of the German homeland in the Volga reflected the gradual Soviet realization that national differences continued to exist and could not be immediately eliminated in the name of "worker solidarity." As relations between the Soviet Union and Germany worsened during the 1920s and early 1930s, the repression of the Soviet Germans increased. Collectivization was particularly harsh, because many of the Germans were small farmers who owned their own lands. As landowners they were considered social parasites and were brutally eliminated. Many others fell victim to the purges of counterrevolutionaries and other suspected opponents of the Soviet system.

## Moldovans

The Soviet government refused to recognize the separation of the Moldovan homeland, Bessarabia, from Russia or the Romanian annexation of the territory. In September 1921 the Soviet government declared war on Bessarabia, which led to skirmishing along the Dniester frontier. The territory east of the Dniester, with its large Moldovan minority, conquered by the Red Army in 1918, was organized as an autonomous republic within Ukraine in 1924 with Tiraspol as its capital. The small Moldovan autonomous republic was organized to propagate communism in Romania and to develop an effective Romanian-speaking Communist elite. The Soviet government initially recognized no difference between Moldovans and Romanians. The first publications in the autonomous republic were printed in Romanian with the Latin script. In the late 1920s, the Russian Cyrillic alphabet was introduced as the official script of the "native" language of the Moldovans. The first Soviet census in 1926 registered the Moldovans as ethnic Romanians. Later Soviet publications "adjusted" the census figures to describe the overwhelming majority of the Romanians counted in 1926 as ethnic Moldovans. The Moldovans formed less than a third of the population of the autonomous republic, which was effectively run by Russian and Ukrainian party functionaries. Suppression of the Moldovans' traditional Romanian culture and language increased in a heavy-handed and brutal campaign during the 1930s.

The annexed Moldovan heartland, the historic provinces of Bessarabia and Bukovina, was treated as a semiagricultural colony under Romanian rule. Powerful Romanian landlords, who moved into the region soon after the annexation, controlled large estates granted by the Romanian government. During the 1920s and 1930s the Moldovans were increasingly dissatisfied with Romanian rule. The region, more developed than most of Romania in 1918, became one of the most backward regions of the Romanian kingdom, and probably the most corrupt, by 1930. The Romanian government, fearing future conflicts with its Soviet neighbor, refused to build roads or maintain communication links in the region, which quickly reverted to subsistence farming or to the political control of absentee Romanian land-lords who controlled large estates worked by Moldovan peasants.

## Siberia and the Far East

The Siberian and Far Eastern territories, although far from the Russian heart-land in European Russia, were devastated when Soviet control was finally es-tablished in the early 1920s. Foreign interventionist forces landed in the Far East and stayed in the region until 1922. The Soviet nationalities policies were applied to the huge area, which was divided into normal provinces with mostly Slav populations and a number of autonomous republics, territories, and districts set aside for the non-Slavic populations, but usually with boundaries that ensured Slav majorities in the populations. The populations of the Siberian ethnic groups declined rapidly. Thousands of shamans and other ethnic leaders, targets of Stalinist repression, were eliminated or dis-appeared into the system of forced labor camps. Cultural organizations, eth-nic schools, and publications in local languages, many established in the first years of Soviet rule, were banned or closed. Assimilation into Russian cul-ture and language, in the guise of Soviet nationalism, paralleled the earlier czarist policies in the region.

Historically populated by non-Russian peoples and political or criminal deportees from European Russia, Siberia again became a center for the re-settlement of deported populations. Forced labor camps spread across the sparsely populated territories, many set up for the deported national elites of ethnic groups that had resisted the Soviet conquest or collectivization. The system of labor and prison camps, known as the gulag, swallowed up mil-lions of Soviet citizens convicted or suspected of anti-Soviet or anti-Stalin views. The Soviet government treated Siberia and the Far East as colonies to be exploited. Drawing on the millions exiled to the infamous gulag, the So-viets used slave labor for mines and the construction of railroads, dams, and cities. The region's enormous natural resources propelled the Soviet Union to great power status, but the living and working conditions of the ordinary Siberians barely attained the levels of colonial Africa during the 1930s.

## Altai

Partly as a punishment for Altai support of the Whites during the civil war, the Soviet authorities designated the Altai Steppe a Slavic resettlement area.

The designation restricted the Altai tribes to the small, newly created autonomous province in the southern Altai Mountains, the Oirot Autonomous Oblast. Soviet industrialization of the region brought a massive influx of Slavic settlers, reducing the Altai to just 50 percent of the total population by 1930. The Altai religion, Burkhanism, and Altai nationalism were tolerated until a crackdown in 1933, when both were denounced as an anti-Soviet conspiracy.

Assimilation policies, similar to those of the earlier czarist regime, were implemented. The Soviets supplemented the traditional Altai alphabet with several Russian characters in 1922 in an effort to convey accurately the growing number of words borrowed directly from Russian. As Soviet policies hardened, the Altai alphabet was replaced with the Latin script in 1931, but in 1938 the Russian Cyrillic alphabet was officially adopted for all the Altai dialects. The small Altai nation, under intense pressure to abandon their traditional culture, devastated by war, and forced to settled and collectivize during the 1930s, began to rapidly decline and to lose population. Alcohol abuse became a major social problem.

## Buryats

The Soviet takeover of Siberia was followed by the creation of autonomous territories, including a Buryat region organized in 1921. The territory was upgraded to an autonomous republic within the Russian Federation in 1923. Initially the Buryats were encouraged to continue their traditional way of life, including the practice of their Buddhist religion. Gradually their rights were molded into the Soviet image. The Buryats' open-pasture pastoralism was forcibly replaced by collective farms and the traditional pursuits of hunting and trapping were outlawed. In 1925, an official campaign against the Buddhist religion was launched. All but a few temples and monasteries were closed, arousing strong resistance. In 1929 the Buryats rebelled against Soviet excesses in an attempt to reverse the seizure and collectivization of their herds. The Red Army quickly crushed the rebels, with more than 35,000 Buryats killed in the fighting and reprisals. Thousands of monks were massacred on Stalin's orders, and irreplaceable ancient documents and cultural treasures were wantonly destroyed.

In 1937, as part of a new purge of the intelligentsia and the religious leadership of the Buryats, Stalin stripped the republic of about half of its territory, arbitrarily separating two Buryat-populated regions as new districts and reclassifying the inhabitants as separate nationalities, the Agün and Ust-Ordün Buryats. Government-sponsored resettlement encouraged Slavic colonists to settle in Buryatia to dilute the Buddhist majority. Accused of acting as Japanese agents, many of the remaining Buryats west of Lake Baikal were expelled from their historic lands. Their cherished Buddhist religion was suppressed, with veneration of Stalin substituted for their traditional respect for the Dalai Lama.

## Sakhas

The Sakhas, living far from the Russian heartland in Europe, escaped the devastation of the civil war, but fell to advancing Soviet troops in 1920. In April 1922, the government established the region as an autonomous republic within the Russian Federation. The attempt to resettle the Sakhas on collectives provoked a widespread rebellion in November 1921, with the last rebels not defeated until 1923. To avoid further confrontations the authorities acknowledged the necessity of a seminomadic way of life for the Sakhas, as guardians of their collectivized herds. In spite of a renewed rebellion in 1928, the Sakhas generally benefited from the early Soviet educational and cultural policies.

The period of Soviet consolidation and collectivization, fiercely resisted in the 1930s, began a long decline in the Sakha population. Thousands disappeared into the prison and labor camps established in the region after 1931. Forced labor, virtual slavery, and the elimination of shamans and other traditional leaders further decimated the Sakha population during the 1930s. The opening of a string of important mining operations allowed the Soviet authorities to force many Sakhas to abandon their traditional pursuits and to accept employment as a workforce overseen by Slavic managers.

## Tuvans

Tuvan independence was finally confirmed by a series of treaties with neighboring states between 1924 and 1926. The establishment of the Tuvan republic helped the Tuvans to resist efforts by the neighboring Mongols to incorporate their small homeland into the new Mongolian republic. Ignoring treaties of peace and friendship, the Soviet government forced the Tuvans to disenfranchise the traditional ruling class and to reorganize Tuvan territory as a Communist state. To reinforce the break with the Tuvan past, the Soviets destroyed nearly all of the region's Buddhist monasteries, killing or imprisoning the monks and traditional healers.

## Central Asians

The overthrow of the Muslim government established in Central Asia and the Bolshevik conquest of the former Russian protectorates of Khiva and Bukhara were partly accomplished with the aid of revolutionary sympathizers among Uzbeks seeking to modernize the feudal nature of Turkestani society. Many of the Uzbek upper classes, long the ruling class in the entire Turkestan region, fled to Afghanistan or joined the rebel groups in the mountains. Khiva and Bukhara continued to exist as Soviet states controlled by groups allied to the Soviet authorities. In 1924, over strong Uzbek objections, the Soviet authorities took direct control of both states, which were included in the division of Central Asia along ethnic lines.

The consolidation of Soviet power in Central Asia was strongly opposed by Muslim guerrilla groups called Basmachi. The Basmachi revolt spread rapidly in opposition to the Soviets' attempts to take complete political control of the region and the Soviet government's strong antireligious stance. Most of the Basmachi groups had been liquidated by 1924, although small bands continued to harass Soviet forces in Central Asia until the early 1930s. The Communist authorities, in order to make a complete break with past polities and leaderships, eliminated the majority of the region's tribal and national leaders and instituted the National Delimitation of 1924, which established national homelands for the Uzbeks and Turkmen based on ethnicity. Autonomous territories established for the Kazakh and Kyrgyz were raised to the status of union republics in 1936. The Karakalpaks, who retained strong clan and regional loyalties, were organized as an autonomous province within the Kyrgyz republic in 1925. Raised to the status of an autonomous republic, the Karakalpak territory was transferred to the Russian Federation in 1932 and became part of the Uzbek Soviet Socialist Republic in 1936.

The Soviet authorities gradually introduced restrictions on the Muslim religion. In 1928 an anti-Islamic campaign was launched in Central Asia, with Islamic schools and courts forcibly closed and thousands of mosques turned into museums, factories, schools, or warehouses. The Soviet collectivization of the region, between 1928 and 1933, was disastrous for the mainly nomadic tribal peoples. Forced to settle in permanent villages, many resisted and fighting erupted. In the ensuing conflict thousands of tribesmen died, were im-

*A Turkoman poses for a portrait. Turkmenia, USSR c. 1930–1934 (Scheufler Collection/Corbis)*

prisoned, or were driven across the border into China. Most of the vast herds that had sustained the nomads were destroyed. Many fled to the cities to escape the brutal collectivization campaign. Alcohol and other Western vices took a great toll during the 1920s and 1930s. The Communist leadership of the Central Asian nations, accused by Stalin of supporting nationalist aspirations, were purged in a series of show trials in 1937–1938 that did away with about three-quarters of the national leaderships.

The huge Kazakh Steppe, in northern Central Asia, became a dumping ground for excess populations and punished peoples from other areas of the Soviet Union. The forced settlement of the Kazakhs, fiercely resisted, was followed by purges and the collectivization of the Kazakh herds. The Kazakhs formed a majority of the population until the late 1930s when the population, representing dozens of ethnic groups, grew rapidly while the Kazakhs, who lost more than 1.5 million people between 1916 and 1939, continued to decline. As in all of Central Asia reliable ethnic Slavs held the positions of power while a few of each nationality were included in local governments to deflect domestic or international criticism of Soviet rule in Central Asia.

## The Stalin Era

Joseph Stalin, having eliminated all rivals, initiated a form of communism later known as Stalinism, which included firm control of all levels of Soviet life, a ruling party hierarchy based on whim, and a personality cult giving Stalin more power than the Romanov czars had. Although Stalin himself was an ethnic Georgian, he embraced Soviet nationalism to the exclusion of all other loyalties. Persecution of national minorities suspected of less than enthusiastic support for the idea of a homogenized Soviet nation increased in the 1930s, but worse was to come. During World War II, when the enemies of the Soviet Union openly supported anti-Soviet and nationalist ideologies, many Russians and non-Russians covertly or openly supported the anti-Communist crusade promoted by invading armies. Stalin's retribution was to affect not only individuals but entire nations.

## Timeline

1921        The Russian Civil War ends with the consolidation of power
            by Lenin and his Bolsheviks. The Soviet conquest of the
            Caucasus is undertaken despite treaties signed by the Soviet

government. Armenia, Georgia, and Azerbaijan are brought under strict Soviet control. The continuation of Lenin's nationality policy leads to the establishment of dozens of autonomous republics, provinces, regions, and districts for the numerous non-Russian national groups.

1922–1923    Armenia, Azerbaijan, and Georgia are consolidated into the Transcaucasian Soviet Federated Socialist Republic. The Union of Soviet Socialist Republics is formed by the union of the Russian Federation, Belarus, Ukraine, and the Transcaucasian Federation. Additional autonomous republics, provinces, and districts are established as Soviet power is extended to the territories inhabited by non-Russian nations.

1924    Lenin's death leads to a power struggle among leading Bolshevik leaders. Additional national groups are granted autonomous homelands. Several autonomous provinces are raised to the status of autonomous republics within the Russian Federation and within the other union republics. The Basmachi Revolt is finally crushed in Turkestan.

1925    The Soviet government begins the consolidation of regional governments in Turkestan.

1926    Stalin wins the struggle for power and takes effective control of the Soviet Union. Stalin's opposition to national autonomy leads to the curtailment of local powers and the rigid control of autonomous territories by reliable members, usually ethnic Russians, of the Communist Party.

1927–1929    New autonomous provinces and regions are created. Stalin institutes the policy of forced collectivization of agriculture. A separatist plot in Ukraine is brutally crushed.

1930–1931    Additional autonomous territories are established, but only limited cultural autonomy is allowed. Periodic purges of the leadership of the many nationalities limits opposition to strict Communist control.

1932    Stalin orders all grain and seed stocks confiscated in Ukraine and the North Caucasus, where opposition to his leadership was suspected. Up to 10 million people die in the ensuing famine.

1933–1934    More nominally autonomous territories are established, including a Jewish Autonomous Oblast, situated in the Far

East, as a national homeland for millions of Jews in the
Soviet Union.

1936    As part of the ongoing consolidation of the Soviet Union,
Turkestan is divided into the ethnically based homelands
named for the titular nationalities, the Uzbeks, Tajiks,
Turkmens, and Kyrgyz. The Transcaucasian Federation is
dissolved and Armenia, Azerbaijan, and Georgia are
admitted to the Soviet Union as union republics.

1938    As part of the consolidation of power among the Russian-
speaking elite of the Communist Party, the Cyrillic alphabet
is imposed on most non-Russian languages, and the Russian
language is made the official language of education in all
Soviet schools.

## Significant People, Places, and Events

AJARS A Caucasian people ethnically related to the Georgians, but with historical and religious differences, because the majority are Sunni Muslims.
In early Soviet censuses they were counted as a separate ethnic group, but
beginning in 1926 they were classified as ethnic Georgians.

AUTONOMOUS REPUBLICS Political territories established under Lenin's nationalities policies to give the larger national groups self-government
within the Russian Soviet Federated Socialist Republic (RSFSR) and the
other constituent republics of the USSR. Territories created for national
groups with lesser powers than the autonomous republics included autonomous provinces, regions, and districts.

BALTIC STATES Also known as the Baltic Republics. The three small states lying on the Baltic Sea, created by the Estonians, Latvians, and Lithuanians
after the Russian Revolution and the outbreak of the Russian Civil War.
The small states, although cut off from raw materials in Russia, established
prosperous economies and promoted regional ties to Finland and the
Scandinavian countries.

CENTRAL POWERS The states, mostly located in Central Europe, that formed
the side opposing the Allies, the Western democracies, the Russian Empire, and smaller states in southeastern Europe, during World War I. The
Central Powers included the German Empire, the Austro-Hungarian Empire, the Ottoman Empire, and the Kingdom of Bulgaria.

COMMUNIST PARTY The name chosen by the Bolsheviks following their
takeover of Russia after the Russian Revolution and civil war. The local

party structures, particularly those of the non-Russian national groups, initially enjoyed considerable autonomy, but by the mid-1920s the Russian Communist Party had centralized power in Moscow.

**GULAG** The extensive system of prisons and labor camps established in northern European Russia and Siberia during the Stalin era. Building on a system of czarist prisons and camps, the Soviet government expanded the number of camps, particularly slave labor camps, which were used to provide slave labor for the massive construction projects decreed by the Soviet government.

**KARAKALPAKS** The smallest of the Central Asian nations. Ethnically and historically related to both the Kazakhs and Uzbeks, they have a weak sense of nationality, with loyalty to the tribe or clan often far more intense than their sense of Karakalpak nationhood.

**LEAGUE OF NATIONS** The most important of the international organizations established by the peace treaties that officially ended World War I. The purpose of the organization was to promote international peace and security, but the absence of the United States and the League's inability to end a series of regional conflicts eventually doomed the effort.

**NAGORNO-KARABAKH** A small territory that officially forms part of the Republic of Azerbaijan. The population, with a large Armenian majority, has long opposed Azeri control of their region. The controversy over the territory has clouded relations between the Armenians and Azeris since the early 1920s.

**OSSETIANS** A mostly Christian Caucasian national group speaking a language related to Iranian. Politically the Ossetians are split between the Russian and Georgian states, with North Ossetia forming a constituent republic within the RSFSR and South Ossetia forming a nominally autonomous district within Georgia.

**RED ARMY** The military forces formed from the soldiers and sailors who initially supported the Bolsheviks following the overthrow of the provisional government in late 1917. The Red Army was greatly expanded with the outbreak of civil war in 1918. Popularly called the Reds, the Red Army fought against the anti-Bolshevik Whites.

**RUSSIAN SOVIET FEDERATED SOCIALIST REPUBLIC (RSFSR)** The largest part of the former Russian Empire that was established as a separate state under Bolshevik control in 1917–1918. Its first constitution was adopted in July 1918, setting out the relationships between the Soviet government and the numerous non-Russian national groups organized into autonomous republics, provinces, and districts. The RSFSR joined the other Soviet republics to form the USSR in 1922.

**SOVIET-POLISH WAR** A conflict between the newly created Polish republic and the nascent Soviet state in 1919–1920. The war resulted from the boundary dispute between the two states. As a result of the war the Poles gained part of the territory they claimed, historically Polish but mostly inhabited by ethnic Ukrainians and Belarussians.

**STALINIST PURGES** The periodic elimination, by execution or deportation, of political rivals, suspect leaders of non-Russian nationalities, and military leaders during the Stalin era, from the late 1920s to 1953.

**TRANSCAUCASIAN FEDERATION** Two historic federations made up of the three Transcaucasian republics of Armenia, Azerbaijan, and Georgia. The first, created in early 1918, was a reaction to the Bolshevik coup in Russia. The second, created after the Bolshevik conquest of the three republics, was admitted as one of the founding member states of the new USSR. The Soviet government dissolved the federation in 1936 and the three republics became separate constituent republics of the Soviet Union.

**UNION OF SOVIET SOCIALIST REPUBLICS (USSR)** Also known as the Soviet Union. The union of the Russian Federation and other Soviet republics formed under Bolshevik control in 1922 as the successor state to the Russian Empire. The USSR was the largest country in the world from its inception in 1922 until its collapse in 1991.

**UNION REPUBLICS** The designation of the member states of the USSR to differentiate them from the subordinate autonomous republics within the Russian Federation and several other union republics. The union republics were the Russian Federation; the Slavic republics of Ukraine and Belarus; the Baltic republics of Estonia, Latvia, and Lithuania; the Romanian republic of Moldova; the Transcaucasian republics of Armenia, Georgia, and Azerbaijan; and the Central Asian republics of Kazakhstan, Kyrgyzstan, Turkmenistan, Tajikistan, and Uzbekistan. The Karelo-Finnish SSR was a union republic between 1940 and 1956.

**ZIONISM** The movement among European Jews to reestablish an independent Jewish state in Palestine. The movement began in the late nineteenth century and gained support in Russia during the upheavals of the early twentieth century.

## Bibliography

Conquest, Robert. *The Great Terror: Stalin's Purge of the Thirties.* New York: Macmillan, 1968.

Fitzpatrick, Sheila. *The Russian Revolution.* New York: Oxford University Press, 1982.

Glaskow, W. G. *History of the Cossacks.* New York: Robert Speller, 1972.

Gonen, Amiram, ed. *The Encyclopedia of the Peoples of the World.* New York: Henry Holt and Company, 1993.

Heller, Mikhail, and Aleksandr Nekrich. *Utopia in Power.* New York: Summit Books, 1986.

Kolsto, Pal. *Political Construction Sites: Nation-Building and the Post-Soviet States.* Boulder, CO: Westview Press, 2000.

Lang, David Marshall. *A Modern History of Soviet Georgia.* New York: Grove Press, 1962.

Nichol, James P. *Stalin's Crimes against the Non-Russian Nations: The 1987–1990 Revelations and Debate.* Carl Beck Papers, Center for Russian and East European Studies, University of Pittsburgh, 1991.

Ulam, Adam B. *Stalin: The Man and His Era.* New York: Viking Press, 1973.

# CHAPTER SIX

# World War II and the Beginning of the Cold War, 1939–1970

JOSEPH STALIN, THE SOVIET DICTATOR from the 1920s to his death in 1953, remained extremely suspicious of any loyalty that might compete with his goal of creating a new national ideal, Soviet man. By suppressing national cultures and eliminating national leaders he sought to assimilate the many Soviet nationalities into a Russian-speaking Soviet nation. When Stalin took power he reversed Lenin's plans for a mosaic of distinct nationalities and began a brutal campaign to eliminate all ethnic and local loyalties. The histories of the various ethnic groups were rewritten to minimize pre-Soviet achievements and cultural institutions. Millions died as a result of Stalin's unwavering assault on national sentiment.

*Three Soviet women guerilla fighting during World War II, c. 1939–1945 (Corbis)*

Alarmed by Germany's expansion on the Soviet Union's western frontier in Europe in the late 1930s, Stalin negotiated a secret nonaggression pact, the Molotov-Ribbentrop Pact, with Germany in August 1939. The pact divided the countries of Central and Eastern Europe into spheres of influence, allowing the Soviet government a free hand in the states assigned to its sphere. The Soviet government was particularly interested in the peoples and territories that had broken free of Russia earlier in the century, the independent states of Estonia, Latvia, Finland, the Romanian province of Bessarabia, later known as Moldova, and the eastern provinces of Poland. In September 1939, the Germans invaded western Poland, while the Nazi ally, the Soviet Union, sent troops to occupy eastern Poland. The Polish invasion was the final spark that ignited World War II.

Stalin's ally, Adolph Hitler, put aside the 1939 nonaggression pact and ordered the invasion of the Soviet Union in June 1941. The war devastated much of the European territories of the Soviet Union. Cities lay in ruins, and industry had either been destroyed or transferred away from the fighting. The human losses, particularly among the Ukrainians and Belarussians, were among the highest in Europe. The loss of national populations to war, on top of the Stalinist terror of the 1930s, emigration, and the massive deportations and repression of the postwar era compounded the dramatic drop in national populations among several national groups. All concessions to national culture and nationality made during the war in an effort to ensure loyalty were quickly abolished in 1945–1946. Campaigns against "bourgeois nationalism" were resumed in all territories in 1946. Even though the Communist Party controlled all levels of government in the national republics, on Stalin's insistence, the Ukrainian SSR and the Belarussian SSR were numbered among the founding members of the new United Nations in 1945.

## Ukrainians

The Soviet occupation of Poland's eastern provinces brought most of Europe's Ukrainian population under Soviet authority. In 1940 the Soviets seized the neighboring Romanian region of Bukovina, also with a Ukrainian majority. The western Ukrainians' long religious ties to Rome and their political and historical ties to the West provoked a severe Soviet repression. More than 1 million Ukrainians from the newly annexed regions were executed or deported between 1939 and 1941. When the Germans launched their attack on the Soviet Union in June 1941, many Ukrainians welcomed the invaders as liberators from the hated rule of the Soviets. Western Ukraine, taken by the Soviets from Poland and Romania in 1939–1940, was quickly overrun and was organized as a German colony with thousands of Ukrainians conscripted or voluntarily inducted into the German army or deported as laborers to Germany and the other occupied territories. The German occupation of Soviet Ukraine further divided the Ukrainian nation, with Ukrainians often facing each other on the battlefield.

The Red Army drove the Germans from Ukraine in 1944. Thousands of Ukrainians were arrested and deported as collaborators. In 1945, the Soviet government annexed the Ukrainian-populated regions of Poland, Czechoslovakia, and Romania. Overlooking the contribution to the war effort by millions of Ukrainians, Stalin accused the entire nation of collaboration. Only their sheer numbers saved the Ukrainian majority from the mass deportations inflicted on many smaller nations. The Uniate Catholic Church, the major religion of the western Ukrainians, was banned and absorbed into the docile Russian Orthodox Church in 1946. The Russian Orthodox hierarchy continued to receive state subsidies, while Uniate Catholic clergy and laymen filled Stalin's gulag. During the late 1940s and early 1950s, many young Uniate Catholics were "voluntarily" moved to development areas in Siberia and Central Asia. At the same time the Ukrainian cities, particularly Kiev, the urbanized coal mining region in the northeast, and L'viv and other cities of the formerly Polish and Romanian territories received an influx of more reliable ethnic Russians.

The death of Stalin in 1953 ushered in a period of relative relaxation. Assimilation, as official policy, was temporarily halted, and the Ukrainian republican government was given some limited powers. In his famous 1956 speech denouncing Stalin's many crimes, Nikita Khrushchev emphasized the crimes against the Ukrainians. The policy of de-Stalinization allowed some additional concessions to Ukrainian culture, but these concessions were not extended to religion, education, or language, where assimilation continued unabated. The replacement of the Stalinist era functionaries allowed some ethnic Ukrainians to fill jobs in the lower levels of the bureaucracy, and several took important positions in the party and republican government.

A Ukrainian renaissance emerged in the early 1960s with many young intellectuals, writers, and artists uniting to promote and safeguard Ukrainian culture. Although the movement was not overtly political, in the Soviet context, language and culture were dangerous issues, and repression was resumed. This in turn stirred demands for the political rights supposedly guaranteed by existing Soviet laws. In 1964, the "Khrushchev Thaw" ended with Khrushchev's sudden removal from power. A new crackdown, in 1965, began more than two decades of repression, show trials, exile, and labor camps.

## Carpatho-Rusyns

The Czecho-Slovak government, threatened by German and Hungarian territorial claims in 1938, sought to bind Carpatho-Rusyn loyalty by finally granting the autonomy promised them in 1919. When the Czechoslovak state was betrayed by its Western allies in the Munich Pact, it was transformed into a federal state made up of autonomous units. Six months later, the dismemberment of Czechoslovakia by the neighboring fascist states gave the Carpatho-Rusyns a unique opportunity: The nationalists mobilized to expel all Czecho-Slovak officials and formed an autonomous government. The Carpatho-Rusyn state, called Carpatho-Ukraine, was declared independent of Czechoslovakia on 2 March 1939. The infant state collapsed following a rapid invasion by Hungarian troops on 14 March. Two days later Hungary annexed the region and suppressed all antifascist and nationalist organizations.

The Soviet invasion and occupation of the region in October 1944 was aided by a vehemently pro-Communist Transcarpathian National Council, which formed as the fascist Hungarian state collapsed. At the end of World War II, in 1945, the Transcarpathian region was ceded by Czechoslovakia to the USSR, where it was added to Ukraine as an ordinary province. One of the most immediate results of Soviet rule in Transcarpathia was the implementation of a policy of Ukrainization. The idea of a distinct Carpatho-Rusyn nationality was outlawed and only Ukrainian identity was sanctioned. The Carpatho-Rusyn language, their Uniate Catholic religion, and unique cultural traditions were immediately banned. The new Communist governments also suppressed the Carpatho-Rusyns still living in Czechoslovakia and in adjacent areas of Poland. Decades of religious, cultural, and political oppression followed.

## Belarussians

The northern districts of the territories taken from Poland in September 1939 were joined to the Soviet Belarussian territories to form an expanded Belarussian Soviet Socialist Republic. As in the other annexed territories, all national, cultural, and religious leaders, including thousands of Roman Catholic priests and nuns, were deported or executed. The Roman Catholic faith, the major religion in Polish Belarus, was ruthlessly suppressed. Like the Ukrainians, many Belarussians welcomed the German invasion in June 1941. The Germans and their allies were hailed as liberators from the Soviet yoke, with many Belarussians voluntarily joining the invading armies. Despite a harsh occupation, the Belarussians were encouraged to collaborate in the anti-Communist crusade. Belarussian nationalists, with German permission, organized some of the trappings of an independent state, including a national guard that helped the invaders to massacre the large Jewish population. A nationalist uprising began with the Nazi defeat in 1944. The poorly armed partisan groups fought the victorious return of the Red Army. Guerrilla bands continued to operate in the republic until the early 1950s.

At the end of the war Belarus was a ruin, having suffered the worst devastation in all of Europe. An estimated quarter of the prewar Belarussian population had perished in the fighting, the postwar uprising, and the deportations of the "ideologically contaminated" survivors. Stalin, intent on the assimilation of the Slavic peoples, instituted a policy of intense Russification. Tens of thousands of ethnic Russians, left homeless by the war, were resettled in the Belarussian regions designated redevelopment zones. The process of assimilation became part of the urbanization and industrialization of the Belarussian republic in the post-Stalin period. The vast majority of the republic's population became bilingual in Russian and Belarussian. Increasing numbers of urbanized Belarussians came to view Russian as their first language. As the Belarussians continued to urbanize, these assimilationist trends accelerated. Attempts at Russification seemed to have succeeded among the Belarussians, and during the Cold War years, Soviet officials did not worry as much about the docile Belarussians as they did about the more nationalist ethnic groups.

## The Baltic Nations

The Soviet occupation of eastern Poland further isolated the three small Baltic nations. A month after the Polish invasion, the Soviet government demanded access to military bases in Estonia, Latvia, and Lithuania. After months of increasing tension, Soviet troops massed on the eastern borders. Unable to resist the overwhelming Soviet military threat, the Baltic governments collapsed and pro-Soviet governments were formed. In June 1940, the newly formed pro-Soviet Baltic governments petitioned the Soviet government for annexation. Hundreds of thousands of Soviet soldiers moved into the Baltic States, quickly suppressing all remaining resistance. Tens of thousands of Baltic nationalist leaders, cultural figures, professionals, and military personnel and their families were deported to prisons and slave labor camps in Siberia. The annexation of the three independent states was denounced as illegal and was never recognized by most Western countries.

The Germans turned on their Soviet allies in June 1941, quickly overrunning the Baltic region as part of their invasion of the Soviet Union. Decimated by a year of Soviet rule, the Baltic peoples often viewed the German invaders as liberators. Many anti-Soviets joined the Germans' anti-Communist crusade, both as soldiers in the military forces and as part of the Nazi program to exterminate the large Jewish population in the region. The German occupation lasted until 1944, when the returning Soviet army drove the Germans out. Hundreds of thousands of Baltic citizens died during the fighting. The Sovietization that began in 1940–1941 was continued. The Soviet political police and special screening commissions investigated the past and the political views of every inhabitant over the age of twelve. The deportations were resumed with tens of thousands of Baltic citizens, deemed a threat to the Stalinist regime, sent to the gulag. A massive in-migration of Russians, sponsored by the Soviet government, replaced the greatly reduced Baltic populations with reliable ethnic Slavs. Russification and collectivization became official policy after the war. Education was only in Russian, and local language publications were banned.

World War II and its aftermath were devastating for the Baltic nations. Hundreds of thousands perished in the conflict and the massive deportations. The local languages were forbidden in schools, publications, and government institutions. The Russian-speaking newcomers were given preferential treatment in housing and employment; however, the Baltic peoples soon constituted a white-collar class with the Slavs mostly working in the heavy industries constructed by the Soviet government. The Baltic national movements virtually disappeared with the brutal suppression of various resistance organizations in the early 1950s. The campaign to regain the independence of Estonia, Latvia, and Lithuania was mostly kept alive by refugees in the West. The Soviets ruled the Baltic States with an iron hand. During the 1950s, 1960s, and 1970s, occasional protests or symbolic acts were condoned as demonstrations of Soviet democracy during the Cold War, but more prominent acts meant certain imprisonment or even death (Olson 1994, 218).

## The Winter War, the Finno-Soviet Conflict

Taking advantage of the nonaggression pact with Germany, the Soviet government also made several far-reaching territorial and military demands on another of the former Russian-controlled nations, Finland. The Finns refused the demands, and negotiations broke down. Alleging a Finnish artillery attack, the Soviet government ordered the Red Army to invade Finland in November 1939. The Finns rallied and repulsed the Soviets. Behind the Soviet lines, the small Finnic nationalities related to the Finns, the Karelians, the Ingrians, and several smaller groups, harassed the Soviet advance. For months the Finns and their Finnic allies within the Soviet Union put up a heroic resistance, but the military might of the Soviet Union proved too forceful. In March 1940, the Finnish government signed a peace treaty that forced the Finns to cede about 10 percent of their national territory, including the Karelian Isthmus near Leningrad (St. Petersburg) and the Finnish shore of Lake Ladoga. Hundreds of thousands of Finns moved west ahead of the Soviet occupation. The Soviet government joined the ceded territory to the Karelian autonomous republic, set up within the RSFSR in the early 1920s, to form the Karelo-Finnish Soviet Socialist Republic, which became the twelfth union republic of the USSR.

The Finns, unreconciled to the loss of so much valuable territory, joined the German assault on the Soviet Union in June 1941. The invading Finnish forces liberated all of Karelia and the other Finnic territories in northwestern Russia. The Finns were welcomed as liberators by the Karels and the other related peoples. The Finnish government, claiming that theirs was a distinct conflict, rejected German demands that they join the attack on Leningrad. Defeated in 1944, the Finnish army withdrew, accompanied by more than 400,000 Karels, Finns, Ingrians, and members of other national minorities fleeing the Soviet advance. The Soviet authorities again divided the Karelo-Finnish republic, transferring much of the territory ceded by Finland in 1940 to Leningrad province and districts in the north to Murmansk. On the grounds that the Karels and Finns formed only a minority in the republic, the government downgraded Karelia's status to an autonomous republic within the Russian Federation in 1956.

The Finns, having declared their neutrality and adjusted their politics to accommodate relations with their giant neighbor, functioned as a conduit for Western goods and advanced technology to the Soviet Union during the Cold War. Their kin, the Karels, Ingrians, Veps, Votes, Ludians, and Izors in northwestern Russia, deprived of their cultural autonomy and under intense pressure to assimilate, underwent a rapid reacculturation into the surrounding Russian population. Karelian language use declined, and the smaller languages nearly disappeared as part of the Soviet policy of absorbing the small nations into the Soviet Russian culture. Some 253,000 people registered as ethnic Karels in the 1939 Soviet census, but their numbers dropped to 167,000 by 1959 as ethnic Karels sought to hide their nationality by registering as ethnic Russians and assimilating into Russian culture. Similar declines in population numbers of the smaller Finnic territories raised fears of the loss of their unique cultures and languages. Emigration to Finland, mostly clandestine, added to the drop in the numbers of Finnic peoples in successive Soviet censuses.

## Moldovans

The nonaggression pact between the Soviet Union and Nazi Germany in 1939 allowed the Soviet government to revive its claim to Bessarabia, in spite of the fact that the Soviets had renounced their historic sovereignty when the USSR established diplomatic relations with Romania in 1934. The Soviet Union, assured that Nazi Germany wouldn't interfere, demanded that Romania cede Bessarabia. The Romanian government, without foreign support, had to accept the Soviet annexation of the region. By August 1940, most of Bessarabia had been amalgamated with part of the small Moldovan Autonomous Soviet Socialist Republic, created in the 1920s, to form the Moldovan Soviet Socialist Republic, which was admitted as a union republic of the USSR. The coastal zones of Bessarabia were transferred to Ukraine to compensate for the loss of the Moldovan autonomous republic. Romania, partly to recover the annexed territory, joined the Axis Powers in October 1940.

The Soviet authorities began a program of rapid "Sovietization" with most industrial and commercial enterprises nationalized. Most of the agricultural land was confiscated and redistributed as part of the collectivization of agriculture. Thousands were summarily executed and more than 100,000 Moldovans were deported to other parts of the Soviet Union in 1940–1941. When Germany and its allies, including Romania, invaded the Soviet Union in 1941, Soviet authorities moved another 300,000 inhabitants and vast quantities of capital goods and livestock to areas farther away from the border before Romanian troops overran the region. The Romanians reported the discovery of mass graves of thousands of executed individuals.

By the summer of 1944, the Soviet forces had retaken Bessarabia and advanced to occupy all of Romania. A pro-Soviet government was installed in Bucharest, which was forced to recognize the Soviet annexation of Bessarabia in 1940. Those Moldovans who had cooperated with the Romanian authorities during the war were liquidated. The Soviet authorities began a program of suppressing the Moldovans' linguistic, ethnic, and cultural affinities to the Romanians. The Cyrillic script was imposed on education and publishing, and many Russian words were introduced into the Moldovan vocabulary. Soviet historians rewrote Moldovan history to demonstrate that the Moldovans' ties to the Romanians were nonexistent or tenuous and historic ties to the Ukrainians and Russians were fabricated. In the more relaxed post-Stalin period, the Moldovans began to reestablish some cultural and personal ties with Romania. The authorities allowed the importation of periodicals, books, and motion pictures from Romania. The trade became so important that books and newspapers in the Romanians' Latin script were seen as a threat. By the late 1960s, the importation of Romanian films and published material had been severely curtailed. In 1970 the importation was abruptly ended. Cultural exchanges between Soviet Moldova and Communist Romania were also ended.

## Armenians

Despite earlier promises, by the late 1930s any expression of Armenian national culture was suspect. The Nazi invasion of the Caucasus failed to reach the southern slopes of the Caucasus Mountains; however, Stalin remained suspicious of the Armenians' ties to the West, particularly the large Armenian population in the United States and Canada. At the end of World War II, the Soviet government, overlooking decades of purges that had eliminated the Armenian political and cultural leadership, began a campaign to attract diaspora Armenians back to their ancestral homeland. More than 200,000 Armenians returned to the region, preferring to live among their own people, even under Soviet rule.

Stalin's death in 1953 began the period known as the "thaw" under Nikita Khrushchev. The Stalinist leadership of the Armenian republic was removed. The new leaders were allowed to combine Soviet rule with loyalty toward Armenia. The popularity of the post-Stalinist changes allowed the new republican leaders to mobilize the people. Despite the campaign to draw the diaspora Armenians to Soviet Armenia, they remained the most widely dispersed nationality, after the Jews, in the Soviet Union. More than 1 million lived in neighboring Georgia and Azerbaijan, many others lived in various parts of the Russian republic.

## Georgians

Georgia, like Armenia, was never reached by the Nazi forces invading the Caucasus, but the loyalty of the Georgians also remained suspect. During the

Stalinist years the nationality question was seldom raised, but the intense loyalty felt by the Georgians to their ancient culture, language, and religion remained, even though driven underground. Indigenous social and political
trends continued to shape the Georgians' attitudes toward the Soviet Union.
Although the Georgians resisted, the fact that Stalin was an ethnic Georgian
in no way softened his attitude toward Georgian nationalism. Lenin's
planned federation of brother republics led by local Communist leaders allowed considerable cultural and linguistic expression until 1934, but the
worst of the Stalinist purges replaced the Georgian Communists with men
personally loyal to Stalin between 1936 and 1938.

After Stalin's death in 1953, Beria was removed as the ruler of Georgia, and
his followers were purged and executed. An ethnic Georgian, Vasilii Mzha-
vanadze, was then elevated to the post of first secretary of the Georgian Communist Party. He remained in power for the next nineteen years, but was finally removed in 1972. During this time the nationality question was rarely
discussed. His successor, Eduard Shevardnadze, another ethnic Georgian, began a new bloodless purge in an effort to eradicate growing corruption.

## Azeris

The elimination of the Azeri national leadership during the Stalinist purges
in the 1930s began a period of intense repression. Militant atheism attacked
all public manifestations of the Azeris' Muslim religion. Mosques were
closed, and public prayers were rarely allowed. Only a token number of the
faithful were allowed to make the annual pilgrimage to Mecca. The Muslim religion, an integral part of the Azeri nation, became part of the underground culture. Assimilation into Russian culture was pressed in an effort to distance the Azeris from their Turko-Persian heritage and to ensure
no interruption to the flow of Azerbaijan's important oil reserves. The Soviet effort to present Azerbaijan as a model to the neighboring Muslim nations mostly failed owing to the repeated purges and the harsh suppression
of the Muslim religion.

Improved medicine and food production nurtured rapid population
growth beginning in the 1930s. The population of Azerbaijan grew a star-
tling 26 percent between the 1939 and 1959 Soviet censuses. The demographic explosion undermined Soviet plans to colonize Azerbaijan, even
though by the beginning of World War II, thousands of non-Azeris had been
settled in the republic, mostly in Baku and the new cities constructed under
successive Soviet economic plans. This situation created islands of multi-

ethnic urbanized populations in an ethnically homogeneous countryside. The rapid growth of the Azeri population worried the Soviet authorities, as it paralleled a drop in the Slavic birthrate in the region. Government attempts to introduce family planning was seen by the Azeris as yet another attack on their persecuted religion and led to violent confrontations in the 1960s.

The Nazis initially listed Baku and its oil fields as a prime objective during the invasion of the Caucasus in 1942, but the reverses that culminated in the defeat at Stalingrad diverted the troops originally charged with the capture of Baku. Soviet expansion during and after the war, although principally into eastern Europe, also targeted the large Azeri-populated region of northern Iran. Soviet troops occupied Iranian Azerbaijan from 1941 to 1946. While suppressing Azeri culture and the Muslim religion in Soviet Azerbaijan, the occupation authorities promoted Azeri nationalism and the common bonds between Soviet and Iranian Azeris in Iranian Azerbaijan. Soviet support led to a nationalist and leftist uprising in Iranian Azerbaijan and the declaration of an independent Azeri republic. The nationalist republic collapsed with the withdrawal of Soviet forces in 1946, reportedly after receiving valuable oil concessions from the Iranian government.

## The Punished Nations

### North Caucasians

The German advance into the Soviet Union in 1941 was accompanied by efforts to promote the oppressed Muslim nations as allies by presenting the war as an anti-Communist crusade. The Germans advanced into the Caucasus in 1942, partly to gain control of the valuable oil fields. They were often met by North Caucasian Muslims with jubilation and were hailed as liberators from the hated Soviet yoke. The Germans won thousands of volunteers to their Turkish League, an anti-Soviet military unit under Nazi command, and other national military forces promoted as German allies. The Germans, in the areas they overran, allowed the restoration of traditional social and religious structures, the opening of churches, mosques, and Buddhist shrines, and the decollectivization of economic activity. Even though many viewed the Germans as saviors, the harsh Nazi methods alienated many others. By early 1943 dozens of small partisan bands had taken up arms against the invaders. In 1943–1944 the Red Army returned to reconquer the occupied territories.

Accused of treason by Stalin, entire nations faced punishment, including soldiers in the Red Army and their families. Expelled from their homes at gunpoint, the deportees were driven to railheads where they were herded aboard waiting trains. Imprisoned in sealed cattle cars, the deportees were shipped east to Central Asia and Siberia, where they were dumped in remote areas without food or shelter. Tens of thousands died in the brutal deportations. Many more died where they were dumped, of hunger and exposure. The survivors were placed under the direct control of the KGB, the notorious Soviet secret police. In exile their cultures and languages were supposed to whither and die.

The deportees included most of the Muslim peoples of the North Caucasus: the Balkars, Chechens, Ingush, Karachai, and the Muslim minority of the Ossetians. The punished nations also included the Crimean Tatars of the Crimean Peninsula farther west. The Kalmyk Buddhists, whose homeland lies north of the Muslim lands in the North Caucasus, were also deported. Unknown in the West until the 1960s, another group, which included a number of small Muslim groups, collectively called Meskhtekians, living along the Turkish border, had also been deported. The autonomous governments erected for most of these national groups in the early 1920s were abolished, and their territories were merged into surrounding provinces and republics. The other Caucasian nationalities, the Circassian peoples (Kabards, Cherkess, Adyge) and the Dagestani peoples, along with the Christian Ossetians, although they suffered tremendous losses, were not singled out for deportation. The Muslim Azkhaz and Ajars of Georgia, although targeted for deportation, also escaped the horrors of the deportations experienced by the related peoples of the North Caucasus.

## Germans

The 1939 Molotov-Ribbenthrop Pact between the Soviet Union and Nazi Germany eased the Stalinist oppression the Germans had suffered for more than a decade. The period of relaxation lasted only until the Nazis launched a surprise attack on the Soviet Union in June 1941, a cataclysmic event for the Soviet Germans. Stalin reacted by declaring all ethnic Germans in the Soviet Union members of a fifth column. In August 1941, some 440,000 Volga Germans and between 250,000 and 350,000 Germans from other regions were rounded up and shipped east in closed cattle cars. The deportees, often forced to leave their homes without adequate clothing or food, were dumped at rail sidings across a large area of Siberia and Soviet Central Asia. In exile they were under the direct control of the KGB. Another 350,000 ethnic Germans, living in the provinces quickly overrun by the advancing German armies, were evacuated to Germany. More than 200,000 of the evacuees were rounded up by Soviet troops in defeated Germany in 1945. They were forcibly repatriated to the Soviet Union and most were sent directly to Stalin's gulag, where they remained until the survivors were released under the terms of an amnesty after Stalin's death in 1953.

The Germans deported to the east in 1941 were not rehabilitated with the other deported nations in 1956–1957. They were finally exonerated in 1964 when relations between the Soviet Union and West Germany began to improve, but unlike some of the other deported nations they were not allowed to return to their homes in European Russia. The Germans circulated petitions, sent appeals, and even dispatched envoys directly to the Kremlin, but all their efforts were met with stony silence. Better relations with West Germany allowed a small number of ethnic Germans to emigrate every year during the Cold War, but the numbers were limited by Germany's inability to absorb all those wishing to leave.

## Koreans

Ethnic Koreans began to move into Russian territory in the mid-nineteenth century, crossing the Tumen River between Korean and Russian territory after the Chinese ceded the Ussuri region of the Far East to the Russian Empire in 1860. A government offer of free land encouraged the Koreans, particularly when famine struck the Korean Peninsula in 1869. By 1910 between 50,000 and 70,000 Koreans had settled in the Russian Far East. Under Soviet rule, many of the industrious Koreans were lured from the frigid lands along the Pacific Ocean with promises of warmer climates and free land in Central Asia.

Korean cultural institutions flourished both in the Far East and Central Asia in the 1920s and early 1930s, until Stalin's drastic policy reversal ended cultural autonomy in 1936. Stalin's increasing paranoia included a deep distrust of the Japanese. Suspecting that the Japanese would try to infiltrate spies from Korea into the Soviet Pacific regions, Stalin ordered all Koreans in the region deported. An estimated 180,000 ethnic Koreans were accused of treason or were simply rounded up, thrown into rail cars, and shipped west to Kazakhstan and Uzbekistan by the end of 1937.

The Koreans' agricultural traditions were quickly put to use for the Soviet state. The deportees turned unproductive marshlands into rice farms in Uzbekistan and pioneered rice and cotton collectives in the arid climate around the Aral Sea. Until Stalin's death in 1953 few details of the deportation of the Koreans leaked out to the West. In the thaw that followed Stalin's death, news of the deported Koreans was finally allowed. They had mostly retained their language, culture, and traditions, even in exile.

## Cossacks

In 1936 several supposedly Cossack regiments were organized within the Red Army, ending the ban on Cossack military training. The Nazi authorities, following the German invasion of the Soviet Union in June 1941, declared the Cossacks descendants of the Germanic Ostrogoths, separating them from the "subhuman" Slavs and elevating them to the status of acceptable allies. Stirred by their suffering under Soviet rule, thousands of Cossacks joined the Nazi campaign against communism, including many from exile communities in other parts of Europe. In Soviet territory many of the Cossacks remained loyal, with Cossacks often facing other Cossack soldiers in battle. At the end of World War II, some 40,000 Cossack soldiers and their families surrendered to the British in Austria. The British authorities, at Stalin's insistence, forcibly repatriated the Cossacks to the Soviet Union, where they were sent directly to perish in the gulag. Cultural and linguistic repression continued in the post-Stalin era. All signs of Cossack culture remained banned throughout the Cold War. In the west, exile groups continued to agitate for recognition, publishing histories, dictionaries, and other materials that could be smuggled into the Soviet Union.

### Demographic Changes

The deportations of millions of people deemed a threat to Soviet rule were not the only demographic changes. The Axis invasion in June 1941 immediately threatened the industrial heartland of the Soviet Union in Europe. In order to continue supplying the Red Army and the civilian population outside the occupied zones, the Soviet authorities began a program to physically transfer whole factories and their workers away from the fighting. Millions of ethnic Slavs were resettled in the ethnic republics of the Volga region, Central Asia, and Siberia. The demographic impact was immediate, reducing to a minority the titular nationality in many of the autonomous republics and inserting large Slavic populations in all others. Stalinist officials even resettled some evacuated Slavs in areas too remote to be a direct part of the war effort, but where the overwhelming majority was made up of a non-Slav nationality. One of the largest influxes of Slavic populations occurred in the Volga region, where many evacuees from the war zones were resettled. The industrialization of this area, both during the war and during the decades of the Cold War, brought in new Slavic migrants in state-sponsored population movements.

## Stalin's Postwar Empire

At the end of the war in Europe, Soviet troops occupied most of eastern Europe. Within two years Soviet troops had installed pro-Soviet governments in Poland, eastern Germany, Czechoslovakia, Hungary, Romania, Yugoslavia, Bulgaria, and Albania. The rapid expansion of communism into eastern and central Europe, accepted by the other wartime Allies, allowed the Soviets to strip much of the region of its manufacturing plants in order to rebuild devastated areas of the Soviet Union.

Western distrust of Joseph Stalin quickly replaced the wartime alliance, as Europe was divided between East and West, communism and democracy. The conflict, called the Cold War, had an intense impact on the nationalities of the Soviet Union. Propaganda and exiled national populations were used in an attempt to undermine Soviet control in the so-called autonomous territories, just one of the many tactics used in an effort to divert the Soviet government from their goal of spreading communism around the globe. Hopes for rapprochement between the USSR and the West were raised by a relaxation in Soviet policies after the death of Joseph Stalin in 1953.

## The Khrushchev Era

The death of Stalin ushered in a new era in Soviet history. A "collective leadership" at first replaced Stalin's one-man rule, but rivalries and discord over Stalin's legacy continued until Nikita Khrushchev became the sole ruler in 1958. Khrushchev denounced Stalin's crimes and modified some of the more dictatorial aspects of Soviet life. Soviet citizens, even the non-Russian nationalities, began to gain a greater degree of personal freedom and civil security.

Stalin's death in 1953 brought a period of relative leniency. Russification was temporarily halted, but soon resumed. Stalin's demise also brought immediate changes in the leadership of the local Communist parties that controlled the autonomous territories. Ethnic leaders began to replace a few of

*A reform-minded leader and champion of "peaceful coexistence," Nikita Khrushchev was an initiator of political and social change during his term as leader of the Communist Party in the Soviet Union, which lasted from 1953 to 1964. (Hulton Archives)*

the Slavs that had filled the local governments since the 1920s. In the 1960s younger intellectuals began to promote the forbidden cultures. At first, their goals were not overtly political, but remained cultural—the promotion and safeguarding of non-Russian cultures and languages. An official backlash brought renewed repression, which in turn brought about demands for the political and national rights enshrined in the existing laws and constitutions. In 1964, the last remnants of the post-Stalin thaw ended with the sudden removal of Khrushchev.

## The Deported Nations Rehabilitated

The small Muslim and Buddhist nations suffered massive losses of up to a third of their total populations during Stalin's 1944 deportations and exile. Khrushchev, as part of his de-Stalinization program, extended an amnesty to the Balkars, Chechens, Ingush, and Karachai in 1956. Strategic and political concerns meant that the Crimean Tatars, the Germans, and the Meskhtekians were overlooked and remained in lonely exile in Central Asia.

### Karachais and Balkars

The Karachais and Balkars are two small closely related nations speaking dialects of the same Turkic language. Already threatened by large-scale Russian immigration during the last half of the nineteenth century, the Karachai-Balkar nation was further threatened by its artificial separation under Soviet rule. In 1921, after the Soviet consolidation of their power in the North Caucasus, they divided the nation into two geographical entities, the Karachais and the Balkars. At that time the Soviet government was bent on suppressing any sense of North Caucasian unity and destroying the resistance to Soviet rule centered in the highlands. In 1922, as part of the Soviet divide-and-conquer policy, the Balkar territory was joined to the neighboring territory of the Caucasian-speaking Kabards to form the Kabardino-Balkar Autonomous Oblast. The combined province was raised to the status of an autonomous province within the Russian Federation in 1936, ignoring appeals by both the Karachai and Balkar leaders for reunification. The Karachais were joined with the Cherkess, a Circassian people closely related to the Kabards, in a joint autonomous province. Dumped at rail sidings across Central Asia and Siberia, the surviving Karachais and Balkars were amnestied by Khrushchev and began to return to their Caucasian homeland. Again they appealed for the creation of a Karachai-Balkar autonomous territory but were not acknowledged. They were again joined with neighboring Circassian peoples in shared autonomies. The Karachai-Cherkess Autonomous Oblast and the Kabardino-Balkar Autonomous Republic were reconstituted in 1957.

## Chechens and Ingush

The Chechens and Ingush, closely related and speaking dialects of the same Caucasian language, had been joined in a shared autonomous republic in 1936. Chechen resistance to Russification presented the Stalinist authorities with one of their most intractable ethnic problems. The Chechens, and to a lesser extent, the Ingush, based their resistance in a strong Islamic folk culture. Although Chechens and Ingush fought on both sides during World War II, Stalin accused the entire nations of collaboration. In exile the Chechens and Ingush clung tenaciously to their languages, cultures, and their Islamic faith. The internal exile lasted for thirteen years before they were officially rehabilitated in 1957. They returned to their homelands in 1957–1958, only to find their homes and properties occupied by others. Rioting broke out in 1958 over the slow place of resettlement and over demands for the return of their predeportation properties. The autonomous republic was reconstituted, but with reduced borders to accommodate territories occupied by the neighboring peoples in 1944. The formerly Ingush region added to North Ossetia began a long conflict between the Muslim Ingush and the majority Orthodox Ossetians. The deportation and the loss of so many of their compatriots deepened the hatred of the Russians that had simmered among the Chechens since their conquest in the mid-nineteenth century.

## Crimean Tatars

In the spring of 1944, when the Soviet Red Army reoccupied the Crimean Peninsula, the Crimean Tatars were targeted for persecution because of their alleged collaboration with the Nazis. Ignoring the fact that the Crimean Tatars collaborated less than any Soviet national group, including the Russians, the entire national population, more than 200,000 people, were rounded up and shipped east. Crimean Tatar academics claim that 110,000 died as a result of the deportation. Russians and Ukrainians resettled the depopulated districts of the peninsula, and all signs of the once-flourishing Crimean Tatar culture were eradicated from their homeland.

Unlike the Muslim nations of the North Caucasus, the Crimean Tatars were not rehabilitated in 1956–1957, although strict KGB control was lifted, more movement was allowed, and Crimean Tatar publications began to be published. Several Crimean Tatar organizations were organized to agitate for complete rehabilitation and the right to return to their strategically important homeland. For the next ten years, national leaders and organizations kept up the pressure, bringing the issue before the United Nations and other international forums. Delegations dispatched to the Kremlin to present their case for return to successive Soviet leaders were simply ignored or ended in prison.

The Soviet government adamantly refused to discuss the possible return of the Crimean Tatars to the strategic peninsula, now populated by more reliable Slavs. Crimean Tatar newspapers, university groups, and publishing firms led a revival of the Crimean Tatar culture in exile. During the 1960s and early 1970s, several hundred families returned to the peninsula without permission, to live in shantytowns around the major Russian cities. Throughout the Cold War era the Soviet government continued to reject all demands for return, persecuting or imprisoning the most outspoken Crimean Tatar activists.

## Kalmyks

The small Kalmyk nation, the descendants of the last Asian people to penetrate Europe in the seventeenth century, was the remnant of a larger Mongol population that had returned to Asia in 1773. When the Russian government attempted to impose direct rule in that year, the Kalmyks east of the Volga River suddenly uprooted and undertook a harrowing return to their original homeland in the Altai Mountains of Central Asia. The Volga River did not freeze over that year, trapping the bands on the west bank, who were unable to join the exodus. The 60,000 Kalmyks left behind accepted Russian rule and eventually formed a military alliance similar to that of the Cossacks. The fervently Buddhist and anti-Communist Kalmyks, their monasteries and shrines destroyed during the height of the Stalinist purges, welcomed the German invaders in 1942. Others joined the Nazi anti-Communist crusade after the occupation authorities allowed the reopening of many temples and monasteries. A Kalmyk army fought as an ally of the Germans, often fighting against Kalmyks serving in the Red Army.

In February 1943, the Red Army regained control of the Kalmyk region. Stalin accused the entire Kalmyk nation of treason and ordered deportation. Often with only minutes' notice, the whole population, including the families of Red Army soldiers, were herded into cattle cars and shipped east. By 1950 over half the prewar Kalmyk population of some 140,000 had died as a result. Officially rehabilitated in 1956, the survivors gradually made their way back to their North Caucasian homeland. In 1958 the Kalmyk autonomous republic was reconstituted, but under strict Communist Party control and with a large ethnic Russian population to ensure continued loyalty and stability.

## Meskhtekians

The Meskhtekians are a nation that formed in exile. They are the surviving descendants of various Muslim peoples deported from the Turkish border region of southern Georgia in 1944. Although they now call themselves by the collective name Meskhtekian, taken from the name of their home region, they include Georgian Muslims called Meskhi, Armenian Muslims known as Khemsils, Shia Muslim Ajars, Kurds, and Karapapakh Turks. Turkey remained neutral during World War II, but Stalin's suspicion of the small Muslim nations, the hereditary enemies of his Georgian ancestors, extended even to peoples in locations far from the area overrun by the invading Germans. More than 130,000 Meskhtekians were driven from their homes in 1944, followed by more than 4,000 Meskhtekian soldiers of the Red Army who returned to their homes in 1945, only to face the same brutal deportation. National leaders claim that about 50,000 of their people died as a direct result of the deportation. They were not included in the 1956 rehabilitation. Eventually they were forgotten in the Soviet Union and remained unknown in the West.

The scattered groups began to establish contact in the early 1960s. Cultural organizations fostered the adoption of a national language, a hybrid combining elements of the Georgian Laz dialect and admixtures from several Turkic languages. Other organizations coordinated petitions, appeals, and continued agitation for the right to return to their mountain homeland in the Caucasus. Following a national congress held in Tashkent, Uzbekistan, in 1964, delegations were sent to Moscow and to the government of Soviet Georgia to plead for the right to return. Officially amnestied and restored to full rights as Soviet citizens only in 1968, many Meskhtekians moved from their scattered exile settlements to the Fergana Valley in Uzbekistan. News of the deportation and the plight of the exiles began to leak out to the West in 1969. International support, mostly by human rights groups, gave the Meskhtekians new hope. The growing prosperity of the energetic Meskhtekian exiles, who advanced more rapidly than their Uzbek neighbors, raised ethnic and religious tensions, which made the Meskhtekian pleas for the right to return ever more urgent.

## Central Asia

The pressures on the Stalinist regime during World War II forced Stalin to adopt a more conciliatory attitude toward religion. Fearing an uprising among the Turkestani peoples while the Red Army was occupied in Europe forced some concessions, particularly religious. Between 1942 and 1944, Central Asian Muslim leaders were allowed to convene a number of congresses, which had been prohibited since the imposition of Soviet rule. At the end of the war, an additional *medresse* (Islamic school) was opened in Tashkent for the training of religious leaders. Some mosques were allowed to reopen during the war and a small number of pilgrims were allowed to make the hajj, the pilgrimage to Mecca, the holy city in Arabia. The creation of what was termed "official Islam" created four regional spiritual boards, the most influential in Tashkent. While appearing to allow Muslims some limited religious autonomy, the establishment of an official religious structure also gave the government increased leverage with Islamic leaders. At the end of the war the concessions to Islam remained in place although considerable resources were still devoted to the eradication of what was viewed as an anachronism.

Nikita Khrushchev was initially greeted as a reformer in Central Asia, but the last years of his regime were marked by harsh repression of religion. In the early 1960s a large number of mosques were again shut down. Antireligious propaganda and atheistic teachings increased up to 1964, when Khrushchev was ousted. Successive Soviet leaders continued the bitter attack on religion during the long years of the Cold War. Muslim authorities from within the hierarchy of Stalinist-era "official Islam" continued to travel abroad, mostly to Muslim states, and as official envoys to international Muslim organizations. Numerous international conferences were held in Tashkent and other Central Asian cities, but by the early 1980s geopolitical considerations, such as the Iranian revolution in 1979 and the Soviet invasion of neighboring Afghanistan in the same year, marked a return to the harsh anti-Islamic approach.

After World War II, as part of the Soviet economic integration, the rich agricultural lands around the Aral Sea and in other parts of Central Asia were turned over almost exclusively to the production of cotton. Cotton production, to the exclusion of traditional crops, disrupted the area and began the environmental disaster that still plagues the region. Local political leaders had only to deliver the annual cotton quota to maintain their near-feudal powers. The drastic political and cultural changes of the Stalin era created a network of Communist functionaries whose clan and family networks gradually took control of the local economies.

## Kazakhs

The Kazakh homeland, made a separate union republic in 1936, retained a sizable Kazakh majority until after World War II. During the course of the war many industries and their workers were transferred to the region, which lay well east of the fighting. In 1953, Nikita Khrushchev decided to transform the fertile but "underutilized" steppe lands of northern Kazakhstan. The aim was to create a new breadbasket region in Kazakhstan and southern Siberia. The so-called Virgin Lands scheme transferred hundreds of thousands of ethnic Slavs and other Europeans to the region, completely changing the demographics of the northern provinces of Kazakhstan. The Kazakh population of the republic, about 57 percent of the total population in 1941, began to decline rapidly, as the ethnic Slav population expanded in a series of government-sponsored settlements.

The rapid increase in population, which stimulated urbanization, even among the indigenous Kazakhs, began a period of cultural awakening for the Kazakh nation. Education also became available for a wider number of Kazakhs. Decimated by the Soviet conquest during the Russian Civil War and the famine and devastation of collectivization, the Kazakhs remained extremely wary of politics, preferring to leave that painful subject to the growing Slavic population.

## Uzbeks

The Stalinist purge of the Uzbek leadership in the late 1930s eliminated some three-quarters of the Uzbek party hierarchy. With the beginning of World War II, the Stalinist terror eased as Uzbek troops were conscripted and sent west to the front. In an effort to win the support of the alienated Muslims, the government granted Islam official status within the Soviet Union in 1942. To administer Soviet Islam, four spiritual directorates were established, the one for Central Asia in Tashkent, the Uzbek capital. Many Uzbeks supported groups that actively opposed the Soviets in alliance with the Germans during the war.

At the end of the war, as part of the proposed economic integration, the rich agricultural lands of Uzbekistan were turned over to lucrative cotton production, usually to the exclusion of all other crops. The Uzbek republican functionaries needed only to deliver the yearly cotton quotas in order to maintain their positions and near-feudal powers. A clannish, authoritarian Communist power structure developed during the Stalin era based on a notoriously corrupt system dubbed by dissidents as "Feudal Socialism."

### Kyrgyz

Slavic settlement of the Krygyz lands was encouraged and became government policy in the early 1930s. The most fertile and productive lands were taken for colonization, leaving the Kyrgyz with only highland grazing lands. Towns and cities in the region became identical to those in European Russia. In 1939 the Kyrgyz were forced to adopt the Russian Cyrillic alphabet in place of the Latin script used since the early 1920s, further distancing them from their past. The Soviet plan for educating a generation of Kyrgyz leaders as Soviets largely failed because the educated Kyrgyz often adopted dissident views or joined the underground nationalist or religious movements. Agitation against Stalinist excesses, before and after World War II, was met with periodic purges and show trials of prominent antigovernment leaders.

During the course of the war many Kyrgyz supported the Turkestan National Committee, which gave covert support to the Germans and any others willing to fight the hated Soviets. In September 1942 the Turkic Legion was formed from Muslim units fighting with the Axis powers. At the end of the war, the region was allocated more resources for development. Education and material advances turned the feudal Kyrgyz leadership into a modern, educated elite, although the majority of the population remained undereducated, clinging to their ancient culture and their Islamic traditions. In 1952 the Stalinist authorities banned the great Kyrgyz epic *Manas,* stimulating demands for the revision of the distorted and falsified Kyrgyz history. The episode marked the beginning of a Kyrgyz cultural revival that remained underground during the decades of the Cold War.

## Turkmen (Turkomen)

The Stalinist repression began in Turkmenistan in the early 1930s. Turkmen nomads, labeled parasites, were forced in bloody battles to give up their herds and settle on Soviet collectives. Far from the centers of Soviet power, the republic was ruled by Communist Party appointees whose only qualification was unquestioning loyalty to Stalin and the Soviet hierarchy. Wielding near-feudal powers, the local bureaucrats, systematically looted the republic, earning for themselves the contemptuous label "Turkmen Mafia."

A massive earthquake struck the Turkmen republic in 1948, destroying the capital and other important centers and leaving more than 110,000 people dead. For the next five years the republic was closed to foreigners, while bodies were recovered and the wreckage cleared. While the republic slowly recovered, cotton cultivation was extended to the most fertile districts, seriously damaging the environment and endangering public health. Even after Stalin's death in 1953, the party leadership in the republic was based on clan, family, and influence ties. The Turkmen leadership, whose loyalty to Moscow was more important than capability, continued as the most notorious and corrupt in Central Asia.

## Tajiks

The Tajiks suffered severe religious repression and periodic political purges in the 1930s even while material and educational standards rapidly surpassed those of the Tajik populations in adjacent areas of Afghanistan and in Iran. Feeling threatened by the rapid changes commanded by Moscow, the Tajiks rebelled in 1941 following a decree changing their Persian alphabet to the Russians' Cyrillic script. Savage Soviet reprisals against rebel areas and areas that remained neutral in the fighting were meant to demonstrate what could happen to ethnic minorities causing trouble while the Soviets were fighting the invading Nazis in Europe. The punishment for the revolt was so far-reaching that it created a leadership vacuum in the republic that lasted into the 1950s.

Considered the most conservative and religious of the Central Asians, the Tajiks retained much of their pre-Soviet culture and traditions despite enormous pressure to adopt Soviet norms. The majority of the Tajiks adhere to the Sunni branch of Islam, with smaller Ismaili and Shia minorities, mostly in the Pamir Mountains. However, religious practices often retained vestiges of the pre-Islamic religious traditions that had become part of the Tajik culture. Attempts to eradicate the Tajiks' strong attachment to their religion in the 1950s and 1960s kept the region in turmoil.

## Jews

Soviet Jewry suffered more than any other Soviet nationality as part of the Nazi effort to exterminate all of Europe's Jews. An estimated 3.1 million Jews lived in the Soviet Union when the war began, but according to the census of 1959, only 2.2 million remained. The beginning of World War II in the Soviet Union in 1941 allowed Soviet Jews to make new advances in their long struggle for equality. Jews had always been disproportionately represented in the hierarchy of the Communist Party, but other professions and trades had been traditionally reserved for ethnic Slavs. Military opportunities particularly opened up with the outbreak of hostilities. During the war, there were several hundred Jewish officers with the rank of lieutenant colonel or above, including more than fifty generals of Jewish descent.

In spite of Stalin's open anti-Semitism, the Jews were granted the right to fully participate in Soviet society, but they had to abandon their religion and their traditional way of life. In theory the Jews gained their longed-for equality, but anti-Semitism did not disappear. Anti-Semitic activity in the Soviet Union increased greatly in response to the creation of the Jewish state of Israel in 1948. Without explanation, Jewish schools, theaters, and cultural institutions were closed down. Leading writers were arrested and executed in 1952. A so-called Doctors' Plot, involving nine physicians, six of them Jewish, was uncovered. The doctors were accused of poisoning leading Soviet politicians. Although the charges were dropped after Stalin's death in March 1953, repression continued to increase.

The Yiddish language, considered the national language of the Soviet Jews, was spoken by nearly all Jews in 1900, but by 1940 that figure had dropped to less than a third. The loss of the language was partly owing to the official policy of assimilation, but was also attributable to the complete secularization of the state. All religious property had been confiscated and religious instruction prohibited. By the early 1930s, very few rabbis remained to carry on the historic cultural and religious traditions. After World War II, the anti-Semitic Stalin led the antireligious, anti-Jewish campaign himself. By 1960 there were fewer than sixty operating synagogues in the Soviet Union, and only one was allowed in Moscow.

## Rom (Gypsies)

In the first years of Soviet rule, the Roms of Russia and Ukraine were recognized as a distinct nationality under Lenin's Soviet policy. The general educational level was raised, newspapers and magazines were published in Rom dialects, and preparations were begun for Rom schools and Rom language education. By the late 1920s most Rom programs had been abandoned and the Rom shared the fate of other deported populations. Thousands were arrested and exiled to Siberia and Central Asia. In 1956, the Soviet authorities announced a decree forbidding the remaining Rom populations to move from the provinces or regions where they had been officially registered.

The Rom populations farther west in Europe came under Nazi rule when war began in 1939. By 1940 thousands had been rounded up and sent to work camps in occupied Poland. By the summer of 1942 the Nazi leadership had decided to exterminate Europe's Roms, putting them into the same category of undesirables as the retarded, the mentally ill, homosexuals, and Jews. When the Nazi armies overran the western part of the Soviet Union in 1941, whole Rom populations were summarily shot; later in the war they were sent to the Nazi concentration camps along with the Jews and other targeted groups. The Gypsy Holocaust, called *Porrajmos* by the Roms, meaning "the devouring," eventually claimed some 2 million lives during World War II. Most died in massacres or of disease and hunger, but more than half a million perished in the Nazi death camps.

## The Siberian Nations

Until World War II, the Soviet government viewed the enormous Siberian territory as a dependent territory, to be colonized and exploited. The indigenous peoples and their rights were not a consideration. During the course of the war, the authorities transferred many industries and large numbers of workers eastward, away from areas threatened by the Nazi advance. The rapid industrialization was accompanied by the need for workers in the more remote areas, so Siberia became the site of the infamous gulag, the string of labor camps to which millions were deported during Stalin's long rule. The deportees, including a large number of non-Russian ethnic groups, were used as slave labor in mines and for the construction of dams, railroads, and cities. An estimated 20 million people perished in the gulag. The construction made possible by the unlimited supply of slaves opened vast areas to exploitation, including the homelands of the Siberian ethnic groups.

## Altai

The Soviet authorities accused the Altai leadership of pro-Japanese leanings during World War II. Many of the Altai leadership, both the traditional hierarchy and the local Soviet functionaries, were liquidated or sent to prison camps. At the end of the war a brief period of leniency gave way to renewed repression. In 1948, the Soviet authorities banned the use of the term *Oirot,* the historical name of the Altai tribes, as counterrevolutionary. The Oirot autonomous province was renamed the Mountain Altai (Gorno-Altai) and the name of the capital was changed from the historic Oirot-Tura to Gorno-Altaisk.

In spite of the many problems created by Soviet rule, the Altai made gains in education and gradually produced a new generation of leaders educated in the Soviet system but well aware of their nation's past glories and injustices. A modest national and cultural revival took hold in the more relaxed atmosphere after Stalin's death in 1953, a revival that began to reverse the long Altai decline. By the 1960s the Altai population again began to increase. Serious social problems, including alcohol abuse, remained as deterrents to development during the 1950s and 1960s.

## Buryats

During World War II many threatened industries and their workforces were transferred from European Russia so that by the end of the war the Buryats constituted a minority of the population in their homeland. Buryat leaders, during the war, started the revival of Buryat Buddhism. The religion was officially reestablished in 1946, but under strict Soviet control. In 1948 a campaign to Russify and Sovietize Buryat culture was launched. Fearing the rebirth of Buryat religion and nationalism, Stalin ordered more than 10,000 Buryat cultural, political, and religious leaders deported or killed. Traditional art forms, including religious tracts, were banned, and Russian-speaking academics took charge of the education and assimilation of the Buryat population. Soviet attempts to separate the Buryats from their Mongol kin included changing the name of the republic from the Buryat-Mongol Autonomous Soviet Socialist Republic to the Buryat ASSR in 1958. The republic was declared a closed region, and access without specific permission was denied, effectively cutting the Buryats off from any outside contact.

## Sakhas

The Sakha homeland was greatly changed by the large number of deported Poles imprisoned in the region following the Soviet Union's invasion on eastern Poland in 1939. The Poles became the main component of the gulag. In Sakha territory they were set to forest clearing and road building. Later German war prisoners and the many others suspected as enemies of the Soviet state arrived in the region. Contact with these new populations, although officially forbidden, had a profound effect on the Sakha population. At the end of World War II the Sakha leadership abandoned their traditional herding life and moved into the professions. The region's enormous natural resources—gold, diamonds, and coal—fueled the Soviet industrialization and drew in a large Slavic population in the 1950s and 1960s. Pollution from the poorly controlled industrial and mining sites scarred the region and left behind dead rivers and polluted grazing lands. The Sakha percentage of the republic's population dropped from 80 percent of the total in 1946 to less than 50 percent in 1965.

## Tuvans

Tannu Tuva remained an independent Communist republic until Soviet troops occupied the major cities in October 1944, ostensibly to prevent a counterrevolution. The Soviet Union officially annexed the Tuvan homeland in 1945, supposedly at the solicitation of the Tuvan population themselves. Although subjected to the Stalinist purges and repression, the Tuvans continued to send petitions and to pressure local officials until the Soviet authorities finally agreed to grant their homeland the status of an autonomous republic in 1961. Their new status gave them some cultural autonomy, although contacts with neighboring peoples were not permitted. Most Tuvans continued to live a traditional way of life, leaving the painful issue of politics to the Russian minority in the region.

## The Cold War

The defeat of Germany and the other Axis powers allowed the Soviet Union to become a world power despite the loss of some 20 million people and the enormous devastation of the war. Soviet authority was extended into Central Europe, effectively dividing Europe into two hostile camps. Soviet ideology and collectivization were imposed by pro-Soviet governments installed in the capitals of the states occupied by the Red Army. In 1949 the USSR became the second state, after the United States, to explode a nuclear bomb, giving it superpower status.

Stalin's death in 1953 began a period of relaxation during the so-called de-Stalinization campaign. This allowed a more lenient view of the many national minorities within the Soviet Union, but determined to retain its control of the Communist bloc, the Soviet government intervened against liberalizing governments in Hungary in 1956 and in Czechoslovakia in 1968. Attempts to install nuclear weapons in newly Communist Cuba in 1962 brought the world close to nuclear war. Although the Soviet government maintained a military stance that required the focus of the Soviet economy, Soviet citizens lived in poverty. In some parts of the Soviet Union, particularly among the national groups in Siberia, the Caucasus, and Central Asia, the standard of living barely exceeded that of developing parts of Africa.

## Timeline

| | |
|---|---|
| 1939 | The Soviet Union and Nazi Germany sign the Molotov-Ribbentrop Pact. Soviet troops occupy eastern Poland, Latvia, Lithuania, and Estonia and begin war with Finland. The eastern provinces of Poland, with Ukrainian and Belarussian majorities, are annexed to the Soviet Union. |
| 1940 | The Soviet Union seizes Bessarabia and northern Bukovina from Romania and annexes Estonia, Latvia, and Lithuania. Territory taken from defeated Finland is added to Karelia to form the Karelo-Finnish Soviet Socialist Republic, which becomes a union republic. |
| 1941 | The Russo-Finnish War ends with a Soviet victory. In June 1941 the Soviets' Nazi allies invade the USSR. All Soviet Germans living in areas not occupied by the invading Nazi forces are rounded up and deported to Central Asia and Siberia. Soviet troops occupy northwestern Iran. |
| 1942 | Axis troops drive into the Caucasus region in an effort to capture the Soviet Union's most important oil-producing regions. Many of the peoples of the region welcome the invaders as liberators from harsh Soviet rule. |

| | |
|---|---|
| 1943–1944 | The Red Army drives the invaders back and returns to the North Caucasus and the Crimean Peninsula. |
| 1945 | World War II ends leaving Soviet troops occupying eastern and Central Europe. Puppet regimes are established in the occupied countries, marking the greatest extent of Soviet territorial power. Disputes in occupied Germany set the stage for the Cold War. |
| 1946 | Stalin abolishes the Uniate Catholic Church in western Ukraine as part of the official repression of religions and national groups that accompanied the end of the war. |
| 1948–1953 | The development of a Soviet nuclear bomb begins the so-called Cold War. |
| 1953 | Stalin dies, setting off a struggle for power that eventually brings Nikita Khrushchev to power in the Kremlin. |
| 1954 | To celebrate 300 years of the union of Ukraine and Russia, the Soviet government transfers the Crimean Peninsula from the Russian Federation to Soviet Ukraine. |
| 1956 | Soviet forces crush an uprising in Hungary as part of the ongoing ideological Cold War. The Karelo-Finnish republic is dissolved, and the Karelian Autonomous SSR is reestablished within the Russian Federation. |
| 1956-1957 | The rehabilitation of the deported nations is begun, allowing the deportees to return to their homes. |
| 1962 | The Soviet attempt to introduce nuclear arms into newly Communist Cuba brings the two Cold War opponents close to nuclear war. |
| 1964 | Khrushchev is overthrown, beginning a period of economic stagnation and massive military spending, as the rivalry between the Communist bloc and the West continues. |
| 1965 | The Soviet Germans are officially rehabilitated but are not allowed to return to their historic homelands. |
| 1967 | The Crimean Tatars are officially rehabilitated but remain under strict control and are not allowed to return to the Crimean Peninsula. |
| 1968 | Soviet troops intervene against a liberalizing movement in Czechoslovakia. The Meskhtekians are rehabilitated but are refused permission to return to their homeland on the sensitive Turkish border. |
| 1970 | Jewish emigration for the Soviet Union to Israel and the United States increases rapidly. |

## Significant People, Places, and Events

AXIS The totalitarian nations opposed to the Allies during World War II. The Axis, united by a number of military pacts and treaties, included Germany, Japan, Italy, Hungary, Romania, and Bulgaria.

COLD WAR The term used to describe the ongoing struggle for power and prestige between the Western powers and the Communist states from the end of World War II until 1989. Although the ideological conflict was of worldwide proportions, the major fields of conflict were in Europe.

DOCTORS' PLOT A suspected plot involving nine physicians, six of them Jewish, announced in early 1953. The doctors were accused of trying to poison leading Communist politicians, setting off a wave of anti-Semitism. The charges were dropped following Stalin's death in March 1953, but the repression of the Jews continued.

IRANIAN AZERBAIJAN The region of northwestern Iran populated by ethnic Azeris, historically, linguistically, and culturally part of a larger Azeri nation that also includes the Azeris of the Transcaucasus. Soviet troops occupied the region during World War II but at the end of the war refused to withdraw. Instead they supported a nationalist uprising in the hopes of eventually reuniting all the Azeris under Soviet rule.

KARELIA The homeland of the Finnish Karels in northwestern Russia. The Karelian Autonomous Soviet Socialist Republic was established in 1923. Originally intended as a model to promote communism in neighboring Finland, in 1940 the autonomous republic was dissolved and was replaced, with additional territory taken from Finland, by the Karelo-Finnish Soviet Socialist Republic, which was admitted to the Soviet Union as the twelfth union republic.

KHRUSHCHEV, NIKITA The Soviet leader who eventually took control by eliminating all rivals following Joseph Stalin's death in 1953.

MOLOTOV-RIBBENTROP PACT A treaty of friendship and nonaggression signed by the Soviet Union and Nazi Germany in August 1939.

OBLAST The Russian name for province. The name oblast was applied to provinces and autonomous provinces both in the Russian Federation and in the various national republics under the Soviet Union.

PUNISHED NATIONS The so-called Punished Nations were the small Muslim and Buddhist nations of the North Caucasus and the other nations deported from their homelands before and during World War II. The nations included the Muslim Balkars, Ingush, Karachai, Chechens, and the Buddhist Kalmyks of the North Caucasus region, and the Meskhtekians of the Transcaucasus, Crimean Tatars of the Crimean Peninsula, the Volga

Germans and other regional German groups of European Russia, the Black Sea Greeks, and the Koreans of the Far East.

**Uniate Catholic Church** The majority religion in the western Ukrainian territory that formed part of the Austro-Hungarian Empire and, between the two world wars, was controlled by Poland.

## Bibliography

Allworth, Edward, ed. *Tatars of the Crimea*. Durham, NC: Duke University Press, 1988.

Caroe, Olaf. *Soviet Empire: The Turks of Central Asia and Stalinism*. London: Macmillan, 1953.

Clemens, Walter C. *Baltic Independence and Russian Empire*. New York: St. Martin's Press, 1991.

Conquest, Robert. *The Nation Killers: Soviet Deportation of Nationalities*. New York: Macmillan, 1970.

Fierman, William, ed. *Soviet Central Asia: The Failed Transformation*. Boulder, CO: Westview Press, 1991.

Lubachko, Ivan S. *Belorussia under Soviet Rule, 1917–1957*. Lexington: University of Kentucky Press, 1972.

Misiunas, Romuald J., and Rein Taagepera. *The Baltic States: Years of Dependence, 1940–1991*. Berkeley: University of California Press, 1991.

Olson, James S. *An Ethnohistorical Dictionary of the Russian and Soviet Empires*. Westport, CT: Greenwood Press, 1994.

Spector, Ivan. *The Soviet Union and the Muslim World, 1917–1958*. Seattle: University of Washington Press, 1959.

# Rebirth of
# Ethnic Consciousness

# Cold War Stagnation and the Rebirth of Nationalism, 1971–1991

THE COLD WAR LEADERS OF THE SOVIET UNION, after the overthrow of Khrushchev in 1964, attempted to maintain the fiction that the country was united and that the many national, ethnic, and religious groups had merged into the idealized Soviet culture. The reality was stagnation on many levels, economic, cultural, and social. The period from the mid-1960s to the mid-1980s was dominated by Leonid Brezhnev, a period sometimes called the period of the benign neglect of the nationalities. As ethnic nationalism intensified during the Cold War period in the Baltics, the Caucasus, and Central Asia, Russian nationalism revived as well. During the 1970s, the Communist Party attempted to propagate its own idea of nationalism to combat the nationalist rebirth that was taking place across the Soviet state. The state and party vigorously promoted the idea of "Soviet man," the culmination of centuries of government assimilationist policies. Marxist theory held that history was marching inexorably toward communism. Society in the Soviet Union, where local nationalisms had, in theory, been eliminated, was becoming international in outlook and was molded by Communist ideals. Misguided parochial perspectives, which were manifested by ethnic nationalism and mistaken religious loyalties, would continue to steadily disappear.

The Brezhnev regime called for a merger of the nations, asserting that government policies could accelerate the elimination of the many insular nationalities. The key to the elimination of local loyalties was Russification, an accelerated version of the policy followed by both czarist and earlier Soviet regimes. The policy was particularly targeted at the Ukrainians and Belarussians, the most closely related, culturally and linguistically, to the Russians. If they could be merged into Russian-Soviet culture, the smaller, non-Slavic nationalities would theoretically follow.

The Soviet Union of the 1970s was very similar to the Russian Empire of

*Russian Party Chief Leonid Brezhnev waves to a crowd during his visit to the White House in June 1973. (Bettmann/Corbis)*

the late nineteenth and early twentieth centuries. Each was imbued with a powerful religious ideology—the Russian Empire with the Orthodox Church, the Soviet Empire with Marxism-Leninism. Both empires were autocratic states with strong suspicions about democratic thought. In order to maintain the Soviet Union as the world's second superpower, the military and the development of military technology increasingly took precedence over the needs of the civilian population, particularly the often-troublesome non-Russian groups. The non-Russian ethnic groups, after decades of suppression, were either assimilating or had been left leaderless by the purges and show trials conducted under successive Soviet leaders. Most ethnic Russians believed that there were powerful economic and cultural reasons for pressing Russification across the Soviet Union. Soviet leaders were also convinced that Russification equaled modernization. Official government and Communist Party policy supported the idea that adoption of the Russian language by all Soviet nationalities would make for a more advanced society able to compete with the affluent West.

Brezhnev's fierce attempt to obliterate all remaining national and religious loyalties led to increased suppression but also increased dissidence. The Helsinki Accords of 1975, which guaranteed various international civil rights, led to the formation of "Helsinki Watch" groups in many parts of the Soviet Union, particularly in areas inhabited by non-Russian nationalities. The Helsinki groups were most active where nationalist sentiment still resisted Soviet pressure. The death of Brezhnev in 1982 and the emergence of Mikhail Gorbachev in 1985 once again altered the situation in the Soviet Union. A new generation of Communist officials took control, determined to reverse the stagnation of the 1970s and early 1980s and to prevent the complete collapse of the Soviet system. Gorbachev's policy of perestroika (restructuring) of the dying Soviet economy was accompanied by a new policy of glasnost (openness) in the secretive Soviet society.

Gorbachev understood that the Soviet Union could no longer maintain its superpower status while its economy remained little more developed than those of the Third World. However, he failed to realize that the rifts in the country were so deep. For seventy years, Soviet unity and its hegemony in the eastern territories of Europe had been based on brutal military power and strong economic inducements. Unable to maintain the economic drain on the Soviet economy, Gorbachev gave the non-Soviet states of Eastern Europe more freedom. Gorbachev's ability to continue the powerful military presence also vanished. With unprecedented speed, Communist governments collapsed throughout Eastern Europe, and steps were taken to bring about the reunification of Germany. New political freedoms in Eastern Europe only strengthened the national aspirations and sentiments of the Soviet national groups. Political mobilization appeared first in the western republics, particularly Ukraine, Belarus, and the Baltic republics, where influences from the liberalizing Communist republics of Eastern Europe were first felt.

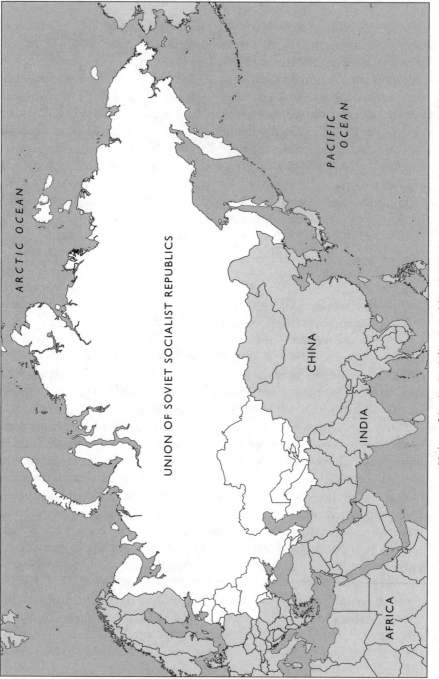

ARCTIC OCEAN

UNION OF SOVIET SOCIALIST REPUBLICS

PACIFIC OCEAN

CHINA

INDIA

AFRICA

*Union of Soviet Socialist Republics (USSR), 1990*

## Ukrainians

The brief relaxation of the Khrushchev period ended in Ukraine with the arrests of numerous intellectuals accused of nationalism, anti-Soviet activities, and other crimes against the state. The crackdown of the 1960s also ended attempts by several dissidents to chronicle Soviet violations of Ukrainian human rights. A number of dissidents resorted to underground samizdat (self-published) manuscripts to publish antigovernment views. The repression intensified in 1972, with a new wave of arrests and a crackdown on further cultural and linguistic concessions. In the late 1970s and early 1980s, Ukrainian nationalism mostly disappeared from the eastern provinces, but in western Ukraine, with its large underground Catholic population, dissent continued to grow despite extremely harsh governmental repression. What remained of the modest national revival of the 1960s was mostly driven underground. Nationalist sentiment, persecuted in the Ukrainian homeland, was centered in the large Ukrainian populations in Canada and the United States, and among exiles living in western Europe.

The Helsinki Accords, negotiated in 1975, guaranteed various national and individual rights and led to the formation of groups affiliated with the movement in Ukraine. Even though some leaders were arrested and sent to prison in Siberia, others persisted, some even drawn from the ranks of committed Marxists. The movement was particularly concerned with religious rights. The government's brutal persecution of the Uniate Catholics in western Ukraine had failed to eliminate the faith, which had gone underground. In 1982, members of the church organized the Committee for the Defense of the Ukrainian Catholic Church, which demanded nothing less than legalization. Ukrainian Orthodox believers also began to resist the domination of their historically separate church by the Moscow hierarchy of the Russian Orthodox Church.

The poor government response to the 1986 Chernobyl nuclear disaster, which affected thousands of Ukrainians and Belarussians living in the path of the radioactive contamination, galvanized the dormant Ukrainian national movement. The liberalization of Soviet life introduced by Mikhail Gorbachev in the late 1980s allowed Ukrainians to again mobilize. Religion, despite decades of suppression, played a crucial role in the rebirth of Ukrainian nationalism in the 1980s. The Uniate Catholics of western Ukraine, having demanded the legalization of their historic church, began to organize to demand other basic rights. Ukrainian Orthodox Christians also stepped up their resistance to domination by the Moscow church hierarchy, seen as part of the Soviet Russification policy. The rebirth of nationalist sentiment, centered in the western Ukraine and Kiev, slowly gained support across the Ukrainian provinces. Nationalists formed the Ukrainian People's Movement for Restructuring, better known by its initials as RUKH, to work for greater autonomy for the Ukrainian republic within the Soviet Union. The first RUKH congress was held in L'viv, the unofficial capital of western Ukraine and the center of modern Ukrainian nationalism. RUKH quickly became an umbrella organization for all progressive forces, including even reform-minded Communists. The new Ukrainian nationalism, based on history, language, and religion, finally forced a change in the leadership of the Ukrainian republic to accommodate popular demands in 1989.

Led by RUKH, nationalists mobilized to denounce the economic and linguistic colonization of Ukraine by the Russians, a colonization, they claimed, that had no historical precedent, not even in colonial Africa. In January 1990, RUKH activists organized a human chain stretching 311 miles from Kiev to the western Ukrainian capital at L'viv to illustrate the unity of the historically divided Ukrainian nation. Mounting pressure on the Communist Ukrainian government to observe Gorbachev's policy of openness included, after more than fifty years of silence, demands for an official accounting of the human-caused famine of 1932–1933. The outlawed Ukrainian Orthodox Church and the Ukrainian Autocephalous Orthodox churches were legalized, as was the Uniate Catholic Church in western Ukraine. In March 1990, Ukrainians voted in a semifree election for their first real parliament since 1918. Although more than two-thirds of the deputies elected to the new parliament were Communist Party members, the parliament declared Ukraine a sovereign state with only six dissenting votes on 16 July 1990. The declaration adopted a four-point program, not only proclaiming Ukrainian sovereignty but also Ukraine's right to a national army and security forces, the supremacy of the republican government in Ukrainian territory, and the intent to transform the Ukrainian republic into a nuclear-free zone.

In October 1990, disillusioned with the slow pace of change and with Gorbachev's perceived shift to the right, the members of RUKH became more radical. Originally they had pressed only for a measure of Ukrainian autonomy, but now some began to talk of even more. In December of the same year, the parliament declared Ukrainian the national language of the Ukrainian state. A vote on a new union treaty among the member states of the USSR produced ambivalent results as the majority favored the renewal of the union but also backed the declaration of Ukrainian sovereignty. Some of the newly legalized political parties interpreted the results as a mandate for complete Ukrainian independence. Some groups recognized the legitimacy of the Ukrainian "government-in-exile," based in the United States. Even the

Ukrainian Communist Party split into "national" and "pro-Soviet" factions as Soviet power began to wane in late 1990.

## Belarussians

A Belarussian national revival, begun as a reaction to Stalin's excesses, particularly in the Roman Catholic western provinces, was ended with the renewed suppression of the Brezhnev era. Assimilation, supported by both the czarist and Soviet governments, had nearly succeeded in the republic. The so-called merger of nations that was adopted by the Soviet regime in the 1970s in support of the ideal of Soviet man was particularly targeted at Belarus. Belief that the cultural merger of Belarus, Ukraine, and Russia would assure the Slavic domination of the rest of the Soviet Empire underlay government actions in the republic. Russification would strengthen the economy and reduce historical ethnic tensions. As in all non-Russian republics, the first secretary of the Communist Party, the republican head of government, must be a Russified Belarussian, and the second secretary had to be an ethnic Russian.

The process of Russification seemed to accompany the urbanization and industrialization of the republic. The increasingly urbanized Belarussians for the most part adopted Russian as their first language, whereas those that remained in rural areas or worked on communal farms retained Belarussian as their primary language. These linguistic trends accelerated with the urbanization of the 1970s and early 1980s. By 1985 only about 70 percent of Belarussians claimed Belarussian as their first language, whereas approximately 30 percent considered Russian their mother tongue. Belarussian was not taught in public schools in the republic. Soviet officials considered the republic as virtually assimilated into Russian-Soviet culture.

The rise of Mikhail Gorbachev and his policies of liberalization began a gradual rebirth of Belarussian nationalism. The Chernobyl nuclear accident in 1986 radically changed attitudes in the republic. Owing to the incompetent management of the nuclear power plant explosion, the poor government response, and the attempts to cover up the full extent of the disaster, the Belarussians began to mobilize. More than 2 million people were exposed to high levels of radioactive contamination. Since management of the nuclear plants was directed from Moscow, many Belarussians blamed the Soviet government for the disaster. A movement demanding the removal of all nuclear weapons from Belarussian soil led to other demands, including linguistic and cultural autonomy and an end to the official policy of Russification.

The nascent national movement, fueled by the growing assertiveness of similar movements in the neighboring Baltic republics, gained momentum in the late 1980s. Small groups joined together as the national movement became more outspoken. The publication of a report on the discovery of a mass grave at Kuropaty near Minsk had a dramatic impact on the growing national movement. The grave, reportedly containing more than 250,000 bodies, was the result of just one of Stalin's purges of university graduates, intellectuals, clergy, people with suspect political loyalties, and even ordinary citizens rounded up to fill killing quotas. The victims, murdered by the NKVD, the predecessor of the KGB, were buried in the mass graves between 1937 and 1941. The discovery that the Soviet government had committed the mass murders, which were officially blamed on the Nazis, added fuel to the growing anti-Soviet movement that was taking hold in what was considered the most obedient of the Soviet republics

In October 1988, several groups established the Belarussian Popular Front, called Adradzhen'ne, meaning rebirth or renewal. Modeled on the movements gaining support in the neighboring Baltic republics, the popular front openly called for national sovereignty, a commitment to human rights, and the legalization of the Belarussian Catholic Church. Other demands included a separate budget for the Belarussian republic, control of the republican economy, cultural and economic autonomy, the right to fly the long-banned national flag, and an open accounting of the crimes committed against the Belarussian nation during the Stalin era. When republican officials refused to allow nationalists to hold meetings in Belarus, Lithuanian officials provided a convention hall, printing presses, and access to newspapers and television. Pan-Slavism was denounced as thinly disguised Russian assimilation amid calls for a revitalization of Belarussian language and culture. Nationalists justified their demands for sovereignty on Belarus's current status as a member state of the United Nations. The conservative Communist rulers of the republic, under ever-increasing pressure from the nationalist movement, reluctantly declared Belarussian sovereignty in July 1990. The declaration proclaimed the republic a nuclear-free zone and designated the entire state a nuclear disaster area.

## The Baltic Nations

Clandestine national groups were unable to do more than small symbolic gestures during the decades of the Cold War. Manifestations of national sentiment were harshly punished. Small exile groups, mostly in the United

States, where embassies representing the independent prewar Baltic republics were allowed to function, tried to keep the issue of Baltic independence alive. Life in the Baltic republics began to change only when Mikhail Gorbachev came to power in Moscow in March 1985. His attempts to liberalize and revitalize the Soviet economy and society were first put into practice in the Baltic region. In 1987 Gorbachev began to discuss the possibility of more political and economic freedom for the Baltic republics, then the most economically advanced in the USSR. What Gorbachev and his advisors did not understand was the depth of anti-Soviet feeling in the region. Held within the USSR by decades of terror and military force, the Baltic republics showed very little loyalty to the tottering Soviet Empire. Political unrest, the unwanted by-product of Gorbachev's glasnost and perestroika, first appeared among the Baltic populations. Gorbachev's policies unleashed political and social forces in the Baltic region over which the Gorbachev regime had little or no control. One of Gorbachev's greatest mistakes was to underestimate the national sentiment still alive among the Baltic nations.

## Estonians

The 1970s were a decade of stagnation and little economic growth in the Soviet Union, but despite the hardships and Communist restrictions, the Estonians managed to become the most advanced and prosperous nation in the USSR. Their homeland, known as Soviet Scandinavia, received television transmissions from ethnically related, prosperous Finland, so the Estonians were well aware of the differences between their relative affluence within the Soviet Union and that of the wealthy, Westernized Finns. The continuing settlement of ethnic Slavs in the republic and the suppression of their cherished culture rekindled Estonian nationalism, which received strong support from Estonian populations in Western Europe and North America. The Estonian economic achievements, although spectacular by dismal Soviet standards, quickly paled as Soviet stagnation spread in the 1970s. By the early 1980s there were regular shortages of services, particularly electric power, industrial goods, and food.

The movement of Slavic settlers into the republic, often in government-sponsored programs, reduced the Estonian population from 97 percent of the total in 1939 to about 65 percent in 1970. The Russian portion of the population, negligible before World War II, reached a quarter of the total in the early 1970s. By 1990 the Estonians represented only 61 percent, whereas

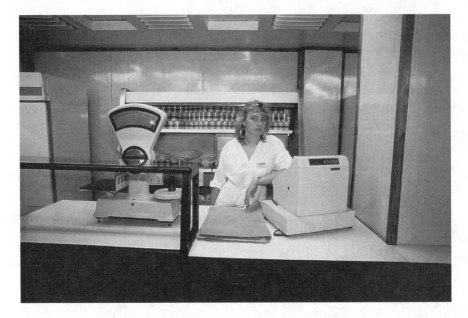

*An Estonian shop clerk stands at the register of a shop with very little to sell, 1991. (Shepard Sherbell/Corbis Saba)*

the Russian portion had risen to nearly a third. As the number of ethnic Slavs increased, the intensity of Estonian nationalist sentiment increased, but official action, opposed by a third of the population, became increasingly difficult. Calls for the Slavs, including the sizable Ukrainian community, to leave the republic were countered by Slavic organizations determined to hold on to their privileges, including housing preferences that would be unthinkable in Russia. What emerged was a society in which the ethnic Estonians made up a high percentage of white-collar and service workers and Slavs were mostly transferred to the republic as blue-collar labor.

The Estonians embraced the liberalization of the Soviet economy and society in the late 1980s as perhaps their last opportunity to regain some control over their lives. The Estonian Popular Front, the first large political organization in the Soviet Union outside the Communist Party, was formed in early 1988. When Eastern Europe threw off the Soviet yoke in 1988–1989, the Estonians began to mobilize. Government plans to construct a huge phosphate-mining industry in north-central Estonia was the spark. The industrial development threatened to pollute the air and water in the entire republic and to bring a new influx of ethnic Slavs to their homeland. Opposition to the project began clandestinely but quickly spread to the universities and other public institutions. The Soviet planners eventually backed down and tabled the project. The significance of their victory stirred Estonian nationalists to demand even more. Soon activists were testing the limits of Gorbachev's policy of glasnost. The Estonian Supreme Soviet, pressured by rising nationalist demands, passed a declaration of state sovereignty in November 1988. The declaration acknowledged the supremacy of Estonian laws within the republic

Working with activists from Latvia and Lithuania, the Estonian nationalists openly demanded autonomy for the Baltic republics. In August 1989, on the fiftieth anniversary of the Molotov-Ribbentrop Pact, more than 2 million Estonians, Latvians, and Lithuanians simultaneously held hands in a human chain stretching across the three Baltic republics. The Estonian nationalists became the most outspoken in the USSR, provoking a backlash by the large Russian-speaking population in the republic. The Internationalist Movement, which represented the interests of the Slavs and other non-Estonians in the republic, demanded the repeal of new Estonian language laws and the outlawing of the Estonian flag, which had quickly replaced the red Soviet banner everywhere but on Soviet government buildings. The Slavs appealed to the Soviet government for annexation of the heavily Russian-speaking northeastern region of Estonia to the Russian Republic, with a few radicals calling for the punishment and deportation of the entire Estonian nation.

A series of locally organized free elections in 1989 and early 1990 gave the nationalists widespread support. In October 1989, the Estonian Popular Front openly announced its avowed objective—the revival of Estonia's pre-1940 status as an independent state. One month later the Estonian government reiterated its earlier declaration of sovereignty, a move immediately condemned by the Soviet government. Political changes came with breathtaking speed. Estonian was declared the official language, the Communist Party lost its dominant role in the political life of the republic, and opposition political groups were recognized. On 30 March 1990, the Supreme Soviet of the Estonian Soviet Socialist Republic voted seventy-three to zero to declare Soviet power in Estonia illegal. They also announced a transition period during which the Estonian republic would move toward complete independence. In April 1990, the Supreme Soviet, renamed the Supreme Council, adopted a new name for the republic, abolishing the Estonian SSR in favor of the Republic of Estonia. Boris Yeltsin, the populist leader of the Russian Federation, visited Estonia in December 1990 expressing his support of Estonian demands for independence.

## Latvians

Latvia, like the other Baltic nations, suffered heavily from the Soviet policy of Russification. In 1939, when war began in Europe, ethnic Latvians constituted about 75 percent of the total population of the republic, but by 1970 Russians made up about 30 percent of the total and the Latvian portion of the population had dropped to just 57 percent. Massive government-sponsored settlement of ethnic Slavs during the 1970s and 1980s further eroded the Latvian majority until in 1990 only 51 percent of the republic's population was ethnic Latvian. As the numbers of reliable ethnic Slavs grew, Latvian national sentiment was diluted. Suppression of Latvian culture, particularly by the Brezhnev regime during the 1970s, forced activists underground or abroad. Small exile groups in the United States and Western Europe maintained the idea of Latvian nationhood. Soviet support for the movement of Slavic migrants to the republic was denounced as slow genocide, but during the delicate balancing act called the Cold War few were willing to listen or help the embattled Latvians against the Soviet policies. Inside Latvia a government crackdown in 1983 led to the arrest of hundreds of members of illegal cultural organizations.

Mikhail Gorbachev's rise to power in 1985 finally allowed the Latvians to voice their grievances. Looking to the Baltic republics as a window on the West, Gorbachev talked of more economic and political freedom for the small nations as part of his plan to revitalize the stagnant, underdeveloped Soviet state. New political freedoms in Eastern Europe strengthened Latvian aspirations to follow suit. Political unrest first appeared in the USSR in the Baltic republics and the first open rebellion emerged among the Latvians. Latvian nationalist organizations quickly mobilized with demands for political and economic autonomy, an end to the Russification policy, the return to Russia of all postwar migrants, and the recognition of the Latvian language as the official language of the republic. A number of the movement's leaders were arrested during a crackdown in 1987, but by 1989 more than half a million Latvians supported a number of democratic organizations. The large Slavic population of Latvia also organized in an effort to counter rising Latvian nationalism and in support of continued tight Soviet control. By 1989 Latvian had been declared the official state language and most Latvians were calling for the reversal of the illegal 1940 annexation of Latvia by the USSR. More radical groups called for the expulsion of all immigrants who had no ties, family or commercial, to the pre-1940 Latvian republic. The more moderate nationalists, realizing the demographic danger, preferred cooperation, and many ethnic Slavs supported the Latvian drive for autonomy.

The Latvian campaign for democracy and independence did not begin in earnest until the Popular Front of Latvia (LTF) was formed in late 1988. In contrast to neighboring Estonia, the Latvian Communist Party, dominated by the Slav minority, adopted an antireform stance. At elections in March 1990, the Popular Front won a convincing victory with the support of the majority of the ethnic Latvians and many of the non-Latvians in the republic. A new Latvian parliament proclaimed the restoration of Latvia's former independence in May 1990. The new Latvian leadership demanded negotiations on Latvia's peaceful secession from the Soviet Union. The large and powerful Slavic minority demanded the repeal of new laws requiring the use of the Latvian language, which very few of them spoke, and for criminal penalties for displaying the Latvian national flag. Although the Slavic groups received support from the Soviet government, they were unable to stop the rapid growth of Latvian nationalism.

## Lithuanians

Throughout the early decades of the Cold War heavy-handed suppression had forced Lithuanian nationalism into a period of dormancy, as the only alternative was arrest, deportation, or death. But in the 1970s, more public forms of political activism began to appear. In 14 May 1972, a young Lithuanian, Romas Kalanta, set himself on fire in the name of Lithuanian independence. His funeral, two days later, set off several days of protests, riots, and demonstrations, the first in the republic since World War II. The demonstrations continued until the Soviet security forces were called out to deal with the growing rebellion. By the mid-1970s demands for national and religious rights were heard. An umbrella group called the Lithuanian National People's Front held clandestine meetings across the republic.

Lithuanian national sentiment, mostly kept alive by underground organizations and exile groups in the West, grew dramatically during the period of the Gorbachev reforms in the late 1980s, quickly pushing far beyond the liberalization instituted in 1987. Gorbachev, realizing that the Soviet Union could no longer maintain its military status based on a Third World economy, looked to the Baltic States, the most developed in the Soviet Union, as an economic window on the West. He even began to discuss the possibility of more political and economic autonomy. As the Soviet economy faltered, Gorbachev was forced to cut off economic subsidies to the satellite states of Eastern Europe. In a breathtakingly short period in 1989, the Warsaw Pact disintegrated and Communist governments collapsed across the region.

The winds of change sweeping across Eastern Europe stimulated similar demands from the Lithuanians. Unlike the Estonians and Latvians, the Lithuanians still constituted a large majority of the population of the republic making mobilization somewhat less complicated. Nationalists formed a popular front group, called Sajudis, in mid-1988. A music professor, Vytautas Landsbergis, emerged as the leader of the rapidly growing Latvian national movement. Sajudis quickly won widespread support for its calls for the reestablishment of Lithuanian independence. Pressed by Sajudis, the Lithuanian Communist government quickly passed legislation annulling language laws, legalizing political parties other than the Communist Party, and adopting constitutional amendments that reversed the 1940 decisions proclaiming Lithuania part of the USSR. In early 1989, the Lithuanian Supreme Soviet voted to replace Russian with Lithuanian as the official language of the republic over the vigorous protests of the Russian minority. In August 1989, hundreds of thousands of Lithuanians participated in a mass protest on the fiftieth anniversary of the Russian-German nonaggression pact of 1939, which had opened the way to Soviet annexation. The Lithuanians, along with the Estonians and Latvians, an estimated 2.4 million people, joined hands in a human chain that extended from the Estonian capital through Riga, the Latvian capital, and on to Vilnius in Lithuania. The demonstrators faced west, toward Europe, with their backs to the Soviet Union. Although Soviet leaders warned the Lithuanians that their nationalist leaders were leading them toward an abyss, they were mostly ignored. In January 1990, in an effort to slow down the Lithuanian activists, Mikhail Gorbachev visited the republic, only to be met by huge crowds demanding immediate Lithuanian independence.

Local elections in February 1990 gave the nationalists a large majority in the Lithuanian legislature. The Communist Party was overwhelmingly rejected. The nationalist majority in the new parliament began to debate Lithuania's complete break with the Soviet state. Gorbachev warned the Lithuanians that secession would mean paying a $33 billion payment for past Soviet services and that the Soviet Union would not give up the naval base and port of Klaipeda should Lithuania secede. The nationalists refused to be intimidated. On 11 March 1990, with widespread support, Vytautas Landsbergis proclaimed the complete restoration of the prewar Republic of Lithuania. The Soviet government immediately demanded the revocation of the legislation and began to apply political and economic pressure. The defiant Lithuanian nationalists refused to be intimidated despite the imposition of a crippling Soviet oil embargo and threatened military action. In June 1990, Landsbergis agreed to temporarily suspend the independence declaration in return for a lifting of the oil embargo while negotiations were undertaken on Lithuanian demands for peaceful secession from the USSR.

## Jews

The Soviet attempt to establish a Jewish homeland in the Far East region of Birobidzhan proved a dismal failure. It never attracted many Jewish migrants, who resolutely refused to voluntarily leave the European Soviet republics. Created as an alternative to the attraction of Zionism—only about 35,000 Jews moved to the region—many forcibly deported from European Russia. Others came willingly, including small numbers from the Americas, Germany, Switzerland, and Poland. Many Jews who moved to the region later left, disappointed and bitter. The Jews who settled in the official homeland suffered the same discrimination and persecutions as the rest of Soviet Jewry. By 1970, the Jewish Autonomous Region had a population of 180,000, with a Jewish population of only 14,000.

The Soviet Jews lost nearly 50 percent of their total population to the Nazi Holocaust, but their suffering continued during the decades of the Cold War. Many Jews intermarried, using non-Jewish names to avoid listing themselves as part of the Jewish nationality and therefore to escape the growing persecutions and restrictions that accompanied the establishment of the state of Israel in 1948. Jewish emigration had been heavily restricted since 1928 when Stalin affirmed his rise to power. Successive Soviet leaders took a very dim view of anyone emigrating from the Soviet paradise.

The Israeli victory in the Arab-Israel War of 1967 rekindled the yearnings of Soviet Jews. Pressure on the Soviet government from the West led to a trickle of emigration during the 1970s and early 1980s when 256,000 Jews left the country for Israel or the United States. The government halted the flow of emigrants in the early 1980s as part of the manipulations of the Cold War. Leonid Brezhnev cracked down on Jewish emigration in the early 1980s, allowing only about 7,000 to receive exit visas between 1982 and 1986. The Gorbachev reforms in the late 1980s opened the floodgates of Jewish emigration. Beginning in 1987, the numbers of Jews leaving grew rapidly, reaching a record of 185,000 Jews leaving the Soviet Union in 1990.

Russian nationalism, which gained strength as chaos overtook the Soviet Empire, often included a strong traditionally anti-Semitic element. Many Russians blamed Jews for the plight of the country. Because many leading Bolsheviks had been Jewish, many radical Russian nationalists saw the Russian Revolution of 1917 as a Jewish conspiracy to destroy Slavic Russia. As the

*A young Jewish Russian boy watches his family's luggage at a Rome refugee processing center while his parents apply for asylum. July 4, 1979 (Nathan Benn/Corbis)*

Soviet economic collapse accelerated in the 1980s, attacks on Jewish cemeteries, synagogues, and homes increased.

## Germans

The Soviet Germans, not rehabilitated with the other deported ethnic groups in the mid-1950s, were finally exonerated in 1964 but were still refused permission to return to their homes in the Volga region and around the Black Sea. Their petitions and appeals were constantly rebuffed, fueling a sense of grievance that continued to grow as the years passed. Their treatment by the Soviet authorities stimulated the growth of a particular nationalism in the 1970s, a movement to win full citizenship rights, including the right to return to their ancestral homelands. In 1975 the German national movement was formalized around a proposal for the recreation of a German national homeland in the Volga region.

A proposal for the official reestablishment of the Volga German territory, first raised by Premier Leonid Brezhnev in 1972, was repeatedly met with demonstrations and strong opposition from the Russians settled in the depopulated districts following the deportation of the Germans in 1941. The idea of a Soviet German homeland was discussed in March 1991, during a conference between President Mikhail Gorbachev and the foreign minister of West Germany, Hans-Dietrich Genser. Subsequent events, including the implosion of the Soviet state, left the question of an autonomous German homeland unsettled.

## Moldovans

The period of Communist brotherhood, during the 1950s and 1960s, which allowed the importation of Latin-alphabet Romanian publications, films and entertainers, and cultural exchanges, was finally ended in 1970. A complete ban on all Moldovan-Romanian contacts was imposed. Even though the Soviet Union and Romania's Communist government renewed a Friendship Treaty in 1970, which recognized existing borders, propaganda from both sides continued the territorial conflict. Both countries signed the Helsinki Accords in 1975, guaranteeing the post-1945 boundaries of European states, but still the issue remained. Soviet pressure on Romania ended most overt references to historic Romanian claims to Moldova in Romanian newspapers and publications.

In the early 1970s it became evident that the Soviet plan to separate the Moldovans from their Romanian kin had succeeded too well. The particular Moldovan nationalism planned and fostered by the Soviet authorities after World War II had gradually moved from a question of government policy to a popular Moldovan movement. During the 1980s a specifically Moldovan nationalism gained support until the Soviet government cracked down on all manifestations of nationalist sentiment. Russification, in the guise of Soviet nationalism, was stressed in Moldova as in the other non-Russian republics.

The Gorbachev reforms reopened the nationality question among the Moldovans in the late 1980s. The liberalization eased the pressure to conform to the Soviet ideals of nationhood and Socialist brotherhood. Calls for linguistic rights, national self-determination, and even union with Romania motivated the rapid spread of nationalist organizations. One of the most important issues was that of language. The Soviet government had imposed the Cyrillic alphabet and stressed the Slavic loan words, calling the Moldovan dialect a distinct language. Nationalists, following a heated debate across the republic, demanded the adoption of the Latin alphabet. Attempts to suppress the movement by republican officials and the Communist Party only sharpened Moldovan determination.

In March and April 1989 thousands of Moldovans participated in mass demonstrations to protest the Russification of their language and culture since the reimposition of Soviet rule in 1944. The huge demonstrations supported demands for the return of the Latin alphabet and for the designation of Moldovan as an official language in the republic. A plan was put forward to replace Russian and the Cyrillic alphabet with Moldovan (Romanian) and the Latin alphabet within five years. The proposed changes to the language laws were vehemently opposed by the large Slavic population in Moldova, particularly in the Slavic majority districts east of the Dniester River. In early 1989, legislation was passed that replaced Cyrillic with the Latin script and gave tacit recognition to the idea that the Moldovans and Romanians were basically one people. The language issue stirred the growth of a national movement, led by the Moldovan People's Front, which opposed Russification, the use of Russian as an interethnic language in the republic, and continued Soviet military conscription. Disturbances spread, growing in intensity. Two laws adopted in August 1989 declared Moldovan the state language, but retained the Russian language as the lingua franca.

In November 1989, nationalist rioting broke out in the Moldovan capital, Kishinev, further splitting the republic between the Moldovans and the non-Moldovans, including a large Slavic population and the smaller, but increasingly nationalist Gagauz community, a Turkic-speaking nation in the south of the republic. A nationalist government was elected in February 1990 on promises to stress the predominance of the Moldovan-Romanian language. In June 1990, the republic's leaders declared the republic a sovereign state and officially changed the name from Moldavian SSR to the Republic of Moldova. Conflict over the status of the Russians and Ukrainians in the Trans-Dniester region in the north and the Gagauz in the south threatened to split the republic. These groups particularly opposed the new language laws making Moldovan obligatory and demands by many Moldovan leaders for eventual reunification with Romania—an idea that had become even more popular following the overthrow of the Communist government of Romania in December 1989. The issue of the non-Moldovan populations, growing ethnic violence, and the question of unification with Romania became serious issues as Moldovan nationalists took control of the republic.

The Soviet government, in an effort to stave off total collapse, proposed a plan for preserving the unitary Soviet state by creating a new structure, a union of thirty-five republics. Fifteen of the republics would replace the fifteen union republics, sixteen new republics would be created within the Russian Federation, and four would be created within the other union republics. Two of the new republican formations were proposed for the Moldovan regions of Dniestria, with its Slavic majority, and Gagauzia, the Turkic-speaking districts in the south. The plan was never implemented owing to the rapid disintegration of the Union of Soviet Socialist Republics. In August 1990 the Gagauz proclaimed their region an autonomous republic, and in September the Slavs, supported by Soviet army units, took control of the region east of the Dniester River and unilaterally proclaimed the autonomy of the Dniestria region under the control of an unreformed Communist government.

## The Volga Region

The Volga nationalities, having lost the best and brightest during the long decades of Stalinist terror, were considered by the Soviet authorities as quiescent and, particularly in the case of the Mordvins, doomed to extinction as assimilation advanced. The large number of Slavs, particularly Russians, settled in the region since the nineteenth and twentieth centuries fostered mixed marriages and cultural fusion. By the early 1970s urbanization and education were clearly favoring further assimilation into Russian culture. Increasing numbers of children were bilingual, speaking both their mother tongue and Russian, especially those going on to institutions of higher education.

## Tatars

The Stalinist purges suppressed the Tatar culture and banned the Islamic religion, but the Tatars maintained both as underground movements. Most Tatars continued to observe Muslim rituals for birth, circumcision, and marriage, with many even observing Muslim dietary restrictions. In the 1970s and 1980s, signs of a revival of nationalist sentiment appeared despite Soviet claims that assimilation had eliminated bourgeois nationalist tendencies among the Volga Tatars. Some evidence of a wider pan-Turkic nationalism also surfaced, reviving the old idea of a great Turkic state that would join all the Turkic peoples of the Soviet Union with their kin beyond the country's borders.

The discovery of large petroleum reserves in Tatarstan during World War II hastened the autonomous republic's industrialization and drew in even more Slav workers. By 1975, the Tatar population of the republic had fallen to just 37 percent of the total. Minority status in their designated homeland quickened the nationalist revival. Language became a nationalist issue in the early 1980s, with condemnations of the Russian language requirements for civil service and university entrance examinations. Activists also attacked the overwhelming dominance of Russian in television and radio broadcasting. They demanded changes in government policies that encouraged Russian-Tatar marriages with rewards of trips or privileged housing assignments. Others condemned the deplorable disrepair of Islamic mosques in the Tatar republic and the decades of antireligious propaganda that had undermined their historic culture. The religious aspect was particularly in focus in 1989 when the Tatars celebrated the 1,100th anniversary of the adoption of Islam. The number of activists remained small as the majority of the Tatars, like the other non-Russian nations of the Volga basin, preferred to avoid politics and to maintain the accommodation that had allowed the peaceful cohabitation of the Volga peoples and the growing numbers of Russian migrants since the de-Stalinization policies of the early 1960s.

The Gorbachev reforms, introduced in 1987, raised expectations among the Tatar population that old grievances might finally be addressed. Many Tatars believed that ancient prejudices among the Russian leadership of the Soviet Union had dictated their status as an autonomous republic within the Russian Federation instead of the status of a full union republic that their numbers would dictate. Demands for union republic status, including the constitutional right to secession, were taken up by a growing number of nationalist activists. Calls for union republic status grew, pressuring the government of Tatarstan to issue a declaration of state sovereignty in August 1990.

## Bashkorts

The Bashkort homeland, as designated by the Soviet government, had a population made up of an estimated 106 distinct ethnic groups in 1970. The Russians constituted more than one-third of the total, Tatars made more than one-quarter, and the Bashkorts slightly less than a quarter. The boundaries of the autonomous republic, drawn to ensure a non-Bashkort majority, left a large number of ethnic Bashkorts living outside the republic where Bashkorts were immersed in Tatar or Russian schools, culture, and media. Even in the urban areas of the autonomous republic the Bashkorts were assimilating, often into the culture of the linguistically, culturally, and religiously related Tatars. Although the rural Bashkort population had preserved their national identity almost intact, the growing urbanized portion of the population had adopted to a considerable degree the culture and lifestyle of European Russia. Even though a majority of the Bashkorts continued to adhere to Islamic traditions, most considered themselves nonreligious and secular in outlook.

Suppressed for more than five decades, Bashkort culture began to revive in the late 1970s. A renewed interest in their Islamic past stimulated a modest Islamic revival among younger Bashkorts. A small but growing number of activists, led by Soviet intellectuals of Bashkort origin, formed a movement that glorified their past and emphasized their language, use of which had been declining since the 1920s. The revival of their rich folk traditions paralleled the resurrection of religious beliefs. The movement demanded the redrawing of republican boundaries to encompass a greater number of ethnic Bashkorts and the improvement of the legal and political status of the Bashkort homeland in 1980. The growing cultural revival coincided with the first attempts to liberalize Soviet society in the late 1980s, stimulating a resurgence of long-dormant Bashkort national sentiment.

## Chavash (Chuvash)

The Chavash, constituting a majority of about 80 percent of the population of their autonomous republic in 1970, experienced an unobtrusive cultural revival in the 1970s, partly owing to increased Slavic migration to their Volga homeland. The modest cultural revival, important in language use, publishing, and cultural studies, reinforced the cultural resistance to the Soviet government's assimilation pressures in the 1970s and 1980s. The revival, which remained carefully free of politics, was expressed in cultural terms with a renewed interest in their unique history and in emphasis on the purification and de-Russification of their language. The Chavash national population of the Volga region grew rapidly in the 1970s and 1980s, dramatically increasing the population of ethnic Chavash living outside the autonomous republic. By 1979, only 52 percent of the ethnic Chavash in the Soviet Union lived within the republican boundaries. The revival was partly triggered by an increased inflow of Slavic migrants to work in the oil and natural gas refineries. By the 1980s the region had several important rail shops and electronic, chemicals, and food-processing industries; however, the majority of the Chavash population remained conservative, rural, and agricultural. The Soviet census of 1979 counted only one city, the capital of the republic, Cheboksary, with a population of over 100,000.

The Gorbachev liberalization in the late 1980s allowed the Chavash to adopt a more nationalist stance. National organizations became active among the Chavash living outside the republic, helping to spread the nationalist cultural revival. The reunification of the Chavash nation into one administrative unit became an important nationalist issue. The Chuvash Public Cultural Center was founded in 1989 to promote Chavash culture both within the republic and among Chavash populations in neighboring republics and provinces.

## Maris

The Maris formed a minority in their autonomous republic by the end of World War II. Massive population transfers during the war and government-sponsored settlement in the 1950s and 1960s increased the Slav portion of the population. Resentment of their minority status and alarm over the decline in the use of the Finnic Mari language sparked a small cultural reawakening. Younger Maris, educated in the Soviet system, were the first to take a new interest in their unique history, language, and the religious beliefs that formed an important part of their culture. The cultural renewal grew slowly but gained support as government pressure to adopt the Russian Soviet culture intensified.

The Mari national revival began to take on overtly nationalist overtones in the late 1970s and quickly grew into a mass movement following the Gorbachev reforms of the late 1980s. Mari cultural and national organizations, unofficial and therefore illegal, pressed for language and cultural rights. Pressure on the republican government led to a change in the official name of the republic from the Mari SSR to the historic name of the territory, Mari El. The republican authorities declared Mari El a sovereign state in October 1990, adopting three official languages—Lowland Mari, Highland Mari, and Russian.

## Mordvins

Separated into small ethnic pockets by the massive immigration of ethnic Slavs into their western Volga homeland during the Stalinist period, the Mordvins were the most assimilated of the Volga ethnic groups by the early 1970s. The Mordvins, divided into five regional and cultural groups, spoke distinct languages and often used Russian as a lingua franca, facilitating the imposition of Russian in education and administration. According to Soviet studies, by 1970 only 78 percent of the total Mordvin population considered Mordvin their first language. The number of Mordvins claiming Mordvin nationality continued to decline as assimilation advanced in the 1970s and 1980s. The liberalization of Soviet society in the late 1980s started a slow reversal of the decades of Russification.

## The Permian Nations

The homelands of the Permian peoples form a vast territory that extends north to the tundra regions but also includes important industrial areas, vast natural resources, and some of Russia's most productive mining operations. The Permian nationalities, the Udmurts, Komi, and Permyaks, in spite of Soviet efforts to acculturate them, have maintained a cohesive sense of their distinct identities. The rapid industrialization of the Permian regions forced large numbers of the Permian peoples to settle in cities and towns where they could work in the mines, mills, and factories. Scattered geographically, surrounded by Slavic populations, and as members of the Russian Orthodox Church, the Permian peoples had begun to lose their cultures and languages. To disseminate information over the large territory populated by the Permian nations, a new alphabet was devised to fit the Permian languages in the

1920s. The alphabet, using mixed Latin and Cyrillic characters, was used in publications and education, but in 1938 the alphabet was outlawed and the Russian Cyrillic script was substituted. Russian was made the only language of administration and education as part of the Soviet policy of assimilation.

The Gorbachev reforms had an immediate impact on the Permian peoples. The relaxation of strict controls sparked massive strikes in 1989–1990 by the region's mostly Russian coal miners demanding higher pay and better working conditions. The strikes by the miners, already handsomely paid by Permian standards, sparked demands for government attention to cultural and economic grievances of the three Permian nations.

## The Caucasus Nations

The Caucasus region, including the Transcaucasian republics and the many smaller national groups of the Transcaucasus and the North Caucasus, remained one of the most volatile in the Soviet Union even after the rehabilitation of the punished nations in the 1950s. Territorial disputes, water rights, and other issues continued to underlay a deceptive calm imposed by Soviet rule and the threat of military intervention.

### Armenians

The Brezhnev era, from the mid-1960s to the mid-1980s, with its focus on the increasingly difficult task of keeping up militarily with the West, allowed the Armenians to become more independent and more nationalistic than had been allowed since the consolidation of Soviet power in the early 1920s. Armenian nationalism, unlike that of other national groups, was directed at the Muslim Turks and the Azeris, their traditional enemies, whereas the Russians were viewed as their traditional friends and fellow Christians. Since the growing national movement did not threaten Soviet rule, it was treated as an internal matter to be dealt with by the local authorities in the Armenian republic.

On 24 April 1965 the Soviet Armenians openly commemorated the fiftieth anniversary of the Armenian Genocide at the hands of the Turks. Ten years later, in 1975, activists began to voice their demand for the unification of Armenia and Karabakh (Nagorno-Karabakh), the Armenian-majority region that was included in neighboring Azerbaijan under Stalin's orders. Some Armenian nationalists in Western Europe and the United States demanded the resurrection of the former Armenian republic, including the traditional Armenian regions of northeastern Turkey. Several terrorist acts were carried out against Turkish targets, but most of the diaspora Armenians rejected violence while continuing to support calls for greater autonomy and a redress of old grievances in the Armenian heartland in the Transcaucasus.

The question of language began a period of greater militancy when the Soviet government proposed eliminating Armenian as the official language of the republic in 1978. Protests and demonstrations persuaded the Soviet authorities to drop the proposal; however, the militants quickly focused on the question of Karabakh, called Artsakh in the Armenian language. The small region, with a population about 80 percent Armenian, did not receive Armenian television, had no institutes of higher learning in the majority language, and remained economically backward as a direct result of policies of the Azeri government. The Karabakh issue provided an emotional focus of the growing national movement.

Mikhail Gorbachev's reforms, introduced in 1987, anticipated some difficulties from the more nationalistic Ukrainians and Baltic peoples, but seemingly no one in the Soviet government anticipated the great outpouring of nationalist sentiment that erupted in Armenia, primarily over the treatment of the Armenian population of Nagorno-Karabakh. In 1987, nationalists collected petitions, and in early 1988, the legislature of the Nagorno-Karabakh autonomous district passed a resolution for the transfer of Karabakh from Azerbaijan to Armenia. In support of the transfer, more than 1 million Armenians attended a peaceful demonstration in Yerevan, the capital of the Armenian republic. Gorbachev promised to review the Karabakh issue at the highest level, but just days later, Azeri mobs tore into the Armenian quarter in the industrial city of Sumgait, near the Azeri capital, Baku, killing more than thirty Armenians and injuring hundreds. From then on the Armenian-Azeri confrontation escalated into open conflict. The Armenians expected the Soviet government to react strongly against Azeri violence toward Armenians in Azerbaijan. When it did not, the Armenians began to lose faith in Russian friendship. In the meantime a popular front organization, the Karabakh Committee, gained credibility and the Armenian Communist elite was increasingly identified with anti-Armenian elements in the Soviet government. Attempts to reach a compromise over Karabakh failed, as neither the Armenians nor the Azeris were willing to negotiate. More than 200,000 Armenians fled the violence in Azerbaijan, pouring across the border into Armenia, only to be engulfed in a new disaster, the most destructive earthquake to ravage the region in more than 1,000 years that struck on 7 December 1988.

The earthquake leveled whole cities and left more than 55,000 dead and half a million homeless. Leaders of the Karabakh Committee, critical of Moscow's slow response and blaming sloppy Soviet planning and construction techniques for the massive death toll, were arrested at the height of the crisis. New Armenian protests erupted, leading to clashes with police and the army. Red Army units, withdrawn from neighboring Azerbaijan to aid in earthquake relief, freed the Azeri militants to renew their attacks on the Armenian minority in Baku and other Azeri cities. Even after the hugely destructive earthquake, trains full of terrified Armenian refugees continued to cross the border. The Azeris then imposed a rail blockade, virtually halting earthquake relief. The Armenians quickly lost faith in the ability of Gorbachev's reformers to protect them from their ancient Muslim enemies.

In January 1990 sporadic skirmishing on the Armenian-Azeri border turned into full-scale war in Nagorno-Karabakh and other districts between Karabakh and the Armenian border. In May 1990 the Armenian legislature, citing the need for local security, suspended the spring draft of Soviet military conscripts. The suspension was declared following massive antidraft demonstrations across Armenia. A coalition of several nationalist organizations, the Armenian National Movement, grew out of the Karabakh Committee organization and rapidly won widespread support, even among committed Armenian Communists. Members of the Armenian National Movement rapidly took over local governments and soon controlled the major organs of the republic. The Armenians, battered by an Azeri economic and rail blockade that crippled the economy and ended earthquake reconstruction, suffered increasingly serious food shortages. The Azeri blockade further aroused Armenian nationalist sentiment as the advantages of Soviet citizenship rapidly withered away.

## Azeris

The relaxation of the post-Stalin era manifested itself in a renewed interest in the Azeri culture and language and in the Muslim religion. The Soviet government viewed the Azeri cultural revival as a return to nationalism. Periodic purges between 1966 and 1969 and again in 1975 eliminated any Azeri leaders suspected of nationalist tendencies. The long prohibition on contacts between the Soviet Azeris and the Iranian Azeris to the south became difficult to enforce as the use of radios became widespread.

The Islamic Revolution that overthrew the Iranian monarchy in 1979 allowed a rapid revival of Azeri nationalism in Iran. While Soviet Azeri radio broadcasts were jammed, broadcasts in Azeri from the Islamic Republic of Iran attempted to stir up Islamic fundamentalist zeal. Although the majority of the Soviet Azeris, after decades of official atheism, rejected the radical Islam of Iran, a new interest in their Muslim religion formed an important part of the continuing Azeri cultural revival. Even though most Azeris found little attraction in the radical and restrictive doctrines of the Islamic Revolution, the Soviet Azeris wishing to visit relatives across the border in Islamic Iran were subjected to lengthy paperwork and thorough scrutiny. The vast majority of the urbanized Azeri population was stirred less by religious fundamentalism than by the demands of an increasingly open economy and the perceived threat from Armenia to Azeri territory in and around Nagorno-Karabakh.

The liberalization of Soviet society under Mikhail Gorbachev in the late 1980s, leading to Armenian claims to Nagorno-Karabakh, fueled a rapid growth of Azeri nationalist sentiment, stimulated by the perceived Armenian threat. Mass demonstrations, strikes, and protests erupted across the republic, as the Karabakh conflict escalated into violence in February 1988. Tensions between the Muslim Azeris and the Christian Armenians, often seen as Russian surrogates in the Transcaucasus region, increasingly focused on the large Armenian minorities in Baku and other Azeri cities. Riots broke out in the industrial city of Sumgait, with mobs attacking Armenians, leaving many dead and wounded. Thousands of Armenians fled the republic. In July 1988 the local legislature of Karabakh, dominated by the Armenian majority, voted for secession from Azerbaijan and union with Armenia, bringing renewed ethnic violence. Soviet troops moved into the region to separate the two sides, but the violence continued to spread. In December 1988 most of the Soviet troops were withdrawn to aid in the rescue effort following the Armenian earthquake, allowing Azeri nationalists to emerge from hiding. The Azeri Popular Front, an umbrella group of cultural and nationalist organizations, called for the establishment of an independent Azeri republic and threatened war if Karabakh was separated from the republic. By mid-1989 the Popular Front had effectively taken control of Azerbaijan, having moved more rapidly from obscurity to power than any similar organization in the Soviet Union.

In November 1989 a more radical faction took control of the Popular Front. The faction, openly separatist, demanded the unification of the Azeri territories in the Soviet Union and Iran. Demands for the opening of the international border and the growing conflict with Armenia stirred new nationalist rioting in late 1989. Azeri demonstrators on the Iranian border tore down border posts and the fence that separated the two Azeri territories. Militants called for Azeri unification and the creation of a reunited "Greater Azerbaijan." In January 1990 nationalists erected barricades around Baku and called for immediate independence. Nationalist control of Baku and the threat of secession provoked a strong Soviet government response. The Islamic government of Iran, faced with growing nationalist activity among Iran's Azeri population, demanded that the Soviet government crack down on the Azeri drive to independence. Security troops smashed through the nationalist barricades and occupied the city, causing many casualties. Officially eighty-three people died resisting the military occupation of Baku, but nationalists claim that the number of martyrs exceeded 500.

The military occupation of Baku ended the de facto rule of the radical faction of the Azeri Popular Front but united the many Azeri factions, including the discredited Communists. By mid-1990 the Communist Party was collapsing and Azeri nationalists represented the only force able to speak for the Azeri majority. The anti-Armenian sentiment quickly evolved into anti-Russian and anti-Soviet sentiments. Even the radical anti-Armenian groups began to view the Soviet government, not neighboring Armenia, as the real enemy of the Azeri nation. The Soviet authorities installed a new government in Baku under a longtime Communist, Ayaz Mutalibov, but Mutalibov, in order to cling to power as national fervor reached its peak, began to outdo the nationalists in supporting Azeri nationalist issues.

The Popular Front negotiated a cease-fire with the Armenians and demanded negotiations with the Soviet government in Moscow on the peaceful secession of Azerbaijan from the USSR. Despite the continuing occupation by Soviet troops, on 2 May 1990, more than 1 million Azeris poured out into the streets to publicly mourn the martyrs killed when the troops attacked Baku. A further act of defiance became another massive popular protest when thousands demonstrated to commemorate the seventy-seventh anniversary of Azeri independence proclaimed in May 1918. A coup attempt, orchestrated by the Communist Party, aimed to return Azerbaijan to firm Soviet control. Tanks in the streets of Baku and other important cities restored calm but further alienated the population. The Mutalibov government embraced a more nationalist platform to retain some support, including a full state border on the frontier with Armenia, replete with customs posts, passport controls, and the other trappings of an international frontier. Mutalibov proclaimed Azerbaijan a sovereign state on 23 September 1990. A week later the republic's first multiparty elections were held. Mutalibov, running unchallenged, led the Communists and their allies to a victory over the nationalists, whose leaders were in prison or had fled.

## Georgians

The de-Stalinization process, begun by Nikita Khrushchev, stimulated a modest national revival in Georgia. A relative moderate, Eduard Shevardnadze, was named first secretary of the Georgian Communist Party in 1972. His policies allowed a limited cultural revival, but nationalist sentiment remained banned. In 1978 a Soviet plan to replace Georgian with Russian as the official language of the republic led to riots and stirred the first manifestations of Georgian nationalism. Zviad Gamsakhurdia, the son of a revered national poet, began to organize dissident Georgian nationalists. Thousands protested in the streets of Tbilisi until Shevardnadze assured Georgians that the official status of the Georgian language would be retained.

The restructuring of the moribund Soviet system by Mikhail Gorbachev fanned nationalist demands by the Georgians but also fueled nationalist sentiment among the national minorities in the republic, not only the Abkhaz but also the Ossetians and the Ajars. Demands by the Abkhaz and Ossetians for secession from Georgia stirred a nationalist backlash that mobilized the Georgian public. A peaceful, proindependence demonstration in the Georgian capital, Tbilisi, was attacked by Red Army soldiers, reportedly using poison gas and sharpened shovels, on 9 April 1989, leaving twenty dead and many injured. The attack on the demonstrators, called Bloody Sunday, provoked a great outpouring of nationalism in the republic. In the months that followed numerous unofficial organizations and cultural groups emerged, many openly calling for Georgian independence.

Although Eduard Shevardnadze was viewed in the West as a reformer, in Georgia he was associated with Moscow and was considered an outsider. Zviad Gamsakhurdia, the charismatic intellectual, quickly emerged as a popular national hero and political leader. In the generally free elections of October 1990, Gamsakhurdia's coalition won an overwhelming victory. On 9 April 1991, two years after Bloody Sunday, the Georgian nationalist government declared the republic's independence of the Soviet Union. In May 1991 Gamsakhurdia was elected to the newly created office of president of the republic. Gamsakhurdia, viewing himself as the savior of the Georgian nation, backed narrow, ethnocentric, anti-Muslim policies that further alienated the republic's sizable minorities. Violence against political opponents, mostly more moderate elements and the leadership of the national minorities, increased as Gamsakhurdia secured his position. While the republic stumbled from crisis to crisis, Gamsakhurdia carelessly reopened old ethnic and regional wounds. Fighting broke out in South Ossetia and Abkhazia between Georgian troops and ethnic separatists.

## The Central Asians

Although Nikita Khrushchev was initially hailed as a reformer, by the early 1960s his regime was marked by bitter repression of religion. A large number of mosques were shut down and antireligious propaganda increased until Khrushchev's overthrow in 1964. Under Leonid Breshnev, in the 1970s, attacks on Islam eased as the Soviet government began to employ the Islamic religion as a tool of foreign policy, particularly to cultivate the Islamic countries of the oil-rich Middle East. Communist appointees and party loyalists throughout Central Asia formed clannish, authoritarian hierarchies based on a notoriously corrupt system dubbed "Feudal Socialism" by the small dissident movements (Gross 1992, 46–72).

In 1979 two events occurred that had considerable impact on the Muslim populations of Kazakhstan, Uzbekistan, Turkmenistan, and Kyrgyzstan—the Islamic revolution in Iran and the Soviet invasion of Afghanistan. The installation of an Islamic government in Iran particularly reverberated among the ethnically and linguistically related Tajiks, although small minorities throughout the region celebrated the resurrection of fundamentalist Islam. Afghanistan borders Soviet Central Asia on the south and has large Uzbek, Tajik, and Turkmen minorities. The Soviet invasion of Afghanistan had even more impact than the Islamic revolution, with many Central Asian military units refusing to fight against their kin in Afghanistan, the first overt signs of opposition to Soviet policies in the Central Asia region. The Iranian revolution and the Afghan war engendered a return to the traditional anti-Islamic policies of the Soviet regime.

Communist Party appointees in Central Asia held firm until the late 1980s. The Gorbachev reforms allowed the growth of opposition groups, and the disclosure of massive government fraud and corruption stirred dormant national movements. Environmental and health issues, particularly the excessive use of chemical agents that accompanied the production of cotton, provided a focus for the nascent nationalists. The facts about the disastrous rates of infectious diseases, cancers, and infant mortality resulting from the government's obsessive drive to produce cotton at the expense of traditional crops came to light. At the same time, revelations about the serious health and environmental damage done by the long series of nuclear tests in Kazakhstan were finally revealed. Even though the Gorbachev reforms were implemented quite slowly in Central Asia and tighter control of unofficial political organizations was maintained than in other areas of the USSR, dissidents began to demand redress of old grievances and even to talk of greater religious and political freedom. The governments of the Central

Asian republics, although still under the control of local Soviet-era strong-men, declared sovereignty of the five states in 1990.

## Russians

Russian nationalism, suppressed for decades by Soviet nationalism, also emerged during the Gorbachev liberalization of government and society. The allowance of the Russian Orthodox Church to regain some of its pre-Bolshevik powers and the adoption of some democratic ways satisfied moderate Russian nationalists, but other groups demanded the restoration of an authoritarian Russian government to hold the multiethnic empire together. The radical nationalists rejected democratic reforms and demanded a strong central government. They blamed the Communists for the destruction of the environment, the plunder of Russia's natural resources, and the rapidly declining population that resulted from the massive number of abortions and from alcoholism and disease. Anti-Semitism, calls for the restoration of the Russian Empire of 1914 (including Finland and eastern Poland), and even calls for the restoration of the monarchy were adopted by the various nationalist organizations that proliferated during the decline and stagnation of the 1980s.

The reemergence of Russian nationalism found political expression when the legislature of the Russian Federation began to debate a declaration of state sovereignty in 1990. The idea of a sovereign Russian Federation was strongly opposed by delegates from the federation's autonomous republics, which objected to provisions that could curtail their own sovereignty. Most of the autonomous republics, along with many autonomous regions and districts, published their own declarations of sovereignty, beginning with the Karelian autonomous republic on the Finnish border. The heated debate over sovereignty revealed the potential for a fracturing of the Russian Federation in imitation of the larger Soviet Union. More-liberal Russian nationalists, led by Boris Yeltsin, the head of the Russian Federation, feared that conservative elements opposed to Gorbachev's reforms, including the Communist Party, the military, and the KGB, might support an authoritarian alternative that would take the Soviet Union back into the dark ages of Stalinist oppression.

The abortive military coup against Gorbachev in August 1991 was supported by the more conservative elements in Soviet society. When Boris Yeltsin took to the barricades in defiance of the coup plotters, Russian nationalism became a potent force. Yeltsin, as president of the Russian Federation, managed to hold the Russian state together as the largest of the successor states to the disintegrating Union of Soviet Socialist Republics, but the other union republics, by mid-1991 mostly under the control of nationalist political parties, reacted to the unsuccessful coup by severing their ties to Russia and declaring themselves sovereign and independent states.

## Timeline

| | |
|---|---|
| 1970 | Jewish emigration, which began to grow after the 1967 Arab-Israeli War, increases dramatically. |
| 1972 | A crackdown on Ukrainian dissent leads to many arrests. |
| 1975 | Leonid Brezhnev consolidates his political power as general secretary of the Communist Party. The Soviet government signs the Helsinki Accords, guaranteeing human rights in Europe. |
| 1976 | Helsinki Watch groups form in many areas of the USSR. |
| 1978 | A Soviet plan to replace Georgian, Armenian, and Azeri with Russian as the official language of the three Transcaucasian republics causes widespread demonstrations and rioting. |
| 1979 | The Soviet Union invades neighboring Afghanistan, beginning a ten-year war that finally ends unsuccessfully. The Iranian monarchy is overthrown and replaced by an Islamic government determined to spread radical Islam to the southern republics of the Soviet Union. |
| 1982 | Brezhnev dies and is succeeded by others determined to continue the same Cold War policies that favored the military over the needs of the civilian population. |
| 1983 | A crackdown in Latvia leads to the arrest of hundreds of members of illegal cultural organizations. |
| 1985 | Mikhail Gorbachev becomes the leader of the Soviet Union, which is increasingly unable to compete with the West. Gorbachev begins to reform the dying Soviet economy. |
| 1986 | Gorbachev announces the policies of glasnost (openness in society) and perestroika (restructuring of the economy). The Chernobyl nuclear disaster occurs in Ukraine and Belarus. Serious rioting in Kazakhstan occurs, following the removal of the ethnic Kazakh head of the republican government. |
| 1988 | Gorbachev officially acknowledges the ethnic suppression and terror imposed during the Stalin era. The Estonian Popular |

Front is formed, serving as a model for popular front groups in many areas of the Soviet Union. The legislature of Karabakh votes for secession from Azerbaijan and for union with Armenia.

1989    The last Soviet troops withdraw from Afghanistan. Gorbachev agrees to withdraw Soviet troops from Eastern Europe. The Communist governments of Hungary, Poland, Czechoslovakia, and East Germany are overthrown or replaced by more democratic regimes. The Berlin Wall is torn down, and the unification of Germany is begun. Independence movements in the Baltic republics openly demand independence. In August 1989 more than 2 million Estonians, Latvians, and Lithuanians form a human chain across the three Baltic republics to show their solidarity and reinforce demands for self-determination. Soviet soldiers attack peaceful demonstrators on Bloody Sunday in Georgia.

1990    Most union republics, including the Russian Federation, declare state sovereignty. The majority of the governments of the autonomous republics, provinces, and regions and many of the ordinary provinces also declare sovereignty. Free elections are held in many republics for local legislatures. On 11 March 1990, the Lithuanian government proclaims the restoration of the prewar Republic of Lithuania.

1991    Boris Yeltsin is elected president of the Russian Federation. On 9 April 1991 the Georgians declare the republic's independence from the Soviet Union.

## Significant People, Places, and Events

AFGHANISTAN The country lying just south of the Central Asian republics of Uzbekistan, Tajikistan, and Turkmenistan with substantial minorities ethnically and linguistically related to the Central Asian peoples.

BLOODY SUNDAY The day that Red Army soldiers attacked peaceful demonstrators with shovels and poison gas during a proautonomy march in Tbilisi on 9 April 1989, killing twenty and injuring many more.

BREZHNEV, LEONID Soviet politician who became head of the Communist Party and therefore of the Soviet Union in 1975. His regime was known for the stagnation and further decline of the Soviet economy and the benign negligence of the needs of the non-Russian nationalities.

**CHERNOBYL** A large nuclear complex in Ukraine close to the border with Belarus that was the scene of a disastrous nuclear meltdown and explosion in 1986.

**GAGAUZ** A small, Orthodox Christian, Turkic-speaking nationality living in several areas of southwestern Moldova and neighboring areas of Ukraine. Activists proclaimed the formation of a separate Gagauz republic in 1990.

**GAMSAKHURDIA, ZVIAD** Soviet dissident turned Georgian nationalist who led the drive for Georgian independence.

**GORBACHEV, MIKHAIL** The Soviet politician who came to power in 1985. His reforms eventually prompted a coup attempt that began the rapid disintegration of the Soviet Union.

**HELSINKI ACCORDS** A series of agreements signed at the 1975 Helsinki Conference on Security and Cooperation in Europe.

**INTERNATIONALIST MOVEMENT** A pro-Russian organization originally organized in the Baltic region to oppose moves toward autonomy or independence in the non-Russian republics and autonomous territories.

**ISLAMIC REVOLUTION** The 1979 revolution in Iran that overthrew the secular government and the monarchy and replaced them with an Islamic state dominated by the radical clergy.

**KARABAKH** Also called Karabagh or Nagorno-Karabakh, and in the Armenian language, Artsakh. A small autonomous republic with an Armenian majority placed under the control of Soviet Azerbaijan by Stalin in 1923 but never renounced by the Armenians.

**KARABAKH COMMITTEE** A nationalist organization originally formed to support Armenian claims to the Karabakh enclave in Azerbaijan. The Karabakh Committee formed the basis of the later Armenian national movement that led the republic to independence.

**LANDSBERGIS, VYTAUTAS** A Soviet-era dissident who led the Lithuanian movement for autonomy and later for independence.

**OSSETIANS** Also known as Alans. An Orthodox Christian Caucasian nation linguistically related to the Iranians and the Tajiks of Central Asia. The Ossetian homeland straddles the border between the Russian Federation and Georgia.

**SHEVARDNADZE, EDUARD** Soviet politician known for pragmatism. He became foreign minister of the Soviet Union in 1985. His implementation of Gorbachev's reforms was lauded in the West. After the dissolution of the Soviet Union, he returned to Georgia, where he served as president of the republic.

**TRANS-DNIESTER (TRANS-DNIESTRIA)** A small region lying mostly on the northern bank of the Dniester River in Moldova. Originally designated a

Moldovan autonomous republic when Moldova, then known as Bessarabia, was united to Romania in 1920, it was later joined to Bessarabia to
form the Moldavian Soviet Socialist Republic.

YELTSIN, BORIS Former Soviet politician. In July 1991, he quit the greatly
weakened Communist Party and later presided over the dissolution of the
party and the Soviet Union after successfully opposing the coup against
Mikhail Gorbachev in August 1991.

## Bibliography

Allworth, Edward, ed. *Muslim Communities Reemerge: Historical Perspectives.*
Durham, NC: Duke University Press, 1994.

Gross, Jo Ann, ed. *Muslims in Central Asia.* Durham, NC: Duke University Press,
1992.

Kotz, David M. *Revolution from Above: The Demise of the Soviet System.* New York:
Routledge, 1997.

Nahaylo, Bohdan, and Viktor Swoboda. *Soviet Disunion: A History of the Nationalities Problem in the USSR.* London: Hamish Hamilton, 1990.

Peterson, D. J. *Troubled Lands: The Legacy of Soviet Environmental Destruction.*
Boulder, CO: Westview Press, 1993.

Plakans, Andrejs. *The Latvians: A Short History.* Palo Alto, CA: Stanford University
Press, 1995.

Smith, Graham, ed. *The Nationalities Question in the Soviet Union.* New York: Longman, 1990.

Tolz, Vera. *Russia: Inventing the Nation.* New York: Oxford University Press, 2001.

Volodymyr Kubijovyc, ed. *Encyclopedia of Ukraine.* Toronto: University of Toronto
Press, 1984.

# CHAPTER EIGHT

# Disintegration of the Soviet Empire and the Emergence of Fifteen Independent States

T HE RUSSIAN-SOVIET EMPIRE REACHED ITS GREATEST EXTENT in both area and power at the end of World War II. At that time the Union of Soviet Socialist Republics and its client states in Eastern Europe made up the so-called Warsaw Pact, but the reality was the old Russian dream of an empire stretching from the Pacific Ocean to the gates of Vienna and Berlin. The empire focused on Moscow in the Russian heartland, although the Russian Federation also included resource-rich Siberia and numerous non-Russian national groups mostly living in officially designated autonomous republics, regions, and districts. Around the edges of the Russian Federation were the homelands of the larger national groups forming separate union republics of the USSR. Then there were the World War II additions to the empire, the client states of Eastern and Central Europe, internationally recognized independent states governed by leftist elites closely controlled by the Soviet authorities. The Soviet government also financed and supported allied leftist governments in Africa, Asia, and the Americas.

Mikhail Gorbachev became the supreme leader of the Soviet Union in 1985, at a time when the empire was virtually bankrupt because of Cold War military and political expenditures. In an effort to halt the empire's rapid decline, he quickly ended military and economic support for the client governments of the Warsaw Pact states. As a result, communism was quickly overthrown in nearly all of Eastern Europe, Germany was reunited, and the Soviet Empire withdrew to the boundaries of the USSR. The so-called outer empire was gone. The post-Soviet euphoria and democratization of Eastern Europe seeped across the Soviet borders, arousing dormant nationalisms and raising myriad demands, including self-government for the long-suppressed Soviet national groups.

Opposition to the attempted liberalization of the Soviet economy and society culminated in an abortive coup against Gorbachev on 19 August 1991. One day after the coup leaders announced their takeover of the Soviet gov-

*Boris Yeltsin signals victory over the failed USSR coup d'etat, August 24, 1991. (Alain Nogues/Corbis)*

ernment, on 20 August, Boris Yeltsin, the president of the Russian Federation, mobilized the Russian public against the plotters then barricaded himself in the parliament building. On 24 August Mikhail Gorbachev resigned as the head of the Communist Party, which was then disbanded in Russia and other union republics. On the same day, President Yeltsin, on behalf of the Russian Federation, recognized the independence of Estonia, setting the stage for the rapid disintegration of the Soviet Union. The fifteen union republics formally declared their independence of the collapsing Soviet Union. Within the newly declared independent Russian Federation the governments of the autonomous territories unilaterally declared their new status as full federation republics, a few even attempted to follow the union republics to independence. Although legally the Soviet government lasted for another four months, its authority was effectively ended.

The failed coup of August 1991 brought an unexpectedly rapid end to the twentieth century's largest extant empire, its most influential political movement, and its most powerful state political party. It also marked the end of the Cold War and the resurgence of quiescent national movements suppressed in the name of Cold War expediency. The simultaneous collapse of Communist ideology and the Soviet Union left hundreds of millions of former Soviet citizens searching for a new national identity. In December 1991 the presidents of Russia, Ukraine, and Belarus signed a treaty creating the Commonwealth of Independent States (CIS), which eventually expanded to include all of the former Soviet republics except the Baltic republics of Estonia, Latvia, and Lithuania.

## The Baltic States

The three Baltic nations resolutely rejected any ties to the other former Soviet republics other than diplomatic ties between sovereign states. Historic ties to Finland, Sweden, and Poland focused Baltic attention to the democratic and prosperous West. Ties were rapidly established with the other states bordering the Baltic Sea and beyond, giving the newly independent Baltic states some measure of protection as internationally recognized sovereign republics.

### Estonia

The Estonians pushed their demands for independence farther than any other Soviet nationality. Throughout 1990 the nationalists took control of various government functions. In March 1990, the 1940 Soviet annexation

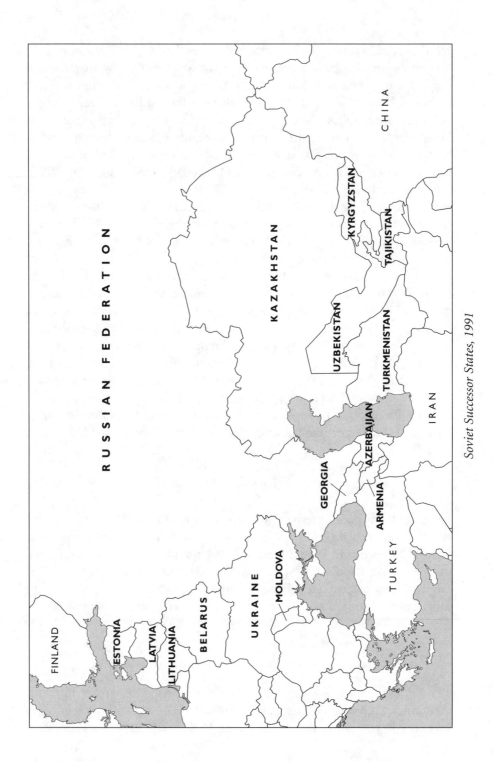

FINLAND

ESTONIA

LATVIA

LITHUANIA

BELARUS

UKRAINE

MOLDOVA

R U S S I A N   F E D E R A T I O N

GEORGIA

ARMENIA

AZERBAIJAN

TURKEY

IRAN

KAZAKHSTAN

UZBEKISTAN

TURKMENISTAN

KYRGYZSTAN

TAJIKISTAN

CHINA

*Soviet Successor States, 1991*

of Estonia was declared illegal, and a transition period for the restoration of independence was organized. By mid-1990 Estonia was virtually independent. The Soviet government attempted to reassert its authority in January 1991 but was opposed by the new Estonian nationalist government. In a March 1991 referendum, 77.8 percent of the republic's population, including many Slavs and other non-Estonians, supported the restoration of Estonia's independence. Immediately after the abortive coup against Mikhail Gorbachev on 19 August 1991, the Estonian government severed all remaining political ties to the Soviet Union. On 20 August the Estonians passed a resolution on national independence and appealed for international recognition. Boris Yeltsin's acknowledgment of Estonian independence on 24 August set the stage for the rapid disintegration of the Soviet Empire.

The Estonians quickly reoriented their economy toward the West. The new government's free trade policies and democratic institutions supported a flourishing cultural revival and increasing prosperity. The new Estonian government refused to extend citizenship rights to what it considered the immigrant population, mostly ethnic Russians settled in the republic under Soviet rule. The large Slav population, concentrated in the east and northeast, continued to demand that all inhabitants of the republic at independence in 1991 be granted Estonian citizenship. In 1992 citizenship laws were adopted that greatly restricted citizenship rights to non-Estonians. The laws, based on a 1939 Estonian law, granted automatic citizenship to all residents who had lived in the republic before the Soviet annexation in 1940 and to their descendants, regardless of ethnicity. Other inhabitants were required to meet a residency requirement and to pass a proficiency test in the Estonian language. In 1995 the residency requirement was extended from two to five years. In 1997 leaders of the Russian Federation government reiterated their dissatisfaction with Estonia's citizenship laws, demanding that all inhabitants of the republic resident in 1991 be granted citizenship rights. Many Estonians resented the large Russian presence in their homeland and continued to resist Russian demands to extend citizenship to the people they viewed as their former oppressors. Changes to the citizenship laws were finally enacted in the late 1990s as part of the Estonians' preparations for membership in both of the important international organizations in Europe—the European Union (EU) and the North Atlantic Treaty Organization (NATO).

## Latvia

The Latvians, like the Estonians, declared the restoration of their former independence on 4 May 1990, but their reduced geographic position in the re-

*A Latvian girl wears a flower crown and holds wildflowers during Herbs Day, a festival in Latvia, 2003. (Niall Benvie/Corbis)*

public, just over 50 percent of the total population, made their position the most precarious in the Baltic region. The new Latvian government, elected in free elections earlier in 1990, demanded negotiations with the Soviet authorities on the peaceful secession of the republic from the Soviet Union. In January 1991 the Soviet government ordered assaults on government and communication buildings in the Latvian capital, Riga, leading to bloody confrontations. A general referendum, organized in the wake of the violence, supported full independence from the USSR.

In the wake of the attempted coup in Moscow in August 1991 the Latvian government quickly followed the Estonians' lead and severed all political ties to the Soviet Union. On 21 August 1991 the Latvian parliament formally proclaimed the independence of the republic, which quickly received international recognition. The major challenge to the new government was to reach a workable accommodation with the republic's large non-Latvian populations, particularly the Russians. In 1992 the language laws were put into full force, with employment, passports, and citizenship dependent on proficiency in the Latvian language. Hundreds of thousands of non-Latvians in the republic were classed as noncitizens. Relations with the Russian Federation swiftly deteriorated over the question of citizenship for the Russian population, which complained of discrimination. Many Slavs left to settle in Russia, Ukraine, and Belarus. The nationalities question remained in the forefront of national politics throughout the 1990s. A new citizenship law, passed in 1994, allowed for the naturalization of non-Latvians. It offered Latvian citizenship to around 50,000 people in 1995 and an additional 180,000 between 1996 and 1999. Preference under the law is given to those who lived in Latvia and their families prior to 1940 or had a Latvian spouse or parent. The law set quotas for naturalization applications after 2000 but was not implemented following severe criticisms by the Russian government as well as some European governments and international organizations. In July 1994 the Latvian parliament, under growing international pressure, abolished the quota system. In the late 1990s, in order for Latvia to qualify for membership in the European Union (EU) and the North Atlantic Treaty Organization (NATO), the language laws were liberalized, reducing the tensions with the Russian government and between the Latvians and the Slavs in the Latvian republic.

The Latvian language, according to leading linguists, had reached the second state of language extinction in the mid-1980s. Since independence in 1991 the language has again flourished, and the threat of language extinction has receded. However, less than a quarter of the large non-Latvian population in the republic was able to speak Latvian in 1997, six years after independence. The majority of the non-Latvians were not allowed to vote in general elections, and new language laws intended to revive the Latvian language excluded the Slavs from full employment and citizenship rights until new laws were adopted after 1999.

Latvia's transformation to a modern market economy, rivaled only by neighboring Estonia, gave the Latvians a standard of living equal to that in many parts of Western Europe. The rapid political and economic changes quickly erased much of the Soviet landscape in Latvia, although the Russian government announced continuing talks with the Latvian government on the purchase of the former naval base at Liepaja. The base, formerly the largest and most important Soviet naval base on the Baltic Sea, was abandoned when the Russian military withdrew from Latvian territory.

## Lithuania

The third of the Baltic nations, Lithuania, also moved rapidly toward secession during 1990. The March 1990 declaration of the restoration of Lithuanian independence was suspended after the Soviet government applied economic and political sanctions. An oil embargo crippled the Lithuanian economy, but few Lithuanians were willing to retract their declaration of independence. In January 1991, the Lithuanian leader, Vytautas Landsbergis, declared the suspension of the independence declaration at an end, provoking an armed Soviet response. Red Army soldiers took control of public buildings in the Lithuanian capital, Vilnius. They later seized the TV tower after overcoming the resistance of a crowd of demonstrators. The confrontation left fourteen Lithuanians dead and several hundred wounded. To demonstrate popular support for independence, the Landsbergis government organized a referendum in February 1991. The results, overwhelmingly in favor, supported the earlier independence declaration. Even though Soviet troops controlled most important buildings and installations, Landsbergis attempted to persuade Western governments to recognize Lithuanian independence but received only sympathy and advice to negotiate with the Soviet authorities.

The August coup in Moscow quickly ended the Lithuanian standoff. Soviet troops initially moved to take control of even more of the city, but returned to their barracks when the coup failed. On 6 September 1991, President Landsbergis reinstated the independence declaration, formally proclaiming the independence of the Republic of Lithuania. Political instability plagued the new state during the first years of independence, particularly over citizenship rights for the non-Lithuanians and the historical territorial dispute with Poland over the Vilnius region. A treaty of friendship and cooperation, signed in 1992, acknowledged Polish recognition of Lithuanian territorial integrity, including Vilnius and its surrounding region, held by Poland from the early 1920s until World War II. The Lithuanian government committed itself to safeguarding the rights of the republic's large Polish minority.

In October 1992, Lithuanian voters, alarmed by a rapidly deteriorating economy, voted for ex-Communist candidates over the nationalists who had led the republic to independence. Governmental instability continued into the late 1990s, aggravated by resignations, dismissals, and scandals involving official corruption. The precarious economic situation and the government's hesitation in implementing reforms hampered Lithuanian efforts to throw off the last vestiges of Soviet rule. An agreement with Russia for the withdrawal of the formerly Soviet troops was completed in 1993, ending more than fifty years of harsh occupation. By the late 1990s the Lithuanians had achieved the economic and political stability necessary to join the European Union and NATO. Membership in the Western organizations is seen by the Lithuanians as their best protection should their giant neighbor to the east again come under the rule of a totalitarian regime intent on recovering territories that once formed part of the Russian or Soviet empires.

In presidential elections in January 2003, a populist challenger surprisingly defeated the establishment politicians who had run the country in various guises since independence. The time when Lithuania needed a well-dressed, English-speaking president seems to have passed as the country matures into a moderately prosperous European state. The rural population, still large by European standards, has not done as well as the urban dwellers since independence and is beginning to exert political pressure.

### The Caucasus Region

The volatile Caucasus was one of the cradles of the separatism that eventually brought about the collapse of the Soviet Union in 1991 but unlike the Baltic region, the Caucasus remains economically underdeveloped and riven by ethnic disputes. The end of Soviet power in the Transcaucasus allowed the dream of independence and international recognition but failed to end the bitter dispute between the Armenians and Azeris or to reconcile the ethnic minorities still striving for greater national sovereignty.

## Armenia

The Armenian national movement, a coalition of several distinct organizations, grew out of the Karabakh Committee. The nationalists gained widespread support, even among longtime Communists. On 23 August 1990 the republican parliament declared sovereignty and changed the name of the republic from the Soviet version to the Republic of Armenia. The declaration, announced as the beginning of a process to regain Armenia's former independence, formally extended Armenian control to the disputed Karabakh territory in Azerbaijan. Support for the Soviet Union was further eroded when, for the first time in the dispute, Soviet troops openly sided with the still-Communist-controlled Azerbaijan against nationalist-controlled Armenia in April–May 1991. A campaign by Azeri and Soviet troops along the border between the two republics forced thousands of Armenians to flee.

The failed military coup in Moscow, in August 1991, was quickly followed by the severing of most remaining political ties to the Soviet government. The Armenians organized a referendum on independence, which showed more than 90 percent in favor. On 23 September 1991 Armenia was formally declared an independent republic. International recognition affirmed Armenia's new status. The new republic, although strongly supported by the Armenian diaspora, faced massive economic and political problems. An economic blockade begun by the Azeris in November 1991 further complicated the situation.

The conflict over Karabakh quickly escalated, with local Karabakh militias, supplied by the Armenians, fighting the new Azeri national army. On 31 December 1991 the Armenian-dominated government of the enclave declared Karabakh independent of Azerbaijan, adding new fuel to the growing war between the newly independent states. Azeri forces besieged Karabakh in November and December 1992, forcing the ethnic Armenian population to live in underground shelters. The enclave's military forces, reinforced by Armenia, went on the offensive to break the siege, finally opening secure corridors between the enclave and Armenian territory to the west. By April 1993 Armenian forces had overrun up to a tenth of Azerbaijan's national territory, including the districts lying between Karabakh and the Armenian republic.

The Armenians, surrounded on three sides by Muslim nations, saw (and still see) themselves as the standard-bearers of Western civilization in the region, a view reinforced by their ties to the large diaspora in the United States and Western Europe. In spite of the conflict with Azerbaijan and a partial blockade by Turkey, the Armenians established a market economy, and despite shortages, industrial production rose rapidly. The Karabakh conflict continues to the present day, but a cease-fire, agreed to in 1994, effectively ended the fighting. Efforts by international organizations to mediate the Karabakh dispute were defeated by hard-liners on both sides, until an agreement, negotiated in 2001, on Karabakh's status and access through a corridor of land from Armenia was tentatively accepted by both governments.

Old authoritarian habits are seemingly difficult to overcome. After a period of relatively democratic government in the 1990s, ballot stuffing, election fraud, and manipulation of the media were again hindering Armenia's efforts to join Europe's democratic countries. The country's presidential elections in February 2003 were particularly notable for their lack of democratic values. Armenian liberals, many from the diaspora, still find it difficult to make headway against Armenia's entrenched political forces and habits formed during decades of dictatorial rule.

## Azerbaijan

The Azeris gained new confidence in the post-Stalin era with a renewed interest in their suppressed culture and language and particularly in their Islamic religion. The modest reculturation that began during the Khrushchev years was again suppressed in the late 1960s and 1970s, leading to periodic purges of the Azeri leadership. In the years after the 1979 Iranian revolution there was some growth in fundamentalist Muslim beliefs, but the majority remained secular and looked more to Turkey than to Iran for inspiration. The liberalization of Soviet society under Mikhail Gorbachev loosened long-simmering ethnic and nationalist tensions across the Caucasus region. In Azerbaijan, in addition to the serious conflict with the Armenians over the Karabakh region, several non-Azeri national minorities, particularly the Avars and the Lezgins living in the northern part of the republic, also demanded greater self-government and an end to Azeri domination. Both groups were divided by internal Soviet borders, the Avars and Lezgins being Dagestani peoples with the majority of their kin living in neighboring parts of the Dagestan republic of the Russian Federation.

Resurgent Azeri nationalism, stimulated by Armenian nationalist claims to Karabakh, was supported by mass demonstrations, strikes, and protests. Following the nationalist uprising in 1990, the Soviets installed a new loyalist government led by Ayaz Mutalibov, but in order to cling to power he too was forced to adopt the Azeri nationalist cause. An August 1990 coup attempt, supported by the Communists, aimed to return Azerbaijan to firm

Soviet control. Soviet tanks in the streets restored calm but further alienated the increasingly anti-Soviet nationalists. In February 1991 the Mutalibov government dropped the "Soviet Socialist" from the republic's name. The failed Soviet coup of August 1991 against the Gorbachev reforms was initially supported by the Mutalibov regime. When the coup failed, Mutalibov embraced popular nationalism, as Azeris demonstrated for immediate independence. On 30 August 1991 the Mutalibov government declared Azerbaijan independent of the collapsing Soviet Union. In October, the Azeri government, threatened by the ever-widening war with Armenia, nationalized all military material in the republic and recalled 140,000 Azeri nationals then serving with the Soviet military forces. Negotiations between the two newly independent Transcaucasian republics failed, and violence escalated as Soviet troops withdrew from the region. The Azeri government, in response to Armenian support for the Karabakh Armenians, abolished Karabakh's autonomy. In response the Karabakh legislature declared the region independent of Azerbaijan in December.

Antigovernment sentiment continued to mount as Armenian victories pushed Azeri troops back and drove thousands of Azeris from their homes. Longtime Communist Party member Heidar Aliyev replaced Mutalibov. Nationalists, led by the Azeri Popular Front, openly opposed Aliyev's neo-Communist government and continued to press for a stronger Azeri response to the Armenian threat. In May 1992 a nationalist uprising overthrew Aliyev and installed a government led by the Azeri Popular Front. The new government, unable to stem the Armenian advance, saw the enemy troops occupy about 10 percent of the republic's territory. In June 1993, local rebels, in turn, overthrew Azerbaijan's nationalist government, reportedly with Russian support. Heidar Aliyev returned as the head of the new government. He was reelected in November 1995 by a majority of Azeris longing for peace and stability. A 1994 cease-fire generally ended the fighting over Karabakh, but the Armenians retained control of up to 20 percent of Azerbaijan's territory, and more than 1 million Azeri refugees continued to languish in squalid camps in the eastern provinces of the republic.

The republic's gross domestic product contracted about 60 percent between 1991 and the late 1990s. Oil production in the Caspian Sea fields brought international oil companies vying for part of the massive oil reserves. The fields, thought to rival those of the Middle East, hold the promise of future Azeri prosperity, but for ordinary Azeris the benefits have yet to be felt. Western governments, ignoring the abuses and dictatorial aspects of the Aliyev government, continue to court the republic's leaders.

In October 2003, amid widespread fraud and intimidation of voters and opposition political parties, the son of Heidar Aliyev, Illham, was elected president of the republic. The lack of a working democracy continues to hinder Azerbaijan's political and economic development. Even though the majority of Western governments deplored the fraudulent election, the development of Azerbaijan's petroleum reserves by Western companies was not affected.

The ethnic conflict with Armenia remains a serious problem, as do the demands of the non-Azeri ethnic groups of the republic. The Azeri and Armenian leaders met in 2001 to discuss an agreement that would return all Armenian-occupied territory to Azerbaijan except Karabakh and a corridor connecting it to Armenia. The final details of the plan had not been agreed upon in mid-2004. Cease-fire violations and occasional fighting in the Karabakh region at times threaten the fragile peace, but neither the Armenians nor the Azeris want or can afford a return to open warfare.

## Georgia

The Georgians' declaration of independence of April 1991 was reconfirmed following the coup against Gorbachev's reforms in August. The nationalist Zviad Gamsakhurdia, elected president of the republic in May 1991, claimed that the Soviet government intended to undermine Georgia's independence through the national minorities. Gamsakhurdia's increasingly paranoiac view of the world also fostered factionalism and fighting between the Georgian regional groups. In response to his growing despotism and erratic behavior, thousands took to the streets to demand his resignation. Gamsakhurdia proved his critics had reason on their side. To quell his opponents he ordered troops to fire on protesters and arrest opposition leaders. By September 1991 his popularity had dissolved, and only a small minority continued to support his presidency. In December open rebellion broke out, and in January 1992 Gamsakhurdia was ousted from power. He and his supporters, after holding out in the parliament building for two weeks, fled to western Georgia in early 1992. In late 1992, Eduard Shevardnadze, whose credentials as an associate of Mikhail Gorbachev aided his campaign, won the new presidential elections. Shevardnadze finally won for Georgia the prize of Western recognition.

Shevardnadze was soon faced with a rebellion in two areas of western Georgia. In Mingrelia, on the Black Sea, supporters of the ousted Gamsakhurdia rebelled, and just to the north a separatist war threatened in Abkhazia. Georgian troops pursuing Gamsakhurdia's supporters rampaged through parts of Abkhazia, leading to heavy fighting between Georgian and Abkhaz troops. More than 160,000 refugees, mostly ethnic Georgians, fled from Abkhazia. The return of Gamsakhurdia to lead the rebels in Mingrelia, just south of Abkhazia in western Georgia, threatened to split the new republic into several parts. The victorious Abkhaz forces, reportedly aided by Russia, drove most of the remaining Georgians from Abkhazia. Eduard Shevardnadze's Georgian government, fighting Gamsakhurdia's supporters in Mingrelia and separatists in other parts of the republic, was finally forced to accept Russian peacekeeping troops on the Abkhaz border in June 1994, effectively bringing breakaway Abkhazia under de facto Russian military protection. Two other minority national groups, the Ossetians on the Russian border and the Ajars in the southwest, also rejected the initial ethnocentric orientation of the Gamsakhurdia government. Eduard Shevardnadze proposed a loose federation of Georgia in June 1998, with Abkhazia, Ajaristan, and South Ossetia given special status, but the agreement was never ratified. The non-Georgian areas continue to function as autonomous states amid the ongoing political instability in Georgia. Russian troops and peacekeepers remain to separate the fighting forces, which ensures the de facto independence of the autonomous regions.

By mid-1995 the republic's gross domestic product was a scant 17 percent of what it had been in 1989. According to some estimates up to 1 million Georgians had left the republic by 2001, mostly younger workers and university graduates seeking economic opportunities. The Georgian state remains fragile and unstable, and although the economic decline of the post-Soviet period has begun to reverse, the economic crisis continues. The status of the non-Georgian national territories continues to plague the republic, but any attempt to impose Georgian government rule in these territories could collapse the republic once again into chaos and war. President Shevardnadze, in spite of numerous handicaps, at first proved to be a democratic and impressive leader. His experience helped Georgia to maintain a fragile stability despite continuing internal ethnic conflicts and international disputes on the borders. Shevardnadze's policies oriented Georgia toward the West while seeking to maintain a necessary balance with its powerful Russian neighbor to the north. In late November 2003 Eduard Shevardnadze, whose rule had increasingly been associated with widespread corruption and poor government, was overthrown in a peaceful movement known as the Rose Revolution. His replacement, elected in January 2004, is the 36-year-old American-educated lawyer, Mikhail Saakashvili, who orchestrated the mass protests that forced Shevardnadze to resign at the end of November.

## The Slav Nations

The three Eastern Slav nations, Russia, Ukraine, and Belarus, like the other ex-Soviet republics east of the Baltic Republics, experienced great difficulties in the transition from authoritarian rule and command economies to democracy and market economies. Totalitarian habits remained strong in Ukraine and Belarus and even in Russia limits were placed on newspapers, opposition political parties, and the economy.

### Ukraine

The Ukrainian parliament, having declared Ukraine a sovereign state in July 1990, continued to pass nationalist legislation unthinkable just a few years earlier, including a law making Ukrainian the national language of the state in December 1990. In the aftermath of the abortive coup in Moscow in August 1991, the Ukrainians proclaimed their republic an independent state. International recognition soon followed. The republic, the second most populous in the collapsed Soviet Union, after the Russian Federation, faced two serious problems. Both problems involved the non-Ukrainian populations, the large Russian population in the industrial heartland in the east of the republic, and the question of the Crimean Peninsula with its large ethnic Russian population, the deported Crimean Tatars, and strategic military bases. The ethnic Russian population of the industrialized eastern provinces considered themselves Russians by culture and language and formed a large portion of the population that opposed Ukrainian independence. The Crimean Peninsula, transferred to Ukraine from the Russian Republic to mark 300 years of union in 1954, quickly became the major problem for the new Ukrainian government.

The Ukrainians' refusal to join a revamped Soviet Union was the final blow to the disintegrating empire. The citizens of Ukraine voted overwhelmingly in support of Ukrainian independence in a referendum on the issue in December 1991. After centuries of Russification, the Ukrainians have a weak sense of nationhood, particularly in the eastern provinces, while in western Ukraine, where Russian domination was only imposed during World War II, the language and culture are most vigorous. The lack of a democratic tradition has hampered the Ukrainians' efforts to create a truly European state with a market economy and democratic values. The democratic transfer of power in 1994 was the first in Ukraine's long history and offered some hope for the future of the state. In 1996 the republic became the third largest recipient of U.S. aid, after Egypt and Israel. American aid

is seen as an effort to offset continuing Russian political and economic influence within the largest territorial state wholly contained in Europe.

Relations with the Russian Federation remain crucial to Ukraine, particularly as Russia could back separatism among the large Russian populations
in eastern Ukraine and Crimea. In 1997 the two countries finally settled the
difficult conflicts over the Black Sea Fleet and the important naval base at Sevastopol in Crimea. The republic faces a continuing economic crisis, the threat
of Russian separatism, the demands of the Crimean Tatars, and vast regional
differences, owing to the distinct histories and cultural development of the
various regional Ukrainian groups. The religious question has also plagued
the new state, with Uniate Catholics in western Ukraine demanding the return of church properties handed over to the Orthodox authorities.

The Ukrainian economy, already in crisis before the collapse of the Soviet
Union, continues to contract under the forces of a free market and the loss
of many of its former markets and sources of raw materials now in the Russian Federation. The euphoria over independence has faded as the ongoing
economic crisis has impacted the Ukrainians' ability to face the challenges of
a democratic system. The authoritarian rule of Leonid Kuchma, Ukraine's
elected president, has disillusioned many Ukrainians. Political scandals, corruption, and governmental instability have further eroded the Ukrainians'
faith in an independent existence. In spite of economic and political unrest,
the majority of the Ukrainians are determined that the republic survive as the
first successful, independent Ukrainian state in modern history.


## Belarus

The conservative Soviet leaders of the Belarus republic, under increasing nationalist pressure, declared the republic a sovereign state in July 1990. The
declaration also proclaimed Belarus a nuclear-free zone and proclaimed the
entire republic a nuclear disaster area as a result of the 1996 Chernobyl explosion. The Belarussians, with their historically weak sense of nationhood,
had, except for a nationalist minority, accepted Russian domination. A referendum on the future of the Soviet Union, organized across the USSR in
early 1991, received a favorable vote in Belarus of more than 83 percent in
favor of retaining the union. The republic's Communist leaders reluctantly
declared Belarus independent of the collapsing Soviet Union on 25 August
1991. A separate member of the United Nations since 1945, Belarus was finally recognized as an independent state in late 1991. Nationalist organizations that had been winning support at the expense of the discredited Com-

its first decade of independence. The Moldovans are now the poorest in all of Europe, behind even the Albanians. Half the people live from subsistence farming. The European Union blocks the import of the only products the Moldovans could compete in—wine, fruit, and vegetables—while undercutting the Moldovans in the Ukrainian and Russian markets with subsidized products of its own. To survive the Moldovans have turned to emigration. The government estimates that between a tenth and a fifth of all Moldovans have left the country, mostly to work in the EU as illegal laborers. In an effort to end the republic's international isolation, the Moldovan government, in June 2003, passed a resolution allowing for the dispatch of Moldovan forces to join the international peacekeeping effort in Iraq.

## The Central Asian Nations

The historic ties of the Central Asian peoples, in particular their common Islamic faith, had maintained a relatively weak national sentiment across the region. Successive czarist and Soviet authorities had lumped the various populations together until they were finally separated into national republics during the Stalin era. The suppression of Islam, which had traditionally been viewed as central to the prevalent sentiment in the region, was gradually replaced by loyalty to the less universal but more tolerated national identities. Kazakhs, Kyrgyz, Tajiks, Turkmen, Uzbeks, and Karakalpaks, no longer allowed to see themselves as part of the great Islamic universe, adopted local identities but still generally rejected the idea of Soviet man. In post-Soviet Central Asia, the historical distrust of the Uzbeks, the traditionally dominant ethnic group in the region, quickly replaced anti-Soviet or anti-Russian feelings.

### Kazakhstan

The Kazakhs had formed a majority of the population of the Kazakh SSR until after World War II. Since the 1930s the Soviet government had dumped unwanted and punished peoples in the region, adding many different ethnic groups to the republic's population. As part of the Virgin Lands scheme of the 1950s and 1960s, millions of ethnic Slavs and other Europeans were transferred to the fertile northern steppe lands of Kazakhstan. As the population of the republic became the most ethnically mixed in the USSR, the Kazakh population of the republic fell from 57 percent of the total in 1941 to just 38 percent in 1979.

Partly stimulated by their minority status in their homeland, a small, educated Kazakh elite, many the graduates of the Soviet hierarchical system, led a national mobilization. By the mid-1980s nationalist organizations, often in the guise of cultural movements, had spread across the Kazakh-populated parts of the republic, particularly in the southern provinces. The attempted replacement of the republic's ethnic Kazakh chairman with an ethnic Russian in 1986 led to Kazakh rioting. The Kazakh protests presented Mikhail Gorbachev with his first serious ethnic challenge. The protests and riots surprised the Soviet authorities and the complacent Kazakh Communist elite. Gorbachev's reforms made little impact on the Kazakhs until 1988 when Kazakh nationalists began to mobilize in response to moves by the republic's large Slav population. A number of distinctly nationalist organizations emerged, some even calling for an independent Kazakh state. The Kazakhs' high birthrate, as opposed to the very low Russian birthrate, and the return of millions of Kazakhs from outside the country, again made the Kazakhs the largest national group in the republic by the early 1990s, giving them new confidence.

The Kazakh republic became effectively independent with the disintegration of the Soviet Empire in August 1991; however, the president of Kazakhstan, Nursultan Nazarbayev, fearing opposition among the large, influential Slav population, hesitated to formally declare independence until the former Soviet republics began to unite in a loose commonwealth, the CIS. On 16 December 1991, exactly seventy-four years after the first Kazakh attempt at independence during the Russian Civil War, Nazarbayev declared Kazakhstan an independent state, the last of the leaders of the union republics to do so. The same month Nazarbayev was elected president of the new state, having run unopposed in the Soviet fashion.

The first serious challenge to the new Kazakh state came from the Cossack population. Cossack leaders called for the country to become part of the Russian Federation and demanded a referendum on the issue. The arrest of several Cossack leaders ended the crisis, but not the underlying ethnic tensions between the Kazakhs and the Slavs. The danger of ethnic violence has been used to curtail democratic government and to extend Nazarbayev's stay in office. The ethnic dimension is not the only problem facing the Kazakhs. More than 400,000 people in the republic suffer from the effects of radiation sickness, a result of the Soviet nuclear tests. Added to the massive pollution of the industrial cities and the ecological disaster left by Soviet policies, health problems will remain a serious challenge for decades to come.

Massive oil reserves, found in the west of the country, helped to reverse the post-Soviet economic decline. The quantity of petroleum, particularly in the Tengiz field, could make Kazakhstan a major oil producer. Western oil companies have invested heavily in the republic, while demanding continued political stability and positive relations between the Kazakhs and the Slavs, Kazakhstan's two largest ethnic groups.

As in other former Soviet republics, the language issue was one of the most difficult problems facing the new Kazakh government. According to a new language law passed in July 1997, the Kazakh language remained the official state language, but Russian was accorded "equal status" in the bodies of local government and at state organizations. The right to use Russian is one of the principal demands of the large Slav population in the northern provinces of Kazakhstan. The 1997 language law was condemned by many Russians who objected to the clauses that provided for 50 percent of all broadcasting in the Kazakh language and required all Slav state officials be proficient in the Kazakh language by 2006. The Cyrillic alphabet, imposed on the Kazakh language in 1940, was abandoned in favor of the Latin script.

In an effort to unite the country, the capital city was moved from Almaty, near the Chinese border in the south, to Aqmola, in the northern Kazakh Steppe, the heartland of the Slav population. The transfer of the seat of power demonstrated the Kazakh determination to hold on to the northern provinces and encouraged ethnic Kazakhs to return to the north, changing the overwhelmingly Slav population of the region. The Kazakh government also reassured the Slavs that the move was undertaken partly to give the Slavs, many of whom feel they were becoming second-class citizens far from the centers of power, better access to the national government.

The long history of authoritarian rule has been difficult to overcome. Pressure on the independent media and a new law on political parties, put into effect in July 2002, were the most criticized aspects of the government's intention to eliminate internal criticism. Of nineteen political parties in the country, less than half, mostly those considered progovernment, were registered in 2003.

### Kyrgyzstan

A Kyrgyz national movement that grew in opposition to the falsification and distortion of Kyrgyz history and the banning of the great national epic *Manas* remained small, with support only among a few dissident members of the Communist elite. Suppressed for decades, the movement again emerged with the liberalization of Soviet society by Mikhail Gorbachev in the late 1980s. The Gorbachev reforms came late to remote Kyrgyzstan, but when they were implemented events unfolded with remarkable speed. The Kyrgyz nationalists pushed for changes still unthinkable in the neighboring Central Asian republics. In 1990 Askar Akayev, a proponent of radical economic reform and the Kyrgyzization of the republic, was elected in an open election. His initial stance on de-Russification was quickly modified to accommodate the large Slavic population in the republic. Kyrgyz tolerance became a model for the other Central Asian republics facing the exodus of the most skilled segment of the society back to European Russia. Although the Kyrgyz nationalists created nothing comparable to the popular front organizations of the European republics, nationalism became a powerful force in the republic. Pressed by nationalist demands, the republican government declared the Soviet republic a sovereign state on 12 December 1990.

President Akayev was one of the few Central Asian leaders to condemn the coup attempt against Gorbachev in August 1991. As the Soviet Union crumbled Akayev declared Kyrgyzstan independent on 31 August. The new republican government, although poorly prepared for independence, attempted to introduce democratic ways to replace the authoritarian habits created during the Soviet era. In the early 1990s the Kyrgyz developed the most democratic and open society in Central Asia. The republic quickly became known as the "crown jewel" of Central Asia for its liberal government and far-reaching economic reforms. Akayev, the only Central Asian leader who is not a neo-Communist Party boss, has attempted to create a democratic, market-oriented state with a multiethnic population. The Kyrgyz have none of the oil or natural resources of the neighboring nations, but they do have abundant water, which may soon be more valuable than oil in the dry plains of Central Asia.

Kyrgyz culture, drawing on the history and culture contained in the *Manas* epic, which tells of a historic Kyrgyz leader who led his people back to their homeland in the Tien Shan Mountains after they had been driven out by the Chinese, has reversed decades of forced assimilation. In August 1995 the whole republic celebrated 1,000 years of the epic poem. An oral encyclopedia, the Kyrgyz epic has up to 500,000 lines and is at least twenty times longer than the *Iliad* and the *Odyssey* combined. The cultural importance of the epic was confirmed by the United Nations, which declared 1995 the Year of the *Manas* Millennium.

Despite efforts to reform the Soviet command economy, the Kyrgyz economy contracted by nearly 40 percent in the first five years of independence. Renewed economic growth began to reverse the long decline only in the late 1990s. In the early twenty-first century the economic successes have been offset by continuing hardships, shortages, and a lack of experience. The democratic character of the Kyrgyz republic has also been somewhat tarnished, with journalists being harassed and imprisoned. The old authoritarian habits continue to surface even while others attempt to build a modern, multiethnic state.

## Tajikistan

Two events shaped Tajik national consciousness in the 1980s: the Soviet war in neighboring Afghanistan and the Islamic Revolution in Iran. Tajik military units sent to fight their Muslim kin in Afghanistan often refused to fight. In 1985 dozens of Tajik soldiers were shot for refusing to fire on Afghan Muslims. The Tajik tribal and clan ties often extended across the border among the Afghan Tajiks. The Iranian revolution had a lesser effect on the secular Tajik population, but it awakened a new interest in the Tajik's long suppressed Islamic religion. Iranian propaganda aimed at the related Tajiks failed to stir an Islamic uprising, although calls to throw off Soviet culture received more attention.

The Gorbachev liberalization of Soviet life was slow to penetrate Tajikistan, which was ruled by a near feudal Communist elite. Tajik nationalism was also slow to emerge, finally being stirred by conflicts over water and resources and by the revival of historic Tajik claims to the ancient cities of Bukhara and Samarkand in neighboring Uzbekistan. The territorial dispute and a growing number of clashes over dwindling water resources led to violence between Tajiks and Uzbeks in 1989–1990. The Tajiks had the lowest per capita incomes in the Soviet Union in 1990 and the highest birthrate. They were considered the least prepared to face the rapid changes that overtook the Soviet Union. The entrenched Communist leaders fought hard to maintain their power as the Gorbachev reforms took hold, finally adopting nationalism as a way of preserving their power and positions. The republican government declared the sovereignty of Tajikistan on 25 August 1990.

The republican leadership, after initially hesitating, reluctantly declared Tajikistan independent on 9 September 1991, but growing instability quickly divided the new state along political, religious, tribal, clan, and regional lines. A coalition government of Communists, religious groups, and regional political leaders was formed, but the Communists again took complete control as violence and insecurity spread. A new power-sharing agreement was implemented in May 1992 but was too weak to prevent the outbreak of civil war just nine months after the collapse of the Soviet Union. Over the next year, tens of thousands died in the fighting that swept the republic and more than half a million refugees were displaced. Cease-fire agreements in 1993–1994 finally ended the fighting and a large, mostly Russian peace-keeping force was sent to divide the warring factions. Further agreements, in 1996–1998, brought religious groups and opposition factions into the government. The Tajiks remain the least developed nation in Central Asia. Their small nation remains split along regional and tribal lines that has allowed Russia and neighboring states, particularly Iran and Uzbekistan, to exert influence.

Much of the tension in Tajikistan stems from regional and clan differences and the fact that the republican government is dominated by just two clans, those from the regions of Kulab and Khujand. The two clans, historically pro-Communist, took control of the republic at independence. Tensions between these two clans and other regional and clan groupings, as well as ongoing strains between the republic's Tajiks and Uzbeks, and between Tajiks and Afghan refugees in the country, continue to undermine attempts at stability. In the early twenty-first century Tajikistan remains the least developed, politically or economically, of all the former Soviet republics. The northern districts are part of Uzbekistan in all but name, and the country remains governed by a neo-Communist regime, supported by a Soviet-style bureaucracy and military factions. The country survives on the credits and loans granted it by the government of the Russian Federation, partly to ensure the security of the large Russian population. Western aid donors, particularly the United States and the European Union, warned the Tajik authorities that a June 2003 referendum on broad constitutional amendments must conform to international standards.

Tajikistan, in 2001–2003, became a major conduit of Afghan heroin and opium. The recovery of the opium-producing areas of neighboring Afghanistan following the overthrow of the Taliban government prompted neighboring Pakistan and Iran to crack down on drug trafficking. The traffickers then turned to Central Asia, particularly unstable Tajikistan and its porous borders, as the new conduit of drugs to Europe.

## Turkmenistan

The Turkmen, during the Soviet era, endured decades of rule by a Communist hierarchy based on clan, family, and regional ties. Known as feudal communism, the Turkmen leadership was notorious for corruption, but loyalty to Moscow counted for much more than honesty or capability. A Communist Party functionary, Saparmurad Niyazov, became head of the

Turkmen Communist Party in 1985. He continued to lead the republic during the era of the Gorbachev liberalization of the late 1980s. His treatment of the nascent national movement in the late 1980s and early 1990s alienated the more modern sector of the population, but his hold on the republic was indisputable.

The Gorbachev decentralization, particularly in terms of giving more responsibility to the republics, only increased the hold of the Communist Turkmen cadres. In the wake of the failed coup in Moscow in August 1991 the Soviet Union collapsed, forcing the Turkmen leaders to embrace nationalism to survive. A referendum was held on independence in October 1991. Passed by 97 percent voting in favor, the referendum was used as the basis to force the reluctant Turkmen leaders to declare independence on 27 October 1991. Saparmurad Niyazov became the Turkmen republic's first president and has fostered a personality cult similar to that of Stalin during the 1930s. After independence the leadership launched a program of Turkmenization. Places with Russian names were changed to Turkmen names or were given Turkmen spellings and pronunciations.

Turkmen nationalism, despite support for independence, has only begun to gather force in the state. Turkmenistan remains a one-party state dominated by Niyazov and his closest allies and has made little progress in moving from a Soviet-style authoritarian state to a democratic system. The country has been run since independence with Stalin-like ruthlessness. A huge golden statue of Niyazov on a revolving stand in the center of the Turkmen capital, Ashgabat, spins so that it is always facing the sun. Some of the months of the year have been renamed after members of the presidential family. President Niyazov even ordered the closure of the academy of sciences and the capital's opera and ballet theater.

The Democratic Party, the renamed Communists, retained a monopoly on power and has suppressed all opposition political activity. The Turkmen, despite the wealth of oil and natural gas in their homeland, remain militarily, politically, and economically dependent on Russia for the continued survival of their first independent state. Although politically the Turkmen state has proved to be the most stable of the Central Asian states, this has come about through authoritarian control and the lack of unity among the Turkmen, still divided into regional and clan groupings. Although Islam remains a powerful force, the Muslim clerics of Turkmenistan are not organized to the point where they might challenge the Niyazov government.

Although petroleum production has begun, Turmenistan's economy remains static. Economic reforms have made little headway. The state continues to dominate nearly all sectors of the economy, and life gets steadily grimmer for the Turkmen population. Education is limited by state decree to just nine years, limiting the number of professionals in the country. Most Turkmen continue to live in dire poverty, although, with extensive petroleum and natural gas deposits, the Turkmen nation should be one of the most prosperous in the region.

## Uzbekistan

Since World War II, Uzbek leaders needed only to deliver the Soviet cotton quotas in order to maintain their positions and near feudal powers. A clannish, authoritarian Communist hierarchy developed in the nation while corruption and waste were widespread. The hold of the Communist clans remained firm until the Gorbachev reforms of the late 1980s. Opposition groups began to form despite harsh suppression. The disclosure of massive government fraud and corruption as well as the publishing of the extent of previously undisclosed environmental disasters stirred dormant Uzbek nationalism. The virtual destruction of the Aral Sea, by drying up and being heavily polluted by chemical compounds used in cotton production, became the focus of nationalist demands. Economic disputes and conflicts over water and other resources led to serious ethnic violence covertly provoked by the Communist authorities as a means of deflecting the increasingly vocal nationalists.

The failed Soviet coup in August 1991 forced the Uzbek leaders to declare independence on 31 August 1991. The new Uzbek republic, beset by massive economic, environmental, and ethnic problems, quickly moved to outlaw the discredited Communist Party. The former Communist loyalists in control of the republic adopted Uzbek nationalism as their new ideology. Although opposed by some of the powerful clan and tribal groups, elections were held in December 1991. Islom Karimov, the former head of the Uzbek Communist Party, was elected the republic's first president. Karimov's authoritarian government began to compete with the Russian Federation for influence in Central Asia. The Uzbeks were traditionally the dominant national group in a vast region, and large Uzbek minorities in the other Central Asian states assured continued influence.

The Uzbek republic, in the Communist Central Asian tradition, continues to be dominated by the regional Tashkent and Samarkand clans, to the exclusion of clans from other parts of the country, particularly the power clan groups in the fertile Fergana Valley. Led by Islom Karimov, the Uzbek government retained much of the authoritarian tradition of the Soviet era. A

March 1995 referendum, approved by a Soviet-style 99.6 percent of the electorate, extended Karimov's term as president. The republic has attempted to exert Uzbek leadership among all the Central Asian republics. The traditionally dominant ethnic group in Central Asia, the Uzbek's central position, their large population, and sizable Uzbek groups in all the neighboring states has intimidated the neighboring Central Asians, who fear Uzbek irredentism and military and political pressure.

The slow pace of economic reform and the continuing suppression of the Uzbek opposition have stimulated an increasing number of protests against the Karimov government and rule by the former Communist bureaucrats. In early 2004 there were an estimated 6,500 religious and political prisoners; all political opposition or press freedom was orchestrated by the Karimov regime. There is increasing criticism of the lack of respect for freedom of religion, the prevalence of torture, and the failure of the judicial system to protect the rights of all Uzbek citizens. Institutions such as the International Monetary Fund (IMF) withheld financial assistance owing to the poor human rights situation in the country.

The Uzbek republic, in the early twenty-first century, differs little from the former Soviet republic. The exodus of thousands of Slavs back to Russia continues to hamper efforts to modernize the economy. The Slavs, despite government assurances that they are welcome in the republic, were reacting to the growing Uzbekization of the society. Emphasis in all levels of republican society is on the Uzbek majority to the detriment of the other ethnic groups in the country.


## Karakalpakstan

The homeland of the smallest of the Central Asian nationalities lies in western Uzbekistan, bordering on the heavily polluted and shrinking Aral Sea. The Karakalpaks, although fewer in number than the other Central Asian nations, have a well-developed sense of their separate culture even though their separate identity is a recent phenomenon. For centuries they have been ruled by neighboring peoples and have had no history of a separate existence. Under the Soviet system, the Karakalpaks formed an autonomous homeland that was finally added to Uzbekistan in 1936. Their homeland is one of the most environmentally devastated of all the former Soviet territories. Since the end of Soviet rule in 1991 the Karakalpaks have focused on the massive problems affecting their small nation, mostly diseases caused by the overuse of chemicals and the diversion of the rivers that once fed the dying Aral Sea.

## The Twenty-First Century

The immense territories that once formed part of the Russian and Soviet Empires have increasingly gone their own way since the collapse of the Soviet Union in 1991. The myth of Soviet brotherhood withered away as quickly as the Soviet Union. The many nations that formed part of the Soviet Union rapidly threw off Soviet culture and embraced older national cultures. The Baltic nations reoriented toward the West, are becoming member states, along with several of the former Soviet client states in Eastern Europe, of both the North Atlantic Treaty Organization (NATO) and the European Union (EU). The Baltic nations want to strengthen their ties to Western Europe to ensure that their giant neighbor to the east is never again the threat it has been in past centuries. The Transcaucasian nations have also oriented themselves toward Europe and the West, although Turkish and Iranian influences are strong in Azerbaijan. The Karabakh conflict between Armenia and Azerbaijan remains unsettled, although the heavy fighting of the 1990s has not resumed. The Slav nations, Belarus and Ukraine, and Moldova remain in a halfway situation between Russia and Western Europe with trade, cultural, and military ties that extend both east and west but with democratic institutions and market reforms that remain weak. The Central Asians have mostly retained their traditional elites under the new guise of nationalists. Clan and tribal ties, long suppressed under Soviet rule, have reemerged as the basis of the Central Asian cultures.

The Russians themselves, having seen their historic empire slip away, remain in control of an inner empire of more than 100 distinct nationalities. Despite warnings that the Russian Federation would soon splinter along ethnic lines much like the Soviet Union in 1991, the federation has held together. The Russian state is now the most decentralized in history, with the republics and other autonomous areas enjoying large measures of self-government. In 1994, in an effort to placate the restive oblasts (provinces), the government granted new provincial powers that gave the oblasts roughly the same rights to self-determination as the republics. Russia's historic anti-Semitism has largely been supplanted by new xenophobias, particularly in relation to the Caucasian peoples. The Jewish population, greatly reduced by emigration, no longer suffers the prejudices and persecutions of the past, although some of the historic antipathy remains. However, the Chechens and other Muslim peoples of the Caucasus region have become the focus of Russian xenophobia. Large Caucasian, in particular Chechen, minorities living in Moscow and other areas outside their homelands, many refugees from the continuing war in Chechnya, suffer from widespread prejudice and often ethnic violence.

The rapid disintegration of the USSR opened a long debate among politicians in all the former Soviet republics on where the borders of the Russian state should be and on the status of the Russian diaspora left outside the new Russian Federation. The attitude of the Russians toward the reduced Russian state and their view of themselves have traditionally been shaped by the existence of the Russian Empire. The Russian Federation is by far the largest of the fifteen geopolitical entities that emerged from the collapse of the Soviet Union. Covering more than 6.5 million square miles (17 million square kilometers) in Europe and Asia, the Russian Federation succeeded the USSR as the largest country in the world. The center of the Russian state, as in Soviet and czarist times, is European Russia, which occupies about a quarter of the country's territory. Thirty-nine percent of the federation's territory but only 6 percent of its population was located east of Lake Baikal, the famed geographical landmark in south-central Siberia. The enormous territorial extent of the federation constitutes a major political and economic problem for the Russian government, which lacks the far-reaching authoritarian clout of its Soviet and imperial predecessors. The ethnic Russians constitute more than 80 percent of the federation's population, and they dominate virtually all regions of the country except the North Caucasus and parts of the Volga basin. Because of Soviet manipulation of boundaries only eight of the member republics have non-Russian majorities and ethnic Russians make up more than half the population of another nine. Ethnic nationalism remains a powerful force in the Russian Federation, but owing to centuries of dispersal, domination, and subjugation, that nationalism is now mostly channeled into gaining greater control of local governments, economic assets, and natural resources.

The breakup of the Union of Soviet Socialist Republics was for the most part the product of mass nationalist movements in the European republics. Spearheaded by the most actively anti-Soviet national groups, the Baltic peoples, nationalism had spread across the other European territories of the Soviet Union by the late 1980s. The implosion of the Communist regime set off a chain reaction. First the Baltic republics were declared independent, setting the stage for the independence of the other union republics, including those with little nationalist sentiment or historical precedent.

## Timeline

August 1991          A coup against Mikhail Gorbachev collapsed after three days. On 24 August, Yeltsin recognized the independence of Estonia, setting the stage for the collapse of the USSR. Latvia, Lithuania, Ukraine, Belarus, Moldova, Azerbaijan, Uzbekistan, and Kyrgyzstan are declared independent of the collapsing Soviet Union. The Russian Federation assumed independent status as the major successor state of the USSR. Within the Russian Federation the governments of the autonomous territories unilaterally declared the upgrading of their status to that of republics within the new Russian Federation.

September 1991 Armenia and Tajikistan declare independence.

October 1991 Turkmenistan is declared independent.

December 1991 Kazakhstan is declared independent. The presidents of Ukraine, Belarus, and Russia form the Commonwealth of Independent States (CIS). The leaders of the Armenian-populated Karabakh in Azerbaijan declare the enclave's independence. Fighting breaks out along the Dniester River between the separatist Slavs and the forces of the new Moldovan government.

January 1992 President Gamsakhurdia is ousted from Georgia.

March 1992 Eduard Shevardnadze is chosen as the head of the new national council in Georgia.

May 1992 A power-sharing agreement, designed to end the growing violence in Tajikistan, is implemented. A nationalist uprising, led by the Azeri Popular Front, overthrows the president of Azerbaijan.

November–December 1992 Azeri forces besiege the Karabakh enclave, forcing the inhabitants to live in underground shelters.

1995 The authoritarian Belarussian government replaces the nationalist flag, adopted as the national flag at independence, with a new flag based on that of the Soviet era. The United Nations declares 1995 the Year of the *Manas* Millennium to mark 1,000 years of the epic Kyrgyz poem.

1997 Russia and Ukraine agree to a settlement ending the conflict over the Black Sea Fleet and the naval base at Sevastopol in Crimea.

1998 Eduard Shevardnadze proposes the formation of a loose federation in Georgia, with Abkhazia, Ajaristan, and South Ossetia given special status.

2002 The Baltic republics of Estonia, Latvia, and Lithuania are invited to join the European Union (EU). In spite of sev-

|  | eral serious cease-fire violations, the 1994 agreement between Armenia and Azerbaijan continues to hold. |
|---|---|
| 2003 | The Baltic republics, along with most of the former members of the Warsaw Pact, sign agreements with the European Union for full integration into the European federation in 2004. |
| October 2003 | Amid widespread condemnation and reports of fraud and intimidation, Illham Aliyev replaces his ailing father as president of Azerbaijan. |
| November 2003 | President Eduard Shevardnadze resigns following massive protests against the corruption and mismanagement that had come to be associated with his government. |
| January 2004 | Mikhail Saakashvili, a young American-trained lawyer and the leader of the so-called Rose Revolution in late 2003, becomes the new president of Georgia. |

## Significant People, Places, and Events

**AKAYEV, ASKAR** The president of the Central Asian republic of Kyrgyzstan.

**ALIYEV, HEIDAR** Longtime Azeri Communist Party member and president of Azerbaijan.

**ALIYEV, ILLHAM SON OF HEIDAR ALIYEV** Aliyev was elected as president of Azerbaijan to replace his seriously ill father. The election was marked by widespread fraud.

**AZERI POPULAR FRONT** The major nationalist organization in Azerbaijan during the early 1990s.

**BLACK SEA FLEET** The Soviet naval fleet stationed at Sevastopol on the Crimean Peninsula in the Black Sea; the object of a bitter dispute between the newly independent Russian and Ukrainian states.

**EUROPEAN UNION (EU)** The political and economic alliance uniting most of the countries of Western and Central Europe.

**KARIMOV, ISLOM** The president of the Central Asian republic of Uzbekistan.

**LUKASHENKO, ALEXANDER** The president of the Republic of Belarus, whose autocratic rule has impeded economic and political reforms.

**MUTALIBOV, AYAZ** Soviet era leader of Azerbaijan installed following the uprising led by the Azeri Popular Front.

**NAZARBAYEV, NURSULTAN** The president of the Republic of Kazakhstan in Central Asia.

**NIYAZOV, SAPARMURAD** The president of the Republic of Turkmenistan in Central Asia.

**NORTH ATLANTIC TREATY ORGANIZATION (NATO)** Military alliance created by the countries of Western Europe and the United States and Canada in 1949.

**RUSSIAN FEDERATION** The name adopted by the government of the former Russian Soviet Federated Socialist Republic (RSFSR) following the declaration of sovereignty in 1990.

**WARSAW PACT (WARSAW TREATY ORGANIZATION)** A mutual defense alliance created in Warsaw, Poland, in 1955 by the Communist governments of Albania, Bulgaria, Czechoslovakia, East Germany, Hungary, Poland, Romania, and the USSR.

## Document

### Statement by White House Press Secretary Marlin Fitzwater on Lithuanian Independence

March 20, 1990

The Lithuanian people have freely expressed their intention to restore Lithuanian independence. The United States has consistently supported the Baltic people's right to peaceful self-determination. The United States notes that the Lithuanian Government has expressed its readiness to address all legitimate Soviet interests, including economic interests, during negotiations.

We also note repeated Soviet statements that negotiations, not force, are the proper course in this situation. We have called upon the Soviet Government to address its concerns and interests through immediate negotiations with the Government of Lithuania. We continue to urge a constructive dialog. This would be complicated by an atmosphere of intimidation and increasing tension.

In this regard, the activities and statements of the Soviet Government over the past few days are cause for concern. We are watching the situation closely.

*Source:* Fitzwater, Marlin. 1990. Daily press briefing. The Museum at the George Bush Presidential Library. http://bushlibrary.tamu.edu (Accessed May 18, 2004).

# Bibliography

Bourdeaux, Michael, ed. *The Politics of Religion in Russia and the New States of Eurasia.* Armonk, NY: M. E. Sharpe, 1995.

Dunlop, John B. *The Rise of Russia and the Fall of the Soviet Empire.* Princeton, NJ: Princeton University Press, 1993.

Dyczok, Marta. *Ukraine: Movement without Change, Change without Movement.* Reading, PA: Harwood Press, 2000.

Hughes, James, and G. Sasse, eds. *Ethnicity and Territory in the Former Soviet Union: Regions in Conflict.* London: Frank Cass, 2002.

Kaiser, Robert J. *The Geography of Nationalism in Russia and the USSR.* Princeton, NJ: Princeton University Press, 1994.

Krag, Helen, and Lars Funch. *The North Caucasus: Minorities at a Crossroads.* Brixton, UK: Minority Rights Group, 1994.

Lieven, Anatol. *The Baltic Revolution: Estonia, Latvia, Lithuania and the Path to Independence.* New Haven, CT: Yale University Press, 1993.

Shlapentokh, Vladimir, Munir Sendich, and Emil Payin, eds. *The Russian Diaspora: Russian Minorities in the Former Soviet Republics.* Armonk, NY: M. E. Sharpe, 1994.

Szporluk, Roman, ed. *National Identity and Ethnicity in Russia and the New States of Eurasia.* Armonk, NY: M. E. Sharpe, 1994.

Undeland, Charles, and Nicholas Platt. *The Central Asian Republics: Fragments of Empire, Magnets of Wealth.* New York: Asia Society, 1994.

# CHAPTER NINE

# The Spread of Nationalist Sentiment beyond the Union Republics

THE STAGNATION OF THE SOVIET UNION, both politically and economically, during the 1970s and early 1980s, was partially brought on by the need to preserve superpower status by maintaining a bloated and expensive military structure. When Mikhail Gorbachev came to power in 1985 the Soviet economy was in sharp decline, the military buildup was unsustainable, and strains were becoming more evident throughout the multiethnic empire. Nationalist sentiment grew out of a cultural revival among the major national groups in the 1970s. By the early 1980s cultural renewal had fostered the growth of nationalist sentiment among the larger ethnic groups and had stimulated parallel movements among many of the smaller ethnic groups. Under Gorbachev the Communist governments of Eastern Europe were cut loose financially and politically as too expensive to maintain. The resulting collapse of communism throughout Eastern Europe in 1989–1990 stimulated further demands by the many ethnic groups of the Soviet Union, including many that were denied union republic status under Soviet rule.

The rebirth of nationalism that rapidly swept through the capitals of the union republics encouraged even smaller ethnic groups to adopt a nationalist ideal. The spread of nationalist sentiment beyond the titular nationalities of the union republics brought to light another factor in the nationalities problem in the Soviet Union. The question was not only one of Russian control and Russification but of the domination of small ethnic groups by neighboring peoples or the titular nationalities of the union republics. Across the Soviet Union ethnic groups, both large and small, released from decades of strict controls, loudly voiced a flood of grievances, some going back to czarist times.

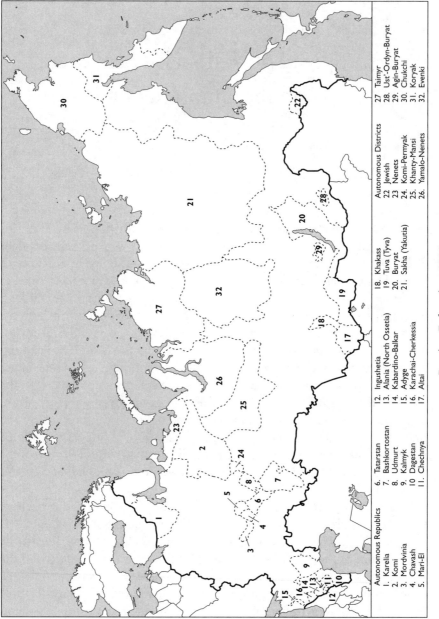

## Russian Federation, 2000

**Autonomous Republics**
1. Karelia
2. Komi
3. Mordvinia
4. Chavash
5. Mari-El
6. Tatarstan
7. Bashkortostan
8. Udmurt
9. Kalmyk
10. Dagestan
11. Chechnya
12. Ingushetia
13. Alania (North Ossetia)
14. Kabardino-Balkar
15. Adyge
16. Karachai-Cherkessia
17. Altai
18. Khakass
19. Tuva (Tyva)
20. Buryat
21. Sakha (Yakutia)

**Autonomous Districts**
22. Jewish
23. Nenets
24. Komi-Permyak
25. Khanty-Mansi
26. Yamalo-Nenets
27. Taimyr
28. Ust'-Ordyn-Buryat
29. Agin-Buryat
30. Chukchi
31. Koryak
32. Evenki

## The Smaller Ethnic Groups in the Russian Federation and the Other Former Soviet Republics

The growth of nationalism below the union republic level rapidly extended to the ethnic groups whose national republics, provinces, and districts had, according to the Soviet constitution and propaganda, wide powers of political, economic, and cultural autonomy. The relaxation of tight political and military control introduced by Mikhail Gorbachev allowed even the smallest ethnic groups to put forth demands, highlighting the many fissures that threatened Soviet society. Ethnic and national groups in the Russian Federation, although numerically insignificant in the overwhelmingly Russian population, had retained much of their national cultures and languages, even though they were submerged and prohibited. By the early 1980s, often in response to growing demands from the larger ethnic groups, nationalist demands were being voiced by groups across the vast territory of the largest of the union republics.

### The Northwest

#### Karels

Deprived of the status of the titular nationality of a union republic by the downgrading of the status of Karelia to that of an autonomous republic within the Russian Federation in 1956, the Karels lost heart and began to assimilate into the surrounding Russian population. The Russification of the Karels, supported by official government policies in the 1960s and 1970s, also had advantages for the Karels in their daily lives. Many adopted Russian identity to escape linguistic and cultural pressure and the political limits placed on non-Russian ethnic groups.

The Gorbachev reforms were followed by a May 1988 official acknowledgment of the campaign of terror unleashed on the Karels during the Stalin era. Renewed contact with the Finns and the large Karel population in Finland spurred a rapid reenculturation and began to reverse decades of assimilation. In June 1991, the first Karel congress in seventy years, held on Lake Ladoga, brought together representatives of the autonomous republic, members of the exile Karel population, and delegates from Karel populations elsewhere in Russia, particularly the sizable population living near the city of Tver'. An executive committee was formed to introduce a bill proposing sovereign Karel districts and territories, areas where the Karel culture and language could be preserved.

## Ingrians

Caught up in the Winter War between Finland and the Soviet Union, a distinct offshoot of World War II, the majority of the Ingrians of the region, having supported the Finns, fled west to escape the victorious Red Army. Thousands, unable to escape, were deported to slave labor camps in 1944–1945. In 1947 Finland formally ceded the Finnish territories west of Leningrad as demanded by the Soviet Union. The Soviet authorities then demanded that the Finnish authorities repatriate all refugee Soviet citizens in Finnish territory. The Finns attempted to shield the refugees, but unable to oppose the Soviets, finally acquiesced. More than 55,000 Ingrians were forced to return to the Soviet Union. Some years after the war, even orphaned Ingrian children adopted by Finnish families were reclaimed by the Soviet Union.

Brutally suppressed during the Stalin era, the Ingrians, claiming a national population of more than half a million in 1917, according to subsequent Soviet censuses, all but disappeared. During the 1950s, some 16,000 of the remaining 140,000 Ingrians were forcibly resettled in neighboring areas of Estonia. Their homes, in the sensitive Narva-Leningrad corridor on the south shore of the Gulf of Finland, were taken over by more reliable ethnic Russians, officially for security reasons. Most of the remainder of the repatriated Ingrians, scattered across European Russia in the late 1940s, were allowed to return to their homeland around the Gulf of Finland in 1956. The Soviet census of 1959 counted only about 5,000 Ingrians, a decrease of more than 97 percent in just thirty years. The Ingrians, as a persecuted nationality, as far as was possible, concealed their identities and attempted to assimilate into the Russian culture in order to survive.

In the Gorbachev era, the small Ingrian population began to demand the revision of their history, falsified by Soviet historians, as a first step toward the stabilization and revival of their national culture. In the 1950s and 1960s the refugee Ingrians in Finland had for the most part disappeared into Finnish society, but in the late 1980s groups began to organize outside help for the Ingrians in the Soviet Union. New interest in their unique history and culture by the Ingrians in Finland was followed by the distribution of books, food, clothing, and other desperately needed goods in the Ingrian areas of Russia. Some of the Ingrians, having registered as ethnic Russians and having adopted Russian names during the years of Stalinist repression, slowly began to rediscover their hidden past. The Ingrian Cultural Society, in rapidly liberalizing Estonia, began to work openly for the revival of Ingrian culture from 1989 onward.

The reform of Soviet life allowed cultural and national groups to proliferate in 1990–1991. Ingrians in Russia began to reestablish ties to the Ingrian populations in Finland and the West, the first such contacts since 1944. Language schools, opened with Finnish and exile Ingrian aid, and thousands of books donated by sympathetic Finnish citizens began to reverse the decades of forced isolation and Russification. An Ingrian congress, held in Estonia in April 1990, and a later congress held in Russia, endorsed the Ingrians' right to self-determination and to closer cultural and political ties to Finland.

### Veps, Votes, and Ludians

The smaller Finnic national groups, although closely related to the Finns, Karels, and Ingrians, maintained their own cultures and languages despite centuries of oppression and Russification efforts by czarist and Soviet governments. Finnish academics who visited the region in 1934 reported a Vep population of more than 50,000 and sizable Vote and Ludian groups. The Stalinist oppression of the Finnish minorities, begun in 1937, ended all cultural activities, eliminated all books in the smaller Finnic languages, and supported assimilation by "accelerated methods" of unspecified means. Finnic language schools were closed, teachers imprisoned, and most intellectuals disappeared or were executed. The national districts, set up a decade before, were liquidated and their local leaderships eliminated. Their territories were parceled out among neighboring autonomies or provinces.

The Finnish occupation of the region during the conflict with the Soviet Union in the 1940s was a period of reenculturation, with schools, organizations, and institutions again operating. Many joined the Finnish military volunteers to fight the hated Soviets. In 1944 the Finns were defeated and were driven back into Finland by the Red Army. Thousands of Finnic refugees fled their homelands as the Red Army advanced, accompanying the Finnish military forces as they fled west. Those that stayed or were unable to escape faced severe collective punishments as suspected collaborators with the Finns.

At the end of the Finnish war and the larger World War II, many of the younger Finnic people began to migrate to the towns, thereby moving into the Russian cultural and linguistic environments. Although Soviet census figures were always suspect, the censuses of 1959, 1970, and 1979 show marked declines in the number of people claiming Vep, Vote, or Ludian nationality. By the late 1970s those claiming these nationalities were mostly over forty years of age, a reflection of the assimilation of younger Finnic people into Russian culture. The social and cultural reforms of the late 1980s began the slow reversal of these trends. Soviet officials acknowledged the Stalinist crimes against the Finnic nations and several national districts were reestablished.

## The Caucasian and Black Sea Nations

### Abkhaz

The Abkhaz, living in the coastal region along the Black Sea in northwestern Georgia, had long resisted Georgian efforts to assimilate them. Their homeland, designated an autonomous republic within Soviet Georgia, had rich agricultural lands and some of the Soviet Union's most popular resort areas on the Black Sea. The region also had a non-Abkhaz majority, largely Georgians and Russians settled in the region under successive czarist and Soviet plans. Anti-Georgian and anti-Soviet rioting occurred in the Abkhazia region in 1957, 1967, and 1979, although these disturbances remained state secrets until the late 1980s.

Stalin suspected the loyalty of the Abkhaz and ordered a plan for the deportation of the Abkhaz to Central Asia in 1943, but the plan was later postponed. Preparations were again put in place for the deportation of the Abkhaz in 1953, but owing to Stalin's death that year they escaped the deportations suffered by other Caucasian nations. However, massive Georgian and Russian immigration to Abkhazia, undertaken during the Stalin era, reduced the Abkhaz to minority status in their ancient homeland by the end of World War II. As early as December 1977, Abkhaz intellectuals officially protested against Georgian attempts to infringe their national rights. The Abkhaz requested that their autonomous republic be transferred from Georgia to the Russian Federation. The request was denied, but they were granted some cultural and economic concessions. Beginning in 1978, the Soviet authorities, in an effort to head off growing demands in Abkhazia for separation from Georgia, set aside 67 percent of government and party positions in the autonomous republic for the indigenous Abkhaz minority.

In 1988, during the liberalization of Soviet society, Abkhaz intellectuals and students formed a nationalist popular front organization called Aiglara (Unity). For the first time since 1921 the Abkhaz National Council was convened as an unofficial shadow government. On 18 March 1989, the nationalists, supported by the council, demanded Abkhazia's separation from Georgia, provoking a strong Georgian nationalist backlash that eventually culminated in Georgian independence in 1991. The new Christian-oriented ethnocentric Georgian government of Zviad Gamsakhurdia claimed Abk-

*This woman is one of thousands of Georgians who lost their homes as a result of the conflict in Abkhazia. Zugdidi, Georgia, 1995 (David Turnley/Corbis)*

hazia as part of its national territory, exacerbating tensions between the Georgians and Abkhaz, whose sense of national identity is as strong as that of the Georgians.

The Abkhaz legislature reinstated Abkhazia's 1925 constitution, effectively declaring the prosperous territory independent of Georgia on 23 July 1992. The Georgian government reacted with the military occupation of Abkhazia, setting off a bitter secessionist war. The Abkhaz separatists, reportedly supported by the Soviet military, drove the remaining Georgian forces from Abkhazia in September 1993. More than 200,000 ethnic Georgians left Abkhazia, fled or driven out during the Abkhaz War. The nationalist Abkhaz government formally declared independence on 26 November 1994, but as of 2004 it had not been recognized by any international organization or government.

In 1997, Georgia's leader, Eduard Shevardnadze, offered increased autonomy but ruled out Abkhaz demands for recognition of the independence of Abkhazia. Renewed fighting between the Abkhaz and Georgian forces broke out in the border region in 1998. New negotiations were undertaken; a cease-fire agreement was signed in mid-1998 but the Abkhaz rejected a plan for broad autonomy within a federal Georgian state. The fragile, armed peace

on the border between Abkhazia and Georgia remains relatively peaceful owing to the presence of Russian peacekeepers, although some new fighting
broke out in 2001.

The breakaway Abkhaz state remains effectively independent even though
its sovereignty has not been internationally recognized. The Abkhaz continue
to exist in a diplomatic no-man's-land, their fragile independent existence
guaranteed only by the presence of the peacekeeping troops on the Georgian
border. Frequent meetings held under the auspices of various international
organizations between Abkhaz and Georgian officials have contributed to a
reduction of tensions and have allowed the cease-fire to continue in force in
spite of violations and incursions by both sides.

## Ajars

The Muslim Ajars, living in an autonomous republic on the Black Sea in
southwestern Georgia, were counted as a separate ethnic group in czarist and
Soviet censuses until 1926, when they were reclassified as ethnic Georgians.
Although less troublesome than the Abkhaz to the Soviet Georgian government, the Ajars also experienced a national revival that began with attempts
by the Soviet Georgian government to curtail their autonomy and to press
assimilation in the 1960s and 1970s. Evidence that came to light after the Soviet collapse indicates that the leadership of Soviet Georgia pursued a long-
term strategy of completely assimilating the Ajars into Georgian culture.

The installation of nationalist, ethnocentric government in Georgia in
1991 fanned ethnic and religious tensions with the Ajars. The attitude of
the radical Georgian nationalists—that the Ajars represented a threat to the
Christian Georgian republic—came to dominate the Ajars' relations with the
Georgians, even after the overthrow of the radicals and the installation of a
more moderate government under Eduard Shevardnadze. In 1993 the Ajar
leader, Aslan Abashidze, declared that the Russian Federation was the protector of the Ajar nation, but later denied that he favored Ajar independence
from Georgia.

In comparison to other areas in the Caucasus, the Ajar homeland has
remained calm and relatively stable. The Georgians, already at odds with
the Abkhaz, have been careful not to incite nationalism in the region. The
government of Aslan Abashidze, although authoritarian and lacking democratic practices, has increasingly separated the region from turbulent
Georgia and has turned Ajaristan into one of the most prosperous areas
on the Black Sea.

## Ossetians

The Ossetians, speaking an Iranian language and mostly Orthodox Christian, live on both sides of the Caucasus Mountains, straddling the international border between the Russian Federation and Georgia. During the Soviet era their homeland was divided into two autonomous territories, the autonomous republic of North Ossetia in Russia and the South Ossetia Autonomous Province in Georgia. The Ossetians, seeing the Russians as fellow Christians and as protection against neighboring Muslim ethnic groups, generally supported Soviet power in the Caucasus region.

The Soviet liberalization in the late 1980s began to change the quiescent Ossetian attitudes. In 1988 the South Ossetians demanded secession from Georgia and unification with North Ossetia. The demands set off violent clashes between Ossetians and Georgians. More than 1,500 were killed and 40,000 Ossetians fled to North Ossetia. On 11 December 1990 the Georgian government unilaterally rescinded the autonomy of South Ossetia. The following day the region's leaders declared the independence of the South Ossetian Democratic Republic.

The disintegration of the Soviet Union, in August 1991, allowed long-suppressed grievances and demands to be aired. The Ingush renewed an old territorial claim to the Prigorodny region transferred to North Ossetia in 1944 when the Ingush were deported on Stalin's orders. The Ossetians reacted by driving the Ingush inhabitants of North Ossetia from the region. As violence spread, more than 60,000 Ingush fled across the border to Ingushetia. Sporadic fighting left many dead and wounded. The Russian government favored the "always loyal Ossetians" over the Muslim Ingush.

The conflicts with the Georgians in the south and the Ingush in the north fueled demands for reunification and greater Ossetian autonomy; however, the majority rejected separatism and the loss of Russian protection. Relations between the South Ossetians and the Georgian government improved in the late 1990s. In June 1998, Eduard Shevardnadze proposed a looser federation of Georgia, Abkhazia, Ajaristan, and South Ossetia. The two sides signed agreements on the return of refugees and on economic reconstruction. As with many other ethnic conflicts in the Caucasian region, the confrontations between the Ossetians and the Georgians in Georgia and the Ossetians and the Ingush in Russia remain unresolved and the continued peace depends on Russian peacekeepers.

## Chechens and Ingush

The resettlement of the deported Chechens and Ingush returning from exile in the late 1950s raised new questions of national rights in the region. The returnees found their villages inhabited by Dagestanis or Ossetians resettled in the depopulated areas by the Soviet authorities. The boundaries of the Chechen-Ingush autonomous republic were arbitrarily redrawn to validate some of the resettlement patterns. Severe rioting, particularly in areas claimed by more than one ethnic group, forced the Soviet authorities to act on some grievances in 1958. During their long exile the Chechens and Ingush had clung to their Islamic religion. Official sources estimated that in the mid-1970s fully half the Chechens and Ingush belonged to outlawed Islamic brotherhoods. Bowing to popular pressure, particularly in Chechen-populated areas, the authorities allowed a number of mosques to reopen in 1978. Many Muslims openly defied the Soviet authorities by making pilgrimages, not to Mecca, which was rarely allowed, but to the shrines of local saints or past military leaders.

Gorbachev's reforms encouraged the peoples of the North Caucasus to demand more self-rule. The Chechens, considered the most anti-Soviet of the many peoples of the Soviet Union, took the opportunity to lay claim to traditional territories, setting off conflicts with neighboring groups. The Islamic religion became a central part of the reborn Chechen and Ingush national movements. The Chechens revolted soon after the abortive Soviet coup in August 1991. Led by a former Soviet general, Dzhokar Dudayev, they overthrew the government of the Chechen-Ingush republic. A new national government, led by Dudayev, declared the republic independent of the Soviet Union on 2 November 1991. The autonomous republic, unlike the union republics, was considered part of Russia, and its independence declaration was rejected by the Russian government and the international community. Although the last Soviet leader, Mikhail Gorbachev, accepted the end of the Soviet Empire, his successor in Russia, Boris Yeltsin, was not willing to see the multiethnic Russian Federation disintegrate in the same way. His main tactic against the Chechen separatists was to use economic sanctions to isolate the small oil-rich republic.

The breakaway Chechen state quickly gained a reputation as a center of Islamic radicalism and as a center of the organized crime spreading throughout the former Soviet Union. Opposition forces in Chechnya, supported by the Russians, attempted to overthrow Dudayev in August 1994 setting off fierce fighting between Chechen rebels and the Russian army. A Russian invasion in December 1994 was expected to easily end the rebellion but

*This image is believed to be of Movsar Barayev, the Chechen rebel who led the seizure of around 700 hostages in a Moscow theater on 23 October 2002. (Reuters/Corbis)*

quickly became bogged down in a guerrilla war after driving the Chechen forces from the major towns and cities. The Chechens, the most implacable enemies of nineteenth-century Russian expansion, again became the major threat to continued Russian rule in the North Caucasus region. A 1996 cease-fire agreement brought an end to the fighting but postponed the question of Chechen independence for a period of five years.

A series of bomb attacks on Russian cities in early 1999 was blamed on Chechen militants, dubbed Muslim terrorists by the Russian government. The crisis deepened following the invasion of neighboring Dagestan by Islamic militants. Russian troops massed on the border of the autonomous republic and were ordered to restore Russian rule. They invaded, but once again Chechen resistance proved stronger than anticipated. The so-called Second Chechen War reduced the Chechen capital and major cities to rubble and killed more than 80,000 people, mostly Chechen civilians. More than 200,000 people fled the republic to squalid refugee camps in neighboring Ingushetia and Dagestan. By 2001 the Russian military controlled all

## TERRORISM AND DISCRIMINATION

On 23 October 2002 members of the Chechen resistance targeted Moscow. A number of Chechen fighters, identifying themselves as members of the 29th Division of the Chechen Army, took control of a Moscow theater during a production of a popular musical. The terrorists, including women, some with explosives strapped to their bodies, immediately released some of the hostages including children but refused to allow the majority to leave and threatened to blow up the theater if the Moscow authorities moved against them. According to a pro-Chechen web site, the terrorists gave the authorities seven days to begin the complete withdrawal of all Russian troops from the Chechen Republic. Even though more than 150 people escaped or were released, the number of hostages was reportedly between 500 and 700, including several foreigners. The hostage-takers' primary demand was for an end to the Chechen war and the withdrawal of Russian forces from their Caucasian homeland.

The Russian authorities attempted to negotiate with the hostage-takers but the negotiations accomplished little. Russian radio broadcast pleas from hostages communicating by cell phone asking the authorities not to storm the building. The terrorists threatened to kill ten hostages for each hostage-taker killed by the police. On 25 October, as the tension around the theater incident mounted, elite troops stormed the theater. Thirty-six of the terrorists were killed, preventing the mass killing of hostages or the blowing up of the building, but a number of hostages also died as a result of the police action.

The taking of the Moscow theater and the presence of suicide bombers added a new dimension to the long-running Chechen conflict. The Chechen homeland was reportedly one of the centers of the radical Islamic groups involved in a number of terrorist acts around the earth. The Chechen terrorists in Moscow seemed willing to die to establish an Islamic republic in the Caucasus region, mirroring similar acts in the Middle East and in terrorist acts perpetrated in the United States and other countries.

The aftermath of the theater incident was particularly felt by the Chechens living outside the ethnic republic. Ethnic Chechens, and other Caucasian peoples, have faced discrimination in Russia since the Caucasian wars of the mid-nineteenth century. But after the Chechen terrorists took hundreds of Russian hostages in the Moscow theater the weight of Russian discrimination and suspicion was felt even stronger than before. The anti-Chechen backlash by the Russian public, angry and fearful following the hostage crisis, led to several violent incidents and general discrimination and even public abuse.

Security was tightened across the Russian Republic with Chechen men often stopped and detained solely on the basis of their ethnic background. The Russian authorities described the detentions as an effort to prevent terrorism, but human rights groups denounced these actions as a virtual license for police to harass non-Slavs and to extract bribes. According to human rights groups there is a well-established pattern of discrimination and abuse by police against Chechens across Russia. Despite calls by the Russian president and other government officials for restraint toward ordinary Chechens, the abuse and discrimination has increased markedly since the October 2002 attack in Moscow.

of Chechnya except the more mountainous south. Chechen fighters, motivated by anti-Russian and Islamic sentiments, carried out a series of attacks on Russian troops within the republic and stepped up attacks on targets in the Russian heartland. In October 2002 Chechen militants seized a theater in Moscow. They threatened to kill hundreds of hostages if their demands for Russian recognition of Chechen independence were not forthcoming. Special troops ended the hostage crisis by using gas and other weapons, but the assault on the theater also killed many hostages. The large Chechen population outside the republic, particularly in Moscow, already targeted for discrimination by the increasingly anti-Caucasian Russians, faced even more persecution and segregation.

A referendum on Chechnya's future, organized by the Russian authorities in March 2003, showed that 477,000, or 88 percent, of registered voters participated, an amazing number in the devastated region. The choice given voters was to approve or disapprove government plans for the future of Chechnya within the Russian Federation. Critical Western human rights organizations and exile Chechens denounced the referendum as an exercise not in democracy but in political control by the Russian authorities. Nationalists dismissed the referendum as just another Russian ploy to placate Western governments and international organizations, particularly in the southern districts where most rebel activity is concentrated. Both the Russian military and the Chechen rebels continue to profit from the conflict. The Russian Army enjoys combat pay, the siphoning-off of budget funds, and arms sales, and kidnapping and general racketeering are profitable for both sides. The losers are the Chechen public, sick of war but distrustful of politicians of all stripes. An amnesty for Chechen rebels, passed by the Russian parliament and implemented in June 2003, met with only limited success.

The Ingush, less traditionally anti-Russian than their Chechen cousins, refused to support the Chechen nationalists. In January 1992 the Ingush homeland, Ingushetia, was officially separated from Chechnya and became a separate member state of the new Russian Federation in June. The focus of Ingush nationalism was the territory transferred to the Ossetians during the brutal Ingush exile in Central Asia from 1944 to 1957. Demands for the return of the remainder of their traditional territory led to violence between Ingush and Ossetians in October 1992. The Christian Ossetians, aided by Russian troops, drove more than 60,000 Ingush into squalid refugee camps. The involvement of government military forces ended Ingush support for the Russian Federation. Nationalist sentiment grew rapidly. In early 1994, on the fiftieth anniversary of their deportation, Ingush nationalist leaders declared their support for eventual Ingush independence.

In early 1999 the governments of Ingushetia and North Ossetia signed an agreement undertaking to return all refugees and forced migrants to their homes by early 2000. The agreement has yet to be fully implemented. The territorial conflict, including the related issues of the Ingush refugees and the final status of the disputed region, remain as the focus of Ingush nationalist interest. Over Ingush protests, North Ossetia has resettled South Ossetian refugees in the disputed district while denying Ingush petitions to return to their homes.

## Dagestanis

The Dagestani peoples inhabit a region that forms one of the member states of the Russian Federation. The Republic of Dagestan is one of the world's most ethnically diverse. The name *Dagestani* is actually a generic term used to designate any of dozens of Caucasian or Turkic ethnic groups living in the eastern part of the North Caucasus on the Caspian Sea. The largest of the Dagestani groups are the Caucasian peoples, the Avars, Dargins, Lezgins, Tabasarans, Laks, Rutuls, Aguls, and Tsakhurs. The Turkic groups, located in the northern part of Dagestan, are the Kumyks and Nogais. The region's mountainous terrain has historically contributed to the ethnic segregation that developed in Dagestan since ancient times. Almost as many languages are spoken in the republic as there are ethnic groups. According to most counts there are thirty-two distinct ethnic groups in the region.

During the Stalinist era, tens of thousands of Caucasians from the high valleys of the Caucasus in the southern part of Dagestan were forcibly removed from their ancient homeland and resettled among the Turkic Kumyk and Nogai groups in the steppe lands farther north. Under successive Soviet regimes, government posts were judiciously divided according to nationality in Dagestan, often with little regard for education or ability. Political power and scarce resources were distributed according to a complicated system of ethnic quotas that conformed to the traditional czarist and Soviet policy of divide-and-rule in the unruly region. Disputes over water and territory, as they did historically, continued to mark ethnic relations.

The Islamic religion of Dagestan, suppressed for decades, became the focus of a national renewal that began during the years of stagnation in the 1970s and 1980s. A religious and cultural revival spread through the thousands of illegal, underground mosques in the 1970s. Resistance to Soviet atheism gradually evolved a more nationalistic stance, particularly among the larger Dagestani groups. Islamic fundamentalism, promoted from revolutionary Iran after 1979, stimulated greater resistance among younger Dagestanis. By 1980 an estimated half of the autonomous republic's male population belonged to illicit Muslim brotherhoods, often with nationalist overtones.

In the more relaxed atmosphere of the late 1980s, religious and national sentiment emerged as harsh Soviet controls ended. The rapid spread of religious feeling forced the Soviet authorities to authorize charter flights to Mecca for believers in April 1990, ending a quota system that allowed just twenty Dagestanis a year to make the important Muslim pilgrimage. The attempted hard-line coup in August 1991 gave new impetus to the revival of the regional Dagestani cultures. One of the most difficult tasks of the Dagestan government was maintaining the unity of the state's territory. Dagestan mirrored the Soviet Union, with some groups, particularly the Avars and Lezgins in the south and the Kumyks and Nogais of the northern steppe, seeking separate national territories. The Russian military attack on neighboring Chechnya in 1994 stirred nationalist and anti-Soviet feelings.

The collapse of the Soviet Union led to the upgrading of Dagestan's status as a member state of the new Russian Federation; however, the Avars, the largest and the formerly dominant ethnic group in the region, saw their traditional power slipping away. Avar political power, tied to Soviet structures, has been declining since the early 1990s. Their loss of status and political position fomented ethnic tensions that led to the mobilization of the Avars in the mid-1990s. In 1995 a territorial conflict with the Kumyks led to the call up of more than 30,000 Avars in a local militia. The dispute, stemming from the Soviet policy of resettling the highland Avars among the Turkic Kumyks in the lowlands, continues to sour relations between the two ethnic groups and fuels demands for the creation of an autonomous Avaristan. Calls for Muslim solidarity are disregarded, as ethnic allegiances are stronger and more historic than the idea of Muslim brotherhood.

The Kumyks feel they are the most disadvantaged of the Dagestani ethnic groups. Soviet policies, which forced many Caucasian mountain people to settle in the steppe lands that the Turkic Kumyks traditionally considered their national territory, completely changed the demographics of the region. The forced resettlements destroyed the traditional settlement patterns and deprived the Kumyks of half their arable lands by the time the Soviet Union disintegrated in August 1991. Tensions between the Kumyks and the settlers, mostly Avars and Laks, freed of Soviet control, became an open conflict. According to Kumyk activists, their group is underrepresented in Dagestan republican structures and is economically deprived. Avar immigration has reduced the Kumyks to minority status in many of their historic districts.

Claiming descent from the early medieval Khazars, the Kumyks also demanded the formation of a separate autonomous territory.

The Lezgins, whose homeland straddles the new international border between Russia's Dagestan Republic and Azerbaijan, are one of the most militant of the Caucasian peoples. Lezgin nationalism exploded with the collapse of the Soviet Union and the independence of Azerbaijan. The border, only administrative during Soviet rule, became a frontier between two sovereign states in 1991, effectively dividing the Lezgin nation into two halves. Tensions with the Azeris are particularly serious. Both governments oppose Lezgin demands for the creation of an autonomous Lezgin state incorporating territories from Russia and Azerbaijan. Some observers believe that the Russian government is encouraging militant Lezgin nationalism in order to increase pressure on the Azeris over oil contracts, production quotas, and pipelines.

## Kurds

The majority of the Kurds of the former Soviet Union live in the Transcaucasus region, in Armenia, Georgia, and Azerbaijan, with other sizable communities in Turkmenistan and Kyrgyzstan. Many of the Kurds, unlike the Sunni Muslim Kurds of the Middle East, are Shia Muslims or are Yezidis, practicing a secretive religion that mixes ancient rites with elements of Zoroastrianism, Judaism, Christianity, Islam, and Manichean dualism. They are considered heretics by Muslims and are often called devil worshipers. Most Kurdish Yezidis live in Georgia. In the nineteenth century nomadic Kurds migrated north from Turkish and Persian territory at the same time as the Russians were expanding to the south.

Stalin at first encouraged the Kurds to develop their national culture, hoping to use them to spread communism to the Middle East. An autonomous homeland, popularly called Red Kurdistan, was formed in the Caucasus. The cultural autonomy disappeared in the late 1930s as Stalin's suspicions of everything non-Russian reached paranoiac levels. In 1937 many Kurds were rounded up in the Caucasus and deported to Central Asia. Two other deportations of Kurds transferred the majority from the borderlands deep into Soviet territory. Stalin seemed to have feared any ethnic group with kinsmen outside the Soviet Union.

The Kurds of Central Asia have somewhat assimilated, but those of the Caucasus remain as an identifiable ethnic group. Allowed to return from exile in the late 1950s, most settled in Armenia and Azerbaijan, near the Kurdish territories in neighboring Middle Eastern states. Armenian and Azeri independence, in 1991, which led to war between the two, quickly involved the Kurds. Each side hoped to employ the Kurds to their advantage, but the Kurds have attempted to remain neutral. In 1992 a Kurdish leader in Armenia demanded the restoration of the autonomous Kurdish state in eastern Azerbaijan that existed under the Soviet nationalities policies from 1923 to 1929.

## Talysh

The Talysh are an ethnic group of mixed Iranian and Caucasian ancestry. Known for their intellectual abilities and literacy, their culture, like that of the neighboring Azeris, combines Caucasian, Turkic, and Iranian traits. The Talysh homeland is divided between Azerbaijan and Iran. Lying along the Caspian Sea the Talysh territory, locally called Talyshstan, rises sharply to the Talysh Mountains, which straddle the Azeri-Iranian border. Like the other Caucasian nationalities, the Talysh of Azerbaijan were slated for assimilation, not into Russian culture but into the greater Azeri culture. According to the 1926 Soviet census, 77,039 Talysh lived in the Soviet Union, but by 1959 relatively few people in the region identified themselves as ethnic Talysh. Soviet ethnographers assumed that the Talysh, as planned, had disappeared into Azeri culture. For several decades the Talysh in the Soviet Union virtually disappeared as a distinct ethnic group, although those in Iran remained as an identifiable ethnic group. Soviet authorities, convinced that the Talysh in southern Azerbaijan had disappeared, did not try to count them in the censuses of 1970 or 1979; however, in the early 1980s, Talysh demands for limited cultural freedom and agitation for group rights forced the local authorities to reconsider.

In the late 1980s, during the liberalization of Soviet society, it became clear that at least a core of Talysh continued to cling to their ancient language and culture and refused to assimilate. The Gorbachev reforms allowed the Talysh to organize and recover their national identity. The revival of the Talysh nationality unleashed a torrent of economic, political, and cultural grievances. The local Soviet authorities, forced to count the Talysh as a separate ethnic group in the 1989 census, were surprised to find that 21,914 people in the region still stubbornly registered themselves as ethnic Talysh.

The independence of Azerbaijan in 1991 began a rapid cultural awakening. Thousands of young Talysh rejected the assimilation of the former Soviet and new Azeri governments. Although Azeri government figures projected the Talysh as 2 percent of the population, nationalists claimed a much higher number, with estimates of around 11 percent of the total population of Azerbaijan. The Azeri government figures are probably based on language, as many ethnic Talysh learned Azeri as their first language under Soviet rule. The revived Talysh culture and language is spreading through the southern districts of Azerbaijan, but are also stimulating a cultural renewal among the Talysh in adjacent areas of Iran. Iranian Talysh, in October 2001, defied the Islamic authorities to meet Azeri Talysh on the international border to demand the opening of border-crossings without excessive formalities.

In 1993 Talysh rebels attempted to set up a separatist republic in southern Azerbaijan, in coordination with an antigovernment uprising in northern Azerbaijan. Many Talysh were arrested and were sentenced to prison. Others fled to Russia. The leaders of the rebellion were sentenced to death for high treason. One of the reasons for the separatist uprising was the discovery of oil in the Caspian Sea in waters claimed by Talysh nationalists. The development of the oil fields in 1998–1999 brought much needed employment but also gave the underground nationalist movement an economic base.

## Circassians

The Circassians of the western Caucasus were divided under Soviet rule into three distinct national groups, the Adyge in the west surrounded by Slavic territory, the Cherkess in the center where they shared an autonomous territory with the unrelated Turkic Karachais, and the Kabards in the east, sharing their autonomous republic with the Turkic Balkars. The easing of strict Soviet control in the late 1980s raised demands for the reunification of historic Circassia and greater political and cultural ties between the three Circassian ethnic groups.

Growing tensions between the Caucasian Circassians and their Turkic neighbors has erupted into violence several times during the 1990s. Demands for the dissolution of the joint autonomies grew as tensions increased. Circassian activism mostly focused on separation from the Turkic peoples until the war in Chechnya began in 1994. Seen as an attack on the Muslims of the Caucasus, the war mirrored the brutal conquest of the region in the nineteenth century. Many young Circassians, disappointed in the slow pace of changes since 1991, have been drawn to Islamic groups as a substitute for the prosperity they feel has been denied them.

## Karachais and Balkars

The Turkic Karachais and Balkars, speaking dialects of the same Caucasian Turkic language, also share cultural traditions, dance troops, and publications. Slow to mobilize following the collapse of the Soviet Union, owing to a weak sense of collective identity, they had first to overcome traditional regional and clan identities. Renewed contacts between the two closely related ethnic groups, forbidden for over three decades, aided the cultural and political revival of the small dual nation.

The Soviet collapse also opened the debate on the political situation and demands for separation from the joint autonomous territories they shared with the Caucasian Cherkess and Kabards. In 1992 Karachai leaders announced the unilateral withdrawal of the Karachai from the joint Karachai-Cherkess region, a move that the Russian authorities have rejected. Ceremonies organized to mark the fiftieth anniversary of the deportation of the Karachai and Balkars to Central Asia were used to reiterate their territorial and political demands. Violent confrontations broke out between Karachai militants and local Cossacks over land rights and Karachai demands for separation in February 2001, and violence has continued sporadically since. Activists claim that only allowing the Karachai and Balkars to separate from the joint autonomies will bring an end to the growing violence.

## Kalmyks

The Buddhist Kalmyks of the steppe lands north of Dagestan are considered among the most antigovernment in the region owing to their treatment by successive czarist and Soviet governments. The Gorbachev reforms stimulated an active religious and cultural revival. The exile Kalmyk community in Western Europe, numbering just 1,500, were served by five temples in 1990, whereas the 200,000 Kalmyks in the Soviet Union had only one active temple. The religious revival was paralleled by a rebirth of nationalism. Militants demanded an apology for the deportation of the Kalmyks during World War II and for the falsification of Kalmyk history by Soviet historians. The Soviet Union's collapse provoked a strong reaction in the autonomous Kalmyk republic. The local government rapidly changed the republican name to the Kalmyk version and unilaterally upgraded the status to that of a member republic of the Russian Federation. Activists also claimed control over the extensive mineral wealth of their republic.

A young Kalmyk millionaire, Kirsan Ilyumzhinov, won republican elections in April 1992 on his promise to convert Kalmykia into a neutral, Buddhist state. Lapel pins bearing his likeness and that of the Tibetan exile leader, the Dalai Lama, the spiritual leader of the Kalmyks, became as common as the hammer-and-sickle once was. Ilyumzhinov's religious views and his peaceful campaign for the rights of the Kalmyks and the Tibetans in China made him the icon of reviving Kalmyk nationalism. Prayer houses were opened and an Institute for the Rebirth of the Kalmyk Language and Buddhism was established. Buddhist holidays are again celebrated. The new Kalmyk University became a center of the Kalmyk revival at the turn of the twenty-first century. Ilyumzhinov set off a crisis when he demanded greater autonomy for his small nation. The crisis deepened until the federal government conceded to new agreements on finances and cultural subsidies. The underlying animosity toward the Russians, a result of past Soviet policies, remains a potent force among the Kalmyks.

## Crimean Tatars

The original inhabitants of the strategic Crimean Peninsula suffered a cruel deportation, discrimination, and repression. Not rehabilitated along with the other deported peoples in the 1950s, the Crimean Tatars remained in exile in Central Asia and Siberia until the collapse of the Soviet Union in 1991. Forbidden to return to their Black Sea homeland, now part of independent Ukraine, they developed a strong culture in spite of their scattered communities and tight control by the KGB and local authorities. A national movement launched a campaign to win official recognition of their right to return to their homeland. Activists staged demonstrations and protests and attempted to bring the issue before the United Nations and other human rights forums. Delegations dispatched to the Kremlin to present their case to successive Soviet leaders were simply ignored or more often were imprisoned. The Gorbachev liberalization finally allowed the Crimean Tatars to be heard. A Soviet commission appointed in 1987 finally addressed the Crimean Tatar issue. Although still forbidden, more than 150,000 Tatars had returned to the Crimean Peninsula by early 1990. Nationalist sentiment, built on decades of suffering, spread rapidly. On 28 June 1991 a Crimean Tatar congress declared their historic right to the Crimean Peninsula as the national territory of the Crimean Tatar nation.

The dissolution of the Soviet Union opened an acrimonious debate between the governments of the newly independent Ukrainian and Russian republics over the fate of the peninsula. Russian claims to the Crimea, particularly the large and important base of the Black Sea Fleet at Sevastopol, quickly strained relations between the two governments. Both the Russians and the Ukrainians attempted to use the Crimean Tatars in the dispute, although neither would agree to talk about the Crimean Tatar claim to the peninsula. The peninsula's Russian majority, with the tacit approval of the Russian government, mobilized to oppose Ukrainian rule. In 1992, the Crimea's Russian leaders proclaimed the peninsula independent of Ukraine; however, just five days later, under pressure from both the Russian and Ukrainian governments, the declaration was rescinded. Crimean Tatar leaders were united in condemning the declaration, which made no mention of the peninsula's indigenous Tatar population.

The Crimean Tatars generally supported Ukrainian claims to the peninsula as the less objectionable of the two alternatives. The returnees, numbering more than 270,000 by the mid-1990s, were mostly relegated to a marginal existence in shantytowns around their former capital and the other large Crimean cities. Militant nationalists continue to demand the resurrection of the civil war era Crimean Tatar republic, pointing out that their claim to the peninsula predates both the Ukrainian and Russian claims. Other leaders demand recognition as the indigenous population of the peninsula, which would give them representation in local governments and easier access to citizenship rights. Around 250,000 Crimean Tatars remain in Central Asia, their plans to return to their homeland curtailed by political and economic constraints.

## Meskhetians

During the 1960s the scattered groups of exiled Meskhetians strengthened their ties, coordinating appeals, petitions, and agitation for the right to return to their homes in the Meskhetia region of Georgia. Delegates from the dispersed communities attended a national congress in Tashkent, Uzbekistan, in 1964. The congress agreed to form the Meskhetian National Movement (MNM), which would coordinate sending representatives to Moscow and Tbilisi to plead their case for the right to return to their homeland.

In the 1970s, the Meskhetian national movement was suppressed, and its leaders were jailed or exiled to remote outposts. Because Meskhetians continued to plead for the right to return to their homes in the Caucasus region, the Brezhnev government accused them of spreading lies against the Soviet Union. Over the next decade, the national movement split between those favoring a return to their ancestral homeland in Georgia and others who wanted to migrate en masse to Azerbaijan, which is ethnically, linguistically, and religiously similar to the Meskhetian traditions.

The rift between the so-called Georgian Meskhetians and the Turkish Meskhetians, those that favored accepting the government's offer of resettlement in Azerbaijan, continued until June 1989, when a serious outbreak of ethnic violence occurred in Uzbekistan. In an incident that began over the cost of a basket of strawberries, Uzbek rioting, led by the man who claimed he had been cheated while buying strawberries from a Meskhetian, turned into a pogrom as the Sunni Muslim Uzbeks turned on the mostly Shia Meskhetians. Uzbek mobs hunted the terrified Meskhetians through a week of violence, rape, and murder. More than 100 Meskhetians died, and over 500 were wounded before the Soviet military evacuated the entire Meskhetian population in the Fergana Valley to guarded camps outside the Uzbek cities. Although they were told that they would be returned to their Georgian homeland within two weeks, the majority of Meskhetians still languish in the evacuation camps.

The collapse of the Soviet Union and the emergence of independent Uzbek and Georgian states further complicated the situation of the Meskhetians. Considered foreigners by the independent Uzbek government, they can obtain neither work nor housing. The first Georgian government, overtly Christian and ethnocentric, refused to discuss the return of the Meskhetians unless they would register as ethnic Georgians and accept repatriation to areas outside their homeland in Meskhetia. A more moderate Georgian government, installed in 1992, was beset by serious ethnic problems on all sides and, although Meskhetian delegations have been received, the government has refused their pleas. By the turn of the twenty-first century, only a handful of Meskhetians had been allowed to return to Georgia. Although the majority of Meskhetians remain in the camps in Uzbekistan, some have accepted offers by the government of Azerbaijan and have been resettled in areas of that country inhabited by the non-Azeri minorities.

## The Volga and Permian Nations

The nations of the Volga River Basin, like those of the Caucasus, were subjected to the same divide-and-rule system so often employed by the Soviet authorities. The Volga nations, although historically separated by language and religion, had maintained close political and cultural ties strengthened by their common position as non-Russian nationalities.

## Tatars

The Gorbachev reforms in the late 1980s raised expectations among the Tatars of the Volga that their long list of grievances would finally be addressed. As one of the largest national groups in the Soviet Union a major demand by the nascent national movement was for Tatarstan, then an autonomous republic within the Russian Federation, to be given the status of a full union republic. The demand, refused on the grounds that Tatarstan did not share an international border, stirred nationalist sentiment across the autonomous republic. Pressed by the nationalists, the Tatar government declared the sovereignty of the republic in August 1990.

The rapid collapse of the Soviet Union in August 1991 stimulated demands for Tatar independence. Huge proindependence demonstrations broke out in the major cities, and a number of nationalist organizations formed. The more moderate groups advocated greater self-determination within a new and democratic Russian federation. Militant groups demanded a declaration of independence and Russian recognition before undertaking negotiations with the new Russian government. Even though the population of the republic was almost evenly split between Tatars and non-Tatars, mostly ethnic Russians, a referendum on independence, in March 1992, resulted in more than 60 percent voting in favor. As a result of the referendum the president of Tatarstan, Mintimer Shaimiev, rejected Russian demands that he sign a new federation treaty. In November 1992 the Tatar parliament approved an amendment declaring Tatarstan a sovereign state freely associated with the Russian Federation. The republic's leaders, after long and often acrimonious negotiations, finally approved the federation treaty in 1994 after the Russian government agreed to Tatarstan's status as a sovereign state freely associated with the federation and the right of legal secession from the federation.

The government of Tatarstan signed a treaty of friendship and cooperation with the breakaway Chechen Republic in May 1997. The subsequent war in Chechnya was a sobering example to the Tatar militants of what could result from pressing their demands for full independence too far. The vicious war against the Chechens also raised religious awareness among the Tatars. The rebirth of Islamic sentiment, although less militant than that of the Chechens, accompanied the continued growth of national consciousness. The Tatars form the largest and one of the most nationalistic of the non-Russian nations of the Russian Federation. The Russian government, fearing another separatist conflict like that in Chechnya, has been careful not to antagonize the large Tatar population.

## Bashkorts

The Bashkort culture, suppressed for more than fifty years and succumbing to assimilation, began to revive in the 1970s. The Islamic religion, the focus of the first tentative moves to revive traditional Bashkort culture, formed the basis of the later explosion of nationalist sentiment when the Soviet Union collapsed. Demands for independence gained widespread support in late 1991. In November 1991 the government of the republic, unilaterally proclaimed a member state of the new Russian Federation, reversed its policy of opposing separatism and announced its support for eventual Bashkort independence. In 1993 nationalists renewed historic claims to "Greater Bashkortostan," including Orenburg province, which would give the republics of the Volga River basin a land border with the newly independent Republic of Kazakhstan.

In 1994, the republic's leaders negotiated extensive political and economic autonomy for Bashkortostan in a power-sharing agreement similar to that signed with neighboring Tatarstan. The agreements allow the Bashkort government to retain a larger share of oil revenue from the Bashkort fields. The power-sharing has benefited the Bashkorts living in Bashkortostan, but the large number living in adjacent areas have not benefited. The first serious clash between the ethnic groups in the republic since 1991–1992 erupted in October 1997. The clash grew from new language laws in Bashkortostan, where the revival of the Bashkort language was given priority. The large Tatar population objected, but was ignored when Bashkort and Russian were adopted as official languages in 1999.

Nationalism among the Bashkorts is not as strong or popular as it is among the neighboring Tatars, but with closer ties between the Bashkort populations, scattered during the upheavals of the twentieth century, plus a continuing migration of ethnic Bashkorts to the republic, ethnic demands have been reinforced. Economic sovereignty raised calls for greater cultural and political autonomy and for the redrawing of the Soviet-era republican borders that artificially divided the Bashkort nation. The uneasy ethnic balance in the republic remains an important issue. Attempts by the Russian federal government to curtail the powers of the member states in 2000–2001 again raised tensions in Bashkortostan.

## Chavash

Nationalist sentiment, although less militant than that felt among the Tatars or Bashkorts, gained support as the Soviet Union imploded in mid-1991. Nationalists forced the republican government to declare the upgrading of the territory to that of a member republic of the new Russian Federation, including officially changing the name of the republic from the Russian to the Chavash-language word. The nationalist backlash greatly reduced support for the Communist Party. In local elections in 1998, the Communists lost all but a few seats in the Chavash legislature. Although the republican government has concentrated on improving the region's fragile economy, Chavash nationalism focuses on the consolidation of their historic homeland and all Chavash into one autonomous state. Nationalists claim a Chavash population of more than 2 million, making them one of the largest of the non-Russian groups in the Russian Federation.

The old idea of joint sovereignty in the Volga basin is again gaining support. Many Chavash are somewhat suspicious of too close ties to the Muslim Tatars and Bashkorts of the region, giving support to a proposed autonomous state of the Christian Volga peoples, the Chavash, Maris, and Mordvins. The national movement remains small, with little overt support for separatism; however, language and cultural issues have become the focus of activists. Demands for the abandonment of the Cyrillic alphabet, the opening of Chavash-language schools, and the creation of a specifically Chavash university continue to motivate national sentiment.

## Maris

A Mari cultural revival took on nationalist overtones in the 1970s and 1980s, growing into a mass movement following the Soviet collapse in 1991. The government of the autonomous republic unilaterally declared Mari-El, the Mari homeland, a full republic within the new Russian Federation. A presidential system had been introduced by the end of 1991, and free elections for the local legislature were inaugurated.

Despite centuries of assimilation efforts, the Maris have maintained a cohesive sense of their distinct identity. In 2000, linguists estimated that more than 80 percent of the Maris continued to use their national language as their first language, whereas only about two-thirds are able to understand Russian. Mari schools have been restored across the republic and among Mari populations living in adjacent areas. The historic animistic religion, which venerates the Mari past, retains a strong influence. Congregations of the indigenous religion have been founded with the approval of the republican and federal governments. That the Russian federal government officially supports a nature religion is unique in all of Europe.

## Mordvins

The collapse of communism, followed by the rapid disintegration of the Soviet Union in 1991, stimulated a rebirth of the Mordvin culture. Demands for the redrawing of internal borders to incorporate the scattered Mordvin populations were put forward in 1992–1993. Outnumbered by the ethnic Russians in their historic homeland, the Mordvin reformers were defeated in local elections in 1993 and replaced by conservative ex-Communists.

The numbers claiming Mordvin nationality and the number of people registered as Mordvin speakers continues to decline, the result of Russian colonization and centuries of assimilation policies. The long decline began to level off in the late 1990s as a new interest in the Mordvin culture took hold, particularly among the young. Younger Mordvins now speak their Finnic dialects as a matter of pride. The focus of Mordvin activism remains the unification of their remaining national population in one autonomous administrative unit.

## Udmurts

The disintegration of the Soviet Union opened a heated debate among the Udmurts. Activists demanded greater cultural and economic autonomy with widespread support, but calls by a small minority for separatism were mostly ignored. The majority feared the uncertainties of too much independence while maintaining that they would reject any attempts to replace Soviet domination with an equally oppressive Russian domination. The Udmurts have retained a surprisingly cohesive sense of identity to the present. Closer contact to the other Permian peoples, the Komi and Permyaks, reinforced their historic ties.

In the years since 1991 the number of ethnic Udmurts has risen dramatically. To escape persecution or to gain economic advantages during the Soviet era, many Udmurts had registered as ethnic Russians, but have now regained their traditional designation as ethnic Udmurts. The decline and low status of the Udmurt language during the Soviet era became the focus of the growing nationalist movement dedicated to the revival of the Udmurt national culture. In 1996 the republican legislature passed an education bill that guaranteed the people the right to receive all forms of education in their own language. Until then Udmurt was taught mainly in rural primary schools, and then only as a preparation for entry into the Russian-language educational system.

## Komis

Several Komi national organizations formed mostly since 1991 demanded autonomy and local control of the region's rich resources and local development projects. The coal reserves in the Komi homeland would give the region a valuable commodity to trade for basic needs. Beginning in 1993 Komi nationalism has focused on demands for the reunification of the Komi homeland in one autonomous state. Activists have repeatedly denounced the flag of the Russian Federation as a symbol of colonialism, as offensive as the red banner of communism. Militants routinely tear down Russian flags and replace them with the Komi tri-color in what has become known as a war of the flags. The Komi flag has come to represent the aspirations and demands for unification, including control of their natural resources that could sustain the Komi nation through the hard economic times.

As among other small ethnic groups, the language issue became important after 1991. The Komi Republic was the first in the Russian Federation to officially adopt a Finnic language as an official language. Emigration of many ethnic Slavs from the republic, particularly from the northern districts, has increased the Komi share of the republic's population and has allowed the Komis to assume greater authority in the republic's affairs. Environmental issues have been put forward in the late 1990s. Widespread pollution, health issues, massive oil spills, and fires caused by discarded pollutants have devastated large areas of the Komi homeland and have become emotional nationalist issues.

## Permyaks

The Permyaks, although for the most part rejecting Komi claims that they form merely a branch of the Komi nation, demanded greater cultural and political ties to the Komi in the wake of the Soviet collapse in 1991. Many Permyaks continue to seek unification of the two related ethnic groups, but others called for the upgrading of the Permyaks' autonomous province to the status of a member republic of the Russian Federation. Republican status would give the Permyaks greater control of the region's mineral resources and lucrative logging operations. Economic demands have grown since the Russian economic crisis in 1998.

## Nenets and the Small Groups of Northern Peoples

The Nenets, Dolgans, Enets, Nganasan, and other small groups of people living mostly within the Arctic Circle in northern European Russia and northwestern Siberia inhabit a huge, although very thinly populated, territory rich in natural resources and therefore of growing importance. Although they are of varied backgrounds, adaptation to their harsh environment and acculturation to reindeer herding made for the development of similar cultures. The Nenets, the largest and most widespread of the small northern ethnic groups, were formerly called Samoyeds.

The northern peoples, strong and enduring, fiercely resisted czarist and Soviet control, but that resistance cost many lives. Communist development plans for the northern regions devastated the fragile environment, which was treated as a classic colony to be exploited. The indigenous ethnic groups were carelessly pushed aside in the rush to develop the region's rich mineral deposits. Hundreds of thousands of Slavs moved to the region, drawn in by higher wages and other benefits offered by the Soviet government.

The liberalization of the late 1980s allowed the Nenets and the other groups to attempt to organize resistance to the devastation of their historic lands. With the Soviet collapse the northern ethnic groups refused to recognize the authority of the Russian-dominated regional governments and began to mobilize in the regions that still have non-Russian majorities. The northern peoples share not only their Arctic homeland but also a sense of outrage at the abuses they suffered and the belief that only by regaining their right to self-determination can they reestablish their identity and begin the rebuilding of their devastated Arctic homeland.

## Carpatho-Rusyns

The Soviet collapse and the emergence of Ukraine as an independent state ended the Soviet suppression and raised Carpatho-Rusyn demands for a return of their status as an autonomous province. In a referendum on Ukrainian independence in 1991, more than 78 percent of the Carpatho-Rusyns also approved demands for autonomy within the new Ukrainian state. Ignored by the Ukrainian government, local leaders formed a provisional autonomous government in 1993. Renewed ties to the Carpatho-Rusyns in Slovakia and Poland since the collapse of communism in Europe has allowed joint programs and close cooperation in cultural, scholarly, and economic planning. The Carpatho-Rusyns of Ukraine, the most numerous of the divided nation, are not recognized as a distinct national group, and therefore the Carpatho-Rusyn language is not recognized as a distinct language, but is considered a dialect of Ukrainian.

## Magyars

The Magyar, or Hungarian, population is concentrated in the Transcarpathian region of Ukraine, a territory that formed part of the Hungarian kingdom prior to 1918. In 1919 the region became part of Czechoslovakia and after World War II was transferred to Soviet Ukraine. Because the Hungarians had fought World War II as German allies, the Magyars of the Transcarpathian territory suffered severe suppression. Their language was outlawed and assimilation to Ukrainian culture was official policy. Only in 1952 was the Hungarian language allowed in public schools, although restrictions remained on the Magyars' Roman Catholic and Protestant churches. Most restrictions were finally lifted in the late 1980s. The end of communism in Hungary and the Soviet Union ended decades of Soviet fraternal friendship and normalized relations between newly independent Ukraine and Hungary. The Hungarian government has demanded fair treatment for Ukraine's Magyar minority, including language and cultural rights.

## Gagauz

The Republic of Moldova, proclaimed independent following the abortive coup in mid-1991, was already faced with the attempted secession of the Gagauz in the southern part of the republic. The new Moldovan authorities attempted to end the secession and to bring the Gagauz under the authority of the new republican government, but by early 1992 Moldovan authority in Gagauzia had virtually ceased to exist. In September 1991 negotiations were begun between the two sides, eventually paving the way for a normalization of relations between the Moldovan government and the Gagauz nationalists. In 1994 the government adopted a constitution that provided for special legal status and broad autonomous powers for the Gagauz, the first time a territorial autonomy had been established for a national minority in the post-Soviet era. In March 1995 the voters of thirty out of thirty-six districts with Gagauz populations voted for inclusion in the autonomous Gagauz Republic, finally ending the five-year separatist crisis. Some of the

Gagauz demanded reunification of the historic Gagauzia, including the eastern districts transferred to Ukraine in 1945.

The Turkic-speaking Gagauz have established close ties to Turkey and to the Turkic peoples of the Caucasus and Central Asia. The Turks have provided economic assistance and even provided a satellite link so the Gagauz can receive Turkish television while encouraging the Gagauz to maintain good relations with the Moldovan government. The fear that Moldova would merge with neighboring Romania fueled the growth of Gagauz nationalism in the early 1990s; however, the Gagauz were reassured by the vote by 95 percent of the electorate that favored continued Moldovan independence in 1997. In 1999 the government reorganized the national territory into nine provinces and two autonomous republics, Gagauzia and Dniestria. Since 1999 nationalist sentiment among the Gagauz has waned, even though such institutions as the European Union (EU) have criticized the Gagauz agreement as providing too much autonomy for a European ethnic group.

## Jews

According to the last Soviet census, in 1989, the Jews were the most dispersed national group in the Soviet Union, although most were concentrated in Europe, in the three Slav republics. The Jewish population, decimated by the Holocaust, declined by another 900,000 between 1959 and 1989 through a very low birthrate, intermarriage, emigration, and concealment of their Jewish identity. Before the collapse of the Soviet Union, many Jews in the United States and Israel believed that once unlimited emigration was permitted, all Jews, except the old, infirm, and committed Communists, would leave, effectively ending the Jewish nationality question in the former Soviet Union. In the early twenty-first century, despite mass emigration from the region, the Russian Federation and Ukraine still have two of the largest Jewish populations in the world.

The relaxation of Soviet strictures on religion since 1991 has allowed the Jews to recuperate much of their religious tradition, but after seventy-four years of official and forced atheism the Jewish religion has been nearly eliminated and the Jews in the countries of the former Soviet Union exist as national minorities rather than as religious minorities. Despite guarantees of the rights and liberties of all national groups, discrimination and acts against the Jews have increased markedly since 1991. Jews continue to face quotas and other social obstacles. A plan to form a Jewish republic as a member state of the reformed Russian Federation was dropped following official opposition. Many Jews still believe that an official homeland in Russian territory would give the Jews the opportunity to recreate a secular Jewish nationality; however, emigration and the large number of assimilated Jews continue to undermine the republican movement.

### Roms

Rom leaders believe that the anti-Communist revolution in Eastern Europe and the Soviet Union in 1989–1991 may have been the Roms' last opportunity to join the world community. In October 1991, after the implosion of the Soviet Union, a conference of Rom leaders put forward a proposal for the recognition of Europe's Roms as a transnational European community, a nation without a state. The Rom proposal would give them the same cultural, political, and economic rights across Europe and would guarantee them the same rights as the other non-Russian ethnic groups of the Russian Federation.

The stereotype of the Roms in Russia has not significantly changed over the centuries. They are still discriminated against in housing, employment, and services and are generally seen as lazy, dirty, stupid, and prone to criminal activity. That Russia's Roms are active in the black market, drugs, and prostitution and have a high crime rate tends to perpetuate this stereotype. The poor economic status of the Roms, which can be tied to these prejudices, is largely responsible for the high Rom crime rate. The Rom populations have been subjected to renewed persecution since the early 1990s, often being blamed for local problems or attacked as scapegoats.

### Germans

The leaders of the new Russian Federation, wary of yet another minority nationalism, were badly in need of Germany's political and financial assistance. In a series of meetings with German officials they finally agreed to the idea of a German national homeland in Russia. The proposal has never been implemented, and more militant groups have begun to form among the scattered German population. Emigration to Germany is one option considered by about 100,000 Germans from Russia and Kazakhstan and other areas of the former Soviet Union each year. However, some of the Germans, mostly farmers speaking antiquated dialects and unaccustomed to modern German culture, have returned to Russia. Economic problems, high unemployment, and the complications of German reunification reduced immigration from Russia in the late 1990s. Germany's intake of the former Soviet Germans, separated from German culture for centuries, was increasingly questioned by German politicians in the late 1990s. In 1999 there were demonstrations in Germany against the economic outlay necessary to retrain the German migrants, often including lessons in the modern German language. Opinion polls showed that around 70 percent of the German electorate wanted controls placed on Russian German immigration and changes in Germany's generous nationality laws, which considered blood over birthplace as the basis for citizenship.

In 1996 representatives of the major cultural and national organizations of the Russian Germans adopted a resolution on national-cultural autonomy, the first of its kind on the territory of the Russian Federation. The German government, increasingly beset by economic problems after 1999, offered to supply financial aid, coal, flour, medicines, and training for the former Soviet Germans who would elect to stay where they were. But for many of the Germans, the prospect of unemployment in a rich, democratic country is still preferable to staying in the poverty and uncertainty of the countries of the former Soviet Union.

## Greeks

The history of the Black Sea Greeks was another of hidden persecution by Soviets and deportation, which came to light only after the collapse of the Soviet Union. Although their existence was denied for decades, the Black Sea or Pontian Greeks, the descendants of early Greek settlements in the region, have emerged from the darkness of Soviet oppression to regain their long history as one of the most important ethnic groups deported from their homelands.

The Greeks were known to have established trade relations with the ancient Scythians. In time a number of Greek city-states were founded around the Black Sea. Later Greek empires, that of Alexander the Great, Pontus on the Black Sea, and the Byzantines, added new Greek communities to the territories around the Black Sea, particularly in the Caucasus and the Crimean Peninsula. Other Greeks migrated to Russia to escape the Muslim rule of the Ottoman Turks between the fifteenth and nineteenth centuries. At the time of the Russian Revolution, in 1917, there were more than half a million ethnic Greeks, often known as Pontian Greeks, in the Russian Empire.

The Axis invasion of the Soviet Union quickly overran territories with sizable Greek populations. Although there is no evidence that the Greeks collaborated, more than 200,000 were deported on Stalin's orders in 1944–1945. Exiled to Central Asia and Siberia, the Greeks were later joined by Greek Communists fleeing their defeat in the Greek Civil War in 1949. The program of de-Stalinization under Nikita Khrushchev in 1956 allowed Greeks to return to their original homes on the Black Sea, although many preferred to leave the Soviet Union for Greece. Others settled in Moscow or other areas of the Russian Federation and Ukraine.

## Bulgarians

The Bulgarians, living mostly in Russia, Ukraine, and Moldova, are the descendants of migrants who settled in Russia after fleeing Ottoman Turkish rule in their Balkan homeland between the fourteenth and nineteenth centuries. They shared the Orthodox faith and a Slavic language, making Russia the natural choice for Bulgarians fleeing wars and oppression, particularly in the eighteenth and nineteenth centuries. By the early twentieth century, there were sizable Bulgarian communities in Moldova, southern and western Ukraine, and in areas of European Russia.

During the years of the Cold War, the Communist Bulgarian government was the most subservient and loyal of all the satellite states of the Warsaw Pact. As a reward, the Bulgarian Communists were allowed to maintain close cultural ties to the Bulgarian communities in the Soviet Union, an unusual leniency on the part of the Soviet authorities. Publications, cultural exchanges, and education in the Bulgarian language were allowed with lesser or greater degrees, fortifying the Soviet Bulgarians against assimilation into the closely related Russian culture. In the early twenty-first century democratic Bulgaria has established good relations with the ex-Soviet republics allowing access to the Bulgarian minorities.

## Altai

The end of the Soviet Union in 1991 stimulated demands by the Altai for the upgrading of their homeland to that of a full member state in the reformed Russian Federation. The Altai territory was granted republic status in the constitution of 1992, but nationalist demands for greater self-rule have been ignored for the most part. Although a free-trade zone was created in the Altai Republic in 1995, the Altai themselves have received little economic benefits.

The Altai intelligentsia has constantly been accused by the Russian authorities of nationalism and anti-Russian sentiment. In the late 1990s, officials in the Russian government reported that corruption in the Altai Republic, which is entirely dependent on federal subsidies, reached astronomically high levels even by the dismal standards of the Russian Federation. The same report also warned of growing support for secession among the Altai. The combination of separatism and corruption, they warned, could create another Chechnya.

Russian archeologists, working in the region in 1993, discovered the mummified remains of a tattooed woman in the region where the Russian, Chinese, Mongol, and Kazakh borders come together in the Altai Mountains. The discovery confirms the long-held Altai tradition of an advanced civilization in the region at the time of Alexander the Great. Altai officials accused the Russians of plundering their heritage when the mummy and other finds were taken to Moscow over Altai protests. Local officials demanded that the Russians stop digging in the hundreds of burial mounds that dot the Altai landscape. The disposition of the mummy and other finds removed from the small republic has become a nationalist issue, with leaders demanding that the mummy and other treasures be returned to the Altai nation.

## Khakass

The liberalization of the late 1980s prompted Khakass demands for the reunification of their historic homeland, artificially divided by Stalin, and began to reverse decades of forced assimilation. Younger militants demanded measures to ensure that the ethnic Khakass occupy the important political posts in the region. Social apathy, drug abuse, alcoholism, and afflictions like tuberculosis and venereal diseases marked Khakass society at the end of the twentieth century. Activists, convinced that only the complete reform of Khakass society would save the small nation from extinction, led the nationalist mobilization that they believe is the first step to national revival. A special feature of the Khakass revival in the 1990s was a deliberate return to their spiritual origins. Shamanism, closely tied to traditional culture, was officially accepted in late 2000 as a parallel spiritual asset alongside Christianity.

## Buryats

The Soviet collapse in 1991 allowed the Buryats to begin the reconstruction of their culture, particularly the Buddhist religion. Intellectuals leading the reenculturation, in 1991, denounced the Soviet crimes against the Buryat nation, particularly the arbitrary divisions dividing the nation into three parts in 1937. Unilaterally declared a member state of the Russian Federation in 1992, Buryatia, after decades of colonization, now has a Russian majority. A new constitution was adopted in 1994, and a bilateral treaty was signed with the Soviet government in 1995. However, in spite of the trappings of autonomy, the republic remains dominated by the Russian majority. In 1998 an ethnic Buryat was elected mayor of Ulan-Ude, the Buryat capital, becoming the highest-ranking Buryat in the republic.

The resurgence of the Buddhist religion, closely intertwined with the Buryat culture, forms an important part of the peaceful movement to reclaim their heritage. The reopened monasteries and temples are now centers of Buryat culture and national sentiment. The Dalai Lama, recognized as the spiritual leader of the Buryats, postponed a planned visit to the region in 1998 because of continuing political instability.

The territorial issue remains the focus of the peaceful nationalist movement. National sentiment favors the reunification of the three Buryat territories in Russia in one political unit with redrawn borders to reflect the historic ethnic geography of the Buryat homeland. In early 2001 activists again demanded the unification of Buryatia. The unification of the Buryat territory was overshadowed in 2003 when a report was issued on the dramatic growth of crime, particularly robbery, which was blamed on the very high unemployment rate among the Buryats. Militants suggested that perhaps secession, which has been ruled out by regional leaders, should be explored because a Buddhist state might well provide greater security and prosperity in an area where there is little of either.

## Tuvans

Tuvan nationalism, dormant under Soviet controls, reemerged in the late 1980s with demands for language and cultural rights and for help in restoring destroyed Buddhist monasteries and temples. In June 1990, large demonstrations erupted in the Tuvan capital with demands for the dismissal of the Russian-dominated republican government. Others denounced the illegal annexation of the free Tuvan state in 1944. Demonstrators clashed with Soviet police who were sent to regain control. The clashes left hundreds dead and injured. More than 3,000 non-Tuvans fled the escalating violence in the republic.

The nationalist resurgence that began in 1991 with the collapse of the Soviet Union raised immediate demands for self-determination. Small militant groups called for the restoration of the former independent republic. In 1992 the Free Tuva Party, the largest of the several nationalist organizations in the republic, agreed to suspend its campaign for secession in exchange for official recognition of Tuvan autonomy within the Russian Federation. However, in 1993, Tuva's parliament amended the republican constitution to include a provision for peaceful secession from Russia. The Tuvans have put particular emphasis on establishing ties to other non-Russian ethnic groups and to peoples outside the Russian Federation. They recall that their small nation-state was annexed by its huge neighbor twice in just thirty years—in 1914 and 1944—annexations made possible by the political and physical isolation of the Tuvan homeland.

### Karakalpaks

The massive environmental damage inflicted on the Karakalpak homeland around the Aral Sea in Uzbekistan by Soviet cotton production became the focus of activism in the region in the late 1980s. Revelations of the extent of the health problems caused by the uncontrolled use of chemical fertilizers both shocked and mobilized the Karakalpaks. Activists condemned the bureaucrats of the Uzbek government and of the Uzbek-dominated government of the Karakalpak autonomous republic for the environmental disaster. More militant nationalists demanded the creation of a separate autonomous Karakalpak republic separate from Uzbekistan in the Soviet Union. Pressed by the activists, the government of the autonomous republic declared Karakalpakstan a sovereign state in 1990.

The independence of Uzbekistan in 1991 was accomplished under the authority of local ex-Communists turned Uzbek nationalists. One of the first undertakings of the new government was to crush the growing Karakalpak national movement in the west of the country. In late 1991 serious ethnic clashes erupted in the Aral Sea region. Rival factions within the national movement formed as Uzbek pressure increased. Some favored a federal relationship with the Uzbek state; others demanded a declaration of independence before opening negotiations with the Uzbeks. The activists, driven underground by police action, continued to demand redress for the health problems caused by Soviet indifference. An estimated 66 percent of all Karakalpaks have serious health conditions as a result of the massive pollution. The Karakalpaks, despite their small numbers, have evolved a sense of identity as strong as those of the other Central Asian ethnic groups and view the physical destruction of their homeland as the result of their lack of control over their own destiny.

## Uighurs

The Uighurs, part of the larger Uighur population of Xinjiang in adjacent parts of China, live for the most part in Uzbekistan and eastern Kazakhstan. Many of the Uighurs are the descendants of refugees from the Manchu conquest of their homeland in the mid-eighteenth century. Chinese rule in Xinjiang has often been extremely oppressive, driving other Uighurs to seek shelter in Russian territory in Central Asia, particularly in the wake of unsuccessful uprisings against Chinese rule in the nineteenth century. Still more Uighurs fled to Soviet territory between the 1920s and 1950s to escape Chinese reprisals of Muslim uprisings and the turmoil of the Chinese civil war in the 1940s.

The Uighurs that settled in the Fergana Valley in Uzbekistan have been assimilating into the closely related Uzbek culture. Those in the north, in the Kazakh republic, have retained their ancient language and culture. The Uighurs were originally encouraged to develop their national culture under Soviet rule in the 1920s, but assimilation into the Central Asian cultures was later stressed. The relative isolation of the Uighurs in Kazakhstan has allowed them to retain their culture. Since the independence of Kazakhstan in 1991 they have reestablished ties to other Uighur groups in Central Asia and in the Xinjiang region of China. Uighur nationalist organizations with ties to nationalists among the Uighurs in China have been curtailed by the Central Asian governments anxious not to antagonize their huge eastern neighbor.

## Koreans

The 180,000 Soviet Koreans ordered by Stalin to be deported from the Far East regions in the late 1930s were resettled in Central Asia. Other Koreans, transported by the Japanese to northern Sakhalin Island before World War II, found themselves under Soviet rule at the end of the war. The Koreans of the former Soviet Union, both the populations in Kazakhstan and Uzbekistan in Central Asia and in the Far East, have assimilated into surrounding cultures more than most ethnic groups. Having no national area of their own, they have no cultural autonomy or national leaders to perpetuate their ancient culture. Assimilation, during the Soviet era, was the only option. The Koreans are also adamant that their children be educated, which meant Russian-language education. Although they still suffer Russian prejudices against Orientals, many Koreans have urbanized and have moved into the professions.

## Sakhas

The Sakhas, forming just a third of the population of their ancestral homeland according to the Soviet census of 1989, began to mobilize against the increasing numbers of Slav workers who came to the region's important mines for a few years, then left having accumulated considerable wealth by Sakha standards. The first Sakha demand, during the reforms of the late 1980s, was to de-Russify their family names, which opened a torrent of other grievances. Many supported demands that control of the lucrative mines be taken from the ministries in Moscow and turned over to officials of the local autonomous government. In 1990 the Sakha territory was declared a sovereign state.

In the wake of the Soviet disintegration, the Sakhas quickly mobilized to take control of their homeland, including abandoning the Russian name for themselves and their homeland, Yakut, and the adoption of their own designation, Sakha. Made a member state of the Russian Federation, Sakha became one of the few producing products, mainly gold, silver, diamonds, and other valuable minerals, that could be exported. Local Russian leaders denounced Sakha demands for cultural and economic autonomy as secessionist and needlessly provocative, but Sakha leaders claimed that they were only taking control of their own future.

The Soviet collapse began a strong outward migration with many workers returning to European Russia as government subsidies disappeared. The number of ethnic Russians fell from more than half of the population to less than 40 percent in 2002. The numbers of Ukrainians and Belarussians also fell dramatically. The Slavic outflow allowed the Sakhas to win control of the local government, which helped to dampen militant nationalism in the region. Although considerable separatist sentiment remains, particularly among the young, this has been tempered by the prospect that the Russian-dominated mining region would stay with Russia should Sakha secede. Although enormous environmental damage has been done to their homeland by the uncoordinated extraction of raw materials, the loss of the richest part of their homeland would be an even greater disaster.

## Khants and Mansis

The Khants and Mansis are two small, closely related ethnic groups living in western Siberia just east of the Ural Mountains. Distantly related to the Hungarians of Central Europe, the Khanty-Mansis developed a distinct social system before the Russian colonization, with their modern culture being a mixture of ancient traditions and Russian customs. In late 1991, the leaders of the two ethnic groups, now forming a very small minority in their ancestral lands, proclaimed sovereignty. Local Russian authorities refused to recognize the declaration, primarily because it would give the Khants and Mansis control of the region's abundant natural resources. The population of the region, about 150,000 in 1970, had climbed to more than 1.5 million in 2000, although the Khants and Mansis together had a total population of only about 50,000.

As in other resource-rich areas of Siberia, the region is beset by oil spills, chemical pollutants, and massive ecological damage. Educated Khants and Mansis have joined cultural and ecological groups that continue to demand the cleanup of the region and for plans to be drawn up for more controlled development. In 1997 Khant leaders in the last contiguous and virtually undeveloped tract of middle Siberian taiga refused to consent to a regional government proposal to auction off lands for oil development. In 1998, realizing that Russian control of their vast former homeland was irreversible, some Khant and Mansi leaders proposed the creation of a small national homeland in the undeveloped region, which would give the two small ethnic groups some control over their lives and would allow them to sustain their threatened cultures. One of the major points of the proposal, which had not been officially addressed in 2003, would be a ban on the development of the new autonomous region's oil and natural gas deposits.

The other small groups of Siberian peoples, particularly the Chukots and Koryaks in the northeast, quickly mobilized as the Soviet Union withered away. Ties to their cousins in North America were gradually established. Organizations based on those of the native peoples of Canada and the United States were formed to represent these small national groups in their dealings with the post–Soviet Russian government. The Association of Peoples of the North absorbed many of the smaller cultural and national organizations into a multinational group representing the smaller national groups in Siberia and the Far East.

The end of the Soviet command economy doomed many of the subsidized industries established in the area during the Soviet era that once drew in workers from Europe with high wages and other benefits. As the uneconomic industries collapsed, thousands of ethnic Russians left to return to Europe, and the native Siberian peoples, often forced to work in the industries by Soviet quotas, began to return to their pre-Soviet lifestyles, herding reindeer on the tundra, fishing, or other traditional pursuits. For the Siberian peoples, like their cousins in North America, the preservation of their traditional occupations and crafts is not a question of culture; it is now a matter of survival.

The collapse of the Soviet system quickly spread from the Russian heartland in Europe to every corner of the vast multiethnic empire. The independence of the former union republics stimulated nationalist demands among the other large national groups of the new post–Soviet Russian Federation. The centrifugal forces let loose with the collapse of the Soviet state quickly resonated throughout the territories of the newly independent states, particularly in the Russian Federation. Many of the national homelands were unilaterally declared full republics of the federation. For a time in the early and mid-1990s, many experts and political observers predicted that the Russian Federation, like the Soviet Union, would be pulled apart by the growing number and popularity of ethnic nationalist movements.

## Timeline

| | |
|---|---|
| June 1991 | A Crimean Tatar congress declares the historic right of the Crimean Tatars to a homeland in the Crimean Peninsula. |
| September 1991 | Armenia and Tajikistan declare independence. The Slav leaders of Trans-Dniestria declare the independence of the region from Moldova. |
| November 1991 | The Chechen government declares the republic independent of the Russian Federation, but recognition is refused. The Ingush reject independence, and their part of the joint Chechen-Ingush republic becomes a separate Russian republic. |
| January 1992 | President Gamsakhurdia is ousted from Georgia. The Ingush homeland, Ingushetia, is officially separated from Chechnya to become a separate Russian republic. |
| March 1992 | Fighting breaks out between Moldovan forces and Slavic separatists along the Dnieper River. Eighteen of the twenty autonomous republics within Russia sign a new federation treaty. Two republics—Tatarstan and |

|            | Chechnya—refuse to sign. Eduard Shevardnadze is chosen as the head of the new national council in Georgia. A referendum on independence in Tatarstan results in more than 60 percent voting in favor. |
| May 1992   | A power-sharing agreement, designed to end the growing violence in Tajikistan, is implemented. A nationalist uprising, led by the Azeri Popular Front, overthrows the president of Azerbaijan. The Russian leaders of the majority population of the Crimean Peninsula declare the independence of Crimea. |
| June 1992  | The Trans-Dniestrian Slavs accept autonomy within the Moldovan state. |
| 1993       | The Abkhaz legislature votes to reinstate Abkhazia's 1925 constitution, effectively declaring the territory independent of Georgia. |
| 1994       | The nationalist Abkhaz government formally declares independence on 26 November. Russian forces invade breakaway Chechnya. The government of Tatarstan finally signs the federation treaty. |
| 1996       | A cease-fire between the Russian and Chechen governments ends the fighting in the region but postpones the question of Chechen independence. |
| 1997       | The government of Tatarstan signs a friendship treaty with breakaway Chechnya. Russia and Ukraine agree to a settlement ending the conflict over the Black Sea Fleet and the naval base at Sevastopol in Crimea. |
| 1999       | A series of bomb attacks in Moscow and other cities is blamed on Chechen militants. Russian troops again invade Chechnya. |
| 2001       | The Russian military invasion of Chechnya gradually turns into a military standoff, even though the rebels retain territory only in the mountainous south. |
| 2002       | The Baltic republics of Estonia, Latvia, and Lithuania are invited to join the European Union (EU). Chechen militants take control of a theater in Moscow and threaten to kill hundreds of hostages before they are overcome by special troops. |
| 2003       | Chechen rebels, perhaps influenced by Muslims in other conflict areas, launch a series of suicide bombs against the Russian military and civilian population in Chechnya. |

## Significant People, Places, and Events

**ABASHIDZE, ASLAN** A former Soviet functionary who remained as the head of the Ajar Autonomous Republic within the new Georgian Republic in 1991.

**ABKHAZIA** An autonomous republic within Georgia declared independent in 1992. As of 2003 Abkhazia, its borders patrolled by Russian peace-keepers, remains a de-facto independent state.

**AVARS** The largest of the Dagestani ethnic groups of the Dagestan Republic in Russia's North Caucasus region. They are concentrated in west-central Dagestan but also extend across the borders into southeastern Chechnya and into northern Azerbaijan.

**BASHKORTOSTAN** The homeland of the Bashkorts in the eastern Volga region. Part of historic Bashkortostan forms one of the twenty-one member states of the Russian Federation. The republic is one of the major petroleum-producing regions of the Russian Federation.

**CHUKOTS** The Chukots are a Paleo-Asiatic people ethnically and historically related to the Native American peoples of North America. Tribal groups, important in the early history of the Chukots, remain as important traditional and cultural divisions.

**CIRCASSIANS** The inhabitants of the ancient region of Circassia in the North Caucasus region of Russia. Geographically and politically separated during the Soviet era, the Circassians are divided into three ethnic groups, the Adyge in the west, the Cherkess in the center, and the Kabards in the east.

**DUDAYEV, DZHOKAR** A former Soviet general who headed a new nationalist government that declared Chechnya independent of the Russian Federation in 1992.

**EVENKS** A Tungus people, one of the small groups of indigenous peoples that are the remnants of a larger Tungus population that once inhabited much of north and northeastern Asia. The Evenks are the most numerous of the Paleo-Siberian peoples of the Russian Federation.

**KALMYKS** A Buddhist, Mongol ethnic group living in the northern North Caucasus on the Caspian Sea. They are related to the Altai tribes of central Siberia, where they originated before migrating west in the seventeenth century.

**KARACHAIS** A small Turkic ethnic group in the central part of the North Caucasus in southern European Russia. Historically, culturally, and linguistically they are closely related to the Balkars living farther west in the Caucasus foothills.

**KHAKASS** The Khakass are of mixed Turkic and Mongol ancestry, physically resembling the Mongols but linguistically and culturally more closely related to the Turkic peoples of Central Asia and Siberia. Loyalty to local clan and tribal groups remains an important part of Khakass culture.

**KHANTY AND MANSI** The closely related Khanty and Mansi peoples of western Siberia speak languages belonging to the Ugrian branch of the Finno-Ugrian languages. Their closest linguistic ties are to the Magyars (Hungarians) of Central Europe. Traditionally the women, whose presence was thought to defile religious idols and tempt tribal members, were forced to wear veils.

**KORYAKS** The Koryaks are a Paleo-Asiatic or Hyperborean nation related to the Native American peoples of North America. Traditionally divided into twelve clans or tribes they have revived since the collapse of the Soviet Union, partially through returning to their traditional lives as fishermen and reindeer herders.

**KURDS** The Kurds of the Caucasus region form part of the larger Kurdish population that is spread across a large region including parts of Turkey, Syria, Iraq, Iran, and Armenia. Many of the Kurds of the Caucasus are Yezidis, the followers of a religious sect considered heretical by Muslims.

**LEZGINS** A Dagestani nation living southwest of the Caspian Sea in Russia's Dagestan Republic and in adjacent areas of Azerbaijan. One of the most nationalistic of the Caucasian groups, the Lezgins support the reunification of their divided nation, either within the Russian Federation or in an independent state separate from both Russia and Azerbaijan.

**MAGYARS** The Hungarian-speaking population concentrated in the Transcarpathian province of Ukraine. The region, once part of the Kingdom of Hungary in the Austro-Hungarian Empire, was transferred to newly formed Czechoslovakia in 1919, but was taken by the Soviet Union in 1945.

**NORTH OSSETIA** Also known as Alania. One of the member republics of the Russian Federation. The homeland of the mostly Christian Ossetians includes North Ossetia and South Ossetia in neighboring Georgia.

**OSSETIANS** Also known as Alans, Ir, or Digor. Their homeland is in the central Caucasus Mountains extending from southern European Russia into Georgia. The majority of the Ossetians, who are related linguistically to the Iranians, are Orthodox, allowing them to maintain a long and beneficial relationship with the dominant Russians.

**SHAIMIEV, MINTIMER** The president of the republic of Tatarstan. Following a referendum on sovereignty in 1992, which resulted in more than 60 percent of the republic's population voting in favor, he rejected Russian demands that he sign a new federation treaty.

**South Ossetia** A former autonomous region in northern Georgia. Fighting broke out in the region in September 1991. On 11 December 1991 the Georgian government rescinded South Ossetia's autonomy. The following day nationalist leaders declared the independence of the South Ossetian Autonomous Republic.

**Talysh** A Caspian ethnic group straddling the border region between Azerbaijan and Iran. They are of mixed Caucasian and Turkic background, but speak a language that belongs to the Iranian language group.

**Tatarstan** The official homeland of the Tatars, the largest ethnic minority in the Russian Federation. The inhabitants of the republic, evenly split between ethnic Tatars and Russians, approved a referendum on sovereignty in 1992. However, in 1994, the republic's leaders agreed to remain within the Russian Federation as a freely associated state with the right of legal secession.


## Document

### Protest in Central Moscow Remembers Deportation of Soviet Germans

Pravda 28 August 2002

Descendents of repressed Soviet Germans have today held their traditional protest in the centre of Moscow. 61 years ago to the day, the Supreme Soviet of the USSR issued an order *On the relocation of Germans living in the Volga Region.* The document marked the beginning of political repression of Russia's Germans. Every year on August 28, victims of the repressions, who lived through a lengthy nightmare, and their relatives, loved ones and friends gather at the 'Stone of Mourning' on Lubyanka Square in Moscow, which was brought from the Solovki prison camp, in order to remember the victims of political persecution.

Participants in the protest expressed their regret that the Duma has still not passed a law on the rehabilitation of Russian Germans. Duma deputy Tamara Pletneva-Shtrak explained that the main problem for Russian Germans remains their rehabilitation. She declared that today 'for Russia, German Germans are her friends, but Russian Germans remain her enemy'. However, June 22, 1941 was just as tragic a date for Russian Germans as for all the other peoples of the Soviet Union. It is worth pointing out, said Pletneva-Shtrak, that in only the first two months of the war, 11 recipients of the honour "Hero of the Soviet Union" were of German origin.

*Source:* On-line Pravda (Accessed May 18, 2004).

## Bibliography

Beissinger, Mark R. *National Mobilization and the Collapse of the Soviet State.* Cambridge: Cambridge University Press, 2002.

Hughes, James, and G. Sasse, eds. *Ethnicity and Territory in the Former Soviet Union: Regions in Conflict.* London: Frank Cass, 2002.

Kolosov, Vladimir Alexsandrovich. *Ethno-Territorial Conflicts and Boundaries in the Former Soviet Union.* Durham, UK: University of Durham, 1992.

Raymond, Boris. *Historical Dictionary of Russia.* Lanham, MD: Scarecrow Press, 1998.

Starr, Frederick S. *The Legacy of History in Russia and the New States of Eurasia.* Armonk, NY: M. E. Sharpe, 1994.

Szporluk, Roman, ed. *National Identity and Ethnicity in Russia and the New States of Eurasia.* Armonk, NY: M. E. Sharpe, 1994.

Warhola, James W. *Politicized Ethnicity in the Russian Federation: Dilemmas of State Formation.* Lewiston, ME: Edmin Mellen Press, 1996.

Wolfson, Zeyev. *The Geography of Survival.* London: M. E. Sharpe, 1994.

# Present and Future

# CHAPTER TEN

# The Russians and the Loss of Empire, 1986–2004

THE RUSSIANS, HISTORICALLY THE DOMINANT ETHNIC GROUP in the multiethnic Russian and Soviet Empires, were alarmed by the profound changes taking place in the Soviet Union as the iron grip of the Communist Party weakened in the late 1980s and early 1990s. Nationalist demands in the union republics and even among the numerous non-Russian nations within Russia itself were often interpreted as calls for greater freedom from Russian domination. Dismay at what they perceived as the ungrateful attitude of the many peoples they had helped lead out of poverty and ignorance incited a backlash of Russian nationalism and the growth of a particular Russian national movement. For decades the Russians had been told that there were powerful economic and cultural reasons for the forced Russification of the non-Russian ethnic groups of the czarist and Soviet Empires. The majority of the Russians were convinced that, since the non-Russian groups were mostly backward and somewhat uncivilized, the imposition of the Russian culture and language would lead to a more advanced, modern society. Proponents of Russification argued that a single, dominant language would ensure greater efficiency in government, the economy, and the sciences and would eliminate the linguistic liability that hampered the efficiency of the Red Army and scientific research. They also believed that centralized political control of the Soviet state would work much better if Russian were the only language used in government affairs. These policies caused not only more resentment among the non-Russian ethnic groups but also a silent indignation that existed just below the surface of Russian culture itself. The feeling that the politics and society of the Soviet Union had somehow subsumed traditional Russian culture grew over decades of Soviet rule. Many Russians believed that Russia and the Soviet Union had fused into a single whole, while the other nationalities had been able to maintain their identities. Many Russians even developed a sense of envy toward the other union

republics because they retained the symbols of nationhood: republican par-
liaments, national histories, distinct Communist parties, cultural traditions,
and national languages. Russians often felt that their culture was completely
obscured by the Soviet shadow.

The upsurge of Russian nationalism in 1990 focused on the debate in the
Russian legislature over the question of state sovereignty. Delegates debated
the question, which was extremely controversial. Delegates from the autonomous republics within the Russian Federation objected to provisions
that would indicate that Russian sovereignty took precedence over their own.
The heated debate revealed the potential for ethnic fracturing within the
Russian Federation as well as within the Soviet Union.

The most conservative elements of Soviet society—the Communist Party,
the military, and the KGB—all opposed Gorbachev's reforms. The collapse
of Communist parties across Eastern Europe, the withdrawal of Russian
troops from the region, and growing demands by ethnic groups within the
Soviet Union itself dismayed and frightened the members of these three institutions. A political backlash against the rapid pace of reform culminated
in the abortive coup d'état against Mikhail Gorbachev in August 1991. The
coup failed for various reasons but mostly because the majority of the Soviet nationalities supported the reforms. When Boris Yeltsin, the democrat-
ically elected leader of the Russian Federation, openly opposed the coup, the
fate of the Soviet Union was sealed. The spasms affecting world communism
reached a climax in the wake of the abortive coup. One day after the coup
leaders proclaimed their takeover of the Soviet state, Yeltsin spoke to a large
crowd from the top of a tank. He denounced the coup and declared his support for Gorbachev and his reforms. On 24 August Gorbachev resigned as
the head of the Communist Party, which Yeltsin promptly outlawed in the
Russian Federation. On the same day, speaking on behalf of the now independent Russian Federation, Yeltsin recognized the independence of Estonia, opening the way for the Russian recognition of the other Baltic republics,
Latvia and Lithuania, and the subsequent breakup of the Soviet Empire. Following the disintegration of the Union of Soviet Socialist Republics, Yeltsin
was left as the elected leader of the Russian Federation, still one of the world's
largest and most populous states. The aborted coup not only splintered the
Soviet Union, it also marked the resurgence of the quiescent Russian nationalism in search of a new national identity. For centuries Russian national
sentiment had been associated with the Russian Empire and its successor, the
fallen Soviet Empire.

The Russian Federation, by far the largest of the successor states of the
Russian and Soviet Empires, laid claim to the territory that formed part of

the Soviet Russian Federation, including the numerous autonomous territories that were the legacy of early Soviet idealism. The reformed Russian
Federation also took over the Soviet Union's permanent seat on the United
Nations Security Council, as well as the bulk of its military and its foreign
assets and debts. In 1992 the Russian government persuaded eleven of the
fifteen former Soviet republics to form the Commonwealth of Independent
States (CIS), which a twelfth state, Georgia, joined in 1993. Russian nation-
alists often looked on the CIS as a means for safeguarding the numerous
Russian populations left behind as the former empire shrank back to its
Russian heartland.

Historically many Russians have blamed "foreigners" for their problems.
The humiliation of losing the Soviet Empire stimulated the growth of this
historic Russian xenophobia. Hard-line nationalists blame the Jews as the alleged agents of both the advent of communism and its demise in 1991. Not
only the Jews are targeted, but anyone not recognizably Slavic, particularly
the darker peoples of the Caucasus and the Roms. Called Blacks and other
derogatory names, the Armenians, Azeris, Georgians, Chechens, and other
Caucasian peoples, along with the scattered Rom population, bear the brunt
of Russian suspicion and blame. The humiliating attempt to quell the rebellion among the Chechens, mirrored to a lesser extent in many of the federation's provinces and autonomous territories, continues to feed the right-
wing xenophobia that has grown as a result of the painful demise of the
centuries-old Russian-Soviet Empire. Russians' xenophobic view of the non-
Russian peoples of the Russian Federation has often vilified the non-Russian ethnic groups as foreigners in their own ancestral lands. Historically the
Russians have been extremely ethnocentric, looking down on non-Russians
as inferior beings in need of Russian patronage to advance. Ethnic epithets
were popular throughout the Russian Empire and the Soviet Union. The
non-Russian nationalities greatly resented Russian arrogance and government policies that they viewed as barely veiled attempts to Russify their cultures. Russian nationalism, which emerged once again with the demise of the
Soviet Empire in 1991, increased as resentment of the Russophobia sweeping the country exploded.

The demise of communism also restored religion as one of the pillars of
Russian nationalism. For more than 1,000 years, the Russian Orthodox
Church, Russian culture, and Russian identity were inseparable; only during
the Soviet era were the three pillars divided. The liberalization initiated by
Mikhail Gorbachev began with religion. The Orthodox Church, firmly es-
tablished among the Slavic populations in Russia, Belarus, Ukraine, Moldova,
Latvia, Estonia, and Central Asia, was to be one of the cultural icons that

would help to hold the Soviet Union together when centrifugal forces began tearing at the edges of the empire.

The peoples of the autonomous territories greeted the gradual collapse of the Soviet Union as an opportunity to regain some control over their lives. The governments of the autonomous republics unilaterally upgraded their status to full republics, member states of the reformed and newly independent Russian Federation. Their new status, along with the greater powers granted other autonomous territories, was confirmed in a new federation treaty signed in 1992 by all of the member republics of the Russian Federation except Chechnya and Tatarstan. The continuing debate over the powers granted to the member republics was finally settled in favor of the Russian majority by granting the same autonomous powers to the ordinary provinces.

The continuing weakness of the Russian federal government and the strength of the republican and regional governments suggest that Russia's future shape may lie somewhere between the complete disintegration of its Soviet predecessor and a genuine federal structure. Attempts to reassert the power of the central government under Vladimir Putin, Boris Yeltsin's' successor, have met with only partial success because the former levers of power—the Communist Party, the KGB secret police, and the Red Army—are no longer available. New democratic tools are not yet in place or remain too weak, partly owing to the deep suspicion of the regional governments toward any attempt in Moscow to regain some of the enormous power it held during the seven decades of Soviet rule.

Russian nationalism is far more complicated than the nationalisms of the non-Russian ethnic groups. The historic Russian culture, like the Communist Party, became the target that unified other national aspirations. The other nationalisms revolved around the ideas of separation from the Russians, independence, reversal of assimilation, and cultural and linguistic revival. Although Russian nationalists were equally resentful of communism and of what Soviet rule had done to Russian identity, their own national movement was divided by intense political and cultural differences. By the time that the Soviet Union began its rapid decline in the late 1980s, Russian nationalism had become a widespread movement, although it was split between three dissimilar ideals—one looked to liberal democracy, another was based on the revival of Russian culture as Soviet culture lost support, and the third rested upon the Russian tradition of political authoritarianism.

The first and more moderate model is based on cultural revival, protection of the severely damaged environment, a market economy, and democratic politics. Initially, during the 1970s, these patriots focused on the restoration of historic monuments, including churches, as cultural and architectural treasures. Even the many nonreligious Russians supported the renovation and saving of churches as a historic part of Russian identity. A small environmental movement also emerged in the 1970s in response to the ecological disasters brought about by the Soviet economic policies. The drying up of the Aral Sea and the Chernobyl nuclear disaster in 1986 were only the most notorious examples of Soviet disregard of the environment. The two groups—the cultural revivalists and the environmentalists—gradually merged in the 1980s to form the moderate faction of Russian nationalism. Mikhail Gorbachev's reforms were exactly what these nationalists had been waiting and hoping for. Liberal Russian nationalists saw Gorbachev as the opportunity, perhaps the last, to bring Russia into the twentieth century and establish closer ties to the affluent and modern West.

Conservative elements, suspicious of the West, had an even longer history in Russian nationalism. Every Russian leader who has looked Westward, from Peter the Great to Mikhail Gorbachev, has had to deal with a fierce backlash from the conservatives. Like the liberals they vehemently opposed communism, but had one thing in common with Soviet ideals: a strong commitment to political authority. But unlike the Communists, they want authority to be based in Russia's ancient institutions, a village-based economy, the Russian Orthodox Church, and Russian freedom from the non-Russian populations they often blame for all of Russia's problems. Central to their view is the restoration of Russian Orthodoxy to its rightful place at the heart of national life. In the conservative view, for 1,000 years, the Russian church, culture, and identity have been inseparable.

In addition to liberal nationalists, committed to democratic reforms, environmental protection, and a market economy, and conservative nationalists, demanding the renaissance of the Russian Orthodox Church and the restoration of a stable, authoritarian government, there was yet another more radical, even reactionary Russian national movement. They hated the Communist Party, modernization, urbanization, industrialization, Western popular culture, and modern technology. This third group flatly rejected democratic niceties and supported the role of authoritarian government as the model for a revived Russia. They were also against large-scale economies and called for all land to be returned to the peasants and for the reconstruction of traditional Russian village life. Communism was blamed for the destruction of the environment and the mindless plunder of Mother Russia's natural resources. Alcoholism and unlimited abortions were blamed for the rapidly declining Russian population. Radical nationalist groups emerged throughout the Russian Federation in the 1980s and 1990s, often taking on another of Russian nationalism's historic trappings, anti-Semitism.

## The Russian Diaspora

The Soviet collapse led to the emergence of fifteen new states, all of which have sizable Russian minorities. The disintegration of the Soviet Union left millions of ethnic Russians in areas that became part of the new national states. The states that emerged from the disintegration of the Soviet Union, called the Near Abroad by the Russians, were still looked on as historically Russian territory. Many Russians had grown into the habit of feeling at home anywhere within the Soviet frontiers. The millions of ethnic Russians settled in non-Russian parts of the Soviet Union, where they were promised better pay, decent housing, and higher social and professional status, were often encouraged by the Soviet government as a means of strengthening the control and cohesion of the Soviet state. These settlers supported the spread of the Russian language as the lingua franca spoken by nearly all non-Russians in the Soviet Union. Suddenly these millions of Russians found themselves a dispersed minority, often unwanted, unwelcome, and despised as reminders of centuries of Russian oppression, and blamed for Soviet repression.

## Russians in Ukraine and Belarus

The largest Russian population outside the Russian Federation is in Ukraine. There they are concentrated in the eastern industrial provinces and in the Crimean Peninsula, which formed part of Russia until 1954. Even though many have adopted Ukrainian ethnicity since 1991, most remain adamant that their Russian identity must be recognized as one of the component nationalities of the Ukrainian state. The leaders of the Russian population in eastern Ukraine often use threats of separatism to win concessions from the Ukrainian government, which is dependent on the industries of the region to sustain the struggling Ukrainian state.

The Russian population of the Crimean Peninsula is the product of a later colonization than that of the eastern provinces of Ukraine. The indigenous population of the Crimean Peninsula, the Crimean Tatars, were accused of collaboration and deported in 1944. The Soviet authorities systematically obliterated all historical, linguistic, and cultural traces of the Crimean Tatars. Ethnic Russians, mostly war refugees from other areas, were

*Tatar man, c. 1990–1993 (Shepard Sherbell/Corbis Saba)*

ian be made an official language in Moldova along with Romanian but were ignored. Strikes and demonstrations grew increasingly violent. A nationalist Moldovan flag, adopted in April 1990, was rejected by the Slav-majority districts, which continued to use the Soviet-era flag.

Fighting broke out along the Dniester in September 1990, shortly after the regional Slav parliament of the Trans-Dniestria region, east of the Dniester River, proclaimed the region independent of the Moldovan state. In November, the Moldovan government sent troops to clear roadblocks set up by the Dniestrian separatists. In the resulting violence six people were killed and another thirty were wounded, greatly escalating tensions. The Dniestrians, with access to Soviet arms stored in the region, began to form self-defense units.

The collapse of the Soviet Union in August 1991 left local Russian military units to assume a political role in the escalating conflict free of Moscow's control. The 6,000 troops of the 14th Army in the Trans-Dniestria territory took on the role of self-appointed peacekeepers, a role that was vehemently rejected by both the Moldovans and the Dniestrian Slavs. In spite of spiraling tensions in the region, the new Russian government refused to withdraw the troops of the 14th Army. The Dniestrian Slavs categorically rejected Moldovan independence and the imposition of the Romanian-Moldovan language and the Latin alphabet. Led by an unreformed Communist, Igor Smirnov, the Dniestrian Slavs demanded that Russian be reinstated as an official language in Moldova and that the east bank of the Dniester become an autonomous territory, either as part of Moldova or Russia, even though it was separated from Russian territory by hundreds of miles of Ukrainian territory.

Demands for Dniestrian separation from the new Moldovan state grew rapidly in late 1991 and early 1992. Even non-Communist Slavs in the east bank region supported the neo-Communist regional government in opposition to the Moldovans. The name of the self-proclaimed republic was changed from Dniester Moldovan Republic to simply the Dniester Republic or Dniestria. A referendum held in December 1991 showed that around 98 percent of those participating supported separation from Moldova. Armed conflict broke out, pitting the separatists, aided by the troops of the Russian 14th Army, against the new army of the Moldovan republic. As the Moldovan government lost control to the better-armed Slavs, the fighting again intensified, leaving more than 700 dead and more than 50,000 refugees driven from their homes.

Representatives of Moldova, Romania, Ukraine, and Russia met in July 1992 in an effort to end the bloody war. Although a final settlement was not can capitals and the industrial cities. They are vital to the young states' economies, as they hold a disproportionate number of the scientific, technical, engineering, and administrative positions, jobs that cannot easily be filled by the Central Asian ethnic groups. Although many Russians, estimated at up to 1 million, have returned to European Russia or Siberia between 1991 and 2001, they still form large and influential minorities across Central Asia.

## Russians in the Caucasus

Like the Russian population of Central Asia, the Russians in the Transcaucasian republics of Armenia, Georgia, and Azerbaijan are primarily urban dwellers. The Russian population, never as large as in the North Caucasus, is now rapidly dwindling, owing to a very low birthrate and emigration. Ethnic conflicts, language requirements, economic hardships, and discrimination are driving many Russians to return to Russia or to immigrate, mostly to North America. The majority of the Russians in the Transcaucasus do not speak the local national languages, which has become a serious problem, excluding them from citizenship or from holding local office.

The majority of the Russians living in the Caucasus region are officially Orthodox by religion, but tend to be less religious than their kin in central Russia. Many of the Russians, descendants of nineteenth- and early twentieth-century settlers, were long isolated from Russian culture and adopted traits and customs from the neighboring peoples. Dissident religious communities such as Molokans, Dukhobors, and Starovers have retained their firm religious beliefs, along with traditions and antiquated dialects that have disappeared elsewhere in Russia.

The only area with a growing Russian population is eastern Azerbaijan, where the opening of oil fields has brought not only Westerners but also Russians. In 1997, in a ceremony attended by both American and Russian government officials, the Azeris officially began oil production in the Caspian Sea. The offshore oil reserves, thought to rival those of the Middle East, have become the focus of Western and Russian economic interests.

## Cossacks

The renewal of traditional Russian nationalism also stimulated the rebirth of distinct groups that, according to Soviet history, had already disappeared. The most notable of these groups are the Cossacks living in territories

*Cossack men and women, c. 1978–1997 (Gregor Schmid/Corbis)*

across the Russian Federation and in Ukraine and Central Asia. The largest and most organized are the Don, Kuban, and Terek Cossacks of the North Caucasus region and the Ural Cossacks, whose homeland lies in territory now forming part of the new Kazakhstan republic.

When Gorbachev called for the restructuring of the Soviet economy, increased entrepreneurial activity, and private initiative, the descendants of the disbanded Cossacks argued that they were uniquely suited to answer Gorbachev's call. Cossack activists, relying on the long tradition of Cossack loyalty, began to reconstruct the Cossack communities virtually destroyed under Soviet rule. An important part of the Cossack revival revolved around the protection of Russian identity. During the nationalist explosion in the late 1980s and 1990s, Cossack groups appeared in places where ethnic conflicts involved ethnic Russians in Moldova, Azerbaijan, Armenia, Siberia, and the Baltic States. The Cossack leaders claimed that the Russians needed a Cossack revival in order to revitalize the Russian military tradition and to resurrect the prosperous private farms once held by Cossacks.

Cossacks nationalists, committed to protecting Russians against outrages by non-Russians, moved to revive military training. The reinstatement of Russian Orthodoxy as the Cossack religion restored yet another traditional part of their heritage. In areas where Cossacks constituted a majority of the population, activists proposed replacing local governments with the traditional Cossack structures. The Don Cossacks restored their Great Circle, the traditional council, as part of the reestablishment of the Don Cossacks as a distinct national group. The Cossack revival reopened the historic controversy over the Cossacks' identity. Were they ethnic Slavs, as claimed by some groups and the Russian government, or distinct ethnic groups that developed through the fusion of Slavs and other groups in the frontier districts of the Russian Empire, as claimed by the increasing number of nationalists?

The largest of the Cossack groups in the North Caucasus, when Gorbachev's liberalization finally allowed them to speak out, at first embraced local issues and environmental concerns, then as mobilization accelerated, they demanded a voice in local government. Factions within the cultural-national revival put forward demands for the recognition of the various Cossack groups as the indigenous nations in their historic homelands, which would give them increased autonomy over cultural and linguistic issues. In mid-1992, a decree signed by Boris Yeltsin rehabilitated the Cossacks and classified them as one of the "oppressed peoples." The decree granted the Cossack hordes the status of ethnic groups and gave them the right to receive land free of charge. The decree also called on the Cossacks to take up their historic task of guarding Russia's borders; however, some Cossacks have refused to serve outside their provincial homelands. The modern Cossacks have taken up their historic military calling as the protectors of the Slav frontiers, but they also insist on another historical pillar of the Cossack identity— the independence of the Cossacks under their own elected leaders.

## The Twenty-First Century

The immense territories that once formed part of the Russian and Soviet Empires have increasingly gone their own way since the collapse of the Soviet Union in 1991. The myth of Soviet brotherhood withered away as quickly as the Soviet Union itself. The many nations that formed part of the Soviet Union rapidly threw off Soviet-Russian culture and embraced older national cultures and languages. The Baltic nations reoriented toward the West, becoming member states, along with several of the former Soviet client states in Eastern Europe, of both the North Atlantic Treaty Organization and the European Union. The Baltic nations want to strengthen their ties to Western Europe to ensure that their giant neighbor to the east is never again the threat it has been in past centuries. The Transcaucasian nations have also oriented themselves toward Europe, although Turkish and Iranian influences are strong in Azerbaijan. The Karabakh conflict between Armenia and Azerbaijan remains unsettled, although the heavy fighting of the 1990s has not resumed. The Slav nations, Belarus and Ukraine, and Romanian-speaking Moldova remain in a halfway situation between Russia and Western Europe with trade, cultural, and military ties that extend both east and west but with democratic institutions and market reforms that remain weak. The Central Asians have mostly retained their traditional elites under the new guise of nationalists. Clan and tribal ties, long suppressed under Soviet rule, have reemerged as the basis of the revived Central Asian cultures.

The Russians themselves, having seen their historic empire slip away, remain in control of an inner empire of more than 100 distinct nationalities. Despite warnings that the Russian Federation would soon splinter along ethnic lines much like the Soviet Union in 1991, the federation has held together. The Russian state is now the most decentralized in history, with the republics and other autonomous areas enjoying large measures of self-government. In 1994, in an effort to placate the restive oblasts (provinces), the government granted new provincial powers that gave the oblasts roughly the same rights to self-determination as the republics.

Russia's historic anti-Semitism has largely been supplanted by new xenophobias, particularly in relation to the Caucasian peoples. The Jewish population, greatly reduced by emigration, no longer suffers the prejudices and persecutions of the past, although some of the historic antipathy remains among reactionary political groups and organizations. However, the Chechens and other peoples of the Caucasus region have become the focus of Russian xenophobia. The large Caucasian minorities living in Moscow and other areas of Russia outside their homelands, many refugees from the continuing war in Chechnya, suffer from widespread prejudice and often are the target of ethnic violence. Russian racism, although historically anti-Semitic, has quickly focused on the Caucasians as the greatest threat to the Russian nation. Although the majority of the Caucasians are Muslim, even Christian Armenians, Georgians, and Ossetians have been targeted, because they are perceived as dark foreigners when they live outside their Caucasian homelands.

Unlike the Russian population, the population of the Muslims of the Russian Federation is increasing rapidly. The Russian Federation has a higher proportion of Muslims than any Western European country, so that Russian xenophobia has a large and growing target. The Muslims have become the stated threat that allows the Russian government to divert attention from social and economic problems. The result is that the ethnic Russian population increasingly fears Islam, and the Muslims' growing distrust of the Russians and the federation authorities does not bode well for the future.

The rapid disintegration of the USSR opened a long debate among politicians in all the former Soviet republics on where the borders of the Russian state should be and on the status of the Russian diaspora left outside the new Russian Federation. The large Russian population in the northern provinces of Kazakhstan in particular demanded their inclusion in Russia when the Soviet Union broke up. Other areas of tension over large Russian populations also saw the formation of pro-Russian organizations and irredentist movements, but changes to any of the fragile borders of the former Soviet Union could stimulate demands for hundreds of territorial transfers and border modifications.

The attitude of the Russians toward the reduced Russian state and their view of themselves have traditionally been shaped by the existence of the Russian Empire. The Russian Federation is by far the largest of the fifteen geopolitical entities that emerged from the collapse of the Soviet Union. Covering more than 6.5 million square miles (17 million square kilometers) in Europe and Asia, the Russian Federation succeeded the USSR as the largest country in the world. The center of the Russian state, as in Soviet and czarist times, is European Russia, which occupies about a quarter of the country's territory. Thirty-nine percent of the federation's territory but only 6 percent of its population was located east of Lake Baikal, the famed geographical landmark in south-central Siberia. The enormous territorial extent of the federation constitutes a major political and economic problem for the Russian government, which lacks the far-reaching authoritarian clout of its Soviet and imperial predecessors. The ethnic Russians constitute more than 80 percent of the federation's population, and they dominate virtually all regions of the country except the North Caucasus and parts of the Volga basin. Owing to Soviet manipulation of internal boundaries only eight of the member republics had non-Russian majorities, and ethnic Russians made up more than half the population of another nine. Ethnic nationalism remains a powerful force in the Russian Federation, but because of centuries of dispersal, domination, and subjugation, that nationalism is now mostly channeled into gaining greater control of local governments, economic assets, and natural resources.

## Which Russian Nationalism?

The rapid collapse of the Soviet Union began a conflict between the opposing views among the Russians themselves. At the beginning of 1992, just after the breakdown of the USSR, Russia's President Boris Yeltsin and his government began a radical economic reform. As the Soviet-era command economy collapsed, Yeltsin's economic reforms were increasingly blamed for the rapidly deteriorating economic situation. Living conditions for a large part of the Russian population plummeted. The ensuing political and economic crisis was made even worse by the struggle for power between Yeltsin and the reformers and his opponents in the Russian Parliament and some members of Yeltsin's own government.

The conflict developed between the traditional Russian nationalism, a product of the Russians' extensive empire, and the new Russian nationalism, as personified by Boris Yeltsin, that emerged with the collapse of the Soviet Union. Yeltsin, although not a democrat in the Western sense, favored a less authoritarian government for the Russian Federation, even allowing the many national minorities to widen their autonomous powers, anathema to previous Russian and Soviet rulers. The view of Boris Yeltsin and other reformers, that Russia must adopt a democratic system and emulate the West in its economic and political systems, was vehemently opposed by conservative Russian nationalists who believed that Russians needed a strong leader and authoritarian rule, both to unite the Russians themselves and to maintain Russian control of the non-Russian minorities in the enormous territories of the Russian Federation.

The growing conflict between the two views of Russian nationalism came to a head in 1992–1993. Hard-liners in the still Soviet-era parliament clashed with Boris Yeltsin in late 1992 over his economic reforms and his presidential powers. In March 1993, the Russian parliament attempted to curb Yeltsin's powers. Yeltsin responded by imposing special rule, which failed to curb his hard-line critics. Some members of the parliament called for Yeltsin's impeachment. A popular referendum, held in April 1993, revealed widespread support for Yeltsin and his economic reforms among the Russian population. Unable to persuade the parliamentarians to pass the needed legislation, Yeltsin dissolved the parliament in September 1993 and revealed plans for free elections to a new Russian federal assembly that would replace the Soviet-era parliament. The parliament responded by voting to replace Yeltsin with his vice-president, the hard-liner Alexander Rutskoi, who announced that he was assuming the office of president. Troops loyal to Rutskoi and the parliament attacked various power centers across Moscow, including the mayor's office and the television and radio stations. The hard-liners and their supporters, including security forces and troops, took control of the parliament building, bringing civil war between the rival Russian factions to the center of Moscow. In early October 1993, while the hard-liners fortified the parliament, their supporters among the city's population clashed with police throughout the center of Moscow.

After a few days of hesitation, several elite divisions of the Russian military finally decided to support Yeltsin. Tanks surrounded the parliament building and following an ultimatum to surrender, began to fire on the building. The assault continued throughout the day and was accompanied by constant sniper fire from the upper stories of several buildings in the city center. Parliamentary troops, equipped with antitank weapons, managed to destroy several of the surrounding machines. In the early afternoon loyal troops stormed the parliament and arrested the hard-line leaders. A few months later, with Yeltsin firmly in control, all leaders of the uprising were pardoned. Official reports placed the toll of the October Uprising at 146 dead and more than 1,000 injured. The conflict ended the open challenge of the radical elements in Russian society against the modernizing reformers.

Yeltsin's precarious health and periods of seemingly irrational behavior allowed the hard-liners to attempt to impeach him once again in 1999, but he finished his term and supervised the peaceful transfer of democratic power to Vladimir Putin, the first such event in Russia's history. The victory of the reformers over the hard-liners, representing the two historic strains of Russian nationalism, could be a temporary victory. Vladimir Putin, although maintaining the trappings of democratic rule, has definite authoritarian tendencies. His handling of the Second Chechen War revealed a philosophy based in the historic Russian mind-set that dictates brutal reprisals against any ethnic group that dares to challenge the Russians' right to rule their historic empire.

Over the past three centuries the leaders of the Russians have turned toward the West, seeking to emulate the economic and social success there. The first five attempts, starting with Peter the Great in the eighteenth century and ending with Lenin's economic policies in the early twentieth century, ultimately failed, and the autocratic Russian tradition reasserted itself. The sixth attempt, begun by Boris Yeltsin in 1991, is still evolving, with the future of the Russians, the more than 100 other ethnic groups in the Russian Federation, and ultimately the rest of the former Soviet Union hanging in the balance.

## Timeline

April 1986        The nuclear power plant disaster at Chernobyl releases
                  large amounts of radiation over parts of Russia,

|                  |                                                                                                                                                                                                                                                                                                                                          |
|------------------|------------------------------------------------------------------------------------------------------------------------------------------------------------------------------------------------------------------------------------------------------------------------------------------------------------------------------------------|
|                  | Ukraine, and Belarus. Gorbachev launches glasnost (openness) in an effort to end the official secrecy that permeated Soviet society.                                                                                                                                                                                                      |
| December 1986    | The first serious anti-Russian rioting in decades breaks out in Kazakhstan.                                                                                                                                                                                                                                                               |
| January 1987     | Gorbachev launches perestroika (restructuring), trying to resurrect the moribund Soviet economy and the Communist Party.                                                                                                                                                                                                                 |
| Winter 1988      | Serious ethnic rioting erupts in the Caucasus, often directed against ethnic Russians.                                                                                                                                                                                                                                                    |
| June 1988        | The millennium of Russian Christianity is officially celebrated in Moscow. Gorbachev formally recognizes the ethnic terrorism of the Stalin era.                                                                                                                                                                                          |
| 1989             | Gorbachev withdraws the Soviet troops from Afghanistan and begins the military withdrawal from Eastern Europe; the Communist governments of Hungary, Czechoslovakia, Poland, and East Germany fall from power. The Berlin Wall comes down, leading to the reunification of West and East Germany. The Cold War is officially declared over. |
| March 1990       | Boris Yeltsin wins seat to the Supreme Soviet of the Russian Federation.                                                                                                                                                                                                                                                                  |
| May 1990         | Yeltsin becomes chairman of the Russian Supreme Soviet.                                                                                                                                                                                                                                                                                   |
| June 1990        | The Russian Federation is declared a sovereign state. Yeltsin is elected president of the Russian Federation in open election. The last Soviet troops are pulled back from Hungary and Czechoslovakia. Gorbachev and the leaders of several of the union republics sign a draft union treaty.                                              |
| October 1990     | The parliament of the Russian Federation passes a resolution proclaiming that no Soviet law can take effect in the Russian republic without the approval of the Russian parliament. The parliament also approves a radical economic plan, effectively undercutting the all-Soviet economic reform package. Gorbachev is awarded the Nobel Prize for peace for his attempts at peaceful reform in the Soviet Union. |
| August 1991      | Hard-line Soviet officials, opposed to liberalization and reform, attempt to remove Gorbachev in a military                                                                                                                                                                                                                               |

coup. The coup fails after three days, greatly elevating Yeltsin's prestige as one of the most active opponents of the hard-liners. The Soviet Union rapidly disintegrates.

November 1991    The Russian parliament grants Yeltsin sweeping powers. Russia gains control of Soviet natural resources on Russian territory and places the Russian economy above that of the Soviet Union, ending any possibility of the Russian Federation remaining in the union. Gorbachev fails in his attempt to win support for a new union treaty.

December 1991    The presidents of the Russian Federation, Ukraine, and Belarus meet to form a loose grouping, the Commonwealth of Independent States (CIS). The Soviet Union officially ceases to exist; the Russian national flag is raised over the Kremlin. Yeltsin takes control of the Soviet Union's nuclear arsenal and military structure.

January 1992    The rift between Yeltsin and hard-line members of the Russian government begins.

March 1992    Eighteen of the twenty autonomous republics of the Russian Federation sign a new federation treaty. The governments of the republics of Tatarstan and Chechnya refuse.

July 1992    Yeltsin is invited to represent the Russian Federation, still the world's largest state in area, one of the largest in population, and a nuclear power, at a Group of Seven (G-7) meeting.

December 1992    Yeltsin clashes with the parliament over economic reform and presidential powers.

March 1993    Parliament attempts to curb presidential powers. Yeltsin then attempts to impose special rule, but fails. Parliamentarians call for Yeltsin's impeachment.

April 1993    A popular referendum shows widespread support for Yeltsin and economic reform.

September 1993    Yeltsin dissolves the parliament and calls for free elections of a new federal assembly. The parliament retaliates by appointing the Russian vice-president to replace Yeltsin.

October 1993    Troops loyal to the parliament attack the mayor's office and a central television transmission station, while the vice-president and parliamentarians hold up in the

|  | parliament building. Military units loyal to Yeltsin end the rebellion by firing on the building. |
|---|---|
| December 1994 | Russian troops invade the breakaway republic of Chechnya. |
| July 1996 | Yeltsin is reelected Russian president. |
| December 1996 | Russian troops are badly mauled by Chechen rebels and begin the withdrawal from the Caucasian republic. The defeat of the invasion is a severe blow to Russian prestige. |
| July 1998 | The remains of Czar Nicholas II and his family, murdered by Bolsheviks in 1918, are interred in St. Petersburg. |
| May 1999 | An impeachment bill against Yeltsin fails in the Russian parliament. |
| August 1999 | Vladimir Putin is confirmed as the new prime minister of Russia. |
| March 2000 | Putin is elected president of Russia to replace the ailing Yeltsin. |
| April 2003 | Russians demonstrate against the American and British invasion of Iraq. Putin's opposition to the Iraqi war places the Russians in opposition to the United States, echoing the rivalry of the Cold War era. |

### Significant People, Places, and Events

HARD-LINERS A section of the Soviet-era political elite that believes in a strong, authoritarian leadership for the Russians, probably modeled on Stalin's totalitarian regime. They include unreformed Communists and members of radical, often xenophobic Russian nationalist organizations.

PUTIN, VLADIMIR The president of the Russian Federation since August 1999, when he replaced Boris Yeltsin. Putin's military background and his more authoritarian style has returned Russia to its historic need for an authoritarian leader, but without losing the democratic reforms put in place by Yeltsin.

RUSSIAN DIASPORA The estimated 25 million ethnic Russians who had emigrated to the other Soviet republics during the czarist and Soviet eras. They formed the largest minorities in many of the new states. Once the ruling elite, after 1991 they found themselves often unwanted, unwelcome, and blamed for Soviet-era repression.

**Russophobia** The hatred of the Russians as the dominant ethnic group during centuries of often-brutal oppression of national societies and cultures. Russophobia, hidden during the decades of Soviet rule, reemerged with the collapse of the Soviet Empire.

**Rutskoi, Alexander** A Soviet-era politician chosen by Boris Yeltsin as his vice-president in an attempt to reconcile the hard-liners to the economic and political reforms put in place after Russian independence. Rutskoi, with the support of radical parliamentarians, attempted to replace Yeltsin in October 1993, but was defeated.

**Sevastopol** The Crimean port city that is the host to the powerful Black Sea Fleet and the center of a vitriolic conflict between the new Ukrainian and Russian governments during the 1990s.

**Smirnov, Igor** The hard-line leader of the Slavs of the Trans-Dniestrian region of Moldova. He rejected Moldovan independence and maintained a Communist state east of the Dniester River, including the Soviet-era flag and the support of the Soviet 14th Army.

**Trans-Dniestria** The self-proclaimed Slav-populated state on the east back of the Dniester River in Moldova.

**Yeltsin, Boris** The first president of the independent Russian Federation in 1991. He led the reform movement that attempted to replace Russia's Soviet-era economy and political society with a more democratic model.

## Bibliography

Breslauer, George W. *Gorbachev and Yeltsin as Leaders.* Cambridge: Cambridge University Press, 2002.

Dawisha, Karen, and Bruce Parrott. *Russia and the New States of Eurasia: The Politics of Upheaval.* Cambridge: Cambridge University Press, 1995.

Laitin, David D. *Identity in Formation: The Russian-Speaking Populations in the Near Abroad.* Ithaca, NY, and London: Cornell University Press, 1998.

McFaul, Michael. *Russia's Unfinished Revolution: Political Change from Gorbachev to Putin.* Ithaca, NY, and London: Cornell University Press, 2002.

Remnick, David. *Lenin's Tomb: The Last Days of the Soviet Empire.* New York: Vintage, 1994.

Saivetz, Carol, and Anthony Jones, eds. *In Search of Pluralism: Society and Post-Soviet Politics.* Boulder, CO: Westview, 1994.

Shlapentokh, Vladimir, Munir Sendich, and Emil Payin, eds. *The Russian Diaspora: Russian Minorities in the Former Soviet Republics.* Armonk, NY: M. E. Sharpe, 1994.

Waller, Michael, Bruno Coppieters, and Alexei Malashenko. *Conflicting Loyalties and the State in Post-Soviet Russia and Eurasia.* London: Frank Cass, 1998.

Williams, Christopher, and Thanasis D. Sfikas, eds. *Ethnicity and Nationalism in Russia, the CIS and the Baltic States.* Aldershot, UK: Ashgate, 1999.

# Index

# About the Author

James Minahan is an independent researcher and writer living in Barcelona, Spain. His books include *Nations without States: A Historical Dictionary of Contemporary National Movements* (1996), *Miniature Empires: A Historical Dictionary of the Newly Independent States* (1998), *One Europe, Many Nations: A Historical Dictionary of European National Groups* (2000), and *Encyclopedia of the Stateless Nations: Ethnic and National Groups around the World* (2002).